"In this excellent volume, Scott Hahn and Curtis Mitch take what is arguably the most difficult book in the New Testament and certainly the most complex of Paul's writings—the Letter to the Romans—and explain it clearly and convincingly. The result is both an accessible verse-by-verse commentary and a sometimes groundbreaking contribution to Pauline studies. The sidebars on patristic and medieval interpretation of controversial passages are by themselves worth the price of the book. If you are looking for a deeply exegetical and robustly Catholic perspective on Romans, then look no further."

—**Brant Pitre**, Notre Dame Seminary, New Orleans

"Hahn and Mitch have written an understandable commentary with clear reasons for their interpretation of key questions in Romans. They have their eyes fully open to the issues that have challenged readers for two millennia, and they engage the reader's mind and heart in order to sound the letter's message more clearly to the Church today. This commentary is worthwhile reading for laypeople, clergy, and academics."

—**Mark Reasoner**, Marian University Indianapolis

"Hahn and Mitch's commentary on Romans is based on current historical studies within biblical scholarship, but they also regularly converse with theologians from throughout the centuries. Accordingly, exegetical positions are built on interaction with ancient sources such as the Dead Sea Scrolls and Josephus, but theological discussions engage a wide range of voices such as Origen, Augustine, Aquinas, the Catechism, and Pope Francis. Since it is Catholic in perspective and ecumenical in spirit, all will be rewarded for attending to this volume."

—**Ben C. Blackwell**, Houston Baptist University

✝ Catholic Commentary on Sacred Scripture

Romans

Scott W. Hahn
and Curtis Mitch

Baker Academic

a division of Baker Publishing Group
Grand Rapids, Michigan

Published by Baker Academic
a division of Baker Publishing Group
P.O. Box 6287, Grand Rapids, MI 49516-6287
www.bakeracademic.com

Printed in the United States of America

Library of Congress Cataloging-in-Publication Data
Names: Hahn, Scott, author.
Title: Romans / Scott W. Hahn.
Description: Grand Rapids, MI : Baker Academic, a division of Baker Publishing Group, 2017. |
    Series: Catholic commentary on sacred scripture | Includes bibliographical references and index.
Identifiers: LCCN 2017021637 | ISBN 9780801036781 (pbk. : alk. paper)
Subjects: LCSH: Bible. Romans—Commentaries. | Catholic Church—Doctrines.
Classification: LCC BS2665.53 .H345 2017 | DDC 227/.107—dc23
LC record available at https://lccn.loc.gov/2017021637

Nihil obstat:
Reverend James M. Dunfee
Censor Librorum

Imprimatur:
Most Reverend Jeffrey M. Monforton
Bishop of Steubenville

January 25, 2017

The *nihil obstat* and *imprimatur* are official declarations that a book is free of doctrinal or moral error. No implication is contained therein that those who have granted the *nihil obstat* or *imprimatur* agree with the contents, opinions, or statements expressed.

The image of the baptismal font in figure 5 is courtesy of the Israel Museum, Collection of the Israel Museum, Jerusalem, and courtesy of the Israel Antiquities Authority, exhibited at the Israel Museum, Jerusalem.

The image of Nero in figure 9 is courtesy of The Greek Ministry of Antiquities and the Ancient Corinth Archaeological Museum, Ancient Corinth, Greece.

In keeping with biblical principles of creation stewardship, Baker Publishing Group advocates the responsible use of our natural resources. As a member of the Green Press Initiative, our company uses recycled paper when possible. The text paper of this book is composed in part of post-consumer waste.

20 21 22 23   7 6 5 4

To Matthew Levering—friend,
colleague, and model scholar

———————

I am gratified by the positive response to this Romans commentary that
has required the publisher to order another printing, which affords the
opportunity to correct a significant omission.

Curtis Mitch has been a good friend and close collaborator for over
two decades. He's worked extensively with me at the St. Paul Center for
Biblical Theology on a number of projects, including this commentary.
As the commentary project went forward, he became to me more than
a collaborator; he became a coauthor.

I asked the publisher to acknowledge Curtis's coauthorial role shortly
before the book was first published, but was informed it was too late in
the production process. I was displeased with this outcome at the time
and have grown increasingly so since the commentary's release. I am
delighted that this printing presents an occasion to right that wrong in
its inclusion of Curtis as the coauthor of the volume. And so it is, after
nearly a quarter century of working with Curtis, that I once again find
myself expressing my gratitude to him, this time for his patience and
humility in accepting this overdue correction.

Contents

Illustrations

Editors' Preface

The Church has always venerated the divine Scriptures just as she venerates the body of the Lord. . . . All the preaching of the Church should be nourished and governed by Sacred Scripture. For in the sacred books, the Father who is in heaven meets His children with great love and speaks with them; and the power and goodness in the word of God is so great that it stands as the support and energy of the Church, the strength of faith for her sons and daughters, the food of the soul, a pure and perennial fountain of spiritual life.

Second Vatican Council, Dei Verbum 21

Were not our hearts burning [within us] while he spoke to us on the way and opened the scriptures to us?

Luke 24:32

The Catholic Commentary on Sacred Scripture aims to serve the ministry of the Word of God in the life and mission of the Church. Since Vatican Council II, there has been an increasing hunger among Catholics to study Scripture in depth and in a way that reveals its relationship to liturgy, evangelization, catechesis, theology, and personal and communal life. This series responds to that desire by providing accessible yet substantive commentary on each book of the New Testament, drawn from the best of contemporary biblical scholarship as well as the rich treasury of the Church's tradition. These volumes seek to offer scholarship illumined by faith, in the conviction that the ultimate aim of biblical interpretation is to discover what God has revealed and is still speaking through the sacred text. Central to our approach are the principles taught by Vatican II: first, the use of historical and literary methods to discern what the biblical authors intended to express; second, prayerful theological reflection to understand the sacred text "in accord with the same Spirit by whom it was written"—that is, in light of the content and unity of the whole Scripture, the living tradition of the Church, and the analogy of faith (*Dei Verbum* 12).

The Catholic Commentary on Sacred Scripture is written for those engaged in or training for pastoral ministry and others interested in studying Scripture to understand their faith more deeply, to nourish their spiritual life, or to share the good news with others. With this in mind, the authors focus on the meaning of the text for faith and life rather than on the technical questions that occupy scholars, and they explain the Bible in ordinary language that does not require translation for preaching and catechesis. Although this series is written from the perspective of Catholic faith, its authors draw on the interpretation of Protestant and Orthodox scholars and hope these volumes will serve Christians of other traditions as well.

A variety of features are designed to make the commentary as useful as possible. Each volume includes the biblical text of the New American Bible, Revised Edition (NABRE), the translation approved for liturgical use in the United States. In order to serve readers who use other translations, the commentary notes and explains the most important differences between the NABRE and other widely used translations (RSV, NRSV, JB, NJB, and NIV). Each unit of the biblical text is followed by a list of references to relevant Scripture passages, Catechism sections, and uses in the Roman Lectionary. The exegesis that follows aims to explain in a clear and engaging way the meaning of the text in its original historical context as well as its perennial meaning for Christians. Reflection and Application sections help readers apply Scripture to Christian life today by responding to questions that the text raises, offering spiritual interpretations drawn from Christian tradition or providing suggestions for the use of the biblical text in catechesis, preaching, or other forms of pastoral ministry.

Interspersed throughout the commentary are Biblical Background sidebars that present historical, literary, or theological information, and Living Tradition sidebars that offer pertinent material from the postbiblical Christian tradition, including quotations from Church documents and from the writings of saints and Church Fathers. The Biblical Background sidebars are indicated by a photo of urns that were excavated in Jerusalem, signifying the importance of historical study in understanding the sacred text. The Living Tradition sidebars are indicated by an image of Eadwine, a twelfth-century monk and scribe, signifying the growth in the Church's understanding that comes by the grace of the

Holy Spirit as believers study and ponder the Word of God in their hearts (see *Dei Verbum* 8).

Maps and a glossary are included in each volume for easy reference. The glossary explains key terms from the biblical text as well as theological or exegetical terms, which are marked in the commentary with a cross (†). A list of suggested resources, an index of pastoral topics, and an index of sidebars are included to enhance the usefulness of these volumes. Further resources, including questions for reflection or discussion, can be found at the series website, www.CatholicScriptureCommentary.com.

It is our desire and prayer that these volumes be of service so that more and more "the word of the Lord may speed forward and be glorified" (2 Thess 3:1) in the Church and throughout the world.

Peter S. Williamson
Mary Healy
Kevin Perrotta

Note to Readers

The New American Bible, Revised Edition differs slightly from most English translations in its verse numbering of Psalms and certain other parts of the Old Testament. For instance, Ps 51:4 in the NABRE is Ps 51:2 in other translations; Mal 3:19 in the NABRE is Mal 4:1 in other translations. Readers who use different translations are advised to keep this in mind when looking up Old Testament cross-references given in the commentary.

Abbreviations

†	Indicates that a definition of the term appears in the glossary
AB	Anchor Bible
ACW	Ancient Christian Writers
AnBib	Analecta Biblica
AYBRL	Anchor Yale Bible Reference Library
BECNT	Baker Exegetical Commentary on the New Testament
Bib	*Biblica*
Catechism	*Catechism of the Catholic Church*, 2nd ed. (New York: Doubleday, 2003)
CBQ	*Catholic Biblical Quarterly*
CCSS	Catholic Commentary on Sacred Scripture
ch(s).	chapter(s)
ESV	English Standard Version
FBBS	Facet Books, Biblical Series
FC	Fathers of the Church
HUCA	*Hebrew Union College Annual*
ICC	International Critical Commentary
JB	Jerusalem Bible
JBL	*Journal of Biblical Literature*
JETS	*Journal of the Evangelical Theological Society*
JSNT	*Journal for the Study of the New Testament*
JSNTSup	Journal for the Study of the New Testament Supplement Series
JSPHL	*Journal for the Study of Paul and His Letters*
JTI	*Journal of Theological Interpretation*
KJV	King James Version
Lectionary	*The Lectionary for Mass* (1998/2002 USA edition)
LNTS	Library of New Testament Studies
LSJ	H. G. Liddell, R. Scott, and H. S. Jones, *A Greek-English Lexicon*, 9th ed. with revised supplement (Oxford: Clarendon, 1996)
LXX	Septuagint
NABRE	New American Bible (Revised Edition, 2011)
NICNT	New International Commentary on the New Testament
NIV	New International Version

NJB	New Jerusalem Bible
NovT	*Novum Testamentum*
NovTSup	Supplements to Novum Testamentum
NPNF[1]	*Nicene and Post-Nicene Fathers*, First Series
NRSV	New Revised Standard Version
NSBT	New Studies in Biblical Theology
NT	New Testament
NTS	*New Testament Studies*
OT	Old Testament
PCNT	Paideia Commentaries on the New Testament
RSV	Revised Standard Version
RSVCE	Revised Standard Version Catholic Edition
SNTSMS	Society for New Testament Studies Monograph Series
SP	Sacra Pagina
TTCS	Teach the Text Commentary Series
v(v).	verse(s)
WBC	Word Biblical Commentary
WTJ	*Westminster Theological Journal*
WUNT	Wissenschaftliche Untersuchungen zum Neuen Testament

Books of the Old Testament

Gen	Genesis	Tob	Tobit	Ezek	Ezekiel
Exod	Exodus	Jdt	Judith	Dan	Daniel
Lev	Leviticus	Esther	Esther	Hosea	Hosea
Num	Numbers	1 Macc	1 Maccabees	Joel	Joel
Deut	Deuteronomy	2 Macc	2 Maccabees	Amos	Amos
Josh	Joshua	Job	Job	Obad	Obadiah
Judg	Judges	Ps(s)	Psalm(s)	Jon	Jonah
Ruth	Ruth	Prov	Proverbs	Mic	Micah
1 Sam	1 Samuel	Eccles	Ecclesiastes	Nah	Nahum
2 Sam	2 Samuel	Song	Song of Songs	Hab	Habakkuk
1 Kings	1 Kings	Wis	Wisdom	Zeph	Zephaniah
2 Kings	2 Kings	Sir	Sirach	Hag	Haggai
1 Chron	1 Chronicles	Isa	Isaiah	Zech	Zechariah
2 Chron	2 Chronicles	Jer	Jeremiah	Mal	Malachi
Ezra	Ezra	Lam	Lamentations		
Neh	Nehemiah	Bar	Baruch		

Books of the New Testament

Matt	Matthew	Rom	Romans	Phil	Philippians
Mark	Mark	1 Cor	1 Corinthians	Col	Colossians
Luke	Luke	2 Cor	2 Corinthians	1 Thess	1 Thessalonians
John	John	Gal	Galatians	2 Thess	2 Thessalonians
Acts	Acts	Eph	Ephesians	1 Tim	1 Timothy

2 Tim	2 Timothy	James	James	2 John	2 John
Titus	Titus	1 Pet	1 Peter	3 John	3 John
Philem	Philemon	2 Pet	2 Peter	Jude	Jude
Heb	Hebrews	1 John	1 John	Rev	Revelation

Introduction to Romans

Few writings have influenced the history of Christian thought quite like Paul's Letter to the Romans. Though the letter is short as far as literary masterpieces go, the impact of Romans has been seismic. It is a work of special magnificence in which Paul's considerable skills as a pastor, evangelist, and theologian are given full display.

The importance of Romans might be measured by the list of scholars and saints who have struggled to elucidate its message. Origen of Alexandria seems to have been the first to attempt a detailed exposition of the letter, and he was followed by St. John Chrysostom, St. Augustine of Hippo, St. Cyril of Alexandria, and St. Thomas Aquinas, to name a few. Likewise, the intellectual architects of Protestantism, Martin Luther and John Calvin, hammered out several of their leading ideas on the anvil of Romans. Today the stream of research and writing devoted to Romans continues unabated. Like the rest of Sacred Scripture, which has God for its transcendent author, Paul's Letter to the Romans has a spiritual and theological depth that is literally inexhaustible.

Author and Date

No one seriously disputes that the apostle Paul authored Romans. From ancient to modern times, only a tiny handful of exegetes, most of them writing in the 1800s, have ever challenged the Pauline authorship of the letter, and none has succeeded in disturbing the settled position of New Testament scholarship on this point. Not only is the name "Paul" attached to its opening line (1:1), but also virtually all agree that the imprint of Paul's extraordinary mind and personality are evident throughout. The author describes himself as an "Israelite" from "the tribe of Benjamin" (11:1), as "the apostle to the Gentiles" (11:13), and as one who spread the gospel "from Jerusalem all the way around to Illyricum" (15:19). Taken together, these details fit the biographical profile of Paul like no other figure known to us from earliest Christianity.

To say that Paul authored Romans is not to say that Paul penned the letter with his own hand. The reader may be surprised to hear at the end of the epistle, "I, Tertius, the writer of this letter, greet you in the Lord" (16:22). Tertius, who is otherwise unknown, served the Apostle as an amanuensis—a scribe who either drafted the letter under Paul's direction or copied it out at Paul's dictation. Either way, Romans is too carefully worded and its arguments too sophisticated to cause us to think that Paul had anything but a very direct involvement in shaping both the content and expression of the epistle.

Paul appears to have sent his Letter to the Romans from the city of Corinth in Greece. There are several indicators that support this. (1) Near the end of the letter Paul indicates that he is making ready to travel to Judea with a "contribution for the poor among the holy ones in Jerusalem" (15:26). This matches the final phase of the Apostle's third missionary tour described in the book of Acts (Acts 18:23–21:16), where we learn that Paul made a three-month stopover "in Greece" (Acts 20:2–3) just before setting out for the Jewish capital (Acts 21:15–16). (2) This correlation between Romans and Acts is reinforced by Paul's comment that Timothy, along with a man named Sosipater, was with him as the letter was being penned (Rom 16:21). In all likelihood, these are the same individuals mentioned in Acts as "Sopater" (a shortened form of Sosipater) and "Timothy," both of whom were with Paul in Greece shortly before the Apostle commenced his journey to Jerusalem (Acts 20:4). (3) Paul tells us that he wrote Romans while staying as a guest in the house of "Gaius" (Rom 16:23). Presumably this is the same Gaius whom Paul had baptized when he founded the church at Corinth only a few years earlier (1 Cor 1:14). (4) Paul sent his letter to Rome by the hand of Phoebe, a deaconess from "the church at Cenchreae" (Rom 16:1). Cenchreae was the Aegean seaport in southern Greece that served the city of Corinth.

Paul most likely wrote Romans in the late winter of AD 57, give or take a year. This is inferred, once again, from the overlap between Paul's remarks in Romans and the testimony of the book of Acts. Again, as indicated by his intent to travel to Jerusalem with a relief offering for Judean Christians (Rom 15:25–26), Paul is at the tail end of his third missionary tour (Acts 18:23–21:16), which may be dated within a small margin of error to the years AD 52–57. And since Acts informs us that Paul left Greece not long before the springtime feast of Unleavened Bread (see Acts 20:6), a date for Romans around March of AD 57 cannot be far off the mark.

Christianity in the Capital

Rome was the largest and most illustrious city in the world known to Paul. As the capital of the vast Roman Empire, its political importance was unrivaled. As a bustling center of cultural and commercial activity, its power to attract intellectuals, merchants, and opportunists from across the Mediterranean world was legendary. It is hardly surprising, then, that a missionary such as Paul should perceive the strategic potential of Rome for the advance of the gospel. By winning and strengthening converts in Rome, he could use the city's considerable influence to reach an entire civilization with the Christian message.

Oddly enough, precious little is known about the beginnings of Christianity in Rome. Questions about when, where, and under what circumstances residents in the capital first made contact with the gospel remain unclear. Nevertheless, there is broad agreement among scholars that Christianity first took hold in the city's synagogue community.

Figure 1. Main hall of the Roman-period synagogue next to the gymnasium-bathhouse complex at Sardis, third century AD.

Historical evidence indicates that Jewish migrants settled in Rome as early as the second century BC; by the middle of the first century AD there could have been as many as fifty thousand.[1] According to one ancient source, a sizable number of Jews living in first-century Rome were descendants of captives taken to Italy from Roman military campaigns in the East and subsequently freed by their masters.[2] These Jews, like those throughout the empire, were accorded special protections and exemptions that allowed them to observe their religious customs without compromise.[3] Their freedoms included the right to assemble for worship, the right to collect the annual sanctuary tax for the temple in Jerusalem, the right to abstain from court proceedings on the sabbath, and the right to decline otherwise compulsory military service. Archaeology has thus far produced the names of more than twelve synagogues established in ancient Rome,[4] along with catacombs, indicating that a Jewish community thrived on the west bank of the Tiber in the first century.

It is not difficult to imagine that faith in Jesus as the Messiah would first find a home in the Roman synagogues rather than among the pagan inhabitants of the city. Ancient testimony suggests that a continuous flow of traffic and communication passed between Rome and Israel in the first century,[5] not least because of the annual pilgrimage festivals, which brought Jewish families from across the Roman Empire to worship in Jerusalem every spring (Passover, Pentecost) and fall (Tabernacles). In fact, the book of Acts states that Roman Jews were in attendance at the feast of Pentecost in AD 30 when the Holy Spirit first drove the apostles into the streets of Jerusalem with the gospel (Acts 2:10). It is certainly possible that some of these Roman pilgrims not only witnessed the event but also returned to Italy as baptized members of the newborn Christian Church (Acts 2:41). Or perhaps Roman attendees at a subsequent feast were the first to carry home convictions about the messiahship of Jesus. Regardless, it would only be a matter of time before "the power of God" released through the gospel (Rom 1:16) would make itself felt in the Jewish quarter of the world's most prestigious city.

1. Harry J. Leon, *The Jews of Ancient Rome*, updated ed. (Peabody, MA: Hendrickson, 1995), 135–36.

2. Philo of Alexandria, *Embassy to Gaius* 23.155.

3. Policies favorable to the Jewish population of the empire were put in place by the Caesars Julius and Augustus. See E. Mary Smallwood, *The Jews under Roman Rule: From Pompey to Diocletian*, 2nd ed. (Leiden: Brill, 1981), 120–38.

4. The evidence, drawn from Jewish burial inscriptions, is briefly surveyed in Wolfgang Wiefel, "The Jewish Community in Ancient Rome and the Origins of Roman Christianity," in *The Romans Debate*, ed. Karl P. Donfried, rev. and expanded ed. (Peabody, MA: Hendrickson, 1995), 85–101.

5. For instance, Acts 28:21 implies that written communication between Roman and Judean Jews was not out of the ordinary. There are also stories of Palestinian rabbis making visits to Rome (†Mishnah *Abodah Zarah* 4.7; *Erubin* 4.1).

There is also a tradition that the apostle Peter came to Rome near the beginning of the reign of Caesar Claudius (AD 41–54).[6] Admittedly, some have questioned whether Peter ever traveled as far as the capital, especially at so early a date, but the relevant sources have not been sufficiently discredited to rule out the possibility that he had dealings with the Roman church at a point prior to the arrival of Paul's letter. The tradition need not mean that Peter founded the Roman church in the sense of making the first converts in the capital.[7] It is just as possible that he helped to organize and encourage a small community of believers that was already in existence.[8]

In any case, Peter was almost certainly not in the capital when Paul wrote his Letter to the Romans. If Peter was, in fact, ministering in Rome in the mid-50s, Paul likely would have referred to him in the epistle, at the very least as someone to be singled out for greeting in the list of names in 16:3–16. Further, nothing Paul says in Romans convincingly undermines the tradition that Peter ministered in Rome in the 40s. Commentators sometimes read Paul's remarks in 15:20—that his missionary policy was not to "build on another's foundation"—to exclude the possibility that Peter or any other missionary could have played a significant role in establishing the Roman church. But if anything, this passage indicates that Paul, in sharing his gospel with believers in Rome, was making an *exception* to his usual practice. Normally the Apostle would steer away from places "where Christ has already been named," but in this case he does just the opposite. Paul is eager both to write to the Roman Christians (1:15) and to visit them in person at his earliest opportunity (15:24, 32).

What is beyond dispute is that the Christian community in Rome was already well-established by the time Paul wrote his epistle. Not only does Paul claim that he has desired to visit the Roman Christians "for many years" (15:23), which presupposes that their church's history stretches back for some time, but also he tells the congregation, "Your faith is heralded throughout the world" (1:8)

---

6. Eusebius, *Ecclesiastical History* 2.14. Jerome, *On Illustrious Men* 1.1, specifies that Peter arrived in Rome in the second year of Claudius.

7. On the one hand, a Christian writer from the fourth century claims that the Romans had not "received their faith in Christ from any of the apostles" (Ambrosiaster, *Commentary on Romans*, preface, in *Commentaries on Romans and 1–2 Corinthians*, trans. and ed. Gerald L. Bray, Ancient Christian Texts [Downers Grove, IL: InterVarsity, 2009], 1). On the other hand, the fifth-century historian Orosius attributes the beginning of the Roman church to the evangelization of Peter (*History against the Pagans* 7.6). Irenaeus, a bishop of the late second century, also states that the church in Rome was "founded and organized" by Peter and Paul (*Against Heresies* 3.3.2), although this is generally taken to refer to the apostles' activities in the mid-60s, when both ministered and suffered martyrdom in Rome. The *Catalogus Liberianus* of AD 354 also names Peter as the founder of the church in Rome.

8. Even scholars who are unpersuaded that Peter was in Rome this early nevertheless find it probable that Christianity had come to the capital by the early 40s. See, e.g., Raymond E. Brown and John P. Meier, *Antioch and Rome: New Testament Cradles of Catholic Christianity* (New York: Paulist Press, 1983), 103.

and "Your obedience is known to all" (16:19). This is a church that has existed long enough to have stirred the admiration of Christians everywhere.

The Christian Community in Rome

Little can be said with certainty about the social and economic situation of the believers addressed by Paul, except that they likely represented a cross section of Rome's urban population. Based on the reception of Christianity in other major cities in the first century, one can probably envision a modest number of affluent and perhaps politically influential persons amid a congregation that consisted mainly of folks from the middle and lower classes, from artisans and merchants to manual laborers, slaves, and former slaves.

More significant for the interpretation of Romans is the question of the ethnic and religious background of Paul's original audience. Views range from identifying the Roman Christians as predominantly Jewish, to predominantly Gentile, to some combination of the two. On this matter scholars rely on a degree of guesswork; but it seems likely that both Jews and non-Jews counted themselves members of the church in the imperial capital.

That some Jewish Christians formed part of Paul's readership is clear from his list of personal contacts in Rome (16:3–16).[9] Three of the individuals he greets are identified as his "relatives" (16:7, 11), by which Paul means his Israelite kinsmen; two more, Prisca and Aquila (16:3), are generally considered a Jewish-Christian couple (Acts 18:2). Beyond this, Paul occasionally speaks in Romans as though Jewish ears were attending to his words. When the Apostle comments in 7:1, "I am speaking to people who know the law," it is fairly certain that he has in mind readers steeped in the teachings of the Torah. Also, early in the letter Paul conducts a rhetorical dialogue in which he speaks to various issues and concerns peculiar to one who professes to be "a Jew" (2:17; 3:1). This is part of a pattern in Romans in which Paul defends himself and his teaching against Jewish objections, whether actual or potential (3:27–31; 9:1–3; 10:1–3). One does not get the impression from Romans that converts from Judaism formed a dominating presence in Rome's Christian community, but they were certainly among the recipients of the letter.

More obvious is that Paul counted his Roman readers "among . . . the Gentiles" (1:13). This is apparent from passages such as 11:13, where Paul declares, "Now I am speaking to you Gentiles," after which he cautions non-Jewish disciples

---

9. I hold that ch. 16 is an integral part of Paul's original Letter to the Romans, even though a few modern scholars dispute this.

against a prideful disdain for unbelieving Israel. Likewise, if the list of Paul's acquaintances in 16:3–16 is any indication, Gentile Christians in Rome must have outnumbered Jewish Christians by a wide margin. Of the twenty-six persons who receive a greeting, a full twenty bear native Greek and Latin names. Still, nothing like an exact proportion of Jews to Gentiles can be determined. The majority of scholars are content to say that the Christians in Rome were mostly Gentiles, with an appreciable number of Jewish believers among their ranks.

Assuming this to be a reasonable judgment, we might then ask: How did the church in Rome come to have more Gentiles than Jews by the time Paul sent his letter? The problem is acute given the common belief that Roman Christianity initially took root in the synagogue community. At least two considerations can help answer this.

First, numerous Gentiles in the Roman world were attracted to Judaism and observed its religious customs in varying degrees. In other words, synagogue communities in the †Diaspora (i.e., in lands outside Israel) were already places where Jews and Gentiles came together for fellowship and worship on a regular basis. Some Gentiles chose to become Jewish converts or proselytes, which means they embraced the full yoke of the Torah, beginning with circumcision. However, a greater number of Gentiles attached themselves to the synagogue in more limited ways. They became what are often called "God-fearers"—persons who admired the moral ideals of Judaism and worshiped the God of Israel but stopped short of circumcision and complete conversion to the Jewish religion. Thus the Roman church, although it originated in the synagogues, probably did not start out as a purely Jewish community. The earliest group of disciples in Rome likely included Jews and Gentiles from the start, even if members of Jewish descent were at first more numerous.

Second, the shift from a Jewish to a Gentile majority in the Roman church by the mid-50s is best accounted for by the Edict of Claudius in AD 49. This imperial decree expelled the Jewish community from Rome because of disturbances in the local synagogues instigated by a certain Chrestus.[10] According to most scholars, "Chrestus" is not the name of a troublemaker in the community, but a variant spelling of the Latin name *Christus*, or "Christ." In other words, it seems that the upheaval in Rome's synagogue community was caused by sharp disagreements between those who believed that Jesus was the Messiah

---

10. The edict is first mentioned by the Roman historian Suetonius (*Life of Claudius* 25.4). The date of the edict, however, is given by the fifth-century Christian historian Orosius (*History against the Pagans* 7.6.15). The latter's testimony agrees with Acts 18:2, which indicates that around AD 51 Paul crossed paths in Corinth with the Jewish-Christian couple Aquila and Priscilla, who had "recently" come from Italy on account of Claudius's eviction.

and those who did not. The book of Acts shows that tensions of this sort could be expressed not only in heated debate but also in persecution and violence.[11]

Whatever the precise nature of the unrest, Claudius found it a nuisance, and so he ousted the Jewish community from the capital. And since Christian Jews were indistinguishable from non-Christian Jews in the eyes of the authorities at this early date, the decree suddenly deprived the Roman church of its Jewish membership, leaving only God-fearing Gentiles behind to carry on without them. It was not until the death of Claudius in AD 54 that the decree effectively expired, allowing Jews to reestablish residency in the capital. For at least five years, then, the church in Rome was a purely Gentile community, and no doubt one that continued to expand and grow with new members. The return of Jewish-Christian exiles in the mid-50s would explain the presence of a Jewish minority in the Roman church as well as the friction between Gentiles and Jews reflected in the letter. Numerous scholars find this to be a plausible reconstruction of the historical situation addressed by Paul.

Reasons for Writing the Letter

Paul had several reasons for writing Romans. Most of these are made explicit in the opening and closing parts of the letter, especially in 1:8–15 and 15:14–33, while others may be inferred from a reading of the letter as a whole. At least three primary aims can be identified.

1. Paul wrote to make *personal contact* with the Roman Christians in advance of an anticipated visit. With the exception of those named in 16:3–16, the Apostle was not directly acquainted with the believers in Rome. His missionary travels had not yet taken him as far west as Italy, and yet he desired to visit the Roman Christians in person and to strengthen them in their faith (1:11–13; 15:23). He felt himself obligated (1:14–15) as "the apostle to the Gentiles" (11:13) to preach the gospel in the epicenter of the Gentile world (15:15–16). In view of these facts, Romans may be considered Paul's letter of self-recommendation, wherein he takes the opportunity to introduce himself and his teaching as a way of preparing for his arrival.

2. Paul wrote to establish a *partnership* with the Romans in bringing the gospel to Spain. Thanks to his tireless efforts in the 40s and early 50s, the foundations of the Church had been solidly laid in the eastern Mediterranean (15:19), and Paul felt it was now time to turn his attention to the West (15:23–24). He saw Rome as a potential base of operations for his projected mission to Spain, much as the

11. Acts 13:16–50; 14:1–7, 19; 17:1–9, 13; 18:5–6, 12–17; 19:23.

church in Syrian Antioch had sponsored his evangelization efforts in the East (Acts 13:1–3; 15:35–41; 18:22–23). In sending the letter, the Apostle hoped to gain the Romans' support—spiritual, logistical, and financial—so that this next phase of missionary activity could be successfully launched (Rom 15:28–32).

3. Paul wrote to sort out a *pastoral problem* that had come to his attention. It is fairly certain that the church in Rome was experiencing internal tensions between Jewish and Gentile believers. Divergent perspectives on the plan of God, exacerbated by mutual struggles with ethnic and religious prejudice, appear to be the leading causes of the trouble. Judging from Paul's comments, it seems that some Jews boasted of being the chosen people of God. They therefore put a high premium on the rituals of the law that served as badges of Israel's †election, things such as circumcision, feast day observances, and dietary regulations (2:23–25; 4:1–11; 14:1–9). Some, in fact, may have considered themselves superior to uncircumcised Christians (2:17–23), perhaps as having a special claim on God, as though he was not equally the God of the Gentiles (3:27–31). A number of Gentile Christians, for their part, apparently came to think of themselves as a replacement for Israel, as though God had rejected his beloved people of old (11:1–24). Theirs was the boast of the latecomer who thinks that he supersedes and supplants the predecessor. The result was that certain Jewish and Gentile disciples were condescending and unwelcoming toward one another (15:7). The influx of returning Jewish Christians into a flourishing Gentile church in Rome likely occasioned or intensified these types of friction and disunity.

Themes and Theology of the Letter

Most scholars agree that Romans is the crown jewel of the Pauline Epistles. It is one of the fullest and richest expositions of the Christian gospel ever captured in writing; some have gone so far as to call it a compendium of all Christian doctrine.[12] This latter assessment is certainly overstated, since too many essential topics are unmentioned in the letter to consider it a synopsis of Paul's whole theology.[13] Still, along with the Letter to the Hebrews, Romans is the closest thing we have to a formal theological treatise in the New Testament.

Romans is all about the drama of sin and salvation. Paul's thoughts range widely over a landscape of theological and pastoral matters, yet each can be

---

12. This was the view of Martin Luther's protégé, Philip Melanchthon.

13. For example, Romans has little or nothing to say about the Church and its various ministries, about the centrality of the Eucharist in Christian worship, about the return of Jesus in glory and the events of the end times, and so forth, even though these are vital subjects of discussion in some of Paul's other letters.

traced back to this inner core of Pauline preaching. Underlying the doctrinal exposition of Romans is a story in which God and the human family are estranged and reconciled again, thanks to the saving righteousness of the Father, the death and resurrection of the Son, and the sanctifying action of the Spirit. Together the Persons of the triune God have done for the fallen race of Adam what it was helpless to do on its own—namely, to raise it from the bondage of sin and death to the grace of new life in the family of God. Paul's achievement in Romans is to showcase this truth as the distilled essence of Christianity. The gospel is nothing if not a message of unmerited grace, of God's love redeeming a world undeserving of such a blessing (5:8; 6:23; 8:15; 11:32).

The theology of Romans may be summarized under four headings: (1) God's righteousness as the basis of salvation, (2) the benefits of salvation for humanity, (3) the salvation of Israel in particular, and (4) the responsibilities that salvation places on the Christian community.

1. The Righteousness of God

Before all else, Paul contends that the gospel reveals the righteousness of God (1:17).[14] By this he means that God has shown himself faithful to his covenant commitments of old by accomplishing his greatest saving work in Jesus Christ (3:21–26). Paul elucidates this theme throughout Romans with an eye toward two developments in the early Church that demanded careful explanation: (a) Christianity's acceptance of Gentiles into the messianic community without requiring their submission to Jewish rites such as circumcision; and (b) widespread unbelief in the gospel among Jews, which could seem to call into question the veracity of the Church's proclamation. Because these missionary situations raised questions about God's plan for Israel and the world, Paul labors in Romans to vindicate the faithfulness of God by delineating the various ways the Lord is accomplishing salvation for all people. He is not content simply to assert God's "fidelity" (3:3), "love" (5:8), "kindness" (11:22), and "truthfulness" (15:8) without support; he shows how God's actions in Christ confirm the divine promises to the patriarchs (15:8), the testimony of the Mosaic law (3:31), and the expectations of the prophetic writings (16:26).

In particular, Paul expounds God's righteousness with reference to God's covenants with Abraham and David. He contends that the Abrahamic covenant,

---

14. Romans has even been called "a large-scale map" of the righteousness of God. See N. T. Wright, "Romans and the Theology of Paul," in *Pauline Theology, Volume III: Romans*, ed. David M. Hay and E. Elizabeth Johnson (Minneapolis: Fortress, 1995), 30–67, quotation from p. 36.

which included promises of Abraham's universal fatherhood (Gen 17:4) and worldwide blessings through his †elect offspring (Gen 22:16–18), reaches fulfillment as Jews and Gentiles come to faith in Jesus Christ and receive his salvation on equal terms (Rom 1:16; 3:28–30). For believing Jews, the true significance of circumcision as a sign of the Abrahamic covenant (Gen 17:10–14) is fulfilled when they exercise the faith of Abraham (Rom 4:12) and observe the Torah from the heart (2:25–29). That only a †remnant of Israel has come to embrace the gospel (11:1–5) is no argument that the word of God has failed, since Scripture reveals that the Israel of faith has always been a chosen subset of Israel according to the flesh (9:6–8). Likewise, in reference to believing Gentiles, Paul insists that their faith is counted as "righteousness," just as Abraham's was before he was circumcised (4:3–5, referring to Gen 15:6), and that their imitation of Abraham's trustful reliance on God makes them his spiritual children, fulfilling the divine pledge that Abraham would become "the father of many nations" (Rom 4:16–17, referring to Gen 17:4). All this was made possible, Paul says, because the Father did not spare his only Son but handed him over to death, just as father Abraham willingly surrendered his beloved Isaac, so that the blessings of the covenant could flow out to all nations (Rom 8:32, alluding to the episode in Gen 22:1–18).

Less appreciated but no less important is Paul's announcement that God has also fulfilled his covenant of kingship with David. This was the Lord's threefold pledge to enthrone David's offspring forever, to make his heir a "son" by royal adoption, and to establish the heir's rule over Israel and the Gentiles together (2 Sam 7:12–14; Pss 2:7–8; 89:3–5, 20–38). It was precisely this complex of promises that defined most of the messianic expectations in the first century, and Paul makes them a vital part of his gospel exposition in Romans. From the start, he gives Jesus the title "Christ" (Rom 1:1), a reference to the "Anointed One" or "Messiah" of ancient Jewish theology.[15] Lest this go unnoticed, Paul affirms that Jesus was born of the royal line of David according to the flesh (1:3) and that God raised him to an immortal life of kingship as "Son of God in power" (1:4). Not only does this verify God's faithfulness to Israel, who received the strongest assurances that the Lord's covenant with David would not falter (e.g., Ps 89:34–36), but the Davidic kingship of Jesus has direct implications for the nations beyond Israel as well: "The root of Jesse shall come, / raised up to rule the Gentiles" (Rom 15:12), Paul reminds his readers, citing Isa 11:10. In Paul's

---

15. The NABRE varies its translation of the Greek *Christos*. It is rendered "Christ" when used as a direct reference to Jesus, but "Messiah" when referring to the chief blessing promised to Israel (Rom 9:5). Readers should be aware that the underlying Greek term is the same in all instances and that Paul uses the title "Christ" with its full messianic significance intended.

vision, the risen Jesus is enthroned as Messiah and Lord "at the right hand of God" (Rom 8:34), where he intercedes for Israel and the nations and summons all to submit to his lordship (10:12) with "the obedience of faith" (1:5).

2. The Reconciliation of the World

Paul establishes in Romans not only the fact of salvation in Christ but also the need for salvation by all. He prepares to announce the good news by reviewing the bad news of human rebellion against God. Paul turns a spotlight on sin in several places in Romans, but especially in 1:18–3:20. Here, at the beginning of the letter, Paul rails against the idolatry and immorality that prevail in the non-Jewish world of Greeks and barbarians (1:18–32); but he brings charges against Israel as well (2:1–3:20). He agrees with fellow Jews that divine judgment rightly comes against pagan depravity (2:2); nevertheless, he contends that his Jewish brethren, by transgressions of the Torah, are likewise "under the domination of sin" (3:9) and in need of salvation (1:16; 11:26–27). This he establishes with multiple quotations from the Psalms (Rom 3:10–14, 18, 20) and Isaiah (Rom 2:24; 3:15–17), so that no one can dispute that "all have sinned and are deprived of the glory of God" (3:23). Ultimately, Paul traces humanity's need for mercy and reconciliation with God back to the first man, Adam, whose primordial disobedience caused sin to infect his progeny on a universal scale (5:12). Thanks to him, death claimed lordship over the entire human race (5:17) and condemnation came to all (5:18). In this fallen state, the descendants of Adam—Jews as well as Gentiles—are branded "enemies" of God (5:10) and left "helpless" to do anything about their predicament (5:6).

But this is not a problem without a solution. For Paul, the tragedy of spiritual bondage is merely a backdrop against which the gospel shines brighter, for it reveals that "God delivered all to disobedience, that he might have mercy upon all" (11:32). Salvation has now come through Jesus Christ, whose sacrificial death brings forgiveness of sins (3:24–25) and opens the way for reconciliation between the Father and the family of Adam (5:10). Paul articulates this vision of salvation primarily in terms of justification and divine adoption. *Justification* is the action of God toward one who believes in Jesus (3:26), an action that pardons the sinner and makes him or her righteous in the sight of God (5:19). This is Paul's way of saying that justification establishes the believer in a right covenant relationship with God. Indeed, he labors in Romans to distinguish the messianic age from the Mosaic age by stressing that membership in the covenant community is secured by faith in Jesus the Messiah and not by observance of

Mosaic ritual laws (3:20, 28). Rather than something that is merited or earned by legal practices such as circumcision (4:2–5), justification is a free gift of grace (3:24) bestowed on the circumcised and uncircumcised alike who believe (3:30). *Divine adoption*, though often underappreciated, is arguably the premiere blessing bestowed on the Christian.[16] Paul has important things to say about this in Romans, where he proclaims that believers united with Christ and led by the Spirit (8:10–11) are the sons and daughters of God (8:15–17). God's adopted children are rescued from the fallen family of Adam, raised to a new standing in the divine family of the Father, and so counted younger siblings of Jesus, "the firstborn among many brothers" (8:29).

Strictly speaking, justification and adoption are two ways of describing the same thing. Not only do they represent two dimensions of a single reality— salvation by grace through faith in Christ—but a close reading of Paul also reveals that both are actualized in the liturgical context of baptism. It is in the sacrament that the benefits of Jesus' dying and rising to new life are applied to the believer in a transformative way (6:3–4; see 4:25; 1 Cor 6:11; Titus 3:5). Once justified as adopted sons and daughters, the community of faith lives at peace with God (Rom 5:1) and is drawn forward by the hope of sharing the glory of God (5:2). Central to this future hope is the final justification of the faithful before the divine judge (2:6–7, 13) along with the resurrection and redemption of their bodies from suffering and decay (8:18–21, 23).

3. The Restoration of Israel

Romans also deals with the relation between the gospel and the people of Israel, a subject to which Paul gives focused attention in chapters 9–11. Reflection on this topic was occasioned by the fact that "not everyone" in Israel "heeded the good news" (10:16). Disbelief in Jesus as Messiah and Lord was common enough that Paul could speak about it in summary terms as Israel's "transgression" (11:11) and "disobedience" (11:30). He charges that many of his kin had stumbled (9:32) and become like branches severed from the trunk of an olive tree "because of unbelief" (11:20). This was a source of "constant anguish" for Paul (9:2), who prayed and worked tirelessly for the salvation of Israel (10:1; 11:13–14).

16. See Trevor J. Burke, "Adopted as Sons (ΥΙΟΘΕΣΙΑ): The Missing Piece in Pauline Soteriology," in *Paul: Jew, Greek, and Roman*, ed. Stanley E. Porter (Leiden: Brill, 2008), 259–87; Martin W. Schoenberg, OSC, "St. Paul's Notion on the Adoptive Sonship of Christians," *The Thomist* 28, no. 1 (1964): 51–75; J. M. Scott, *Adoption as Sons of God: An Exegetical Investigation into the Background of ΥΙΟΘΕΣΙΑ in the Pauline Corpus* (Tübingen: Mohr Siebeck, 1992).

The widespread failure of Israel to accept the righteousness of God in Jesus (10:3–4) raises theological questions about the justice and reliability of God, which Paul is anxious to defend and clarify. As usual, he tackles these issues by turning to the Old Testament. There he finds a consistent pattern in the way God accomplishes his purposes in history. Paul demonstrates, for example, that the Lord advances his plan of redemption through an elect remnant of Israelites (9:27–29; 11:2–5). These are the chosen recipients of his mercy, while others among the covenant people are hardened (9:16–18). God, according to biblical teaching, is sovereignly free to dispense his blessings, just as a potter is free to determine the shape to be given a lump of clay (9:19–23). Indeed, he is now extending his grace to Gentiles as well as Jews (9:24–29), since he is Lord of both (10:12). The point of these observations is to demonstrate that God is not unjust in his ways (9:14) and that his word to Israel has not failed (9:6).

Paul's reading of Scripture is intended to show that Israel's stumbling in the present follows the pattern of Israel's stumbling in the past. One should not be surprised—much less skeptical of Christian claims—to witness Israel resisting the gospel, with only a remnant responding in faith (11:5–7). The Lord brings a "hardening" upon part of Israel (11:25) so that salvation might come to the Gentiles (11:11). But Israel is not thereby a rejected people (11:1–2). On the contrary, the chosen people are still "beloved because of the patriarchs" (11:28). In fact, as they watch the nations come to faith in the Messiah, God aims to provoke Israel to a jealous imitation of Gentile belief (10:19; 11:13–14) that will reattach them to the olive tree of the Lord's messianic community (11:23–24). Paul stands in awe of "this mystery" and its glorious realization when "all Israel will be saved" (11:25–26). He marvels at the way God uses even disobedience, first among Gentiles and then among Israel, to bestow his mercy on all (11:32).

4. The Requirements of the Christian Life

Intermittently throughout Romans, Paul translates his theological vision into practical instructions for Christian living. Speaking generally, he urges readers to walk "in the newness of life" they received in baptism (6:4). Believers must fight against the enslaving power of sin (6:12–14) and yield themselves to obedience, which leads to righteousness (6:16), sanctification (6:19), and ultimately eternal life (6:22). To achieve this, they must offer body and mind as a sacrifice to the Lord (12:1–2) and remain steadfast in prayer (12:12). Suffering plays a critical role in this as well, as Paul ascribes to it the power to sculpt a Christian's character (5:3–4) and conform the believer more closely to

Christ (8:17). Regarding particular attitudes and actions, Paul urges disciples to practice humility (12:3, 16) and generosity (12:13) and so conquer evil with what is good (12:21). As members of the body of Christ, believers are expected to use their spiritual gifts for the upbuilding of the whole community (12:4–8); as citizens in the world, they are bidden to pay taxes and to honor rightful government authorities (13:1–7). Those who observe these standards will become more like Jesus, who "did not please himself" (15:3) but made himself a "servant" to all (15:8 RSV).

Fundamental to Paul's moral and spiritual catechesis in Romans is the conviction that Christian living is possible only by the grace of the Spirit (8:11). Once empowered from within, the children of God can finally put to death the sinful deeds of the flesh (8:13) that impede their ability to obey the law of God (8:7). In other words, the Spirit enables the baptized to fulfill "the righteous decree of the law" that was otherwise unattainable for fallen human nature (8:4). Paul appears to have in mind the specific decree to "love one another" (13:8), which constitutes the fulfillment of the law (13:10). This level of obedience, which comes from the heart (6:17), is the outworking of divine grace, since "the love of God has been poured out into our hearts through the holy Spirit that has been given to us" (5:5). The love required by the law is a love powerfully and abundantly supplied by the Spirit.

Challenges for Interpreting the Letter

Many readers find Romans to be almost as frustrating as it is fascinating. It is one of the most loved of the Pauline Letters, and yet it does not yield its secrets willingly. Critics say this is because Paul is a clumsy and confused thinker. The truth of the matter, however, is just the opposite. Paul is one of most brilliant theologians the Church has ever known, and so his thoughts frequently soar at an altitude that few others are able to reach or sustain.

Romans is a demanding read. This seems to have been evident already in apostolic times—possibly Peter had Romans in mind when he admitted that "there are some things hard to understand" in Paul's Letters (2 Pet 3:16). All of us are sure to find parts of this letter that make for slow sledding. But this is not a bad thing. Taking the time to read carefully through Romans and to ask intelligent questions along the way can bring tremendous rewards. After all, Paul did not write with the intention of being obscure or of having his teaching misconstrued. He has precious wisdom to offer, but we won't receive it without some exertion.

A few things should be kept in mind when reading Romans: (1) Paul's writing style is terse and tightly packed. Few have the ability to stuff a maximum of meaning into a minimum of words like the apostle to the Gentiles. Consequently, the impression derived from a surface reading of his words rarely penetrates to the depths of what he is trying to say. This is an argument for mulling over Romans and reading it attentively several times over. (2) At the same time, we need to be careful not to lose sight of the forest for the trees by fixating on words and phrases to the neglect of the whole message of the letter or its larger units. Paul is notorious for building his arguments over the course of several chapters at a time. If we fail to see this, we risk missing the big picture of what Romans is all about. (3) From start to finish, Paul measures the truth of his gospel against the teaching of Scripture. In fact, of the whole collection of Pauline Letters, none is more densely concentrated with references to the Old Testament than Romans. And despite occasional charges to the contrary, he is not guilty of mere proof-texting—of plucking verses from the Bible that appear to support his assertions regardless of what they actually mean. On the contrary, Paul's biblical exegesis in Romans is contextual exegesis. This means, on the one hand, that Paul is aware of the original contexts and meanings of his scriptural references and, on the other, that he generally considers that information relevant. Readers who are less familiar with the Old Testament than Paul will need to go back and investigate the original contexts of his biblical citations. A precise understanding of his teaching often depends on our willingness to do this type of background work.

Structure and Outline

The literary structure of Romans is simple and straightforward. In chapters 1–11 Paul presents readers with an *exposition* of Christian faith, and in chapters 12–16 he offers a range of *exhortations* regarding Christian life. Belief and behavior, or catechesis and conduct, thus form the two main panels of the epistle. These, in turn, are framed by a formal introduction (1:1–15) and a lengthy conclusion (15:14–16:27). For additional divisions of the letter, see the outline below.

The Messiah and the Gospel of Salvation

Romans 1:1–32

Romans begins with an unusually full introduction. This should not be surprising, since Paul is introducing himself to a Christian community that, for the most part, he does not know personally. The Apostle sets forth his credentials, recites a confession of faith, and is generous with compliments for the Roman believers. He concludes these formalities with a word of thanksgiving, and then begins the theological exposition of his gospel.

The Opening Address (1:1–7)

¹**Paul, a slave of Christ Jesus, called to be an apostle and set apart for the gospel of God, ²which he promised previously through his prophets in the holy scriptures, ³the gospel about his Son, descended from David according to the flesh, ⁴but established as Son of God in power according to the spirit of holiness through resurrection from the dead, Jesus Christ our Lord. ⁵Through him we have received the grace of apostleship, to bring about the obedience of faith, for the sake of his name, among all the Gentiles, ⁶among whom are you also, who are called to belong to Jesus Christ; ⁷to all the beloved of God in Rome, called to be holy. Grace to you and peace from God our Father and the Lord Jesus Christ.**

OT: 2 Sam 7:14; Ps 2:7
NT: Acts 2:29–33; 13:32–33; 2 Tim 2:8; Heb 1:2–5
Catechism: slaves of Christ, 876; risen glory of Christ, 445, 648; son of David, Son of God, 496; obedience of faith, 143, 2087
Lectionary: 4th Sunday of Advent (Year A)

Paul leads off with a salutation typical of those found in Greco-Roman letters: he names the sender, identifies the addressee, and expresses a greeting along with a wish of well-being for the recipient(s). But he adapts and expands the conventional format with Christian elements. To his name, Paul attaches titles and qualifications intended to resonate with believers in Rome; and instead of wishing readers good health or a windfall of material prosperity, he prays for an outpouring of grace and peace in their lives.

1:1   **Paul** introduces himself as a **slave** whose entire life is dedicated to serving **Jesus**. In a secular context the Greek term *doulos* might insinuate something degrading; but here Paul is using a term given to those many "servants" of the Lord whose faithfulness is celebrated in the Old Testament, figures such as Moses (Josh 1:1), Joshua (Josh 24:29), David (Ps 89:4), and the prophets (2 Kings 17:23).

But more than a servant, Paul is an **apostle**. He has seen the risen Jesus (1 Cor 9:1) and has received a personal commission from him to preach the gospel (Gal 1:1, 11–12). This makes Paul a royal messenger, an ambassador vested with the authority of the one who sent him.

Paul was **called** and **set apart** for this service by the Lord. He uses nearly identical language in Gal 1:15 to say that God consecrated him from his mother's womb to be a minister of the Word, much as God had done for the prophet Jeremiah (Jer 1:5) and for the †Servant of the Lord who appears in Isaiah (Isa 49:1). Paul is aware, in other words, that apostleship is not volunteer work—something one does out of personal interest or a magnanimous desire to make the world a better place. Apostolic ministry is a vocation, a calling from the Lord that brings with it a solemn responsibility. Paul was "a chosen vessel" handpicked by the Lord to be a missionary for the Messiah (Acts 9:15 KJV).

Paul's task was first and foremost to proclaim **the gospel**. Here the word "gospel" does not refer to the written Gospels of the New Testament (Matthew, Mark, Luke, John). Rather, the Greek term *euangelion* is a single-word summary for "the good news of salvation" accomplished by Jesus. In the ancient world, a *euangelion* was the announcement of a world-changing event, often a spectacular military triumph or the accession of a new ruler—the kind of screaming headline that would get wall-to-wall coverage in today's media. Beyond that, the word evokes a prominent theme from the book of Isaiah (expressed by the related verb *euangelizō*) that speaks of the Lord redeeming his people Israel and extending his salvation to the ends of the earth (see the †Septuagint version of Isa 40:9; 52:7; 60:6; 61:1). These associations add dimension and depth to the good news announced by Paul.

But to understand Paul's mission in life, one must ultimately consider the focus of his life, which is Jesus. And the first thing the Apostle tells us about Jesus is that he is the **Christ**. This word is familiar to us—maybe too familiar. We tend to think of it as a second name and forget, perhaps, what it signifies. "Christ" is a title meaning the "Anointed One" or "Messiah" of Jewish expectation, a title heavy with theological significance, as the texts and traditions of the Old Testament manifest. Although there was some variety in Jewish thinking, most of the messianic hopes in Paul's day clustered around the promise of a future Davidic ruler, an ideal king from the dynastic line of David and Solomon.[1] Verses 3–4 will show that Paul attaches this messianic title to Jesus with a full awareness of its royal Davidic overtones.

Paul affirms that the gospel was **promised previously** in the texts of the **holy**   **1:2** **scriptures**, what Christians call the Old Testament. The good news about Jesus is not a new story: he is the glorious realization of a divine plan set in place from the beginning. In fact, one of Paul's aims in Romans is to show that his preaching is fully in line with the Scriptures of Israel, all of which prepare for this climax of history in some way or another. Roughly sixty times in Romans the Apostle will reference texts of the Old Testament, and in numerous other instances he will allude to their message or adopt their wording in more subtle ways.[2] Paul hopes that by the time he reaches the end of the letter, he will have shown how the mystery of salvation in Christ is "manifested through the prophetic writings" of the Bible (16:26).

Scholars frequently contend that verses 3–4 are taken from an ancient Chris-   **1:3–4** tian hymn or confession of faith. This is a possibility but not a certainty. Whatever their origin, Paul is strumming a chord of great theological importance. He makes two assertions about Jesus that constitute his messianic credentials: according to human genealogy, Jesus is a royal descendant of **David**; and since rising from death to new life, he has been designated **Son of God in power**.

Paul's point is not that Jesus became the divine Son of God at his resurrection, a theological error known as "adoptionism." Nor is he summarizing the Church's faith in the human and divine natures of Christ, a theological truth known as "the hypostatic union." Rather, Paul is centering his thoughts on the messiahship of Jesus in relation to the miracle of Easter.[3] In his mortal humanity,

---

1. Relevant texts of the Old Testament include Isa 9:5–6; 11:1–5; Jer 23:5–6; 30:9; Ezek 34:23–24; 37:24–28; Hosea 3:5. Extrabiblical witnesses include *Psalms of Solomon* 17.1–46 and the Dead Sea Scroll fragment called 4QFlorilegium (= 4Q174).
2. The figure comes from Steve Moyise, *Paul and Scripture: Studying the New Testament Use of the Old Testament* (Grand Rapids: Baker Academic, 2010), 3.
3. Thomas R. Schreiner, *Romans*, BECNT (Grand Rapids: Baker Academic, 1998), 41–43.

Jesus fulfilled the expectation that God's Anointed would come from the royal line of David (2 Tim 2:8); and in his risen humanity, now rendered immortal by the glory of God, Jesus actually became the king that God swore would rule upon David's throne "forever" (Ps 89:4–5, 30–38; see Luke 1:31–33). Death had prevented every other Davidic successor from fulfilling this seemingly impossible oath. But ever since the dawn of the third day, "Christ, raised from the dead, dies no more; death no longer has power over him" (Rom 6:9).

The title "Son of God" thus has a messianic significance anchored in the Lord's covenant of kingship with David. Especially relevant are two passages, 2 Sam 7:14 and Ps 2:7, which describe David's anointed heir as a "son" adopted by God on the day of his coronation as king of Israel.[4] Paul contends that Jesus, raised and enthroned in his Davidic humanity, has come to occupy this permanent kingly office in fulfillment of the Lord's oath.[5] He now reigns forever "at the right hand of God" (Rom 8:34). Peter made precisely this point in his Pentecost sermon in Acts 2:29–36, and Paul himself touched on it in his inaugural preaching in Acts 13:30–37.

None of this means that the divinity of Jesus is unimportant to Paul or irrelevant to his remarks. On the contrary, the two assertions that delineate the status of Christ's humanity before and after the **resurrection** are both affirmations about the divine **Son**. One can therefore say that the risen humanity of Jesus has blossomed into a more perfect *image* of his divine Sonship and become a more perfect *instrument* of his divine sovereignty. From now on the splendor of the eternal Son of God is manifest in and through Christ the risen man.[6]

Paul further relates the Son's resurrection to **the spirit of holiness**, which is a Semitic way of saying "the Holy Spirit" (the Hebrew equivalent occurs in Ps 51:13; Isa 63:10–11; and multiple times in the Dead Sea Scrolls). Paul will explain in chapter 8 how the miracle of the resurrection will be replicated when the "Spirit" of the Father imparts glory and life to the "mortal bodies" (Rom 8:11) of all who are sons and daughters of God by adoption (8:15).[7]

4. Christopher G. Whitsett, "Son of God, Seed of David: Paul's Messianic Exegesis in Romans 1:3–4," *JBL* 119, no. 4 (2000): 661–81.

5. Interpretation hinges on the meaning of the Greek participle *horisthentos*, which the NABRE renders "established" and other contemporary translations render "designated" (RSV), "declared" (NIV), or even "proclaimed" (JB). Here the term most likely means "appointed," with an office or position in view, as in Acts 10:42; 17:31.

6. See F. X. Durrwell, *The Resurrection: A Biblical Study*, trans. Rosemary Sheed (New York: Sheed & Ward, 1960), 45–47, 131–33.

7. Resurrection of the dead is linked to the work of the Holy Spirit also in the Old Testament (Ezek 37:13–14) and in early rabbinic theology (†Mishnah *Sotah* 9.15).

Paul returns briefly to his accreditation as an apostle. This is not an office   **1:5**
that one merits or earns; it is a **grace** that God freely bestows. And the words
we have received indicate that Paul is conscious of being part of a larger group.
Others are apostles as well, such as the Twelve (Luke 6:13–16), along with a
wider circle of individuals (1 Cor 15:5–7), some of whom were sent forth as
representatives from local congregations in the earliest days (Acts 14:14; 2 Cor
8:23). As an evangelist and founder of churches, Paul holds an **apostleship** with
plenary authority, on the level of the original Twelve.

His mission is to promote **the obedience of faith** throughout the world (see
Rom 15:18). The expression forms a literary *inclusio*—a thematic statement that
stands like two bookends at the beginning (1:5) and end of the letter (16:26).
With this device Paul signals that "the obedience of faith" embraces and holds
together much of his teaching in Romans.

The expression can be understood in different ways. Some argue that it
means "the obedience that flows *from* faith." Others contend that it means
"the obedience that *is* faith." Of the two options, the second is more likely
Paul's intended meaning, since he virtually equates obedience with believing
in the gospel (see 10:16, where "heeded"—literally, "obeyed"—and "believed"
both indicate acceptance of the good news). Conversely, the Apostle considers
unbelief or rejection of the Christian message a form of disobedience (10:21;
11:23, 30–31).

Throughout Romans, "faith" and "obedience" stand in the closest relationship. Despite claims to the contrary, these terms are not polar opposites that
represent competing ways of salvation—the true path of trusting acceptance
of Christ's redeeming work (faith) versus the prideful path of trying to gain
heaven on our own power by following moral and religious commandments
(obedience). There is some truth in this contrast, insofar as salvation cannot
be attained by sheer human effort. But to emphasize faith to the exclusion of
obedience is like saying that one wing of the airplane does all the flying or one
blade of the scissors does all the cutting. Faith and obedience go together in
Pauline preaching, just as they do in real life. This is why the Apostle praises
the Romans for their Christian faith (1:8; 11:20) as well as for their Christian
obedience (6:17; 16:19).

Finally, the introduction names the recipients: the believers **in Rome**. Paul   **1:6–7**
can pay them no finer compliment than to celebrate the blessings already bestowed on them. As Christians, they are an †elect people of God (**called**), an
object of the Lord's special affection (**beloved**), and a community set apart to
glorify him through the witness of their lives (**holy**). Readers versed in the

Among All the Gentiles

Often lost on modern readers is the connection between the coming of the Davidic Messiah and the destiny of the Gentiles. Scripture reveals this link when it describes the founding of the Davidic kingdom as a time when Israel first extended its dominion over Gentile nations. King David subjected several foreign states to Israelite rule (2 Sam 8:1–14); then King Solomon enlightened many pilgrims and dignitaries from distant lands with his wisdom (1 Kings 5:14; 10:1–7, 24). For this brief period, Gentiles were welcomed into fellowship with the God of Israel and encouraged to pray toward his temple in Jerusalem (1 Kings 8:41–43). Pious Israelites prayed that nations near and far would come to fear the Lord (Ps 2:11) and serve the royal son of David (Ps 72:11–13). Unfortunately, sin put an end to this outflow of grace, and it fell to Israel's prophets to announce a more perfect and definitive kingdom to come. The Lord pledged to rebuild "the fallen hut of David" so that it might possess "all nations" (Amos 9:11–12). The future would bring "an everlasting covenant" in fulfillment of God's loyalty to David (Isa 55:3–5), and the nations beyond Israel would once again seek the Lord's instruction (Isa 2:1–3). That Paul is tapping into these hopes is clear from Rom 15:12, where he quotes Isa 11:10: "The root of Jesse shall come, / raised up to rule the Gentiles." In Paul's mind, bringing the nations to faith is a mission that flows directly from his conviction that Jesus is the risen Davidic Messiah.

Old Testament will recall similar descriptions of Israel as a people "holy" and "chosen" and "loved" by the Lord (Deut 7:6–8).

Ancient letters ordinarily offered "greetings" (Acts 23:26) or, in Jewish correspondence, wishes of "peace" (2 Macc 1:1). Paul's prayer here for **grace** and **peace** to fill the hearts of the Roman disciples is uniquely Christian. He refers to the blessings that represent the cause (grace) and result (peace) of our reconciliation with God (Rom 5:1–2), blessings that come not from the world but **from God our Father and the Lord Jesus Christ**.

Words of Thanksgiving (1:8–15)

⁸**First, I give thanks to my God through Jesus Christ for all of you, because your faith is heralded throughout the world. ⁹God is my witness, whom I serve with my spirit in proclaiming the gospel of his Son, that I remember you constantly, ¹⁰always asking in my prayers that somehow by**

God's will I may at last find my way clear to come to you. [11]For I long to
see you, that I may share with you some spiritual gift so that you may be
strengthened, [12]that is, that you and I may be mutually encouraged by one
another's faith, yours and mine. [13]I do not want you to be unaware, brothers, that I often planned to come to you, though I was prevented until
now, that I might harvest some fruit among you, too, as among the rest of
the Gentiles. [14]To Greeks and non-Greeks alike, to the wise and the ignorant, I am under obligation; [15]that is why I am eager to preach the gospel
also to you in Rome.

OT: 1 Sam 12:5–6; Dan 3:31–45; 7:1–28
NT: Rom 11:13; 15:22–25; Acts 19:21; 28:14–31; Phil 1:8
Catechism: prayer of thanksgiving, 2637–38; primacy of the Church of Rome, 834

Paul moves from his salutation to a prayer of thanksgiving, which he offers **1:8**
through the mediation of **Jesus Christ**, our intercessor at the Father's right
hand (8:34). The Apostle is grateful not for some personal favor rendered by
the Romans but for their public witness to the gospel. Their **faith** has become
known and admired throughout the Christian **world**. Their heroic adherence
to Jesus, especially in pagan Rome, can only inspire fellow believers to a deeper
religious commitment.

Paul's statement that the Roman church's faith is **heralded throughout the**
world seems to hint that the Roman church occupies a unique place in the
plan of God. Rome was the seat of the greatest earthly power in history up to
that point, and its Christianization could only send shock waves through the
world about the claims of Jesus Christ. Rome's importance to Paul may also
be traced to the book of Daniel, where the prophet envisions a succession of
four Gentile empires oppressing the covenant people, the last of which falls in
defeat before the messianic kingdom of God (Dan 2:31–45; 7:1–28). Daniel's
prophecy is significant because, in early Jewish and Christian tradition, the
fourth and final kingdom was identified as imperial Rome.[8] Did Paul sense
that the Roman church, by advancing the kingdom of God in the heart of the
pagan empire, was playing a role in the fulfillment of these visions? Perhaps. In
any case, it is indisputable that the reputation and leadership role of the Roman
church continued to grow from this point forward, not least because Peter and
Paul were both martyred in Rome in the mid-60s. Christian writings from the
second century describe the church in Rome as one that "presides in charity"

---

8. For Jewish texts, see *4 Ezra* 11–12; *Leviticus Rabbah* 13.5; *Pirke de Rabbi Eliezer* 28; also Josephus,
Jewish Antiquities 10.276. For Christian texts, see Hippolytus, *Commentary on Daniel* fragment 2; Cyril
of Jerusalem, *Catechesis* 15.13; Jerome, *Commentary on Daniel* 7:7.

(St. Ignatius of Antioch, *Letter to the Romans*, salutation) and holds a place of "preeminence" as the standard-bearer of Christian orthodoxy (St. Irenaeus, *Against Heresies* 3.3.2).

1:9–10   Paul's affection for the Roman community surfaces in his **prayers**. Using an oath formula—**God is my witness**—he insists on what cannot be verified by his readers, namely, that he turns his thoughts **constantly** to their well-being when he comes before the Lord. One of his petitions has been that, **by God's will**, a way will be cleared for him to visit the Romans in person. By putting the matter in this way, Paul reaffirms his status as a "slave" (1:1). He can pursue his own aspirations only in the measure that God's plan allows.

The language that Paul uses to describe his service to God is distinctively cultic, as commentators rightly note. The verb **serve** (Greek *latreuō*) frequently appears in Scripture to designate the service of divine worship (e.g., Matt 4:10; Heb 12:28; Rev 7:15). For the Apostle, serving Christ through prayer and **proclaiming the gospel** is a liturgy in which he plays the role of a priest offering the faithful to God. He will make this point explicitly in Rom 15:15–16.

1:11–12   Paul's longing to see the Romans includes a desire to share **some spiritual gift** with them. He speaks specifically of a *charisma*, what he elsewhere calls a "manifestation of the Spirit" (1 Cor 12:7). This is a charismatic or ministerial gift that individual believers receive as a grace from the Lord, not primarily for private benefit but for the upbuilding of the Church. Paul will revisit the subject of spiritual gifts in Rom 12:6–8. Here he hopes for the mutual encouragement that comes when Christians encounter **one another's faith**.

1:13   More than once Paul planned to visit Rome but was **prevented** by the demands of his missionary work (15:18–22). His desire was to **harvest** some spiritual **fruit** in the Roman capital, just as he had done **among the rest of the Gentiles**—that is, among the churches he founded in Asia Minor and Greece. Here he expresses optimism that an opportunity is **now** presenting itself. Unfortunately, things did not work out this way. Little did Paul know that during his planned stop in Jerusalem (15:24–25) he would be arrested and held prisoner for the next two years (Acts 21–26). When he finally set foot in Rome, it was as an accused citizen awaiting trial before Caesar (Acts 28:11–16).

1:14–15   Paul felt himself under **obligation** as "the apostle to the Gentiles" to evangelize the Romans (Rom 11:13), bound by God to take the gospel to **Greeks and non-Greeks alike**. The expression—literally, "both Greeks and barbarians"—is not one that Paul coined for the occasion. Other ancient authors used it to distinguish between those who were educated in the language and traditions of classical Greece and those who were unenlightened by this cultural heritage.[9] The human race is thus swept into two categories: the civilized and the uncivilized, **the wise** and **the ignorant**. Paul uses the expression, not to say that Greeks are better than everyone else, but rather that "all Gentiles without exception" constitute his assigned mission field, regardless of their ethnicity, education, language, or social standing.

The Power of the Gospel (1:16–17)

> [16]For I am not ashamed of the gospel. It is the power of God for the salvation of everyone who believes: for Jew first, and then Greek. [17]For in it is revealed the righteousness of God from faith to faith; as it is written, "The one who is righteous by faith will live."

OT: Gen 15:6; Hab 2:4
NT: Mark 8:38; Luke 9:26; Acts 3:26; Gal 3:11; 2 Tim 2:8; Heb 10:38
Catechism: the gift of faith, 1814–16; eternal life for the righteous, 1038, 2002

Verses 16–17 constitute the thesis statement of Romans. They are Paul's way of punching in the coordinates for the rest of the letter, setting its trajectory, plotting its course. Much of what he says hereafter will elucidate this important announcement in one way or another.

1:16   Paul transitions from introduction to exposition by centering attention, yet again, on the **gospel** (1:1, 9, 15). Here he intends the fullest meaning of the term, which covers the whole gamut of Christian revelation and redemption made effective in the lives of believers. Paul is **not ashamed** of it, despite the mockery and opposition that greet him wherever he goes. Some think Christianity is an absurd way of life and worship; others find it boorish and unsophisticated (1 Cor 1:22–24). Either way, Paul is not embarrassed to spread the faith boldly, nor is his ministry hamstrung by a fear of personal rejection.

For Paul, the gospel is **the power of God** in action. Proclaimed in words, administered through sacraments, and received as grace, it changes the world from above. Miraculous transformations take place when hearts and minds are touched by **salvation**, and Paul has witnessed these firsthand. He will explore the wonders of God's work in us in chapters 5–8.

These benefits are **for Jew first, and then Greek**. Notice that Paul has shifted from the Hellenocentric (Greek-centered) perspective of verse 14 to a

9. E.g., Plato, *Theaetetus* 175a; Strabo, *Geography* 16.2.38; Philo of Alexandria, *On Abraham* 267; Josephus, *Jewish Antiquities* 4.12.

Judeocentric (Jewish-centered) perspective in verse 16. In this worldview one is either a Jew or a non-Jew, a follower of the one true God guided by his law or a pagan stumbling through life in spiritual darkness. Though Paul himself is "an Israelite, a descendant of Abraham, of the tribe of Benjamin" (11:1), he adopts a Jewish way of speaking to say something quite different—namely, that God is now offering salvation to **everyone who believes**. Christianity is to be a faith of international and global proportions.

Nevertheless, the equality of the Greek (= Gentile) as a candidate for salvation does not cancel out the priority of the Jew. Salvation history leading up to Christ was God's long-term investment in the nation of Israel, and it is unthinkable that the Lord would cast aside his covenant people and replace them with Gentiles (11:1). The historical privilege of the Jews puts them first in line to receive the blessings of the Messiah, even as these are extended to Gentiles as well (15:27). This conviction helps to explain why Paul, each time he ventured into a new missionary territory, preached in synagogues before taking the gospel out to the wider world (e.g., Acts 13:5, 14; 14:1; 17:1–3).

1:17   The gospel also manifests **the righteousness of God**. This is a theme of supreme importance in Romans. Much of the epistle represents Paul's effort to explain what this means (see the sidebar "The Righteousness of God").

Paul further indicates in verse 17 that God's righteousness proceeds **from faith to faith**. Some argue that this is an idiom of emphasis, meaning "by faith from start to finish," but the assertion is problematic.[10] The preposition sequence (Greek *ek . . . eis . . .*) tends to designate either a *progression* from one state or degree to another, or else a *range* from one point of time or space to another. For this reason, some commentators say that Paul is summarizing the work of salvation as something that originates with God's faithfulness manifested in Christ's redeeming work and culminates with the believer's faith in Christ. Most likely, the expression designates the Christian's progressive growth in faith as the basis for growth in righteousness. Later Paul will forward Abraham as a model of growing strong in faith (4:19–21) and will urge believers to advance in righteousness (6:16–19).

To verify the saving power of faith, Paul cites the words of the prophet Habakkuk: **The one who is righteous by faith will live** (Hab 2:4). Few passages of Scripture state more clearly that God promises life to those who are righteous by faith. Paul will expand on this theme in the next chapter by affirming that "eternal

10. Charles L. Quarles, "From Faith to Faith: A Fresh Examination of the Prepositional Series in Romans 1:17," *NovT* 45, no. 1 (2003): 1–21, was unable to find a single instance in ancient Greek literature where the two prepositions Paul employs here are combined to form an emphatic idiom.

The Righteousness of God

BIBLICAL BACKGROUND

The Letter to the Romans is punctuated with the language of "righteousness" (in Greek, *dikaiosynē*). Most scholars agree that Paul has in mind the Hebrew notion of *tsedeq* or *tsedaqah*, which signals "conformity to a standard or norm." In the Bible, the standard of measurement is typically the covenant, the bond that unites God with his people and spells out the obligations that govern this relationship.

Scripture speaks of righteousness when a covenant relationship is in good order, with its stipulations observed and upheld by the partners involved.[a] The righteousness of God, then, is another way of speaking about God's covenant faithfulness. The Lord displays his righteousness when he keeps his promises (Neh 9:8) and renders just judgment on human actions (Ps 50:6; Dan 9:14). Even more, he reveals it through mighty acts of deliverance. God shows himself righteous when he exercises his power and will to save, as noted especially in the Psalms (Pss 31:2; 71:2; 143:11) and Isaiah (Isa 45:8; 56:1; 61:10).

For Paul, the righteousness of God is a double-sided concept. On the one hand, it refers to the righteousness *demonstrated by God* in the events of salvation history. Divine righteousness in this sense is an "attribute of divine activity."[b] On the other hand, the righteousness of God designates the gift of righteousness that *comes from God* in the form of grace imparted to the believer.[c] It is his merciful gift of putting sinners right once again by establishing them in a covenant relationship and entitling them to his blessings. Believers who receive the gift of God's righteousness are forgiven and "made righteous" before him (Rom 5:19; 2 Cor 5:21; Phil 3:9).[d] These two aspects are tightly interwoven in Romans, especially in 3:21–26, where we learn that God manifests his righteousness precisely by justifying (= making righteous) the one who puts faith in Jesus. Thus, the righteousness of God in Romans is the covenant faithfulness of God experienced as salvation by his people.

a. On the language of "righteousness" as covenantal language, see Stanley E. Porter, "The Concept of Covenant in Paul," in *The Concept of the Covenant in the Second Temple Period*, ed. Stanley E. Porter and Jacqueline C. R. de Roo (Leiden: Brill, 2003), 269–85.
b. Joseph A. Fitzmyer, SJ, *Romans*, AB 33 (New York: Doubleday, 1993), 262.
c. St. Augustine, *On the Trinity* 4.15; St. Thomas Aquinas, *Commentary on Romans* 1.6.102.
d. The Dead Sea Scrolls also connect the righteousness of God with the forgiveness of sins. See, e.g., the *Community Rule* (1QS 11.2, 12).

life" awaits the faithful at the final judgment (Rom 2:7). A preview of this future scenario presented itself in Habakkuk's day, when Israel faced the chastening judgment of God. The prophet foresaw the Babylonian invasion and conquest of Judea in 586 BC as a manifestation of the Lord's wrath against his errant people, a wrath that only the person who kept faith would escape. Paul likewise sees faith as the path to deliverance and life on the coming day of judgment.

Reflection and Application (1:16–17)

Probably few of us can say as adamantly as Paul, "I am not ashamed of the gospel." At one time or another we have all felt timid, maybe even terrified, before the world's seething disdain for Christianity. The gospel is frequently mocked in cultural and political discourse, and much of the secular media jumps at the opportunity to poke fun at its most cherished truths and expressions. At the very least, a line is drawn in the sand that makes our options clear: we can shrink with embarrassment before this onslaught, or we can stand up and be counted. To be ashamed or not to be ashamed—that is the question.

It is tempting to think that Paul faced opposition that was less determined and less diabolical than we face today. But history indicates otherwise. Every generation of Christians has had to count the cost of following Jesus. Every believer has had to internalize the Lord's words: "Whoever is ashamed of me and of my words in this faithless and sinful generation, the Son of Man will be ashamed of when he comes in his Father's glory with the holy angels" (Mark 8:38).

But the gospel of Jesus Christ does not cease to be good news, no matter how many denounce or oppose it. Paul understood this well. Everywhere he witnessed "the power of God" transforming people's lives for the better. There is no shame in working for the salvation of others. There is great satisfaction in watching God renew the face of the earth through our feeble efforts. The challenge before us is one of courage. Yes, much of the world will reject the gospel and its messengers with hostility. But our lot is thrown in with Jesus, who has already "conquered the world" (John 16:33).

Idolatry: The Corruption of Religion (1:18–23)

[18]The wrath of God is indeed being revealed from heaven against every impiety and wickedness of those who suppress the truth by their wickedness. [19]For what can be known about God is evident to them, because God made it evident to them. [20]Ever since the creation of the world, his invisible attributes of eternal power and divinity have been able to be understood and perceived in what he has made. As a result, they have no excuse; [21]for although they knew God they did not accord him glory as God or give him thanks. Instead, they became vain in their reasoning, and their

senseless minds were darkened. [22]**While claiming to be wise, they became fools** [23]**and exchanged the glory of the immortal God for the likeness of an image of mortal man or of birds or of four-legged animals or of snakes.**

OT: Deut 4:16–18; Pss 19:2–5; 106:20; Wis 13:1–10
NT: John 3:36; Acts 14:15–17; 17:26–28; Eph 4:17–19
Catechism: knowledge of God from creation, 31–35, 1147; the virtue of religion, 1807, 2125; idolatry, 2113

Starting with verse 18, Paul begins a long section in Romans, running to 3:20, in which the entire world is shown guilty before God. The corruption of religion, leading to the corruption of personal and social morality, is the tragic story of our race that both Gentiles and Jews played a part in. And neither had a legitimate excuse: Gentiles had the natural revelation in creation to light their way (1:18–32), and Jews had the supernatural revelation of the Torah as a lamp unto their feet (2:1–3:20).

No sooner does Paul declare that the righteousness of God is revealed in   **1:18**
the gospel (1:17) than he adds that the **wrath of God** is likewise **revealed from heaven**. Technically, the notion of divine wrath is an *anthropopathism*, a metaphorical description of God as though he had human passions and emotions. In reality, God is eternally unchanging; he does not lose his cool or boil over with rage as you and I sometimes do. Hence, when Scripture speaks of divine indignation or anger, it means God's fixed response to sin—sin being completely at odds with his justice and holiness.[11] The Bible routinely employs such humanlike descriptions for the purpose of making the infinite mystery of God more understandable to finite minds.

Paul says that heaven's wrath is provoked by **wickedness** and **impiety**, particularly of those who **suppress the truth** about God. It is a question not of ignorance but of people's willful efforts to smother the truth under a heap of sinful choices and distractions. Failure to acknowledge a personal God—one Supreme Being, Lawgiver, and Intelligence—is first and foremost a moral problem. Only secondarily can it be called an intellectual problem.

Notice too that God's wrath is manifesting itself in the present flow of history. It is true that Paul forecasts a "day of wrath" in connection with the last judgment (2:5). But the Lord's just response to sin is not simply held in reserve until the end of time. Even now it is painfully visible in the degeneracy of human society. Paul will explain the meaning of this when he relates how God hands sinners over to their wanton desires in 1:24, 26, 28.

---

11. St. Thomas Aquinas holds that "wrath" is metaphorical when attributed to God and interprets it to signify the divine "punishment" that comes upon the sinner (*Summa Theologiae* I.19.11).

1:19–20   In point of fact, God made himself **evident** through "the greatness and the beauty of created things" (Wis 13:5). Theologians call this God's natural revelation, which Paul claims has been accessible in every age and to every thinking person through the use of reason: **Ever since the creation of the world, his invisible attributes of eternal power and divinity have been able to be understood and perceived in what he has made.** By a process of observation, reflection, and deduction, the mind is capable of rising to the knowledge of an almighty Deity who transcends the material universe and yet is necessary to account for its existence and organized complexity. The world, to paraphrase the Apostle, is covered with the fingerprints of God.

Persons who refuse this knowledge **have no excuse.** Before God's tribunal, they are simply defenseless. Even the notion of "culpable ignorance" seems too weak to capture what Paul is saying. For him, it is a matter of knowledge pushed aside and rejected rather than knowledge unattained because of negligence.

1:21   Not surprisingly, once people turned their backs on the witness of God in creation, **they did not accord him glory as God or give him thanks.** Implicit in Paul's words is the notion that human beings have a moral obligation to worship the Lord with gratitude, since all that we have comes from him. Tradition calls this "the virtue of religion." Without it, men and women spiral downward into the vice of idolatry.

Thereafter **reasoning** becomes **vain** and **senseless.** In other words, rejecting the natural knowledge of God has debilitating effects on the human faculties, including the intellect. People who are otherwise rational begin to lose touch with reality; their capacity to see the truth about God and themselves becomes **darkened** when they shield their minds from the light of divine revelation refracted through creation.

1:22–23   The consequence of this is the perversion of religion known as idolatry. Idolatry in the abstract means elevating the creature to the place of the creator, as Paul puts it in 1:25. Idolatry in the concrete is what history witnesses every time **the glory of the immortal God** is traded away and **exchanged** for lifeless images, which peoples in the biblical world shaped into a menagerie of **mortal man** and **birds** and **four-legged animals** and **snakes.** Paul appears to have in mind Greeks and Romans, who represented their deities in human form, as well as Egyptians, who also gave their gods and goddesses animal forms.

Paul's thinking on idolatry is formed by Scripture, especially by passages such as Deut 4:16–18, where Moses forbids the manufacture of idol images fashioned to look like people, animals, birds, or crawling creatures. Moreover, Paul borrows key expressions from Ps 106:20, which tells how Israel "exchanged" the "glory"

The Natural Knowledge of God

LIVING TRADITION

Paul affirms the possibility of "natural theology," of coming to know God's existence, power, and goodness through reflection on the world around us (1:19–20; see Acts 14:15–17; 17:26–28). He was not the first to make such a claim, since the same thing is stated in the Old Testament (Ps 19:2–5; Wis 13:1–10); nor was he the last, for several Christian thinkers and saints devised rational proofs for demonstrating the existence of God apart from faith (St. John of Damascus, St. Anselm, St. Thomas Aquinas). Even pagan philosophers reasoned their way upward on a scale of perfection to a single Supreme Good (Plato) as well as backward in time to a single Prime Mover (Aristotle).

Despite a barrage of philosophical and atheistic objections put forward in modern times, the Catholic Church continues to insist that God and his perfections are knowable by reason apart from the supernatural revelation of Sacred Scripture and Sacred Tradition. This was declared in 1870 at Vatican I, which stated: "Holy Mother Church holds and teaches that . . . God, the beginning and end of all things, can be known with certainty by the natural light of human reason from a consideration of created things" (*Dei Filius* 2.1). Likewise, Vatican II reaffirmed in 1965 that "God, who creates and conserves all things by his Word, provides men with constant evidence of himself in created realities" (*Dei Verbum* 3).[a]

a. For classical and contemporary arguments for God's existence, with a focus on rebutting the claims of the New Atheism, see Scott Hahn and Benjamin Wiker, *Answering the New Atheism: Dismantling Dawkins' Case against God* (Steubenville, OH: Emmaus Road, 2008); Timothy Keller, *The Reason for God: Belief in an Age of Skepticism* (New York: Dutton, 2009); and Michael Augros, *Who Designed the Designer? A Rediscovered Path to God's Existence* (San Francisco: Ignatius, 2015).

of the Lord for the "image" of a bull—a reference to the golden calf apostasy at Mount Sinai (Exod 32:1–6). By slipping in this allusion, Paul offers a subtle reminder that Gentile idolatry is not the only idolatry the world has ever seen. Time and again Israel succumbed to the very same temptation. In fact, Scripture documents how the covenant people, in their darkest hours, also worshiped images of men (Ezek 16:17), beasts (Lev 17:7), and reptiles (2 Kings 18:4).

Immorality: The Corruption of Life (1:24–32)

[24]**Therefore, God handed them over to impurity through the lusts of their hearts for the mutual degradation of their bodies.** [25]**They exchanged**

the truth of God for a lie and revered and worshiped the creature rather than the creator, who is blessed forever. Amen. [26]Therefore, God handed them over to degrading passions. Their females exchanged natural relations for unnatural, [27]and the males likewise gave up natural relations with females and burned with lust for one another. Males did shameful things with males and thus received in their own persons the due penalty for their perversity. [28]And since they did not see fit to acknowledge God, God handed them over to their undiscerning mind to do what is improper. [29]They are filled with every form of wickedness, evil, greed, and malice; full of envy, murder, rivalry, treachery, and spite. They are gossips [30]and scandalmongers and they hate God. They are insolent, haughty, boastful, ingenious in their wickedness, and rebellious toward their parents. [31]They are senseless, faithless, heartless, ruthless. [32]Although they know the just decree of God that all who practice such things deserve death, they not only do them but give approval to those who practice them.

OT: Lev 18:22; 20:13; Ps 81:13; Wis 14:26–27
NT: 1 Cor 6:9–10; Gal 5:19–21; Eph 4:17–19; 1 Tim 1:10; 2 Tim 3:2–5
Catechism: chastity and homosexuality, 2357–59

Idolatry is "the reason and source . . . of all evil," says the book of Wisdom (Wis 14:27). Paul adopts this perspective as his own in Rom 1:18–32, where he shows that the aftereffect of serving idols is an explosion of immorality. Nothing is more disorienting for the human person than rejecting the creator in favor of the creature, which sets off a domino cascade of societal degeneration that seems to have no end short of hatred for God (1:30).

Figure 2. Cult statue of the Ephesian Artemis, first century AD. In Ephesus, Artemis and Cybele were blended into one goddess connected with fertility, birth, nature, and the hunt. Her dress is decorated with winged figures, lions, bees, mythical creatures, and bull testicles.

Heading the list of evils spawned by idolatry is sexual **impurity**. Paul teaches   **1:24**
that **God** sometimes brings judgment on godless men and women by handing
them over to **the lusts of their hearts** without restraint. He simply stands back
and allows the base desires of the flesh to gain mastery over right reason. As a
result, fornication, adultery, prostitution, and an appetite for the pornographic
take deep root in society. Those who are caught up in these disordered pursuits of
pleasure treat their **bodies** (as well as others') in degrading and disrespectful ways.

Idolatry is thus exposed as a **lie**—a deception that misconstrues the true   **1:25**
nature of reality and the true object of human fulfillment. If accepting the truth
about **the creator** rightly orients a person's life, then diverting religious veneration to **the creature** throws life into confusion and sets it on a path toward
progressive disintegration.

Having touched on sexual "impurity" in general (1:24), Paul narrows his   **1:26–27**
focus to homosexuality.[12] He seems to consider this a textbook example of
what happens when men and women suppress the natural revelation of God
inscribed in creation. And again, Paul's thoughts are indebted to the Jewish
Scriptures, which strenuously disapprove of homosexual behavior, declaring it
an abomination (Lev 18:22). According to the biblical vision, God intended sex
for married persons, who are sexually differentiated and can reciprocate one
another's love in a procreative way (Gen 1:27–28). Deviation from this standard is **unnatural**—literally, "against nature."[13] It is rebellion against the divine
purpose of human sexuality, which is discernible from the complementarity of
man and woman and the design of their physical anatomy.[14]

Paul's denunciation falls on *acts* of sexual intimacy between persons of the
same gender. Both **females** and **males** are guilty of giving up **natural relations**[15] with the opposite sex and doing **shameful things** with one another. In
the Apostle's judgment, both are disordered forms of sexual expression that
are contrary to God's design and thus morally unacceptable. It is fair to say

12. For a thorough discussion of this issue, see Robert A. J. Gagnon, *The Bible and Homosexual
Practice: Texts and Hermeneutics* (Nashville: Abingdon, 2001).

13. The notion that homosexual behavior is "unnatural" or "contrary to nature" is also found in
Jewish sources roughly contemporary with Paul (see Philo of Alexandria, *Special Laws* 3.39; Josephus,
Against Apion 2.275; *Testament of Naphtali* 3.4).

14. Some argue that Paul's polemic against homosexual acts is not relevant to a moral evaluation of
gay couples in loving and committed relationships, since persons in this situation are merely following
their natural inclinations. It is important to understand, however, that Paul defines what is natural not by
the experience of desires that arise unbidden and seek satisfaction but by the testimony of Scripture and
human reason regarding the divine order of creation. Otherwise, everything from covetousness to hatred
would have to be reclassified as natural movements of the soul rather than disordered desires forbidden
by divine law. Even the urge for sexual gratification within marriage must be regulated and controlled.

15. The expression in Greek is "the natural use," which is shorthand for "the natural use of the
opposite gender as a sexual partner."

He "Handed Them Over"

Three times in this section Paul uses the expression "God handed them over" to describe the divine punishment of idolaters (1:24, 26, 28). These words hold the key to his understanding of "the wrath of God" manifest in history (1:18). We may, however, find Paul's thinking on this subject strangely counterintuitive. We tend to associate divine wrath with the dramatic and the destructive, with thunderbolts, cyclones, floods, and earthquakes. Yet there is a more subtle and dreadful form of divine wrath that few seem to be aware of.[a] This is what Paul explains in Rom 1: sometimes God punishes godless sinners by allowing them to bind themselves in the captivating pleasures of sinful passion.[b]

Admittedly, this sounds at first like an absence of divine wrath, like a failure on God's part to take punitive action against sin. But this is not the case. When people are determined to satisfy their lusts and the Lord stands by without intervening, he is allowing them to disgrace themselves by forming attachments to forbidden pleasure. In essence, God's punishment for unrepentant sin is attachment to sin, precisely because the more one indulges in sin, the more one drifts away from God and the more one squelches any desire to repent and return to him for mercy. Paul would say that such a person is "storing up wrath" for himself (2:5).

The takeaway lesson is that you and I must resist the temptation to sin, and when we fail we must be quick to repent and to renounce the wrong we have done. This is what keeps us from sliding down into the addictions that make us "slaves to impurity" (6:19) and other evil habits. Otherwise we will begin to experience desires for wrongful pleasure that slowly intensify over time, reaching a point where they become almost irresistible. Furthermore, we must come to see that when God disciplines us for sin, when he injects suffering, adversity, and disappointment into our lives in the wake of our bad choices, these are the signs of his mercy. They are taps on the shoulder that invite us to seek forgiveness and to straighten out our way. Given the prospect of eternal damnation, the last thing we *really* want is to prosper and flourish in a lifestyle of sin, for that is a sign that God is letting us have what we want rather than giving us what we need. That is a sign that God, in his wrath, is "handing us over" to iniquity.

a. See also Ps 81:12–13 and Acts 7:41–42.
b. Scott Hahn, *Lord, Have Mercy: The Healing Power of Confession* (New York: Doubleday, 2003), 85–88.

that Paul does not address the question of homosexual inclination or same-sex attraction per se, and to this extent he does not speak to all the issues that concern modern readers. Even so, he is unambiguous about the grave sinfulness of homoerotic sexual acts and further points out that **lust** is ordinarily part of the equation.

Paul adds that perpetrators of these sins **received in their own persons the due penalty for their disordered behavior**. One might think of the physical consequences of such behaviors—for example, sexually transmitted diseases. In all likelihood, however, Paul's comment has little to do with health risks. Instead, the "due penalty" points to a spiritual consequence experienced as moral confusion and sexual addiction. Just as virtue is its own reward, so vice is its own punishment. In sum, we forge our fetters by habitually giving in to inordinate passions.

In a final salvo, Paul exposes the ugly variety of human iniquity. He has examined religious rebellion (1:19–23) and sexual rebellion (1:24–27); now he looks at moral rebellion more broadly. There are several such vice lists in the New Testament, but arguably none so raw and hard-hitting as what we read in Rom 1. His point, once again, is that life unravels on all fronts when people do **not see fit to acknowledge God**. Humanity's attempt to manage its own affairs without God has proven wildly unsuccessful, since creatures turned away from the creator inevitably think and do what is **improper**. **1:28–31**

Most agree that in verses 29–31 Paul is not attempting to classify godless behavior category by category. Some literary arrangement is noticeable in the Greek, but it is likely that Paul is rattling off vices unsystematically. What he describes is nothing less than the eruption of moral chaos in personal, family, and social life. Everywhere people have fallen from their dignity as human beings made to love God and one another. Instead, they have become selfish (**greed**), slanderous (**gossips**), arrogant (**insolent**), untrustworthy (**faithless**), irrational (**senseless**), excessively competitive (**rivalry**), insubordinate (**rebellious toward their parents**), impressed with themselves (**boastful**), insensitive to others (**heartless**), and downright violent (**murder**), among other things.

If any item in the list can be called a standout, it is that people have come to **hate God**. This is the basement floor of human depravity, the dankest depths to which our race has been known to lower itself. And yet, something about it is predictable: once forbidden desires become like deities that must be served at all costs, then the God who prohibits them will be branded the enemy.

It is surprising to hear Paul say, on the heels of verses 29–31, that godless men and women still have some awareness of right and wrong. That is the implication of saying **they know the just decree of God**. No matter how completely an individual is mastered by vice, there remains a lingering perception of the natural moral law that God inscribes on the heart. Even persons deep in sin have **1:32** an understanding that rebellion against God **deserves death**. Some speculate that Paul is talking here about capital punishment, but that is unlikely. Instead he seems to indicate something primal that lives on in the human conscience, something like a faint echo of the divine decree regarding "the tree of knowledge of good and evil" in Gen 2:17: "From that tree you shall not eat; when you eat from it you shall die." It is difficult to be more precise than this, and many commentators admit that the meaning of Paul's statement is not entirely transparent.

Finally, Paul hints that moral decay reaches an advanced stage when people **not only** commit sins of godlessness **but give approval to those who practice them**. Societal degeneration sinks to crisis levels when adulation—applauding others for their wrongdoing—is added to the heap. Once the stigma of iniquity is taken away and wanton misbehavior becomes socially acceptable, people are emboldened in their evil ways rather than deterred from them. The prophet Isaiah laments this as a time when people call evil good and good evil (Isa 5:20).

Reflection and Application (1:18–32)

Throughout this initial section of the letter, Paul is slamming down the gavel and declaring the world guilty before God. It is not that he has some morbid fixation with sin or that he enjoys railing against our fallen race from some lofty, spiritual pulpit. Paul is rather preparing to announce the good news of salvation (3:21–30) by speaking first of the bad news of human sinfulness (1:18–3:20). It is hard to fully appreciate a cure for cancer unless one sees firsthand the devastation it causes in the lives of real people. So too the greatness of our redemption cannot be measured unless the gravity of our predicament has been honestly and painfully examined. Exposing the reality of sin is thus a vital preliminary to a full understanding of the gospel.

We should keep in mind, therefore, that 1:18–32 is simply the first stage in a larger argument. A good story moves from conflict to resolution. Paul is telling just such a story—and it happens to be the true story of human history. Tension and suspense are built up by probing the depths of our plight, but only as a prelude to the saving intervention of God in Jesus Christ, who alone can rescue us from the awful mess we have made of our lives.

The Judgment and the Law of God

Romans 2:1–29

Romans 2 reads like a mirror reflection of Rom 1, where Paul's exposé of pagan depravity is matched in kind by a stinging indictment of disobedience among the covenant people. His point is that sin is not simply a Gentile problem; it is a Jewish problem as well. A close reading of the two chapters in tandem reveals this thematic continuity: both Gentiles and Jews are guilty of provoking the "wrath" of God (1:18; 2:5) by rebellion against what they "know" to be true (1:21, 32; 2:18), and so both are without "excuse" for failing to do what is right (1:20; 2:1).

The Just Judgment of God (2:1–11)

[1]Therefore, you are without excuse, every one of you who passes judgment. For by the standard by which you judge another you condemn yourself, since you, the judge, do the very same things. [2]We know that the judgment of God on those who do such things is true. [3]Do you suppose, then, you who judge those who engage in such things and yet do them yourself, that you will escape the judgment of God? [4]Or do you hold his priceless kindness, forbearance, and patience in low esteem, unaware that the kindness of God would lead you to repentance? [5]By your stubbornness and impenitent heart, you are storing up wrath for yourself for the day of wrath and revelation of the just judgment of God, [6]who will repay everyone according to his works: [7]eternal life to those who seek glory, honor, and immortality through perseverance in good works, [8]but wrath and fury to those

who selfishly disobey the truth and obey wickedness. ⁹Yes, affliction and distress will come upon every human being who does evil, Jew first and then Greek. ¹⁰But there will be glory, honor, and peace for everyone who does good, Jew first and then Greek. ¹¹There is no partiality with God.

OT: Deut 10:17; Ps 62:13; Prov 24:12; Wis 11:23; Sir 5:4–6; Zeph 1:15
NT: Matt 16:27; 25:31–46; John 5:28–29; 2 Cor 5:10; Col 3:25; 1 Pet 1:17; 2 Pet 3:9
Catechism: presumption, 2091–92; particular judgment, 1021–22; last judgment, 1038–41

The opening verses of Rom 2 mark a shift in Paul's historical viewpoint. In 1:18–32, he explained the manifestation of divine wrath in the present. In 2:1–11, he turns toward the future, to the †eschatological "day of wrath" (2:5) when Jews and Gentiles alike will stand before God to be judged impartially (2:11) according to their actions (2:6–10).

2:1-3   Readers coming fresh to Rom 2 are likely to feel lost at first, since Paul is already in the thick of an argument that began in 1:18. The opening word **There-fore** is an indicator that we are catching the Apostle in midthought. At this point Paul also initiates a "diatribe" with an imaginary conversation partner, called an interlocutor. †Diatribe was a rhetorical convention developed in classical antiquity in which a teacher or writer promoted his views by making assertions, formulating questions, and anticipating objections, all in the format of a lively debate. Paul dialogues with an unnamed individual whom he addresses simply as **you**. In verse 17 we discover this person is a self-professed "Jew."

Notice that Paul is not directing his comments toward any particular Jew but to **every** Jewish person who passes **judgment** on Gentile sinners. Evidently some, inflated with a sense of moral superiority, felt justified in playing **the judge** and condemning the non-Jewish world for its wickedness. No doubt Paul agrees that pagan abominations are worthy of condemnation, since he says **the judgment of God on those who do such things is true**. However, he immediately criticizes his debate partner for holding others to a **standard** that he himself struggles to attain. Indeed, Paul charges his fellow Jews with doing some of **the very same things** that are exampled in the pagan world! A glance back at 1:18–32 shows how piercing this rebuke must have felt.

The judgmental Jew is therefore left **without excuse**. Paul's use of this ex-pression[1] is no accident, since he leveled the same charge against Gentiles in 1:20. The parallel is notable: just as pagans are inexcusably culpable for sinning against God's revelation in creation, so Jews have no defense for transgressing God's revelation in the Torah.

---

1. Greek *anapologētos*.

Presumption and Judgment

Paul issues some stern warnings in Rom 2 against the dangers of presumption. Even though his words address the problem of Jewish presumption, they are no less applicable to the problem of Christian presumption. Believers in Jesus should never despair of God's mercy, but neither should they convince themselves that salvation is guaranteed to all who place faith in Christ, regardless of how they live. The prospect of a future judgment by God urges the baptized to work out their salvation "with fear and trembling" (Phil 2:12). These ideas are nicely threaded together in the following admonition by St. Caesarius of Arles:

> We must fear lest someone believes so strongly that he will receive God's mercy that he does not dread his justice. If a man does this, he has no faith. Likewise, if he dreads his justice so much that he despairs of his mercy, there is no faith. Since God is not only merciful but also just, let us believe in both. Let us not despair of his mercy because we fear his justice, nor love his mercy so much that we disregard his justice. Therefore, we should neither hope wrongly nor despair wickedly. A man who hopes wrongly thinks he can merit mercy without penance and good works; one who despairs wickedly does not believe he will receive mercy even after the performance of good works. Therefore, above all, we should consider and fear lest we believe that faith without good works can suffice for us.[a]

a. St. Caesarius of Arles, *Sermons* 12.5. Adapted from *Saint Caesarius of Arles: Sermons*, vol. 1, trans. Sister Mary Magdeleine, OSF, FC 31 (New York: Fathers of the Church, 1956), 72.

But the indictment does not stop there. On top of hypocrisy and infidelity Paul adds the sin of presumption. This is the prideful overconfidence that the Jewish people will **escape the judgment of God**. Reading 2:17–29 in light of passages such as Matt 3:9, it seems that some Jews regarded their ethnic ties to the patriarchs, along with the privilege of being counted among God's people, as an insurance policy against the fiery day of judgment. It was a false confidence that every Israelite was guaranteed mercy, no matter what.[2] Of course, Paul did not need to convince fellow Jews that they had sinned at one time or another in their lifetime. Rather, his point is that personal disloyalty to the covenant will count against each individual transgressor at the final judgment unless repentance comes first (Rom 2:4). Membership in the covenant does not make faithful observance of the covenant optional for salvation.

2. This type of presumption is also cautioned against in Sir 5:4–6.

2:4–5   Paul next poses a question that invites self-examination. If the Jewish moralist is guilty of spiritual pride, then, whether or not he realizes it, he is holding the Lord's **kindness** and **forbearance** and **patience** in contempt. Presuming upon God's future mercy has led him to overlook God's present mercy in allowing him opportunities for deeper conversion. In fact, God's tolerance of misbehavior is aimed at bringing about **repentance**, which, in Pauline terms, entails both a "godly sorrow" for past sins (2 Cor 7:10) and a lifelong commitment to seeking "glory, honor, and immortality" (Rom 2:7).

Those who spurn this mercy reveal the **stubbornness**—literally, "hardness"—of their **heart**. Hardheartedness is biblical language for a human will that resists the Lord and his law (Exod 8:15; Prov 28:14; Ezek 3:7; Matt 19:8). Paul will speak of the solution to this problem in Rom 2:26–29.

For the moment, however, he warns the **impenitent** Jew against **storing up wrath** for the future.[3] In Paul's thinking, "wrath" is the exact opposite of "salvation" (5:9; 1 Thess 1:10; 5:9). And **the day of wrath** is an Old Testament expression for the dreadful day of reckoning, when God will manifest the full measure of his justice in opposition to evil (Zeph 1:15, 18; 2:3).

2:6–10   The all-important line in Paul's discussion is the claim that God **will repay everyone according to his works**. This statement has occasioned controversy among Christian groups today, but it would have seemed commonplace to Paul's readers. "Judgment according to works" is a classic tenet of Jewish theology rooted deep in the teaching of Scripture.[4] This is the belief that God will hold every person accountable for his or her actions, public or private, and assign each person a corresponding destiny. One will either receive **eternal life** at the final judgment, or face the **wrath and fury** of the God who punishes evil.

Everlasting life awaits those who pursue **glory, honor, and immortality**. These terms summarize the teaching of Scripture, which reveals that humanity was made to be crowned with "glory and honor" (Ps 8:6) and to experience a life that is "imperishable" (Wis 2:23). Those who seek these things seek the full realization of God's plan for the human race. But this reward is not for the uncommitted. Paul goes on to speak of **perseverance in good works**, by which he means a steady persistence of moral and spiritual effort over the long haul. For Paul, faith is the structural foundation that underlies and supports the entire Christian life from beginning to end. It is thus an indispensable element in

3. James D. G. Dunn, *Romans 1–8*, WBC 38a (Nashville: Nelson, 1988), 84, suggests that Paul's statement may be a reversal based on the wording of Tob 4:9–10.
4. E.g., Job 34:11; Eccles 12:14; Sir 16:12–14; Jer 17:10.

Public domain / Wikimedia Commons

Figure 3. *The Last Judgment* by Michelangelo (1475–1564).

all matters pertaining to salvation, including the performance of good works. Believers are no more justified by works *alone* than they are justified by faith *alone*. Hence Paul elsewhere defines Christian living as "faith working through love" (Gal 5:6).

Opposite salvation and life is the prospect of **affliction and distress**. These terms point to the panic and dread that will seize unrepentant sinners when God sits in judgment over their lives. Paul again borrows language from the Old Testament, this time from the †Septuagint translation of Deut 28:53, 55, 57, which announces the curses of the covenant set to fall on Israel should they forsake the Lord and his law.[5] Such is the destiny that awaits those who **selfishly[6] disobey the truth**. This statement implies that God's truth, once

---

5. The Hebrew terms are translated "siege and distress" in the NABRE. The same word pair appears in Isa 8:22 and 30:6 in the LXX, but these passages appear to be drawing from the same curse threats in Deuteronomy that Paul evokes.

6. The Greek *eritheia* designates either "selfish ambition" or "strife." Modern translations vary in rendering it "self-seeking" (NRSV, NIV), "factious" (RSV), or "unsubmissive" (JB).

revealed, imposes expectations and accountability on those who receive it. One not only assents to divine truth with the mind; one also consents to live by the demands of that truth with the will. Refusal to obey what is true is thus equivalent to obeying **wickedness**.

Paul's main point in this section is that **Jew** and **Greek** will be held to the same standard of judgment. Israel is not automatically guaranteed salvation; condemnation is not automatically reserved for all other nations. By the same token, Paul neither contests nor depreciates the †election of Israel as a chosen people. Indeed, he will later acknowledge the many blessings that the Jewish people possess because of their special relationship with the Lord (Rom 3:1–2; 9:4–5; 11:28–29). The Jew's privileged position among the nations is precisely why he stands **first** in line to receive recompense from God. The recipient of more revelation, he is the more accountable for his response to it. The words of Jesus explain Paul's reasoning here: "Much will be required of the person entrusted with much, and still more will be demanded of the person entrusted with more" (Luke 12:48).

2:11   In summary, Paul declares: **There is no partiality[7] with God.** His words echo an important biblical teaching, showing its full agreement with the gospel. Foremost in mind is probably Deut 10:17, which defines impartiality to mean that God "has no favorites" and "accepts no bribes" when he renders his judgment (see also 2 Chron 19:7; Wis 6:7; Sir 35:15). Its restatement in Rom 2 indicates that God will not give preferential treatment to Jews over Gentiles when a final reckoning is made of their lives. Whoever does good or evil, irrespective of genealogy or nationality, will receive a just recompense from the Lord.

The Doers of the Law (2:12–16)

---

[12]All who sin outside the law will also perish without reference to it, and all who sin under the law will be judged in accordance with it. [13]For it is not those who hear the law who are just in the sight of God; rather, those who observe the law will be justified. [14]For when the Gentiles who do not have the law by nature observe the prescriptions of the law, they are a law for themselves even though they do not have the law. [15]They show that the demands of the law are written in their hearts, while their conscience also bears witness and their conflicting thoughts accuse or even

---

7. The Greek term *prosōpolēmpsia* is related to a Hebrew idiom ("to lift the face") that is used to warn judges not to show favoritism in the courtroom and thereby compromise a fair administration of justice (Lev 19:15; Ps 82:2; see Deut 16:19).

defend them [16]**on the day when, according to my gospel, God will judge people's hidden works through Christ Jesus.**

OT: 1 Chron 28:9; Wis 17:11; Jer 17:10; 31:33
NT: Matt 12:37; Acts 10:42; 1 Cor 4:5; 2 Cor 5:10; Heb 4:12; James 1:22
Catechism: natural law, 1954–60, 2070–71; moral conscience, 1776–1802; Christ the judge, 679, 682

In these verses, Paul discusses the law of Moses for the first time in Romans. It is a subject to which he will return many times throughout the letter. Here he wishes to preempt an objection from his hypothetical Jewish respondent, who is likely to charge that Paul's foregoing description of judgment has left the Torah out of consideration. It is one thing to say that good works are necessary for salvation. But doesn't the Mosaic law define what is good? And aren't the Gentiles, by and large, ignorant of its precepts?

Paul begins by distinguishing between those who live **outside the law** and those who live **under the law**. This is a traditional Jewish way of characterizing the life of Gentiles and Jews respectively. However, contrary to this convention, Paul sees no difference between the fate of sinful Gentiles and the fate of sinful Jews. Wicked Gentiles will **perish without reference to** the Mosaic law, since they "know" by natural revelation that evildoing merits "death" (1:32), just as rebellious Jews will **be judged in accordance with** the Mosaic law.
2:12

The point is that explicit knowledge of the Torah will afford no protection against condemnation. Having and knowing the law will be no substitute for keeping the law. Jews **who hear the law** read aloud in the synagogue every sabbath are not considered righteous or **just** on that account. They must **observe the law** in the varied circumstances of life, and only then will they be **justified** by the Lord.
2:13

Paul here introduces the concept of justification, which is one of the ways he speaks about salvation in Christ, especially in Romans and Galatians. To be justified is to be established in a right relationship with God. (For further discussion, see the sidebar, "Justification," in Rom 3 [pp. 50–51].)

Paul next tackles the issue of Gentile obedience to the law. He states that, surprisingly, some non-Jews, without formal knowledge of the Torah, have been known to live according to its decrees. What exactly he means by this is debated.
2:14–15

Many hold that Paul is describing pagan **Gentiles** who manage to lead virtuous lives by observing the natural law **written in their hearts**; according to this reading, the expression **by nature**[8] means something like "by following

---

8. The NABRE preserves the ambiguity of the Greek, which leaves us guessing whether "by nature" modifies what precedes ("the Gentiles who do not have the law by nature") or what follows ("by nature

the guidance of their God-given conscience."[9] Certain Gentiles actually observed **the prescriptions of the law**, despite having no explicit knowledge of the commandments of Moses.

Others hold that Paul is discussing the moral transformation of Christian Gentiles in the New Covenant.[10] The reference to God's law "written in their hearts" is taken as an allusion to the prophet Jeremiah's New Covenant oracle, where the Lord declares of his messianic people: "I will place my law within them, and write it upon their hearts" (Jer 31:33). In this interpretation, the expression "by nature" means "by circumstances of birth and upbringing." Paul is thus interpreted to say that the Torah is no longer the exclusive possession of the Jews, for Gentile converts to Christianity are now being instructed in its teachings, and thanks to the indwelling of the Spirit (Rom 2:29) they are fulfilling its righteous **demands** in their lives (8:4).

Deciding between these two options is difficult. On the one hand, Paul acknowledges that a natural moral awareness operates in pagan nonbelievers (1:32) through the witness of their **conscience** (2:16). On the other hand, Paul is building toward a discussion of how Gentiles, in their native circumstances, lacked the advantages that come with Jewish circumcision (2:27), but, having come to believe in Christ, they are now recipients of an inner circumcision "in the spirit" (2:29). Either way, Paul contends that Gentiles who live in accord with the law **are a law for themselves**. Scholars have noted that similar statements appear in Greek writings to describe persons of exceptional moral character who conduct themselves virtuously by following the light of reason.[11]

Additionally, Paul contends that the conscience of the Gentile will **accuse** or **defend** his actions as blameworthy or praiseworthy at the last judgment, and thus **bear witness** to the justice of God's final verdict. Paul does not say much about conscience in his letters, but he clearly understands it as an interior judge that applauds our good moral choices and faults us for sinful ones. Without saying so explicitly, Paul presupposes that the law of conscience operates according to the same moral standards as the law of Moses.[12]

---

observe the prescriptions of the law"). Modern translations such as the RSV, NRSV, JB, and NIV prefer the latter rendering.

9. It is generally agreed, among ancient and modern commentators alike, that "by nature" does *not* mean "by the strength of human nature apart from grace."

10. An ancient proponent of this view is St. Augustine; see *On the Spirit and the Letter* 44–47. For a modern defense, see N. T. Wright, "The Law in Romans 2," in *Paul and the Mosaic Law*, ed. J. D. G. Dunn (Tübingen: Mohr Siebeck, 1996), 131–50.

11. E.g., Aristotle, *Nicomachean Ethics* 1128a; Philo of Alexandria, *On Abraham* 46.276.

12. Catholic theology has commonly taught that the dictates of the natural law are fundamentally no different than the Ten Commandments (Catechism 2070–71).

Finally, Paul informs readers of something essential to the teaching of his 2:16 gospel—namely, that **God will judge people's hidden works through Christ Jesus**. Both halves of this statement warrant careful consideration. First, the judgment of secret deeds is based on the scriptural belief that "the LORD searches all hearts and understands all the mind's thoughts" (1 Chron 28:9). God's gaze penetrates all things, thus making him uniquely qualified to pass sentence not only on our outward actions but even on "the motives of our hearts" (1 Cor 4:5). Second, Paul speaks in unison with other New Testament passages in saying that Jesus "is the one appointed by God as judge of the living and the dead" (Acts 10:42; see Matt 25:31–46; John 5:27; 2 Thess 1:5–10).

Reflection and Application (2:1–16)

For many Christians, Paul's remarks on "judgment according to works" in Rom 2 is a square peg that finds no place in the round hole of their theology. The reason: it is thought to contradict the Apostle's teaching elsewhere in Romans on the subject of salvation. Two points in Rom 2:1–16 have proven to be troublesome. First, Paul asserts in Rom 2 that eternal life is for those who persevere in doing "good works" (2:7), but elsewhere he teaches that eternal life is a "gift of God" (6:23). Second, Paul states in Rom 2 that "those who observe the law will be justified" (2:13), but elsewhere he says that "a person is justified by faith apart from works of the law" (3:28). Although skeptics would have us believe that Paul contradicted himself on these matters, most have tried to work out a more satisfying solution to the problem.

One attempt to resolve the tension is the "hypothetical" reading of Rom 2, which holds that Paul is describing an impossible scenario. In theory, he admits that one could gain eternal life by good works and a perfect obedience to the law. However—so the argument goes—Paul proceeds in the next chapter to show that no one is actually capable of doing this, since all are "under the domination of sin" (3:9). Understood in this way, the affirmations in Rom 2 are dismissed as theoretical rather than doctrinal.

Despite the simplicity of this solution, there is no evidence that Rom 2 is a hypothetical exercise designed to clear the deck for Paul's *real* thinking on salvation to be set forth in Rom 3.[13] On the contrary, it is a sober expression of Christian truth and an integral part of his "gospel" (2:16). The key is to recognize

13. Hence, this is not a universally held opinion among Protestant scholars. According to one, Klyne R. Snodgrass, "Justification by Grace—To the Doers: An Analysis of the Place of Romans 2 in the Theology of Paul," *NTS* 32 (1986): 72–93, "the passage is assertive in character and has every indication of being meant seriously" (p. 74).

that Paul speaks of salvation in relation to our first justification as well as our final justification. The two cannot be disconnected, of course, since the grace of God is the engine that drives the whole process from beginning to end. When a person is first justified, he receives God's righteousness as a free gift of grace through faith (as stated in 6:23) apart from any merits gained by observance of God's law (as stated in 3:28); and when a person is justified at the last judgment, he is found to be righteous and receives eternal life as a reward for cooperating with divine grace, expressed by putting his faith into action through good works (as stated in 2:7) and observance of God's law (as stated in 2:13). Simply put, our first justification takes place in the missiological context of conversion and baptism, whereas our final justification takes place in the †eschatological context of God's judgment on the last day.[14]

Given this distinction, there is no actual conflict between "judgment by works" in Rom 2 and "justification by faith" in Rom 3. We need not choose one over the other, since Paul teaches both. They stand at two different points along the same spectrum. Justification is a process that begins with faith in Christ and unfolds over the course of life as a commitment to expressing that faith in good works.[15]

The Law and True Circumcision (2:17–29)

[17]Now if you call yourself a Jew and rely on the law and boast of God [18]and know his will and are able to discern what is important since you are instructed from the law, [19]and if you are confident that you are a guide for the blind and a light for those in darkness, [20]that you are a trainer of the foolish and teacher of the simple, because in the law you have the formulation of knowledge and truth—[21]then you who teach another, are you failing to teach yourself? You who preach against stealing, do you steal? [22]You who forbid adultery, do you commit adultery? You who detest idols, do you rob temples? [23]You who boast of the law, do you dishonor God by breaking the law? [24]For, as it is written, "Because of you the name of God is reviled among the Gentiles."

[25]Circumcision, to be sure, has value if you observe the law; but if you break the law, your circumcision has become uncircumcision. [26]Again, if an uncircumcised man keeps the precepts of the law, will he not be considered circumcised? [27]Indeed, those who are physically uncircumcised

---

14. Jesus likewise spoke of justification in connection with the final judgment (Matt 12:37 RSV).

15. The absolute necessity of grace to perform good works is also an essential part of the picture, as Paul will make clear in Rom 6–8.

but carry out the law will pass judgment on you, with your written law and circumcision, who break the law. ²⁸One is not a Jew outwardly. True circumcision is not outward, in the flesh. ²⁹Rather, one is a Jew inwardly, and circumcision is of the heart, in the spirit, not the letter; his praise is not from human beings but from God.

OT: Gen 29:35; Deut 30:6; Isa 42:6; 49:6; 52:5; Jer 9:23–25; Ezek 36:20
NT: Matt 12:41–42; 23:3; Rom 7:6; 1 Cor 7:19; 2 Cor 3:6; Col 2:11–12
Catechism: hallowing God's name, 2807–15; obedience in the Spirit, 1966, 1972

The next step in Paul's imaginary debate is to push the issue of hypocrisy into the foreground. His Jewish conversation partner takes pride in being a member of the covenant people and boasts that he is enlightened by the Mosaic law. Paul, however, injects painful reminders that Israel has often failed to practice what it preaches. Once again, he stresses that keeping the law is what really matters, not just possessing it, knowing it, or teaching it.

Paul addresses the zealous **Jew** who places his hope in **the law** and boasts of   2:17–18
his special relationship with **God**. This is sometimes taken to mean that ancient Jews were self-righteous, that they tended to brag about their success in observing the 613 commandments of the Torah. Perhaps there is some measure of truth in this, but Paul's immediate concern lies elsewhere. The boasting in view concerns Jewish *possession* of the law, not Jewish *performance* of the law. Paul is taking aim at a national pride within Israel that borders on religious snobbery. His target is an elitist attitude of Jewish superiority over the Gentiles, based on the fact that Israel is **instructed** by divine revelation about the **will** of God.

Paul's partner in this hypothetical dialogue, a religious Jew, views the Gentiles   2:19–20
as **blind** in spiritual and moral matters, as living in **darkness**, as people who are **foolish** and **simple**; he considers himself a **guide** and a **light** to godless humanity, a **trainer** and **teacher** of the ignorant masses. Paul would agree that Israel's vocation was to be "a light to the nations" (see Isa 42:6; 49:6). Unfortunately, Israel often crippled its witness to the world by transgressing the very law it paraded before others. It is the perennial problem of hypocrisy and scandal, and Christianity is no more immune to it than Judaism or any other religious faith.

It should be noted that Paul agrees with the conviction that an inspired **formulation of knowledge and truth** resides in the Torah. In other words, he remains persuaded as a Christian that God's wisdom has been given a permanent and privileged expression in the law of Moses (Deut 4:5–8; Sir 24:1–23; Bar 4:1–4). Paul will likewise endorse the Jewish belief that the law's commandments are "holy and righteous and good" (Rom 7:12). Paul's deep appreciation for Old Testament revelation has been shared and defended by the Church from the beginning.

2:21–23   Without finishing the sentence he began in verse 17, Paul fires off a series of incriminating questions. His objective is to deflate Jewish pride in the law by singling out instances of Jewish lawbreaking. Paul is not accusing all Jews of flagrant violations of Torah. That would be unfair to the many devout in Israel who kept the law down through the ages. Rather, he is illustrating that sin has taken hold among the covenant people, despite the advantage of having the law.

Paul first indicts the Jew who fails to **teach** himself to observe the Torah. Then he gives a sampling of transgressions that apparently no one questions have taken place at one time or another in the Jewish community. He alludes to the †Decalogue, which prohibits **stealing** (Exod 20:15), **adultery** (Exod 20:14), and the veneration of **idols** (Exod 20:4–5).

Somewhat unclear is the third item: What does he mean by **rob temples**? The expression could refer to plundering idol shrines of their cultic paraphernalia (2 Macc 9:2), to stealing from annual tax revenues that were sent to Jerusalem for the ministries of the temple,[16] or to "committing sacrilege" in general. Whatever the precise nature of this sin, clearly Paul sees his fellow Jews as guilty of **breaking** the very law they **boast** of possessing.

2:24   Paul backs these multiple indictments with the testimony of Scripture: **"Because of you the name of God is reviled among the Gentiles"**—a quotation based on the †Septuagint translation of Isa 52:5. Isaiah bemoans the scandal caused by Judah's exile to Babylon in the sixth century BC. The unstated premise, which Paul expects readers to know, is that rebellion against the law is what forced the covenant people into exile in the first place. There the shame that covered the Jews as a deported and subjugated people attached to the reputation of their God. The Lord had wanted to manifest his mercy to the world through Israel; instead, he had been forced to manifest his wrath against their disobedience. Paul's accusation is thus supported: the Jew, by defaulting on his obligation to keep the law, dishonors God in the eyes of the nations (Rom 2:23).

2:25–27   Paul targets the one requirement of the law that many considered the most important: **circumcision**. For Jewish males, this was the mark of divine favor par excellence, the physical sign that set Israel apart from other nations. Paul affirms the **value** of circumcision as a claim to the blessings of the covenant, and yet he cautions that it entitles the Jew to this benefit only **if** he is careful to **observe the law**. In other words, circumcision obligates the Jew to obey

16. Josephus, *Jewish Antiquities* 18.81–84.

"the entire law" of God (Gal 5:3). Otherwise, physical circumcision becomes equivalent to **uncircumcision**.

It is hard for Christian readers today to feel the force of this statement. Paul is basically telling the Jewish lawbreaker that, in God's eyes, he is no different from a Gentile!

Paul does not stop there. He also proposes the converse: **if an uncircumcised** Gentile walks the moral high road by keeping **the precepts of the law**, then God will regard him as **circumcised**. He will even be in a position to **pass judgment** on the unfaithful Jew, despite the Jew's advantage of possessing the **written law** and **circumcision**.

Paul concludes the chapter by revising the common understanding of **Jew**   **2:28–29** and **circumcision**. His contemporaries would normally think in terms of **the flesh**, supposing that Jewishness is a matter of ethnic descent, religious practice, or both and that circumcision is a physical procedure. But Paul finds this conventional view in need of adjustment. His own definitions are put forward with the help of two antitheses: outward versus inward, and letter versus spirit.

First, Paul insists that one is ultimately **a Jew inwardly**. By this he means that religious commitment to the Lord must come from deep within. Family genealogy and the surgical removal of foreskin are secondary matters; being outward and visible, they only elicit respect **from human beings**. Here Paul alludes to a biblical wordplay on the name "Judah," which resembles the Hebrew verb for "praise" (Gen 29:35). Paul reserves the name "Jew" for one whose **praise** comes **from God**. Only God, after all, can see that a person's **heart** is circumcised and compliant with his law.

Second, Paul claims that **circumcision** of the heart is accomplished **in the spirit**. This is not a reference to the "spiritual" nature of true circumcision (as in the RSV); nor is it a reference to its effect on the human "spirit" (as in the NABRE). Instead, it describes the work of the Holy Spirit in the believer (as in the ESV). Paul's contrast of letter and spirit elsewhere strongly suggests this (Rom 7:6; 2 Cor 3:6).[17] It summarizes the distinction between the Old Covenant and the New. The Torah came as written **letter**, as a book that reveals God's will but is external to God's people and provides them with no internal assistance for obedience. The Spirit, however, makes his home in the believer, filling his heart with love for God (Rom 5:5) and empowering him from within to obey God's righteous decrees (8:4).

17. See the classic study by Bernardin Schneider, OFM, "The Meaning of St. Paul's Antithesis: 'The Letter and the Spirit,'" *CBQ* 15 (1953): 163–207.

Circumcision of the Heart

BIBLICAL
BACKGROUND

Circumcision is one of most important badges of Jewish identity. In the Bible, the cutting away of the male foreskin is a sign of the Lord's covenant with Abraham (Gen 17:9–14) that was taken up into the Lord's national covenant with Israel (Lev 12:3). Circumcision was not just one requirement among many; it served as a rite of initiation into the whole liturgical life of the covenant people. Its importance was heightened even more in Paul's day, as it marked off Jew from Gentile and signified the Jewish privilege of being the †elect people of God. Some Jews held that no covenant relationship with God was possible without circumcision (*Jubilees* 15.26).

Paul first raises the issue of circumcision in Rom 2:25–29, where he differentiates between circumcision of the flesh and circumcision of the heart. Some allege that Paul is spiritualizing circumcision as a convenient way to justify Christian nonobservance of the Mosaic ritual laws (such as dietary restrictions, animal sacrifice, and sabbath observance). But this is a misunderstanding. Paul is expounding a theme introduced already in the Old Testament.

The Scriptures teach that circumcision is an outward sign of an inward commitment. Circumcision of the foreskin imposes on the recipient the moral and spiritual obligation to circumcise the heart—to cut away the stubbornness of the will that resists obedience to the Lord (Deut 10:16; Jer 4:4). If a Jew is uncircumcised in heart, it means he is unwilling to live by the law of the covenant, even if he bears the sign of the covenant in his flesh (Lev 26:41).

This was a recurring problem in biblical Israel, but it was not a problem without a solution. Moses, looking into the future, promised the Israelites that God "will circumcise your hearts . . . so that you will love the Lord, your God, with your whole heart and your whole being" (Deut 30:6). Ezekiel announced a similar divine action to come: "I will sprinkle clean water over you. . . . I will give you a new heart, and a new spirit I will put within you . . . so that you walk in my statutes, observe my ordinances, and keep them" (Ezek 36:25–27). Paul ties these ideas together in Rom 2 and declares their fulfillment in the New Covenant. He speaks of Christians who keep the precepts of the law (2:26) because they have received a "circumcision . . . of the heart" that is "in the spirit" (2:29). Elsewhere he relates this hidden work to the sacrament of baptism, through which God administers "the circumcision of Christ" (Col 2:11). For the Christian, then, circumcision of the flesh no longer functions as a sign of membership in the covenant (1 Cor 7:19; Gal 5:6; 6:15). Once the promised reality has come, the rite that prefigured it is laid aside.

Why is Paul stressing these points? Because his thoughts in Rom 2 are turned toward the final judgment. Only "those who observe the law will be justified" (2:13), and "God will judge people's hidden works through Christ Jesus" (2:16). Being a Jew outwardly affords no guarantee that all will be well in the end. The work of the Spirit in the circumcised heart is the only effective preparation for divine judgment.

Reflection and Application (2:25–29)

It is easy for Christian readers to conclude that a text like Rom 2:28–29 has little relevance for our lives. After all, we don't call ourselves Jews, nor do we boast of circumcision. This section of the letter may hold a certain historical interest for us, but its practical application can easily elude us.

But imagine Paul had said that "one is not a Christian outwardly" and that "true baptism is not outward, in the flesh." This might grab our attention, and rightly so. Paul's indictment of Jewish presumption and disobedience is no less applicable to Christian presumption and disobedience. The name "Christian" means something much more than attending a weekly liturgy and going through the motions when it comes time to pray or receive the sacraments. Commitment to Christ must come from the heart, and our concern must be with God's approval of our choices and decisions, regardless of what others think. Just as circumcision required the Jew to observe "the entire law" (Gal 5:3), so too does baptism obligate us to obey the entire gospel, and the sacrament is attended by solemn promises to live out the demands of our faith until the end.

Judgment on Sin and Justification in Christ

Romans 3:1–31

The transition from Rom 2 to Rom 3 is seamless. Paul continues his †diatribe with an imaginary debate partner who speaks on behalf of traditional Judaism. Likewise, Paul preempts a misunderstanding that being a Jew counts for nothing in the Christian scheme of salvation. He is adamant that circumcised Jews have distinct advantages over pagan Gentiles, even though these are mitigated by the fact that Jews and Gentiles alike are captive to the power of sin. The good news is that God has demonstrated his righteousness in Jesus Christ for the redemption of the entire world and the justification of all who believe.

The Faithfulness and Justice of God (3:1–8)

¹What advantage is there then in being a Jew? Or what is the value of circumcision? ²Much, in every respect. [For] in the first place, they were entrusted with the utterances of God. ³What if some were unfaithful? Will their infidelity nullify the fidelity of God? ⁴Of course not! God must be true, though every human being is a liar, as it is written:

"That you may be justified in your words,
and conquer when you are judged."

⁵But if our wickedness provides proof of God's righteousness, what can we say? Is God unjust, humanly speaking, to inflict his wrath? ⁶Of course not! For how else is God to judge the world? ⁷But if God's truth redounds to his glory through my falsehood, why am I still being condemned as a sinner?

[8]**And why not say—as we are accused and as some claim we say—that we should do evil that good may come of it? Their penalty is what they deserve.**

OT: Gen 18:25; Pss 51:6; 107:11; 116:11

NT: Rom 9:4–5; 14:10–11; 2 Tim 2:13

Catechism: truthfulness and trustworthiness of God, 215, 2465; evil may not be done to bring about good, 1789

Paul is anxious at the outset of Rom 3 to affirm the "fidelity" (3:3), "righteousness" (3:5), and "truth" (3:7) of God over against the "infidelity" (3:3), "wickedness" (3:5), and "falsehood" (3:7) of God's chosen people.[1] His point is that unfaithfulness among the Jews does nothing to alter or undermine God's own faithfulness to his covenant commitments. Nor is God "unjust" to bring his wayward people to judgment (3:5).[2] Much of what Paul says here anticipates his fuller discussion of God's righteousness in Rom 9–11.

Paul's Jewish respondent would likely take issue with the revised definitions   **3:1–2** of circumcision and Jewishness put forward in 2:25–29. So Paul responds preemptively with a series of questions. In chapter 2 it could almost seem that Paul is downplaying, if not discarding, the whole notion of Jewish privilege—the belief that Israel is chosen by God and set apart for his special purposes. Paul anticipates this mistaken inference with a blunt question: **What advantage is there then in being a Jew? Or what is the value of circumcision?**

His response is unhesitating: **Much, in every respect**. Paul holds that the blessings conveyed to the covenant people give the Jew a real advantage over the Gentile. Careful readers might have anticipated this answer, given that Paul continues to put the Jew "first" in relation to the Gentile in matters related to the gospel (1:16; 2:9–10).

The **first** indicator of a Jewish advantage is that Israel was **entrusted with the utterances of God**. Some speculate that Paul has particular divine oracles in mind, such as the promises to the patriarchs, the commandments given by Moses, or the pronouncements of the prophets. It is more likely that Paul is referring to the Old Testament as a whole. This expression "utterances of God"[3] appears in other writings of the Hellenistic period[4] as a reference to the Hebrew Scriptures in general. The point is that Israel, as the custodian of divinely

---

1. Richard B. Hays, "Psalm 143 and the Logic of Romans 3," *JBL* 99, no. 1 (1980): 107–15.

2. According to Hays, "Psalm 143," 111: "The idea of the covenant is not explicitly mentioned here, but it is unmistakably present: the righteousness of God consists in his persistence in keeping his covenant intact in spite of human unfaithfulness."

3. Greek *ta logia tou theou*.

4. Ps 107:11; Heb 5:12; Philo of Alexandria, *On Rewards and Punishments* 1.1.

inspired writings, had a privileged knowledge of God's will and God's ways; no other nation had this before the coming of Christ.

3:3–4   At this point Paul veers away from the list of Jewish advantages. Readers will have to wait until 9:4–5 for Paul to resume his discussion of the blessings bestowed on the chosen people.

His next question rests on the assumption, already implied in 2:17–24, that knowing God's will comes with the responsibility of doing it. This raises the issue of what happens when **some** prove **unfaithful**. How does this affect the covenant between the Lord and his people? Will **infidelity** among the Jews **nullify the fidelity of God**? Possibly Paul had been accused of teaching, or at least insinuating, that God had abandoned his obligations of love and loyalty to Israel—something he strenuously denies both here and in 11:1 with the expression **Of course not!** His gospel announces the fulfillment of God's saving designs, not their abrupt termination.

As usual, Paul is not content merely to assert that God is trustworthy and **true**; he is careful to establish the point from the Bible. He lifts the expression **every human being is a liar** from the Greek translation of Ps 116:11 (= LXX 115:2). Then he appeals to Ps 51:6, which in the †Septuagint reads: **"That you may be justified in your words, / and conquer when you are judged."** The passage articulates a clear contrast between the Lord, who is vindicated of wrongdoing, and his penitent people, who openly acknowledge their sins. Long-standing tradition regards Ps 51 as David's prayer of confession after his adultery with Bathsheba (Ps 51:2; see 2 Sam 11:2–5; 12:9–14). The king laments his sin, accepts responsibility for his iniquity, and pleads for forgiveness. At the same time, he affirms God's justice in a metaphorical way by insisting that no assembled court could ever find blame in God's actions. This is precisely the message that Paul wants to convey at this juncture in Romans.

3:5–7   A clever debater might question whether sinners should be held accountable to God's judgment if one result of their **wickedness** is to magnify **God's righteousness**. Isn't it **unjust** for God to **inflict his wrath** when the failures of Israel have occasioned such a positive outcome? Paul flattens this proposal, too: **Of course not!** The very thought of God acting unjustly is unthinkable to Paul. In fact, it is possible that the parenthetical remark—**humanly speaking**—serves as a mild apology to readers who may be scandalized by the suggestion.

God acting unjustly is an offensive proposition because it collides with the biblical doctrine that **God** will someday **judge the world** in righteousness (Rom 2:6–11; Gen 18:25; Job 34:10–12; Ps 94:2). While it is true that God is faithful in upholding his covenant with an often unfaithful people, it hardly follows that Israel should be exonerated on this account. Human **falsehood** may well throw **God's truth** into greater relief, but the Lord is still bound to enforce his covenant by imposing its sanctions on disobedience. The exercise of divine mercy does not set aside the demands of divine justice.

Another question follows, only this time Paul treats it as a slanderous distortion of his gospel. Apparently some had charged the Apostle and his collaborators with teaching that Christians **should do evil that good may come of it**. The allegation is that, according to Paul's preaching, human rebellion against God may be said to bring greater glory to God because it moves him to exercise his mercy and saving power. One might recognize some theological validity in this deduction ("O happy fault . . ."),[5] but not the moral inference that is drawn from it. Encouraging evildoing in the name of the gospel is a severe twisting of the Apostle's message. **3:8**

Paul does not take the time at this point to rebut the accusation directly.[6] Still, it is clear that he finds it repugnant and contrary to his teaching.[7] His use of the expression **we are accused** could just as well be translated "we are blasphemed" or "we are slandered" (RSV, ESV, NRSV, NIV). Readers are left in no doubt about Paul's view of the allegation: persons who act wickedly and prove false to the Lord, regardless of their privileges, bear the **penalty** they justly **deserve**.

The Universal Dominion of Sin (3:9–20)

[9]**Well, then, are we better off? Not entirely, for we have already brought the charge against Jews and Greeks alike that they are all under the domination of sin,** [10]**as it is written:**

> "**There is no one just, not one,**
>   [11]**there is no one who understands,**
>   **there is no one who seeks God.**
> [12]**All have gone astray; all alike are worthless,**
>   **there is not one who does good,**

5. The expression, known in Latin as the *Felix culpa*, is sung in the Roman liturgy as part of "the Exsultet" for Easter Vigil. In the 2010 edition of the *Roman Missal*, International Commission on English in the Liturgy Corporation, the relevant portion reads: "O truly necessary sin of Adam, destroyed completely by the death of Christ! / O happy fault that earned so great, so glorious a Redeemer!" (see also Catechism 412).

6. He will do so in 6:1–23.

7. Catholic moral theology infers from Paul's response that "the ends do not justify the means," meaning that objectively sinful acts can never be considered a morally acceptable way to achieve an objectively desirable outcome in personal or social life (Catechism 1789).

[there is not] even one.
¹³Their throats are open graves;
  they deceive with their tongues;
the venom of asps is on their lips;
  ¹⁴their mouths are full of bitter cursing.
¹⁵Their feet are quick to shed blood;
  ¹⁶ruin and misery are in their ways,
¹⁷and the way of peace they know not.
  ¹⁸There is no fear of God before their eyes."

¹⁹Now we know that what the law says is addressed to those under the law, so that every mouth may be silenced and the whole world stand accountable to God, ²⁰since no human being will be justified in his sight by observing the law; for through the law comes consciousness of sin.

OT: Pss 5:10; 10:7; 14:1–3; 36:2; 140:4; 143:2; Eccles 7:20; Isa 59:7–8
NT: Rom 3:23; 11:32
Catechism: reality of sin, 386–87; proliferation of sin, 1865–69; the law reveals sin, 708

Paul has been building to verses 9–20 since 1:18. It is the rhetorical finale of the first part of Romans, which has sought to demonstrate that rebellion against God is the common fault of all humanity. Few would object to Paul's indictment in 1:18–32 that accuses the Gentiles of plunging into moral and spiritual darkness. The bigger challenge was to demonstrate that Jews were in the same boat. Paul thus made it his aim, beginning in 2:1, to show that sin had taken a firm hold among the covenant people as well. He now makes this point with resounding emphasis by summoning the witness of the Old Testament.

3:9   Paul continues his †diatribe with a Jewish conversation partner (engaged in since 2:1) by posing the crucial question in need of an answer: **Well, then, are we better off?** At issue is whether the Jewish people enjoyed privileges that were sufficient for salvation. To this Paul responds: **Not entirely.**[8] Basically he is qualifying his remarks in 3:1–2 without negating them. On the one hand, he acknowledges that Jews possess notable advantages over the Gentiles; on the other, he denies that these blessings gave the chosen people a pre-Christian admittance into the fullness of messianic grace.

The reason for Paul's qualification is simple: he realizes that **Jews and Greeks alike** share the same plight of being **under the domination of sin**. Despite their

8. Unlike the NABRE, which renders the Greek *ou pantōs* as a qualified denial, most modern translations render the expression as an emphatic denial: "Not at all" (NIV, JB) or "No, not at all" (RSV, ESV, NRSV).

advantages, the Jews are trapped in the same predicament as the rest of the fallen world. They are as much in need of a savior as everyone else.

To substantiate this claim, Paul summons texts from the Jewish Scriptures **3:10–18** that document the grim reality of Jewish sinfulness. He links together a *catena* (Latin for "chain") of six or seven quotations from the Old Testament, most of them in agreement with the wording of the †Septuagint. The passages in order of citation are Pss 14:1–3 (the word **just** in Rom 3:10 may be taken from Eccles 7:20); 5:10; 140:10; 10:7; Isa 59:7–8; and Ps 36:2.[9]

Paul's citations are usually said to prove that every single Jew and Gentile, without exception, is a sinner living in opposition to God. On first reading, this might appear to be his main point. However, there is reason to think that Paul is bringing charges against the Jewish nation collectively, not against every Jewish man, woman, and child individually. It is true that the whole human race is implicated in the sin of Adam and is forced to live with the consequences of his fall from grace. This touches every person's life, as Paul will make clear in Rom 5. But we must be careful not to run ahead of his argument. The point *here* is that sin has breached the defenses of God's chosen people, just as it has all other nations.

Several points support this reading. (1) Paul's citations from the Psalms and Isaiah make use of poetical exaggeration as a way of giving the message greater impact. This would not have escaped Paul's notice. As a careful interpreter of Scripture, he would not have felt free to impose a rigidly literal meaning on obviously hyperbolic texts or rhetorical overstatements. (2) To insist that Paul reads these verses literally amounts to saying that Paul places Scripture in opposition to Scripture. Statements such as **There is no one just** (3:10) and **no one . . . seeks God** (3:11) and **There is no fear of God** (3:18) serve well as shocking generalizations, but they are blatantly inaccurate if treated as exceptionless statements of fact. The Bible speaks of numerous figures who are deemed "righteous,"[10] who earnestly "seek" the Lord,[11] and who reverently "fear" God.[12] It hardly seems credible that Paul, an avid student of the written Word, could think of no exceptions whatsoever to his far-reaching verdict. Besides that, Paul could not have hoped to convince readers—least of all Jewish ones—to accept his interpretations if they were propped up by a cavalier handling of Israel's sacred texts. (3) Most telling of all, Paul quotes from several psalms that actually

---

9. The references listed correspond to the NABRE translation of the OT, which differs at points from the chapter and verse numbering of the Septuagint.

10. Gen 6:9; Wis 10:6, 10, 13; Dan 13:3; see also Matt 1:19; Luke 1:6; 2 Pet 2:7.

11. 2 Chron 11:16; 15:12; 34:3; Pss 27:8; 63:2; 119:10; Isa 51:1.

12. Gen 22:12; 42:18; Exod 1:21; Job 1:1; Ps 22:24; Mal 3:16.

distinguish those who are "righteous" in Israel from those who are "wicked" (Pss 5; 14; 36; 140). No doubt these references support Paul's contention that sin has established a beachhead in Israel. But that is not the same thing as saying that every member of the covenant people is a godless rebel, down to the last woman or man. How, then, can Paul deny the possibility of even a single Jew being righteous when he draws from psalms that affirm the distinction between righteous and unrighteous Jews in no uncertain terms? Again, his argument works as a collective indictment of Israel, viewed as a nation alongside other sinful nations, but not as a distributive indictment of every single Jew considered individually.[13]

It is also notable in verses 13–18 that Paul singles out passages that link the manifestation of sin to various parts of the human body. Mention is made of **throats**, **tongues**, **lips**, **mouths**, **feet**, and **eyes**. On the one hand, Paul is showing how the body participates in human rebellion against God, with its members acting as slaves under the command of a corrupted human will. He will return to this idea in Rom 6, when he urges Christians to renounce the bondage of the "sinful body" (6:6) and the inclination to use the parts of the body as "weapons for wickedness" (6:13). On the other hand, Paul seems to suggest an analogy between the physical body and the fallen human race, both of which have come under the domination of sin, and both of which have witnessed evil spread to its many members.[14]

3:19   Paul submits the chain of biblical passages quoted in verses 10–18 as evidence of **what the law says**. The statement is curious since none of the citations is taken from the Torah in the narrow sense of the five books of Moses. Paul is using a shorthand expression for the full collection of Israel's Scriptures, which was sometimes identified in a broad sense as "the law" (John 10:34; 15:25; 1 Cor 14:21). The indictment, then, being aimed at **those under the law**, is directed at the covenant people, whose faith and life are defined by the teachings of the Old Testament.

Paul's recourse to the Bible is meant to reduce **every mouth** to silence and to declare **the whole world accountable to God** for its guilt. His conviction is that no legitimate protest can be made against the verdict of inspired Scripture; all are left speechless and defenseless when the incontrovertible evidence of the written Word is put forward.

3:20   Paul closes his argument with the sweeping assertion that **no human being will be justified in his sight**, a paraphrase of the Septuagint translation of Ps

---

13. For related considerations, see commentary on 3:23.
14. Frank J. Matera, *Romans*, PCNT (Grand Rapids: Baker Academic, 2010), 85.

143:2 (= LXX 142:2). The allusion sums up where Paul has brought his readers at this point. He has led them to see that Jews no less than Gentiles have no solid grounds for confidence in facing the Lord's judgment. Thanks to the pervasiveness of sin, which knows no national or territorial boundaries, none can hope to be found guiltless in God's eyes.

Paul adds that justification before the divine judge cannot be attained even **by observing the law**—literally, "by works of the law."[15] This way of putting the matter must have raised an eyebrow or two among the Jewish believers in Rome, since Scripture states that keeping the commandments would establish Israel in "righteousness" or "justice" (Deut 6:25). Indeed, it was commonly believed among ancient Jews that faithful observance of the Torah made a person righteous or just—that is, a person of good standing in the covenant.[16]

For Paul, however, **the law** of Moses is not an instrument of justification, a means of acquiring the saving righteousness of God. Given that all nations, including Israel, have fallen short of God's original purposes, its function is to prepare the way for salvation by imparting a **consciousness of sin**. This is not to deny that the law is "holy and righteous and good" (Rom 7:12). It is only to say that the Torah reveals the problem of sin rather than providing a remedy for it. Paul even says that the law was "powerless" in helping people to fulfill its demands, given the weakness of our fallen nature (8:3). Enlightenment rather than enablement is the principal function of the Mosaic law in the progressive †economy of salvation.[17]

The Righteousness of God Manifested (3:21–26)

> [21]But now the righteousness of God has been manifested apart from the law, though testified to by the law and the prophets, [22]the righteousness of God through faith in Jesus Christ for all who believe. For there is no distinction; [23]all have sinned and are deprived of the glory of God. [24]They are justified freely by his grace through the redemption in Christ Jesus, [25]whom God set forth as an expiation, through faith, by his blood, to prove his righteousness because of the forgiveness of sins previously committed, [26]through the forbearance of God—to prove his righteousness in

---

15. For the meaning of this expression, see commentary on 3:28.
16. Examples include Luke 1:6; Qumran fragment 4QMMT 3–7; Josephus, *Against Apion* 2.293.
17. St. Thomas Aquinas affirms this when he teaches that the Old Law *instructs the mind* in the knowledge of God's will and its opposite—that is, sin—while the grace of the New Law *assists the will* in the performance of God's will and avoiding its opposite. See the entire discussion in *Summa Theologiae* II-II.90–114.

**the present time, that he might be righteous and justify the one who has
faith in Jesus.**

OT: Exod 25:17–22; Lev 16:1–34; Wis 11:23

NT: Rom 1:16–17; 3:9; 10:12; Heb 2:17; 9:11–22; 1 John 4:10

Catechism: Christ is expiation for sin, 433; justification is a gift of grace, 1996; justification
is merited by Christ's passion, 1992; justification involves a real communication of righteousness, 1987, 1991

Verses 21–26 bring us across the threshold of a new section of Romans. Having
rendered his verdict of guilt on the world, Paul shifts gears to consider how God
has redeemed the world from this sorry state. His words serve as a fuller elabo-
ration of the announcement in 1:16–17, explaining how God's righteousness
has been manifested through the death and resurrection of the Messiah and
made effective in the lives of all who believe.

3:21 The first two words of this verse—**But now**—signal to the reader that Paul is
about to make a transition. Since 1:18, he has been stewing over the bad news
of human sinfulness. Starting in 3:21, the Apostle turns to consider the good
news of human salvation.

This shift in discussion follows a shift in history. The **righteousness of God**,
which denotes the saving action of God as well as his saving grace,[18] has come
into view in a new way. Specifically, this has occurred **apart from the law** of
Moses and the efforts of Israel to observe its precepts. Paul stresses that saving
righteousness is not something that people are capable of attaining or producing
themselves. It is something properly divine—it belongs uniquely to God and
can only come to us as a gift from him. Nevertheless, we learn of it through the
witness of **the law and the prophets**, which is another way of referring to the
writings of the Old Testament (Matt 5:17; Acts 24:14; 28:23).

3:22–23 At this point Paul's extremely terse language begins to cause some difficulty.
Clearly he intends to unfold the meaning of **the righteousness of God**; but it
remains unclear what exactly the expression **faith in Jesus Christ** (the Greek is
literally "faith of Jesus Christ") is supposed to convey. The NABRE, along with
most modern translations, understands Paul to say that Jesus is the *object* of
our faith and the mediator of God's righteousness. This is perfectly acceptable
and in certain ways preferable. But as modern scholars have correctly pointed
out, the expression could also mean that Jesus is the *subject* whose faithfulness
makes God's righteousness manifest in history.[19] Deciding between "our faith
in Jesus Christ" and "the faithfulness of Jesus Christ" is difficult, since both

---

18. See the sidebar, "The Righteousness of God," in Rom 1 (p. 11).

19. See Luke Timothy Johnson, "Romans 3:21–26 and the Faith of Jesus," *CBQ* 44, no. 1 (1982): 77–90.

make sense in the context. Indeed, Paul seems to exploit both possibilities in the following discussion.

But first Paul retraces the movement from plight to solution, from sin to salvation. He contends that **no distinction** can be made between persons because **all have sinned**. Countless readers of Romans take this to mean that every member of the human family, without exception, stands before God as a sinner. However, this popular reading is imprecise on two counts. (1) Paul uses the phrase "no distinction" instead of the phrase "no exception." Paul's issue is whether there is a *difference* between the two groups of people up for comparison.[20] The two groups, of course, are Jews and Gentiles. In fact, the only other time that Paul uses the expression[21] is in Rom 10:12, where he says: "There is no distinction between Jew and Greek; the same Lord is Lord of all." Thus, when the Apostle says "all have sinned," he is implicating Jews together with Gentiles.[22] (2) The more obvious fault of the popular reading is that *there are exceptions* to the statement. Notice that Paul is talking about sins committed by deliberate choices. There is no denying that the human race is born into this world in a state of spiritual alienation from God. Paul teaches as much elsewhere (5:12; Eph 2:3). But the saying "all have sinned" does not apply to persons incapable of willful transgression. What of miscarried fetuses, infants in arms, children younger than the age of reason, the mentally disabled? For that matter, what of Jesus Christ himself? He too was born into the human family of Adam, and yet he passed through this world without the slightest taint of sin (Heb 4:15; 1 Pet 2:22; 1 John 3:5).[23] If even a single exception can be found, then the popular interpretation must be wide of the mark. Paul's point, yet again, is that Jews have been no more immune to wrongdoing than Gentiles.

Because all have sinned, all are **deprived of the glory of God**.[24] Paul typically associates glory with immortality (Rom 2:7) and thus with the future hope of believers (5:2). Glory is what awaits the faithful when the Lord completes his work of salvation for all creation (8:18). It is nothing less than our participation in God's undying life.[25] Beyond this, the Apostle appears to have in mind

20. The NIV captures this nicely with the translation "There is no difference between Jew and Gentile."

21. Greek *ou gar estin diastolē*.

22. According to James D. G. Dunn, *The Theology of Paul the Apostle* (Grand Rapids: Eerdmans, 1998), 372–73: "'All' is one of the really key words in Romans . . . 'all' consistently means Jew as well as Gentile, Gentile as well as Jew."

23. Catholic tradition adds that Mary, the Mother of Jesus, was likewise preserved sinless throughout her life by a special grace of God (Council of Trent, *Decree on Original Sin* 6; *Canons on Justification* 23).

24. As indicated in modern translations, Paul can be taken to mean either "lack the glory of God" (NJB) or "fall short of the glory of God" (RSV, NRSV, NIV).

25. Ben C. Blackwell, "Immortal Glory and the Problem of Death in Romans 3.23," *JSNT* 32, no. 3 (2010): 285–308.

the Jewish notion that Adam's fall disrobed humanity of God's glory.[26] Once lost, the glory of divine incorruption has never been successfully regained by our wayward race.

3:24   That glory cannot be regained until men and women are **justified** by God (8:30). Being justified means having sins remitted, the grace of divine life imparted, and membership in the covenant family of God granted.[27] All of this takes place **freely** and **by his grace**, which is to say that justification is an unmerited gift (5:15–16). It is a free bestowal of God's merciful love; it is not something earned or deserved like a wage (4:2–4; 6:23).

The basis for our justification is **the redemption** accomplished **in Christ Jesus**. In the biblical world, "redemption" referred to the manumission of slaves, whose freedom could be purchased by a wealthy patron or relative. Even more, redemption brings to mind memories of the biblical exodus, the epic story of God, the redeemer of Israel, delivering his people from the captivity of Egypt (Exod 15:13; Deut 7:8). This was remembered as the most spectacular feat of divine redemption in Old Testament times. But now something greater still has happened. A new exodus has occurred through the blood of the Messiah. It is a new act of redemption that benefits all nations, offering them spiritual freedom from the slavery of sin (Rom 6:6; Eph 1:7; Col 1:14).

3:25–26   In close connection with the exodus theme, Paul also evokes the ritual of Yom Kippur, the great Day of Atonement, described in Lev 16:1–34. This is achieved through a cluster of terms central to this liturgical event: **expiation**, **blood**, and **forgiveness**. Yom Kippur was the day in Israel's calendar when the Lord's mercy poured forth in greatest abundance, when all was made right again for the covenant people. For Paul, the Day of Atonement paved the way for a Christian understanding of Good Friday.

Specifically, Paul envisions the crucified Jesus as †"expiation"—in Greek, *hilastērion*. This is the term used in the †Septuagint for the "mercy seat" (RSV) of pure gold that covered the ark of the covenant as a lid (Exod 25:17–22).[28] This

---

26. See *Life of Adam and Eve* 21.6 (Greek); *Genesis Rabbah* 12.5–6; *3 Baruch* 4.16 (Greek).

27. See the sidebar "Justification" (pp. 50–51).

28. A significant debate surrounds the translation and interpretation of Paul's use of *hilastērion*. It is sometimes rendered "propitiation" (KJV, ESV) and thought to signify that Christ's death turns away God's wrath from sinners. Other times it is translated "expiation" (NABRE, RSV) and said to mean that Christ's death takes away the guilt incurred by sinners. A few modern translations avoid taking sides in the debate by rendering the expression "a sacrifice of atonement" (NIV, NRSV). Catholic tradition recognizes the theological validity of both ideas in elucidating the doctrine of the atonement. Still, the notion of expiation as "removal of sin" seems closest to Paul's intended meaning. See Joseph A. Fitzmyer, SJ, *Romans*, AB 33 (New York: Doubleday, 1993), 120–21, 349–50; Toan Joseph Do, "The LXX

Figure 4. Early sixteenth-century painting of King David accompanying the ark of the covenant into Jerusalem (artist unknown).

sacred item was the focal point of the Day of Atonement liturgy and, prior to the incarnation, the most privileged place of God's holiness and presence on earth. Every year the high priest of Israel gained "forgiveness" for the transgressions of his people by sprinkling the "blood" of sacrificial animals on the top surface of the ark, the golden "mercy seat" or "expiation." Paul recognized that the ancient rite of the Day of Atonement prefigured something far greater. His words indicate (1) that the death of Jesus was an act of sacrifice, (2) that the animal offerings of Israel have been superseded by the offering of Christ's life-blood on the cross, and (3) that human sin and divine love have made contact in the bleeding and dying of Jesus in such a way that definitive forgiveness is now open to all who believe.[29]

According to Paul, then, the crucifixion of the Messiah was a public demonstration of God's **righteousness**. Through it God acted to fulfill his covenant, which promised blessings for the whole world. But what of all the **sins previously committed** in the long stretch of history that passed before Good Friday? These were not overlooked or forgotten or treated lightly. Rather, God had been exercising divine **forbearance**: in his mercy, he deferred or held back the full measure of his judgment on sin until a uniquely effective atonement could be made by his Son. Paul locates this era of messianic grace and fulfillment **in the present time**.

Background of ΙΛΑΣΤΗΡΙΟΝ in Rom 3, 25," in *The Letter to the Romans*, ed. Udo Schnelle (Leuven: Peeters, 2009), 641–57.

29. For these points, see Pope Benedict XVI, *Saint Paul: General Audiences, July 2, 2008–February 4, 2009*, trans. *L'Osservatore Romano* (San Francisco: Ignatius, 2009), 104–5.

Paul then ties together his exposition of the **righteousness** of God by summarizing its two principal aspects.[30] First, righteousness involves God showing himself to **be righteous** in his saving deeds, which project his fidelity and mercy onto the screen of human history for all to see. Second, it refers to his action to **justify the one who has faith in Jesus**. Unfortunately, due to limitations in our English vocabulary, there is a tight connection between these two sides of divine righteousness that is not easy to capture in translation.[31] Basically, Paul is saying that the righteousness of God means both that "God himself is righteous" and that "God makes righteous" the believer in Jesus.

Justification by Faith (3:27–31)

[27]**What occasion is there then for boasting? It is ruled out. On what principle, that of works? No, rather on the principle of faith. [28]For we consider that a person is justified by faith apart from works of the law. [29]Does God belong to Jews alone? Does he not belong to Gentiles, too? Yes, also to Gentiles, [30]for God is one and will justify the circumcised on the basis of faith and the uncircumcised through faith. [31]Are we then annulling the law by this faith? Of course not! On the contrary, we are supporting the law.**

OT: Deut 6:4; Jer 9:22–23
NT: Rom 2:17, 23; 3:20; 15:17; Gal 2:15–16; James 2:18–26
Catechism: justification by faith and baptism, 1987; initial grace of justification cannot be merited by works, 2010; God is one, 200–202

Everything Paul says in Rom 3 revolves around Jews and Gentiles in relation to the gospel. In 3:1–20, he stresses that together they are equal culprits in sin. In 3:21–26, he indicates that together they are equal candidates for salvation. Finally, in 3:27–31, he contends that together they are justified in Christ on equal terms. The essential condition for all peoples is faith, a subject that will occupy Paul's attention here and in the next chapter.

3:27   Paul transitions to the final verses by asking whether anyone has sufficient reason for **boasting**. In saying this, he is reconnecting with his critique of Jewish presumption in Rom 2, where he noted the tendency of some to "boast of God" (2:17) and "boast of the law" (2:23). The problem is not that Jews are bragging

30. See the sidebar, "The Righteousness of God," in Rom 1 (p. 11).
31. Michael J. Gorman, "Romans: The First Christian Treatise on Theosis," *JTI* 5, no. 1 (2011): 13–34, speaks of justification as "righteousification" in order to make this connection clearer (p. 27).

about their personal adherence to God's law—a form of self-congratulating moralism. Paul is instead taking aim at a form of Jewish nationalism that absolutizes the importance of Israel's divine †election and possession of the Torah. However, now that a universal "redemption" (3:24) has been accomplished by Jesus in "the present time" (3:26), boasting about such things is **ruled out**. The religious prerogatives of the Jewish people no longer determine the scope of God's favor. Salvation history has moved beyond that preliminary stage.

Paul draws a contrast between two different grounds for boasting. The NABRE's marginal note points out Paul's wordplay on the Greek *nomos*, which normally means "law" but is translated "**principle**" both times it is used in this verse. The Jew should not boast in a law of **works** that has no power to justify and no longer serves to identify the people of God (3:20). Confidence should rather be placed in the law of **faith**, which appropriates the gift of salvation and unites all who believe in the Messiah. The implied premise is that "faith" is itself a grace from God rather than a human "work" that would give cause for boasting (Eph 2:8–9; Phil 1:29).

3:28   Paul follows with a formal statement of Christian belief on the *means* of justification. Speaking on behalf of himself and his missionary collaborators, he addresses the question of how **a person is** initially **justified** in Christ. For clarity he couples an affirmation with a denial. Justification, he affirms, takes place **by** means of **faith**. Faith is what reaches out to God and accepts the gift of righteousness that is offered in Jesus. Contrary to Martin Luther and others, faith is not the *sole* instrument that brings this about, since Paul elsewhere contends that one is justified through the sacrament of baptism (1 Cor 6:11; Titus 3:5–7).[32] Likewise, the Apostle defines faith as something that acts in love (Gal 5:6) and obedience to the gospel (Rom 1:5; 16:26). Indeed, Paul has a very broad concept of saving faith: it is nothing less than the total response of the human person to God and his loving initiative. It is exercised when we entrust ourselves to God, when we trust in the promises that God makes, when we assent to the truth that God reveals, and when we consent to live as God requires.[33]

Hard on the heels of this affirmation in verse 28, Paul adds that justification takes place **apart from works of the law**. What he means by "works of the law," an expression that appears twice in Romans (3:20, 28) and six times in

---

32. The Council of Trent identifies baptism as an "instrumental cause" of justification (*Decree on Justification* 7). Even in the New Testament, James makes the categorical statement that "a person is justified . . . not by faith alone" (James 2:24).

33. For Catholic teaching on faith, see Vatican I, *Dei Filius* 3; Vatican II, *Dei Verbum* 5–6; and Catechism 150–65.

Justification

Paul speaks much about "justification" in his Letter to the Romans. It is one of the primary ways that he expounds the mystery of salvation in Christ. Justification is the merciful action of God that places us in a right relationship with him. It is a transformational event that grafts us into the New Covenant and makes us inwardly righteous. Paul understands justification as a process that begins in baptism (1 Cor 6:11), when a believer first professes faith in Jesus (Rom 3:28), and culminates when God rewards the righteous at the last judgment (2:13).

The language of justification is juridical, derived from the ancient courtroom. In this setting, a judge "justifies" an individual standing trial when he vindicates him, ruling in his favor and exempting him from the punishment that would otherwise be imposed. One who was justified was thereby restored to an honorable standing in the community.[a] Many scholars hold that justification was enacted through a declaration of acquittal, a verbal statement by the judge declaring the defendant "not guilty" of the allegations against him.[b] In Israel, where cases were adjudicated on the basis of the Mosaic law, a person who was found righteous was judged to be standing securely within the covenant and entitled to its blessings.

How Paul understands justification against this background is disputed. Does he envision God as the divine judge pronouncing the believer righteous at baptism? If so, then justification is best viewed as a transformative utterance. After all, Scripture teaches that God's word is the instrument of his will, and so God does whatever he declares in the very act of declaring it. When God

continued on next page

Galatians (Gal 2:16; 3:2, 5, 10), has challenged the minds of ancient and modern scholars alike. Opinions divide into two main camps, and both are worthy of serious consideration.

The first camp maintains that Paul is referring specifically to the *ceremonial observances* of the Mosaic law, which long defined the Jewish way of life and outwardly distinguished Jews from Gentiles.[34] The "works" in question would include such things as circumcision, dietary regulations, sabbath observance, purity codes, and sacrifices. On this view, Paul denies that the sacrificial and purity rites of the

---

34. A modern proponent is James D. G. Dunn, "The New Perspective on Paul," reprinted in *The New Perspective on Paul*, rev. ed. (Grand Rapids: Eerdmans, 2008), 99–120. Ancient and medieval advocates of this interpretation include Origen of Alexandria, *Commentary on Romans* 8.7.6; St. Jerome, *Commentary on Galatians* 1.3.2; Ambrosiaster, *Commentary on Romans* 3:28; Theodoret of Cyrrhus, *Commentary on Galatians* 2:15–16; Peter Abelard, *Commentary on Romans* 2.3.20; *Glossa Ordinaria* on Rom 3:20.

speaks, everything changes—quite literally. New realities burst into being when the word of the Lord goes forth in power.[c] Hence, justification must not be reduced to a pronouncement that imputes a legal status of righteousness but effects no actual change in the sinner. On the contrary, righteousness is the gift of spiritual life that God imparts through the Messiah (5:17 RSV). Justified believers are "made righteous" by incorporation into Christ, just as they were "made sinners" by virtue of their genealogical ties with Adam (5:19). If our fallen condition in Adam deeply affects our nature and touches the innermost core of our being, then justification in Christ can do no less.

Justification is thus a multifaceted mystery. Believers who share in Christ's righteousness experience a remission of sins (6:7), a reconciliation with God (5:1–11), a resurrection to new life (6:4), and a reception of the Spirit of adoption, by which we are made God's children (8:14–16).[d] Arguably no one has distilled the essence of Paul's teaching on justification as clearly as the Council of Trent, which explained in 1547 that justification "is a transition from that state in which a person is born a child of the first Adam to the state of grace and adoption as children of God through the agency of the second Adam, Jesus Christ."[e]

a. F. Gerald Downing, "Justification as Acquittal? A Critical Examination of Judicial Verdicts in Paul's Literary and Actual Contexts," *CBQ* 74, no. 2 (2012): 298–318.

b. Joseph A. Fitzmyer, SJ, "Justification by Faith in Pauline Thought: A Catholic View," in *Rereading Paul Together: Protestant and Catholic Perspectives on Justification*, ed. David E. Aune (Grand Rapids: Baker Academic, 2006), 77–94.

c. Gen 1:3; Ps 33:6; Isa 55:11; Ezek 12:25. See George T. Montague, SM, *The Living Thought of St. Paul* (Milwaukee: Bruce, 1966), 170–71.

d. Catechism 654, 1992.

e. *Decree on Justification* 4, adapted from Norman P. Tanner, SJ, *Decrees of the Ecumenical Councils* (Washington, DC: Georgetown University Press, 1990), 2:672.

Torah serve as instruments of justification; they have no power to justify the sinner and no longer function as badges of religious identity that mark out the covenant people of God from the rest of the world. Paul's developing discussion in Rom 2–4, with circumcision near the center, lends support to this reading. Collapsing the religious distinction between Jews and Gentiles is the burden of his argument in these very same chapters. And Paul has just spoken of a sacrifice, the expiatory death of Jesus (3:25), that supersedes the liturgical rites of Israel.[35]

The second camp argues that Paul is referring to the *observance of all the commandments* of the Mosaic law. The "works" in question are not restricted to the ceremonial rites of the Torah, but include its moral commandments as

35. It should also be noted that the Hebrew equivalent for Paul's phrase "works of the law" appears twice in the Dead Sea Scrolls (4QFlorilegium 1.6–7; 4QMMT 3). The point is debated, but both instances seem to have a primary connection with the ceremonial prescriptions of the Torah.

Justification by Faith, but Not by Faith Alone

It has been said that Martin Luther's doctrine of justification by faith alone was something of a theological *novum* of the sixteenth century. This is true if we mean that he was the first to give a full account of human salvation in these terms. However, the insufficiency of "faith alone" as the sole condition for salvation was contemplated long before the founding of Protestantism. Besides the New Testament, which denies justification by faith alone in James 2:24, theologians of the patristic and medieval periods such as Origen, Augustine, and Aquinas were careful to caution believers against this misunderstanding of Paul's teaching.

> Let believers be edified so as not to entertain the thought that because they believe, this alone can suffice for them. On the contrary, they should know that God's righteous judgment pays back to each one according to his own works.[a]

> We feel that we should advise the faithful that they would endanger the salvation of their souls if they acted on the false assurance that faith alone is sufficient for salvation or that they need not perform goods works to be saved. . . . When Saint Paul says, therefore, that man is justified by faith and not by observance of the law, he does not mean that good works are not necessary or that it is enough to receive and to profess the faith and no more. What he means rather and what he wants us to understand is that man is justified by faith, even if he has not previously performed any works of the law.[b]

> Some have been frequently deceived about sinning with impunity . . . believing that faith alone is sufficient for salvation, according to John 11:26: "Whoever lives and believes in me shall never die"; others believing they will be saved solely by Christ's sacraments, on account of what is said in Mark 16:16: "He that believes and is baptized will be saved"; and John 6:54: "He that eats my flesh and drinks my blood will have eternal life." Still others suppose that they can sin with impunity on account of the works of mercy they perform, inasmuch as it says in Luke 11:41: "Give alms for those things which are within you; and behold, everything is clean for you." . . . But they do not understand that all these things are of no benefit without charity, for it says in 1 Corinthians 13:2–3: "If I have all faith; if I give away all I have to the poor, and I have not charity, I gain nothing."[c]

a. Origen of Alexandria, *Commentary on Romans* 2.4.7. Adapted from Origen, *Commentary on the Epistle to the Romans, Books 1–5*, trans. Thomas P. Scheck, FC (Washington, DC: Catholic University of America Press, 2001), 111–12.

b. St. Augustine, *On Faith and Works* 14.21. Adapted from St. Augustine, *On Faith and Works*, trans. Gregory J. Lombardo, CSC, ACW 48 (New York: Newman, 1988), 28–29.

c. St. Thomas Aquinas, *Commentary on 1 Corinthians* 6.2.285. Adapted from St. Thomas Aquinas, *Commentary on the Letters of Saint Paul to the Corinthians*, trans. Fabian R. Larcher, Beth Mortenson, Daniel Keating (Lander, WY: The Aquinas Institute for the Study of Sacred Doctrine, 2012), 107.

well.[36] According to this view, Paul contends that no act of obedience to any of the Mosaic laws can merit the justification of the sinner; we simply cannot work our way into God's family and earn the eternal life that he offers as a free gift (6:23). A proper understanding of justification should lead us to see that God has done for us what we could never have done for ourselves. Like the first opinion, this too appeals to the wider context of the letter for support. Paul's critique of the law in Romans extends beyond circumcision and the ritual obligations imposed by Moses to an examination of the moral precepts that man is so often unable to keep (2:21–22; 7:7–12). Likewise, the law's role as a moral informant that exposes sin is also brought out in the letter (3:20; 7:7).

Both interpretations of "works of the law" tie in with critical themes in Romans, and both express important theological truths. One might say that our understanding of this verse depends on the force of the preposition translated "apart from"[37] in the sentence "We consider that a person is justified by faith apart from works of the law." If Rom 3:28 is a statement about *the complete process of justification*, then the first meaning of "works of the law" fits best. That is, the ceremonial laws play no role at all in justification; the whole thing, from start to finish, takes place without them. However, the same cannot be said about the moral laws, such as the Ten Commandments, which Paul expects believers to observe (13:8–10; 1 Cor 7:19) if they would be justified at the last judgment (Rom 2:13). However, if Rom 3:28 is a statement about *initial justification*, then the second meaning of "works of the law" seems preferable. Paul would then be saying that justification, which takes place when one believes and is baptized, is absolutely gratuitous; not a single work of obedience to God's law could ever give us a claim on the grace we receive at this moment. Yet the conditions of our first justification must be distinguished from the conditions of our final justification, which requires Christians to be doers of the law (2:13) and to perform the "good works" that God has prepared for us (Eph 2:10). That both interpretations are found in ancient and modern scholarship should not surprise us, since both in their different ways touch on authentic facets of the Christian gospel.

Paul's next move is to draw out the consequences of denying his teaching. If **3:29–30** justification comes by "works of the law," then is **God** the exclusive possession of the **Jews**? If Israel is the sole possessor of the Mosaic law, does it follow that

---

36. A modern proponent is Joseph A. Fitzmyer, SJ, "Paul's Jewish Background and the Deeds of the Law," in *According to Paul: Studies in the Theology of the Apostle* (Mahwah, NJ: Paulist Press, 1993), 18–35. Ancient and medieval advocates of this interpretation include St. Augustine, *On the Spirit and the Letter* 23, and St. Thomas Aquinas, *Commentary on Romans* 3.4.317.

37. Greek *chōris*.

Israel is the sole possessor of the God who gave that law? Does not this same God **belong to Gentiles, too?** Indeed he does, and so immediately Paul adds: **Yes, also to Gentiles.**

Paul's reasoning is expressed in terms of Israel's monotheistic faith, the belief that **God is one**. This is a reference to Deut 6:4 as rendered in the †Septuagint. The Apostle seems to infer from this text that one God can have only one people, who enter his covenant in one way. So even though the human family was once divided into the **circumcised** and the **uncircumcised**, the time has come to dismantle the partitions that once separated Jews from non-Jews (Eph 2:11–14). Salvation is found not in Israel's law but in Israel's Messiah, with the result that all are "one in Christ Jesus" (Gal 3:28). It cannot be tied to the legal obligations of the Torah, since these had the function of separating Israel from the nations. But with the dawn of messianic times, neither circumcision nor uncircumcision counts as a badge that identifies members of the family of God (1 Cor 7:19; Gal 5:6; 6:15). The gift of **faith**, expressed in baptism (Rom 6:1–4), is what counts, since it gives entrance into the Lord's covenant community regardless of one's race or prior religious affiliation.

3:31   The final verse of Rom 3 is transitional. It draws one phase of Paul's gospel exposition to a close, even as it points toward another. At this juncture, a Jewish reader may be concerned that Paul's doctrine of **faith** results in **annulling the law**. Lest this conclusion be drawn, the Apostle fires back with an emphatic denial: **Of course not!** Paul is not invalidating or undermining the inspired revelation of the Torah. **On the contrary**, his gospel message is actually **supporting the law**. The righteousness of God has indeed been manifested "apart from the law" (3:21), but this does not mean it is opposed to the law. Jewish Torah and Christian gospel stand in a relationship of essential continuity. Paul will spend the better part of Rom 4 setting out the evidence that supports this assertion.

Reflection and Application (3:27–31)

Protestants and Catholics have long butted heads over the meaning of Paul's teaching in these verses. Luther and his followers, on the basis of Rom 3:28, formulated an absolute antithesis between "faith" and "works" that made Christian charity and obedience incidental to salvation. Catholic theologians, on the contrary, stress the equal necessity of "faith" and "works" for salvation. Unfortunately, this historic disagreement has spawned the common misperception that Protestants think we are saved by faith alone and Catholics think we are saved by good works.

Of course, there is a kernel of truth in this caricature. Many Protestants do believe that Christians are saved by faith alone, although they typically acknowledge that believers have a duty to live according to the gospel. Catholicism, however, has never accepted the premise that one can reach heaven simply by being a good person. A staggering number of ill-catechized Catholics may think and act this way, but no such doctrine is taught by the Church. Virtually all Christian communities agree, at least in their official statements of faith, that we are saved by the grace that is received through believing in Jesus.

As Catholics, we need to rediscover the priority of faith in our vision of Christian salvation. Stressing the necessity of good works is entirely proper, since our final judgment will be based on whether we have lived a life of faithful obedience (2:6–7). But faith is even more foundational. Scripture is clear that "without faith it is impossible to please [God], for anyone who approaches God must believe that he exists and that he rewards those who seek him" (Heb 11:6). Faith is the front door into a living relationship with God. It is how we embrace God and attach ourselves to him. Beyond that, faith enables us to see that salvation is primarily God's work—*he* does the heavy lifting, even though he asks us to respond to his love with obedience. Good works are crucial to our salvation, to be sure. But we must not minimize the role of faith and our need to grow in faith. No real relationship with the Lord is possible without it.

The Faith and Fatherhood of Abraham

Romans 4:1–25

Romans 4 revolves around the figure of Abraham. Jews have always looked to Abraham as a forebear in faith and the founding patriarch of the covenant people, the rock from which they are hewn (Isa 51:1–2). Paul does not deny his kin this ancestral privilege, yet he does something that must have shocked them: he claims that Abraham is the spiritual father of believing Gentiles no less than believing Jews! Initially the assertion seems fanciful and unbiblical. But Paul shows otherwise by examining the Abraham story in Genesis. His argument, pushing off from Rom 3:31, is designed to show that the gospel of justification by faith for Jews and Gentiles alike confirms rather than conflicts with the written law of Moses.

The Justification of Abraham (4:1–12)

¹What then can we say that Abraham found, our ancestor according to the flesh? ²Indeed, if Abraham was justified on the basis of his works, he has reason to boast; but this was not so in the sight of God. ³For what does the scripture say? "Abraham believed God, and it was credited to him as righteousness." ⁴A worker's wage is credited not as a gift, but as something due. ⁵But when one does not work, yet believes in the one who justifies the ungodly, his faith is credited as righteousness. ⁶So also David declares the blessedness of the person to whom God credits righteousness apart from works:

> [7]"Blessed are they whose iniquities are forgiven
>   and whose sins are covered.
> [8]Blessed is the man whose sin the Lord does not record."

[9]Does this blessedness apply only to the circumcised, or to the uncircumcised as well? Now we assert that "faith was credited to Abraham as righteousness." [10]Under what circumstances was it credited? Was he circumcised or not? He was not circumcised, but uncircumcised. [11]And he received the sign of circumcision as a seal on the righteousness received through faith while he was uncircumcised. Thus he was to be the father of all the uncircumcised who believe, so that to them [also] righteousness might be credited, [12]as well as the father of the circumcised who not only are circumcised but also follow the path of faith that our father Abraham walked while still uncircumcised.

OT: Gen 15:6; 17:1–14; Pss 32:1–2; 106:31
NT: John 8:39–40; Rom 9:6–8; Gal 3:5–9; Heb 11:8–10; James 2:21–23
Catechism: faith of Abraham, 145–46, 2572; justification by faith, 1993; fatherhood of Abraham, 762

In the opening section of Rom 4, Paul reaches back to Genesis for answers to two basic questions: First, *how* was Abraham justified? And second, *when* was Abraham justified? Clarity on these matters leads to a new appraisal of Abraham's fatherhood and a more precise determination of Abraham's family. Paul's conclusions may seem novel from a traditional Jewish viewpoint, yet his handling of Scripture is both careful and compelling.

The opening line of the chapter is the key to understanding Paul's discussion. **4:1** Unfortunately, the grammatical intent of the passage—what Paul meant by the words he used—is not easily determined. Modern translations often render 4:1 as a single question about what **Abraham found** (NABRE) or "discovered" (NIV) or "gained" (NRSV, ESV).[1] However, there are solid reasons for punctuating the verse as two questions rather than one, and for thinking that Abraham is the object of discovery rather than the subject who finds or obtains something for himself.[2] Retranslating the passage along these lines yields the following: "What then shall we say? Have we found Abraham to be our forefather according to the flesh?" The question is whether we—meaning

---

1. The RSV differs in following a manuscript tradition (Codex Vaticanus) in which the infinitive "to have found" does not appear in the text.
2. Richard B. Hays, "'Have We Found Abraham to Be Our Forefather according to the Flesh?': A Reconsideration of Rom 4:1," *NovT* 27, no. 1 (1985): 76–98.

"we Christians"[3]—are constituted the children of Abraham by circumcision, which was the sign of the Abrahamic covenant inscribed "in the flesh" (2:28). Paul's answer is no. Abraham's progeny are those who share his faith, whether uncircumcised Gentiles or circumcised Jews.

4:2–3   Understanding verse 2 is just as important for following Paul's argument as understanding verse 1. He reasons that **if Abraham was justified on the basis of his works, he has reason to boast**. However, Paul will show from Genesis that **this was not so in the sight of God**. Abraham was *not* justified by "works" such as circumcision; therefore he had *no* basis for boasting in his covenant relationship with God.

Immediately Paul turns to **the scripture** to certify his position. The statement **Abraham believed God, and it was credited to him as righteousness** is a nearly exact quotation from Gen 15:6 as it reads in the †Septuagint. The passage is significant because it spells out the basis of Abraham's justification before God: it was his trustful belief in the Lord and the Lord's promise, not dutiful observance of a covenant requirement. Abraham was deemed righteous because of his faith, quite apart from the flint knife of circumcision (Rom 4:9–10).[4]

But more is involved here than the status of Abraham as an individual, and Gen 15:6 is more than a doctrinal proof text. The larger context of this verse reveals that Abraham's faith in Gen 15 is set against the background of a twofold crisis over his *fatherhood* and his *inheritance*—interrelated themes that will occupy much of Paul's attention in the remainder of Rom 4.

In Gen 15 Abraham reminded God that he had "no offspring" and that his domestic servant would be his "heir" in the absence of a son (Gen 15:3). Years earlier the Lord had declared his intention to make Abraham a "great nation" (Gen 12:2), but thus far this promise had remained unfulfilled. Abraham still had not fathered a child, so his inheritance seemed destined to pass outside his family. Therefore the Lord reassured him: Abraham would be given his "own offspring" as his "heir," and his future "descendants" would be as numerous as the stars of the sky (Gen 15:4–5). This is the promise that Abraham believed with the full strength of his faith. As a result, he was reckoned as righteous and drawn into a covenant with the Lord, who pledged to give the promised land

---

3. N. T. Wright, "The Letter to the Romans," in *The New Interpreter's Bible*, ed. Leander E. Keck (Nashville: Abingdon, 2002), 10:489.

4. It is apparent from Gen 12–14, and made explicit in Heb 11:8, that Abraham had been living by faith long before Gen 15:6. In fact, the Hebrew expression used in this verse (*he'emin be*, "believe in, have faith in") is often thought to be frequentative, suggesting an action that is habitual or customary rather than one that is undertaken for the first time. In view of these considerations, Gen 15:6 should not be read as Abraham's initial coming to faith but as his passing a critical test in his ongoing journey of faith.

Pope Francis on Abraham, Our Father in Faith

LIVING TRADITION

Faith opens the way before us and accompanies our steps through time. Hence, if we want to understand what faith is, we need to follow the route it has taken, the path trodden by believers, as witnessed first in the Old Testament. Here a unique place belongs to Abraham, our father in faith. Something disturbing takes place in his life: God speaks to him; he reveals himself as a God who speaks and calls his name. Faith is linked to hearing. Abraham does not see God, but hears his voice. Faith thus takes on a personal aspect. God is not the god of a particular place, or a deity linked to specific sacred time, but the God of a person, the God of Abraham, Isaac, and Jacob, capable of interacting with man and establishing a covenant with him. Faith is our response to a word which engages us personally, to a "Thou" who calls us by name.[a]

a. Encyclical Letter *Lumen Fidei* (*Light of Faith*) 8.

as an inheritance to his descendants (Gen 15:7–21).[5] Readers are thus prepared to see that God's promise to give Abraham both heirs and an inheritance came not through the law but "through the righteousness that comes from faith" (Rom 4:13).

Paul's commentary on the righteousness of Abraham, like his remarks on the **4:4** righteousness of God in 3:24–26, stresses the gratuitous nature of the blessing. Justification is not a **wage** paid out to an employee as **due** compensation for his labors. Rather, God confers it as a **gift** that he is not obligated to bestow. That Paul felt the need to clarify this suggests that some had come to view circumcision in precisely these terms—as a work that God credits as righteousness.

Against this, Paul insists that Abraham's **faith** was the basis of his **righ-** **4:5** **teousness**, echoing the words of Gen 15:6. The patriarch received this blessing because he believed in the **one who justifies the ungodly**. This way of describing God is surprising, especially in view of the Old Testament, where the Lord declares: "I will not justify the wicked" (Exod 23:7, literal translation). On the contrary, the Lord pledges to hold the godless accountable for their godless ways. But Paul says something quite different. Salvation history has entered a

---

5. Readers should keep in mind that "righteousness" has to do with membership in the Lord's "covenant." Genesis 15:6 thus appears to indicate that Abraham, by putting his faith in God and his word, showed himself worthy of a covenant relationship with the Lord, just as the similarly worded passage in Ps 106:31 relates how Phinehas's loyalty to God was met in return with the bestowal of a divine covenant (see Num 25:1–13). For an analysis of these parallel texts, see R. W. L. Moberly, "Abraham's Righteousness (Genesis XV 6)," in *Studies in the Pentateuch*, ed. J. A. Emerton (Leiden: Brill, 1990), 103–30.

Paul, a Rabbi by Training

Romans 4 reveals that Paul's training as a Jewish rabbi was put to good use in his proclamation of the gospel. In several ways he shows himself adept at utilizing the techniques and traditions of Jewish theology to expound a Christian vision of salvation from Scripture.

This is apparent first in the Jewish *techniques* of biblical interpretation that he employs. In the initial verses of Rom 4, Paul presents two passages from the Old Testament, Gen 15:6 and Ps 32:1–2, which he treats as mutually illuminating. Modern readers might see these quotations as unrelated. But scholars have noted that Paul is following a rabbinic rule of interpretation known as *gezerah shawah* ("equivalent regulation, analogy").[a] According to this rule, two passages that share a significant word in common, often called a "catchword," may be used to explain each other. This is why Paul brings Ps 32:1–2 into conversation with Gen 15:6—both citations have the Greek verb *logizomai* ("credit, record, reckon"), with God as the stated or implied subject. Likewise, Paul insists that justification takes place apart from circumcision by showing that Abraham himself was called righteous prior to his circumcision. In arguing from chronology, Paul is following another rabbinic rule of interpretation known as *dabar halamed me-inyano* ("word of instruction from its context").[b] According to this principle, the meaning of any given verse of the Bible must be ascertained from

continued on next page

new phase with the death of the Messiah as an †expiation for sin (Rom 3:25). God is now revealing his righteousness as mercy toward the one who **believes** in him. Thanks to the atoning sacrifice of Jesus, he is pardoning past offenses and restoring sinners to a right relationship with himself.[6]

4:6–8   Paul continues to make his case by appealing to Ps 32:1–2 as it reads in the Septuagint. Both the Hebrew and Greek Psalters ascribe this text to King **David**, "the sweet psalmist of Israel" (2 Sam 23:1 RSV). This time the gospel is preannounced in the form of a double beatitude: **Blessed are they whose iniquities are forgiven and whose sins are covered**, followed by **Blessed is the man whose sin the Lord does not record**.[7] Paul proposes that the **blessedness** described in the psalm sheds light on the **righteousness** credited to Abraham in Gen 15:6. Although undetectable in the NABRE, the

6. See the sidebar, "Justification," in Rom 3 (pp. 50–51).

7. It is often remarked that this is metaphorical language drawn from the world of bookkeeping and business contracts. An accountant performs this action when making an entry on a ledger sheet to record a client's credits and debits.

the context in which it appears, with due attention given to the surrounding sequence of events.

Paul's allusion to Jewish *tradition* about Abraham likewise enhances his theological argument. Genesis indicates that Abraham, from the standpoint of his physical condition, was as uncircumcised as a Gentile at the time he was justified. But what about his prior spiritual condition? Scholars have suggested that Paul shares the Jewish belief, deriving from reflections on Josh 24:2, that Abraham was the archetypal proselyte from idolatry, the premier example of one who converted from the veneration of many gods to a monotheistic faith in the one true God.[c] Thus, when Paul says that Abraham believed in the God "who justifies the ungodly" (Rom 4:5), he has in mind how Abraham himself was ungodly before the Lord called him, since "ungodliness" is characteristic of the Gentile world in general (1:18 RSV). Readers are invited to see that Gentile Christians in Rome, once immersed in the idolatry of classical civilization, have more in common with Abraham in the matter of justification than do Jewish Christians who are descended from the patriarch according to the flesh and share the mark of circumcision!

a. Seven rules of interpretation are attributed to a pre-Christian rabbi known as Hillel, although these are attested only in later writings (*Aboth de Rabbi Nathan* 37; Tosefta *Sanhedrin* 7.11).

b. For Paul's use of these rules, see Richard N. Longenecker, *Biblical Exegesis in the Apostolic Period*, 2nd ed. (Grand Rapids: Eerdmans, 1999), 101.

c. *Jubilees* 12.1–21; Josephus, *Jewish Antiquities* 1.155; *Apocalypse of Abraham* 1–8. See Edward Adams, "Abraham's Faith and Gentile Disobedience: Textual Links between Romans 1 and 4," *JSNT* 65 (1997): 47–66.

Greek verb *logizomai* appears both in Gen 15:6 LXX ("credited") and in Ps 32:2 LXX ("record").

Paul wants to show before all else that justification includes a merciful act of pardon. He makes a tight correlation between God's actions of *crediting* righteousness, *forgiving* iniquities, *covering* sins, and *not recording* sins. Readers are led to see that remission of guilt and release from condemnation are bound up with the notion that justification renders the believer righteous. Theologians sometimes compare this transaction to light dispelling darkness. As righteousness is imparted to the believer, sin and guilt are simultaneously driven out.

But what does it mean that "sins are covered" and that God "does not record them"? It sounds as if God fails to acknowledge our transgressions by cloaking them from his sight, or that he chooses not to keep track of them.[8] But is

8. Martin Luther mistakenly inferred from the nonimputation of sin in Rom 4:8 that justification was simply an external imputation of righteousness to the sinner rather than an interior renewal.

justification simply a matter of willful blindness and a neglect of bookkeeping on God's part? Does it take place in such a way that it leaves the inner condition of the believer unaffected? Not at all. God truly cleanses us through justification. Yet there is one sense in which our sins cannot be undone or obliterated: they are forever events of history. God can remove the guilt of our sins; likewise, God can withhold the punishment that our sins deserve. But their occurrence remains forever inscribed in the annals of past time. This is something that God's mercy must simply overlook.[9]

4:9–10 Besides the gift of forgiveness, Paul detects another layer of significance in Ps 32 when he asks, **Does this blessedness apply only to the circumcised, or to the uncircumcised as well?** He finds it telling that nothing in the psalm suggests that David's beatitude is restricted to the circumcised of Israel. The mercy of justification is open to anyone who carries the burden of sin. Paul has already demonstrated in Rom 1–3 that sin has corrupted all nations; it knows no ethnic or territorial boundaries. Divine forgiveness must then be accessible to Gentiles as well as to Jews.

Paul underscores the point by looking again at **Abraham**, who was **credited** with **righteousness** because of his **faith**—yet another reference to Gen 15:6. Only this time Paul would have us note the *timing* of Abraham's justification. Assuming readers are familiar with the Abraham story, he asks, **Under what circumstances was it credited? Was he circumcised or not?** In case anyone is stumped, he quickly supplies the answer: **He was not circumcised, but uncircumcised**.

Paul is pointing out that Abraham was justified in Gen 15 even though he was not circumcised, which did not occur until Gen 17. More than a decade separates these two events, and the implications of this fact are crucially important.[10] Paul has just established from Scripture that justification—even for Abraham's biological descendants—has never been tied to circumcision. Even more, he has just demonstrated that Abraham was *no different from a Gentile* when he was justified by faith! This helps to explain why Paul is so adamant that justification takes place apart from "works of the law" (Rom 3:28).

4:11–12 Nevertheless, this does not make **circumcision** irrelevant. Echoing the words of Gen 17:11, Paul affirms that circumcision was a **sign** of God's commitment

---

9. St. Thomas Aquinas, *Commentary on Romans* 4.1.338. For discussion, see Bruce D. Marshall, "*Beatus vir*: Aquinas, Romans 4, and the Role of 'Reckoning' in Justification," in *Reading Romans with St. Thomas Aquinas*, ed. Matthew Levering and Michael Dauphinais (Washington, DC: Catholic University of America Press, 2012), 216–37.

10. Ishmael was not yet conceived in Gen 15 and is circumcised in Gen 17 at thirteen years of age (Gen 17:25).

to the descendants of Abraham, as well as an outward indicator of the **righteousness** that Abraham had possessed while still an **uncircumcised** partner in God's covenant. It served as something like a **seal** testifying to the Lord's approval of the patriarch's **faith**.

The immediate purpose of these reflections is to address the question of Rom 4:1: "Have we [Christians] found Abraham to be our forefather according to the flesh?"[11] The answer is no. But since Abraham was to have countless descendants, many of whom were circumcised, the question remains how to identify the family that was promised to him. Paul responds that the fatherhood of Abraham is primarily spiritual. Abraham's fatherhood, in other words, is founded on faith rather than biology. He is **the father of all the uncircumcised who believe**—that is, Gentile Christians—as well as **the father of the circumcised who not only are circumcised but also follow the path of faith that our father Abraham walked**—that is, Jewish Christians. Note carefully Paul's language of "not only . . . but also." Neither circumcision nor natural descent has been rendered meaningless for Abraham's offspring; at the same time, these will not suffice as substitutes for exercising the same faith as Abraham.

The Promise to Abraham (4:13–17)

[13]It was not through the law that the promise was made to Abraham and his descendants that he would inherit the world, but through the righteousness that comes from faith. [14]For if those who adhere to the law are the heirs, faith is null and the promise is void. [15]For the law produces wrath; but where there is no law, neither is there violation. [16]For this reason, it depends on faith, so that it may be a gift, and the promise may be guaranteed to all his descendants, not to those who only adhere to the law but to those who follow the faith of Abraham, who is the father of all of us, [17]as it is written, "I have made you father of many nations." He is our father in the sight of God, in whom he believed, who gives life to the dead and calls into being what does not exist.

OT: Gen 15:4–6, 18–21; 17:5; 2 Macc 7:28; Ps 72:8; Sir 44:19–21
NT: Matt 5:5; Rom 3:20; 5:13, 20; Gal 3:7–9
Catechism: God's promise to Abraham, 706; the law discloses sin, 1963; creation out of nothing, 296–98, 318
Lectionary: 4:13, 16–18, 22: St. Joseph, husband of the Blessed Virgin Mary

11. See commentary on 4:1 for this translation.

The central verses of Rom 4 continue Paul's discussion of Abraham's fatherhood, only now the issue of Abraham's inheritance is moved into the foreground. Throughout this short section, one cluster of ideas (faith, promise,
and gift) is played off against another (law, wrath, and violation) with the aim
of setting the record straight on a critical question: Who are the beneficiaries
of the inheritance promised to Abraham? The pillars of Paul's argument are
sunk deep in Scripture, but the interpretive connections that make it work
are not always explicit. A degree of detective work is thus needed to appreciate his explanation.

4:13   Paul first centers attention on **the promise** that God made **to Abraham
and his descendants**. This promise is clearly attached to the **righteousness
that comes from faith**—another allusion to Gen 15:6—but clarity shades into
obscurity when Paul describes it as a promise that Abraham will **inherit the
world**. Readers who flip back to Genesis will search in vain to find the Lord
making this promise explicitly. One way around the difficulty is to posit that
Paul is thinking in typological terms. Genesis tells us that God swore an oath
to grant Abraham's heirs "the land" of his sojourning, which at that time was
occupied by ten nations (Gen 15:18–21). Perhaps Paul views Canaan as an
image of the world at large, which is home to all nations. A similar †typology
is sometimes thought to underlie Jesus' saying, "Blessed are the meek, for they
shall inherit the earth" (Matt 5:5 RSV).[12]

In any case, a global extension of the promise to Abraham is already envisioned in the Old Testament.[13] The key passage is Sir 44:21: "God promised him
[Abraham] with an oath / to bless the nations through his descendants . . . /
Giving them an inheritance from sea to sea, / and from the River to the ends
of the earth." Ben Sira appears to view the oath to Abraham in Gen 22:16–18,
which promises blessings for "all the nations," through the prism of Ps 72:8,
which petitions the Lord to broaden the rule of the Davidic king "from sea to
sea, / from the river to the ends of the earth." The Abrahamic covenant is thus
linked to the territorial dimensions hoped for in the Davidic covenant. For Paul,
however, neither covenant is fully realized until the messianic reign of Jesus,
"the son of David, the son of Abraham" (Matt 1:1).[14] Now we have reached
the point where Christians, being joint heirs with Christ (Rom 8:17), stand to
inherit "all things with him" (8:32 RSV).

---

12. Matthew 5:5 borrows language from Ps 37:11, which originally designates the "land" of Israel
as the inheritance of the Lord's faithful ones (so RSV, NRSV, ESV, NIV, JB).

13. Likewise, nonbiblical Jewish works express the belief that Abraham's descendants would "inherit
the earth" (*1 Enoch* 5.7; *Jubilees* 22.14; see also Philo of Alexandria, *On Dreams* 1.175).

14. See the sidebar, "Among All the Gentiles," in Rom 1 (p. 6).

With some emphasis, Paul clarifies that the promise of a worldwide inheritance did not come **through the law**. By this he means that no legal or ritual conditions were attached to the pledge that Abraham would become the father of many nations. It was his **faith** that secured its fulfillment. Once again, Paul's argument is constructed on the grounds that Abraham was still an uncircumcised man when the promise was made to him.

This leads to a short discussion of the **law**, its adherents, and its effects. Paul **4:14** is working from the premise, stated in verse 13, that the Torah plays no part in identifying the heirs of the promise to Abraham. The law calls for "works," which were required of the Jews, the people **who adhere to the law**; the **promise**, however, calls for a trusting **faith** in God, which is open to all, even to Gentiles, who are "outside the law" (2:12).[15] To make keeping the law a necessary condition for reception of the inheritance is to make faith **null** and the promise of God **void** and ineffectual.

Paul touches on the argument developed in Rom 1–3: If the **law** of Moses plays **4:15** no role in identifying Abraham's heirs, then what does it do? Among other things, it **produces wrath**. The logic of this statement is highly compressed and requires some unpacking. For Paul, the Torah is what makes **violation** or transgression possible because, in the name of God, it erects definite boundaries between prohibited and praiseworthy actions, imparting a clearer "consciousness of sin" among the Jews (3:20) than the general awareness of right and wrong that lies open to pagan Gentiles (1:18–32).[16] As a result, the Jewish lawbreaker stores up "wrath" for himself when he violates the Torah and refuses repentance (2:5). Conversely, **where there is no law, neither is there violation**. Paul wants to drive home that the promise made to Abraham came at a time in his life (Gen 15:4–5) when there was **no law** of Moses, not even the command to be circumcised (Gen 17:10).

At this point, readers are primed for Paul to state his conclusion. Abrahamic **4:16** sonship, and the inheritance that goes with it, **depends on faith**, which means that God bestows it as a free **gift** rather than a payment rendered **to those who only adhere to the law**. Abraham's heirs are not those who follow the way of life defined by the Torah but those who follow **the faith of Abraham**, who is **the father of all of us**, Jewish and Gentile Christians together. Just as faith made Abraham a father, so faith makes believers his sons and daughters.

---

15. Hays, "Have We Found," 92, makes the important point that Paul employs "an associative logic" in Rom 3:27–4:22 such that works of the law, circumcision, and fleshly descent from Abraham are so closely related as to be virtually equivalent motifs.

16. Paul maintains that "sin was in the world" before the law of Moses, but sin in pre-Mosaic times was not counted as a legal trespass apart from Adam's violation of an explicit commandment (see Rom 5:13–14).

4:17   Paul supports this thesis by citing the words of Gen 17:5: **I have made you father of many nations.** There are two things to notice about this verse. First, God declares that Abraham is the father of *many* nations, not just *one* nation. The inclusion of Gentiles in the family of Abraham is thus validated from the Lord's own words. Second, Paul gives close attention to the narrative context of this divine pronouncement. God announced that he had *already* made Abraham the father of a multinational family *before* circumcision was commanded (Gen 17:10–14). He is referring to a blessing announced in Gen 15, before the covenant of circumcision was even introduced.

The critical moment for Abraham's fatherhood came in Gen 15:6, when he **believed** in God and his divine ability to do the humanly impossible—to give him a son in his old age and countless descendants thereafter. These are the circumstances that prompt Paul's description of the Lord as one **who gives life to the dead and calls into being what does not exist.**[17] Only God, the creator and giver of life, could have made good on his promise to Abraham, whose body at nearly one hundred years old was as good as "dead" (Rom 4:19).

The Faith of Abraham (4:18–25)

[18]**He believed, hoping against hope, that he would become "the father of many nations," according to what was said, "Thus shall your descendants be."** [19]**He did not weaken in faith when he considered his own body as [already] dead (for he was almost a hundred years old) and the dead womb of Sarah.** [20]**He did not doubt God's promise in unbelief; rather, he was empowered by faith and gave glory to God** [21]**and was fully convinced that what he had promised he was also able to do.** [22]**That is why "it was credited to him as righteousness."** [23]**But it was not for him alone that it was written that "it was credited to him";** [24]**it was also for us, to whom it will be credited, who believe in the one who raised Jesus our Lord from the dead,** [25]**who was handed over for our transgressions and was raised for our justification.**

OT: Gen 15:5; 17:5, 17; 18:14; Isa 53:11–12
NT: Rom 6:4; 15:13; 1 Cor 10:11; 15:17
Catechism: hope of Abraham, 1819; faith embraces God and his truth, 150; perseverance in faith, 162; participation in Christ's passion and resurrection, 1988
Lectionary: 4:13, 16–18, 22: St. Joseph, husband of the Blessed Virgin Mary

---

17. Paul holds the emerging Jewish doctrine of creation out of nothing (2 Macc 7:28; Philo of Alexandria, *Special Laws* 4.187), which is likewise a tenet of Christian faith (Catechism 296–98).

Romans 4 concludes with Paul drawing a line from the faith of Abraham to the faith of the Christian believer. Prior to this point, he has analyzed the circumstances surrounding the patriarch's extraordinary act of trust in Gen 15:6. Here he probes more deeply into the spiritual and psychological drama of the event. Paul's reflections form a bridge carrying the discussion into the time of messianic fulfillment, when faith is again placed in the God who overcomes death with his power to bring forth new life.

Continuing the conversation in progress, Paul fixes one eye on Gen 17:5, **4:18–19** where God called Abraham **the father of many nations**, and the other on Gen 15:5, where God turned the patriarch's gaze to the starry heavens with the promise, **Thus shall your descendants be**. As Paul has reminded us several times now, this is the divine word that Abraham **believed**.

But now Paul draws attention to another virtue in play. Alongside faith, he notes that Abraham was **hoping against hope**—from a human perspective, hoping in something utterly hopeless.[18] Abraham and his wife **Sarah** had been a childless couple for the duration of their married life thus far, and they were both past the normal age for conceiving a child. He thought of his **own body** and the **womb** of his wife as **dead** from a reproductive standpoint, for he was **almost a hundred years old** (Gen 17:17). Utterly hopeless indeed.

Nevertheless, Abraham **did not doubt God's promise in unbelief**.[19] Genesis **4:20–22** does not state this explicitly, but Paul extrapolates from Abraham's unhesitating response that he was **empowered by faith**[20] and thus **fully convinced** that the Lord was **able to do** everything **he had promised**. In effect, Abraham already recognized the truth of the words spoken later to Sarah in Gen 18:14: "Is anything too marvelous for the LORD to do?" Unlike most of fallen humanity, Abraham had a clear perception of the power of God and so **gave glory to God**, whereas the Gentiles typically failed on both counts, according to Rom 1:20–21. This is precisely why Gen 15:6 says that Abraham's faith **was credited to him as righteousness**. He did not allow his vision of the creator to be cramped by the calculations of human reason and historical probability.

In these verses Paul leaps from the life of Abraham to the life of the believer. **4:23–24** Scripture, as a divine word, is more than a history of God's involvement with the world of the distant past. The Old Testament has a contemporary relevance

---

18. Brendan Byrne, SJ, *Romans*, SP 6 (Collegeville, MN: Liturgical Press, 1996), 160.

19. At first glance, Paul's assertion appears to contradict Gen 16:1–4, where Abraham seeks to fulfill the promise of a son through Hagar, his wife's handmaiden. But his resort to surrogate motherhood need not amount to positive doubt, even if it involved some rationalizing on Abraham's part. In point of fact, the divine promise in Gen 15:4–6 did not specify who the *mother* of Abraham's natural son would be.

20. Other translations render the expression "grew strong in faith" (RSV, NRSV, ESV), "drew strength from faith" (JB), and "was strengthened in his faith" (NIV).

that offers encouragement (15:13) and instruction to the Christian community (1 Cor 10:11). When Paul refers to the expression **it was credited to him** in Gen 15:6, he points out that it was not concerning Abraham **alone** that this statement **was written**. Indeed, **it was also for us**—the family of Jewish and Gentile believers living in messianic times. Christians too are **credited** with righteousness when they **believe in the one who raised Jesus our Lord from the dead**.

This last statement is significant for understanding the parallel that Paul sees between the faith of Abraham and the faith of the Church. First, he points to a correspondence in the *divine object* of faith, which in both cases is God the Father. Paul can just as well speak of putting faith in Christ the Son (e.g., Gal 2:16), but here he wants to underscore that justifying faith is directed toward God the creator. Second, his stress on this point implies a further correspondence touching on the *historical object* of faith. Paul never comes out and says it, but note the implication in his argument: the miracle of Isaac's conception is akin to the miracle of Jesus' resurrection. His stress on the deadness of Abraham's and Sarah's bodies (Rom 4:19), coupled with his assumption that readers know the miraculous outcome of the story (the birth of Isaac), makes this conclusion all but inescapable. Just as faith once accepted that God could bring new life to the sterile and aging humanity of Abraham and Sarah, leading to the birth of a son, so now faith accepts that God has given new life to the crucified humanity of Jesus, leading to his glorious rebirth in the resurrection. In short, Christian faith has the same essential character as Abrahamic faith. This is why Paul can insist that what happened to Abraham when he believed in God happens to every one of his heirs who places faith in the Lord as he did.

4:25   The final verse of Rom 4 is often said to derive from an early Christian confession of faith. It states in parallel formulas that Jesus **was handed over for our transgressions** and that he **was raised for our justification**. It may be that the early Church recited such a summary of the paschal mystery and its benefits in the liturgy. But speculation aside, it is certain that Paul takes full ownership of the statement. Whether or not he coined the expression, it conveys his belief that Christ's passion and resurrection are the two events most critical in our redemption.

Additionally, many contend that the wording of the statement is indebted to the fourth Servant Song in Isa 52:13–53:12. This prophetic poem concerns a mysterious figure, identified only as the Lord's Servant, who surrenders himself to the rejection and abuse of his own people. He even makes his life an atoning sacrifice by being "handed over to death . . . for their sins" (Isa 53:12 LXX). Not surprisingly, the earliest Christians read the song as a prophetic preview of the suffering and dying of the Messiah for the salvation of the world (Matt 8:17; Luke 22:37; Acts 8:32–35). Paul will have this same passage in mind in Rom 5 when he contrasts the obedience of Jesus with the disobedience of Adam.

It is significant, moreover, that both verbs in Rom 4:25 are in the passive voice ("was handed over . . . was raised") without the agent of the action being specified in the text. Commentators typically designate such verbs as "divine passives," meaning that God is the implied subject who handed Jesus over to death and raised him from the grave. These are standard affirmations of the New Testament, even though the Gospels tell us that Judas Iscariot handed Jesus over to hostile authorities (Matt 26:14–16) and that Jesus spoke of having the power to raise himself from the dead (John 10:17–18). Focusing on the actions of the Father ties the events of the Triduum to the larger scheme of God's righteousness being revealed in the history of salvation (Rom 1:17; 3:21–26).

No less significant is the link that Paul forges between the resurrection of Christ and the justification of the Christian. It is true that the miracle of Easter morning serves as a motive of credibility for the claims of Christianity, a vindication of Jesus and the supreme validation of his message. It is also true that Paul views the event as having implications for the moral life of the baptized, who are called to die to their sins and walk "in newness of life" (6:4). But here the Apostle describes the resurrection as a saving event in its own right. His words, whether traditional or crafted for the occasion, assert a *causal* connection between Jesus rising again and the sinner's justification.[21] As one theologian says of Rom 4:25: "If we are to be faithful to the parallelism of the statement, we must place our Lord's resurrection beside his death as fully effective for our salvation."[22] Careful study of Paul's writings reveals that the resurrection is no minor addendum to the gospel of a crucified Messiah; on the contrary, it is the crowning truth sounded in the earliest Christian preaching.[23]

Reflection and Application (4:1–23)

Judaism and Christianity agree that Abraham is a living example of godliness. He is a man whose life and actions are held out for reflection and imitation. Of

---

21. Bruce Vawter, CM, "Resurrection and Redemption," *CBQ* 15, no. 1 (1953): 11–23.

22. F. X. Durrwell, *The Resurrection: A Biblical Study*, trans. Rosemary Sheed (New York: Sheed & Ward, 1960), 27.

23. David Michael Stanley, SJ, *Christ's Resurrection in Pauline Soteriology*, AnBib 13 (Roma: Editrice Pontificio Istituto Biblico, 1961).

Resurrection and Justification

Few theologians have made the effort to grapple with Paul's insight that Jesus Christ "was raised for our justification" (4:25). Among the exceptions stands St. Thomas Aquinas, who explains:

> Two things are implied in the soul's justification, the remission of sins and the newness of life which is the result of grace. In both cases the effect brought about by the power of God is said to be caused by Christ's death and resurrection. More specifically, in the field of exemplary causality, the passion and death of Christ are properly the causes of the remission of our faults, for we die to sin. The resurrection, on the other hand, more properly causes the newness of life through grace or justice. Therefore, we read that *he was put to death for our sins*, that is, to take them away, and *he was raised for our justification*.[a]

a. *Summa Theologiae* III.56.2, adapted from St. Thomas Aquinas, *Summa Theologiae*, Blackfriars vol. 55, trans. C. Thomas Moore, OP (New York: McGraw-Hill, 1976), 75.

his many admirable virtues, Paul singles out his faith. Careful attention to Rom 4 suggests that Paul sees three essential aspects to faith in the Abraham story.

Faith is first and foremost *personal*. It is not a mere mental acceptance that life is directed by a nameless cosmic force, but an act of the mind and heart reaching out to the One who reveals himself as creator and redeemer. Time and again in the Bible, God presents himself to the world as a person to be believed, trusted, glorified, and loved. God is someone with whom we can have a genuine relationship that grows and deepens over time. The Catechism teaches this when it states, "Faith is first of all a personal adherence of man to God" (150).

Faith is also *propositional*. Adherence to the all-knowing God means taking him at his word. It means committing ourselves to him by trusting in all that he says. For Abraham, this meant believing in the Lord and relying on the divine promise of future offspring despite natural obstacles. Abraham trusted that what is humanly impossible is nevertheless possible with God. Again the Catechism reminds us that faith entails "a *free assent to the whole truth that God has revealed*" and that it "is right and just to entrust oneself wholly to God and to believe absolutely what he says" (150).

Lastly, faith is *persevering*. Invariably there is a lag between the promises made by God and the time when those promises are fulfilled. The purpose of this interval is to provide the believer with opportunities for faith to grow stronger and purer. In the case of Abraham, many years separated the pledge of a son and the day of the son's birth, during which time Abraham had to sustain his trust in the Lord, reposing the full weight of his hopes and dreams in the word that God had spoken. Thus, Paul is not tossing out some throwaway line when he urges believers to follow "the footsteps" of Abraham's faith (4:12, literal translation). He recognizes that faith in God and his promise characterized Abraham's entire path of life in good times and in bad. The Catechism touches on this aspect of faith as well: "To live, grow, and persevere in the faith until the end we must nourish it with the word of God; we must beg the Lord to increase our faith" (162).[24]

24. See Mark 9:24; Luke 17:5; 22:32.

Reconciliation in Christ the New Adam

Romans 5:1–21

Chapters 5–8 constitute the next major section of Romans. For the time being Paul sets aside his effort to explain the relation of Jews and Gentiles to the gospel. Now his concern is to expand on the blessings and struggles of the Christian life going forward from initial justification to final salvation. This shift in focus is matched by a shift in approach: the Apostle transitions from theological argumentation, grounded in a profusion of Old Testament texts, to a theological contemplation of the "grace" that believers possess in the present and the "glory" they hope to possess in the future. In the interim, disciples are faced with many challenges, especially the ongoing realities of sin and suffering. But thanks to the ministry of the Son and the Spirit working in the hearts and lives of believers, the Father enables us to "conquer overwhelmingly" (8:37), so that nothing may "separate us from the love of God in Christ Jesus" (8:39).

Peace with God through Christ (5:1–5)

¹Therefore, since we have been justified by faith, we have peace with God through our Lord Jesus Christ, ²through whom we have gained access [by faith] to this grace in which we stand, and we boast in hope of the glory of God. ³Not only that, but we even boast of our afflictions, knowing that affliction produces endurance, ⁴and endurance, proven character, and proven character, hope, ⁵and hope does not disappoint, because the love of God has been poured out into our hearts through the holy Spirit that has been given to us.

OT: Pss 22:5; 116:10; Isa 32:15; 44:3; Ezek 36:25–26; Joel 3:1

NT: John 14:27; Acts 14:22; Rom 3:23; 8:18–25; Eph 2:14–18; Titus 3:5–6; 1 John 4:16

Catechism: God's peace, 1829; the theological virtues, 1812–29, 1991; love is God's gift and our response, 733, 2658

Lectionary: Trinity Sunday (Year C); St. Blaise; Common of Martyrs; 5:1–2, 5–8: 3rd Sunday of Lent (Year A); Confirmation

How do we know that Rom 5–8 is an identifiable unit within the epistle? In the opening verses of chapter 5 and the closing verses of chapter 8, Paul repeats key themes, terms, and ideas (5:1–11; 8:18–39).[1] Paul begins and ends the section with attention to God's love, the tribulations of this life, the need for endurance through suffering, and the hope of future glory.

Using the word **therefore**, Paul signals his intent to draw out the implica-   5:1
tions of his teaching in chapters 1–4. Having already described the *basis* of justification, he moves on to consider the *benefits* of justification. Everything that follows in chapters 5–8 can be traced back to the conviction that **we**—Paul and his Christian readers—**have been justified by faith**. On the one hand, our initial justification is viewed as a past event; on the other hand, it is a fact that gives rise to other facts that call for closer attention.

The first is that **we have peace with God**,[2] which means having a proper relationship between the Father and the human family restored. It certainly includes an absence of hostilities, and yet it has a positive dimension as well. Paul probably has in mind the Hebrew notion of *shalom*, which indicates a state of covenant communion and well-being.[3] Peace of this sort may come with a sense of inner tranquility, but its essence is relational more than experiential. It comes **through** the Messiah and mediator of the New Covenant, **our Lord Jesus Christ** (John 14:27).

Another result of justification is that Christians **have gained access [by**   5:2
faith][4] **to this grace in which we stand**. Christ's actions in history have made it possible for believers to enter the sphere of God's presence and mercy. This sounds rather abstract, but Paul's thoughts may well be more concrete. The

1. Douglas J. Moo, *The Epistle to the Romans*, NICNT (Grand Rapids: Eerdmans, 1996), 293.
2. A majority of manuscripts read "let us have peace with God" (subjunctive) at 5:1; however, most scholars judge that "we have peace with God" (indicative) is more likely the original reading. One reason is contextual: the paragraph consists of a series of affirmations and otherwise lacks even a single exhortation. See Bruce M. Metzger, *A Textual Commentary on the Greek New Testament* (New York: United Bible Societies, 1975), 511.
3. N. T. Wright, "The Messiah and the People of God: A Study in Pauline Theology with Particular Reference to the Argument of the Epistle of the Romans" (DPhil diss., Oxford University, 1980), 136, says the peace of 5:1 "refers to all the blessings which accrue to the covenant family."
4. Brackets indicate that the editors of the NABRE consider these words textually uncertain—i.e., there remains some doubt about whether they come from Paul or a later scribe inserted them.

term "access" (Greek *prosagōgē*) can suggest admittance into the presence of a king[5] as well as entrance into a temple (see Eph 2:18). Access to both the throne and the temple was restricted to an authorized few. For Paul, these associations are not alternative ways of conceptualizing our approach to God but more like two sides of the same coin.[6] In the Old Testament, the Lord is the divine king whose invisible presence was believed to sit enthroned not in a war tent or a royal audience hall but atop the ark of the covenant (2 Sam 6:2; Isa 37:16) in the innermost chamber of the temple in Jerusalem (1 Kings 6:19). Paul may well envision our access to grace as a spiritual admittance into the sanctuary of heaven, the eternal throne room of God, which was represented architecturally by the sanctuaries of biblical Israel (Exod 25:9; Wis 9:8). Gospel scholars often detect a similar message about newly gained access to God signaled by the tearing of the temple veil at Jesus' crucifixion (Matt 27:51; Mark 15:38; Luke 23:45).

In any event, justified believers **boast** or exult in the **hope** of attaining **the glory of God**. By this Paul means the heavenly immortality that awaits the saints, who will come to participate fully—body, soul, and spirit—in the luminous splendor of divinity that belongs eternally to God. Believers wait for this glory "in joyful hope" because it is not something they already see with their eyes and hold in their grasp (Rom 8:24–25). Christian hope is neither a vague optimism nor a presumptuous assurance about the outcome of God's final judgment. Rather, it is the confident expectation of receiving what God has prepared for those who love him, provided they conform themselves to Christ and so confirm their status as God's children and heirs (8:17).

5:3-4   From here Paul's thoughts take a surprising turn. Divine glory is not the **only** thing in which Christians exult. They **even boast** of undergoing **afflictions**! Paul has not misspoken; he attaches tremendous significance to suffering, as is evident in his missionary preaching: "through many tribulations we must enter the kingdom of God" (Acts 14:22 RSV). For the Apostle, suffering is integral to God's redemptive purposes. It is part of the Christian path because it sculpts us into the image of Jesus, who passed into glory by way of the cross.[7]

Paul will say more about the saving purpose of suffering in Rom 8. For now he outlines a process of Christian growth and maturation in four steps.[8] Why is **affliction** an occasion for boasting? Because it **produces endurance**, meaning

---

5. Xenophon, *Cyropaedia* 7.5.45.

6. James D. G. Dunn, *Romans 1–8*, WBC 38a (Nashville: Nelson, 1988), 248, is cautiously open to this possibility, given that "cult and court could be readily merged in such imagery."

7. See especially Siu Fung Wu, *Suffering in Romans* (Eugene, OR: Pickwick, 2015).

8. Paul employs a rhetorical device in which each successive statement of an interconnected series picks up a word from the preceding line and makes it the basis for a new assertion. For other examples in the Bible, see Wis 6:17–20 and 2 Pet 1:5–7.

a steadfast will to do what is right and to hold fast to the faith in the midst of adversity. And perseverance, in turn, generates the **proven character** of one who has been tested and found faithful. Finally, having emerged from the fires of tribulation, our **hope** for heavenly glory is made the more firm. Of course, none of this would be possible on the paltry strength of fallen human nature. It is owing to the "grace in which we stand" (5:2) that virtues such as these are able to blossom and grow in our lives.

Paul's rhetorical buildup, begun in verse 3, ascends to its climax in verse 5. **5:5 Hope**, he says, **does not disappoint**, or "does not put to shame." Clearly he wants to encourage readers in their struggles and to assure them that hope refined by affliction will not lead to disillusionment or humiliation in the end. Although he does not quote a specific passage, Paul derives this conviction from Scripture—for example, "To you [my God] they cried out and were saved, on you they placed their hope and were not put to shame" (Ps 22:6 LXX).

Hope has this confidence because the **hearts** of believers have been filled with **the love of God**. There is some debate about whether this means "God's love for us" or "our love for God." Many scholars argue that Paul intends at least the former, and verse 8 seems to bear this out. More than anything, Paul wants to strengthen believers with the certainty that God loves them. This is all the more crucial in times of anguish and woe, when it can feel as though God is distant and unconcerned with our plight.

But could Paul be talking about *our* love for God as well, as theologians such as St. Augustine maintained?[9] There are solid reasons for thinking so. Paul affirms elsewhere that a new capacity to love God is produced in believers by the **Spirit** (Gal 5:22; Col 1:8).[10] In fact, Rom 5:1–5 seems to reference the triad of signature Christian virtues: faith (v. 1), hope (vv. 2, 4), and love (v. 5), all of which are produced in believers by the Lord's grace (1 Cor 13:13; 1 Thess 1:3). It is doubtful that Paul could single out faith, hope, and love in the short compass of five verses without any intended reference to these mainstays of gospel living.

At any rate, hope grows in confidence because of this inpouring of divine love. The more the Spirit increases our love for God, the more firmly the Spirit attaches us to God. And as love for the Lord intensifies, fear of his condemnation diminishes (1 John 4:17–18). The Spirit, who **has been given** to dwell in the hearts of the justified, is thus a first installment toward the fullness of God's eternal blessings (2 Cor 1:22).

9. See, e.g., *On the Spirit and the Letter* 5.
10. This is also affirmed in the Catholic Church's tradition (Second Synod of Orange, Canon 25).

Poured Out in the Spirit

In Rom 5:5, Paul links the indwelling of divine love in the Christian heart with the indwelling of the divine Spirit. This is a truth believed by faith and experienced in the joys and consolations of the Christian life. Note the biblical texture of Paul's language. He is subtly announcing the fulfillment of God's saving designs revealed in the Old Testament, particularly the prophecies of a future time when the Spirit will flow down in generous measure on the people of God.

A clear signal of this intent is the expression "poured out." Several prophecies of the Old Testament liken the Holy Spirit to water that streams downward from heaven and gives life to the world. Sometimes a reference to water is explicit, as in Isa 44:3, where the Lord promises: "I will pour out water upon the thirsty ground. . . . I will pour out my spirit upon your offspring." Other times a representation of the Spirit as water is implicit, as in Joel 3:1, where God announces, "I will pour out my spirit upon all flesh"—a prophecy fulfilled at the first Christian Pentecost (Acts 2:17). In Isa 32:15 the pious of Israel wait on the Lord "until the spirit from on high / is poured out upon" them. One passage even combines the triple imagery of Spirit, water, and human hearts in a way similar to Rom 5:5. It is Ezek 36:25–26, where the Lord says, "I will sprinkle clean water over you. . . . I will give you a new heart, and a new spirit I will put within you." The impression is strong that Paul's thinking is indebted to passages such as these and that he views prophetic hopes of the Spirit's outpouring coming to fulfillment in the messianic age (Rom 1:1–4).

This is first of all linked to the events of Pentecost (Acts 2:14–36), and then to the initial reception of the Spirit by Gentile converts, which was an aftershock of the Pentecost event (Acts 10:45). But is Pentecost all that Paul has in mind in Rom 5:5? Not likely. The normative context for the outpouring of the Spirit in the life of the Church is baptism. No sooner did Peter preach on the Spirit's descent at Pentecost (Acts 2:17) than he urged the crowds in Jerusalem to "Repent and be baptized, every one of you, in the name of Jesus Christ . . . and you will receive the gift of the holy Spirit" (Acts 2:38). Paul's doctrine is no different: baptism is the occasion when justification takes place (1 Cor 6:11) and the Spirit of the Lord streams into the lives of believers in a powerful way (1 Cor 12:13). We see this clearly in Titus 3:5–7: "He [God] saved us through the bath of rebirth / and renewal by the holy Spirit, / whom he richly poured out on us / through Jesus Christ our savior, / so that we might be justified by his grace / and become heirs in hope of eternal life." The waters of baptism render the cleansing work of the Spirit visible, fulfilling prophetic expectations of the Spirit being "poured out" on the Lord's people.

Reconciliation with God through Christ (5:6–11)

---

⁶**For Christ, while we were still helpless, yet died at the appointed time for the ungodly. ⁷Indeed, only with difficulty does one die for a just person, though perhaps for a good person one might even find courage to die. ⁸But God proves his love for us in that while we were still sinners Christ died for us. ⁹How much more then, since we are now justified by his blood, will we be saved through him from the wrath. ¹⁰Indeed, if, while we were enemies, we were reconciled to God through the death of his Son, how much more, once reconciled, will we be saved by his life. ¹¹Not only that, but we also boast of God through our Lord Jesus Christ, through whom we have now received reconciliation.**

NT: John 3:16; Rom 3:24–26; 2 Cor 5:18–20; Eph 2:1–3; 1 Thess 1:10; 1 John 3:16

Catechism: justification through the death of Christ, 617, 1992; reconciliation through the death of Christ, 613–14; God's love manifest in the death of Christ, 604

Lectionary: 5:5–11: Mass for the Deceased; Commemoration of All the Faithful Departed; 5:5b–11: Sacred Heart (Year C)

Verses 6–11 look back in time to Christ's death as the basis of our salvation and then forward in time to Christ completing his work of salvation within us. In discussing these matters, Paul invites us to consider the logic of God's actions. If the Father has gone to all the trouble of surrendering his Son for the benefit of his enemies, how can we doubt his desire to save those who are now his friends? The strong affirmations in this passage are meant to dispel whatever uncertainties about God's love or saving intentions may be lingering in the minds of readers.

Paul begins by thinking back to the spiritual condition of our race **at the appointed time**, at the moment in history when the Messiah went to his death in fulfillment of God's plan. This was a time when humanity was both **helpless** and **ungodly**. The first term indicates that we were "weak" or "infirm" with respect to salvation, powerless to extricate ourselves from sin and separation from God. A pitiable condition indeed, but a sinister one as well. So Paul adds the second term to indicate that we were habituated to godless ways. The world lived in a more or less continual state of opposition to God. So we were not only sickly but also stubbornly sinful. And yet **Christ** laid down his life **for** the salvation of these very people.

Paul regards the severity of our predicament as a measure of God's extravagant love. Experience knows that **only with difficulty does one die for a just person, though perhaps for a good person one might even find courage to die**. Everyone has an instinct to live, and so people find it hard to forfeit their

5:6

5:7–8

77

lives, even for a noble cause. Consent to death requires a valiant act of the will that is calculated, in part, by the worthiness of the beneficiary. This makes it all the more remarkable that **while we were still sinners Christ died for us.** The rebellious human race was not worthy of such a sacrifice. Quite the contrary, it was unworthy in every way imaginable—not only devoid of merits, but loaded down with sins and demerits.

The heroic generosity of Jesus thus **proves** the intensity of God's **love** for us. Paul is talking about the species of love known in Greek as *agapē*, which is neither a mutual affection between friends (*philia*) nor a romantic passion between lovers (*erōs*). It is the kind of love that wills what is best for another no matter the cost. It is an unconditional love that pours itself out in acts of service and sacrifice. The New Testament describes this love originating with God and enacted in giving: "God so *loved* the world that he *gave* his only Son" (John 3:16, emphasis added).

In saying this, Paul sheds light on another dimension of the cross. Earlier he called the Messiah's death proof of God's "righteousness" (Rom 3:24–26). Now he adds that the Messiah's death is proof of God's "love" (5:8). Both are made visible in Christ's sacrifice of his life.

5:9–10   Paul next makes two comparisons that pivot on the words **how much more.** The logic of these back-to-back statements proceeds from a lesser fact to a greater fact—a rhetorical device popular among rabbinic teachers under the name *qal wahōmer* (Hebrew for "light and heavy").[11] Paul employs it elsewhere in his writings (Rom 5:15; 2 Cor 3:11), as does Jesus in his preaching (Matt 6:30; 7:11; 10:25). Here it serves to bolster confidence in the final salvation of Christians.

Both verses mention the work that God has already accomplished in believers, and then both consider the work that God has yet to accomplish in them. At present we are **justified by his blood** and have been **reconciled to God through the death of his Son.** These are two ways of saying that the crucifixion was an atoning sacrifice that reestablished believers in a covenant relationship with God. The first expression echoes Paul's remarks in Rom 3:24–26, while the second introduces a new element into the discussion: the concept of reconciliation. Reconciliation refers essentially to a mended relationship. It is what happens when **enemies** become friends, when family members once estranged are reunited. Here Paul means the removal of animosity between God and sinful humanity, and so forgiveness is a crucial part of the picture (2 Cor 5:19). One could say that reconciliation encapsulates the whole notion of being "justified" and at "peace with God" (Rom 5:1).

---

11. Classical rhetoric refers to this as an "a fortiori" argument.

In view of the staggering depths to which God has lowered himself for our redemption, Paul expresses great confidence that Christians **will be saved** in the end. His use of the future tense points to something too often underappreciated—namely, that Paul views the Christian life as a continuum of salvation with a beginning, a middle, and an end. The Apostle can thus speak of the *past* as a time when Christians "were saved" (8:24), of the *present* as a time when Christians "are being saved" (1 Cor 1:18), and of the *future* as the time when Christians "will be saved" (Rom 5:9–10; see 13:11).

Paul's view of salvation is further brought into focus by his use of prepositional phrases. By saying that believers will be saved **through him**, he underscores that Jesus is the mediator of God's efforts to reconcile the world to himself. By saying that believers will be saved **from the wrath**, he alludes to the final judgment, "the day of wrath" (2:5) when the Lord will reveal the full measure of his justice. To be saved from this is to be rescued from final condemnation. By saying that believers will be saved **by his life**, Paul specifies that salvation is a participation in the risen life of the Messiah.

Paul rounds off his preface to Rom 5–8 with another reference to Christian boasting. He already stated that believers boast in their hope "of the glory of God" (v. 2), at which point he added a reference to boasting of "afflictions" (v. 3). Now he tacks on a third object of Christian exultation: believers **boast of God through our Lord Jesus Christ**. Paul does not mean that God's people should strut around bragging about the blessings they have received. This boast is directed entirely to God, who has achieved our **reconciliation** with him in the Messiah. It is the Lord's work that calls for celebration.

5:11

Sin and Death through Adam (5:12–14)

---

¹²**Therefore, just as through one person sin entered the world, and through sin, death, and thus death came to all, inasmuch as all sinned—** ¹³**for up to the time of the law, sin was in the world, though sin is not accounted when there is no law.** ¹⁴**But death reigned from Adam to Moses, even over those who did not sin after the pattern of the trespass of Adam, who is the type of the one who was to come.**

OT: Gen 2:16–17; 3:1–19; Ps 51:7; Wis 2:24; Sir 14:17
NT: Rom 4:15; 1 Cor 15:22, 45–49; Eph 2:3
Catechism: sin in the world, 386–89; first sin and original sin, 397–406; all are implicated in Adam's sin, 402; death as consequence of sin, 1008; typology in Scripture, 128–30
Lectionary: 5:12–19: 1st Sunday of Lent (Year A); 5:12, 17–19: Common of the Blessed Virgin Mary

St. John Chrysostom on Boasting in God

LIVING TRADITION

People who brag about deeds cite their own works as a model. In contrast, those who take pride in their faith in God offer a better reason for boasting, since they glorify and praise the Lord rather than themselves. For when, through their faith in God, they discover things that cannot be known through the physical world, they show their true love for God and clearly proclaim God's power. The noble soul, the lofty mind, and the lover of true wisdom all share this attribute. While anyone might avoid stealing or killing, to believe that God can accomplish what appears impossible requires an exceptional soul, one that is deeply attached to God. . . . The person who fulfills the commandments honors God, but the person who lives virtuously through faith glorifies God even more.[a]

a. St. John Chrysostom, *Homilies on Romans* 8.1. Cited from *Romans: Interpreted by Early Christian Commentators*, trans. and ed. J. Patout Burns Jr. with Constantine Newman (Grand Rapids: Eerdmans, 2012), 86.

Paul segues into one of his deepest and richest reflections in Romans. The whole passage, extending from verse 12 to verse 21, sets forth a typological antithesis between Adam and Christ. Paul's point is that the Messiah's obedience more than compensates for the first man's disobedience. To set the stage for this contrast, he addresses the *causality* of sin and death as well as the *universality* of sin and death. The passage ranks as a major theological breakthrough on the origin and diffusion of our sinful human condition, one that goes beyond the insights of the prophets and even beyond the express teaching of Jesus. The full weight of Paul's gospel rests on the truth of these few tightly worded sentences.

5:12   Romans 5:12 bristles with difficulties. The first of these concerns the word **therefore**. It suggests that Paul is about to draw a conclusion from verses 1–11, and yet the logical relationship between the preceding section and the present discussion is somewhat unclear. Perhaps Paul felt that his reference to the two states of humanity, one at enmity with God (5:10) and the other at peace with God (5:1), demanded a fuller explanation. Verses 12–21 could thus be read as an explanation of how the world came to find itself in this divided situation.

Another difficulty is that verse 12 is an incomplete sentence. Paul introduces the first half of a comparison between Adam and Christ with the expression **just as**, but instead of completing the analogy with a balancing statement introduced by "so also," the sentence breaks off. It appears as if Paul's thoughts were racing ahead of his pen. Evidently he was more anxious to spell out the differences between Adam and Christ than to establish the essential similarities.

Readers will have to wait until verse 18 before the thought of verse 12 is brought to completion.

Thankfully, some light reflects off Paul's words **through one person sin entered the world**, which all agree is an allusion to the story of the fall in Gen 3. The "one person" is the first man, Adam, and the "sin" in question is Adam's primal transgression in the garden (Gen 3:6).[12] Although creation was fully aligned with the purposes of the creator in Gen 1 and 2, this original harmony was shattered in Gen 3 when the first couple violated the covenant stipulation in Gen 2:15–17.[13] Adam, by the misuse of his will, opened a way for sin to make its dreadful debut in the world.

Paul then adds that, through the breach made by **sin**, another enemy invaded our history: **death**. The idea of death entering the world was probably suggested to Paul by the wording of Wis 2:24: "By the envy of the devil, death entered the world." The parallel with Rom 5:12 is striking but only partial. Whereas the book of Wisdom blames death on the diabolical serpent and its cunning manipulation of the first couple, Paul puts the responsibility for death squarely on the shoulders of Adam, who was forewarned of the consequences of disobedience (Gen 2:17).

The critical question is what Paul means by "death." On the one hand, we can safely assume that Paul has Gen 3:19 in mind, where the curse of mortality is pronounced on Adam, dooming his body to dissolution. To this extent Paul stands arm in arm with ancient Jewish theology, which also blamed Adam and Eve for the universal experience of death.[14]

But is biological death primarily what Paul is talking about? Is Adam's legacy reducible to a limitation on the human life span? Not by a long shot. Bodily demise is a symptom of a more serious problem, and so the statement **death came to all** is not the commonplace observation that everyone eventually dies. Experience teaches that much. Paul is touching instead on a mystery of faith: the tragedy and transmission of *spiritual* death.[15] He is talking about the death of our original union with God, which only secondarily results in physical death.

---

12. Paul is also aware of Eve's role in the fall, as evidenced by 2 Cor 11:3, but for theological reasons his concern is with Adam as the progenitor of the human race.

13. Genesis does not explicitly identify the arrangement in Eden as a "covenant," yet Jewish and Christian tradition has often done so. For example, the LXX rendering of Sir 14:17 reads: "For the covenant from of old [says]: 'You shall surely die'" (referring to Gen 2:17).

14. E.g., Sir 25:24; *4 Ezra* 3.7; 7.118; *2 Baruch* 23.4; 54.15.

15. Joseph A. Fitzmyer, SJ, *Romans*, AB 33 (New York: Doubleday, 1993), 412, acknowledges that Paul's meaning "includes spiritual death." Likewise Dunn, *Romans 1–8*, 273, contends that Paul's concern in this verse is with "original death more than original sin." Perhaps it would be better to say that "original death" is the way that Paul speaks about "original sin."

Adam's relationship with the Lord was pronounced dead at the very moment he committed the first sin, long before the years left his body lifeless.[16] This is the full scope of "death" that Paul sets in opposition to the gift of "eternal life" (Rom 6:23).

The question, then, is how to understand the words **inasmuch as all sinned** at the end of verse 12. Modern translations such as the NABRE make it seem as though Paul considers each person's sin the cause of each person's death. This idea had some currency in ancient Judaism, which held that everyone replicates the fall of Adam by following his example.[17] But is this Paul's point? Apparently not, since he goes on to say in verse 14 that death claimed dominion over everyone who lived between Adam and Moses, "even over those who did not sin after the pattern of the trespass of Adam."

The discovery of Paul's meaning probably requires an alternative translation of the passage. Instead of the rendering "inasmuch as all sinned" or "because all sinned," evidence has come to light that supports the translation "with the result that all sinned."[18] The idea is that spiritual death came to all of Adam's descendants, and as a *consequence* of this, all of them became sinners. Taken in this way, the causal relationship between sin and death is different for Adam, on the one hand, and his progeny, on the other. Sin caused the spiritual death of the first man, and yet the spread of spiritual death caused sin to reign over the lives of his descendants. Death in this sense is an inherited condition that gives rise to universal sinfulness.

It is here that Paul parts company with his native Jewish theology and ventures into uncharted territory, theologically speaking. Judaism had embraced the idea that mortality is passed down from Adam. But Paul goes beyond this to say that Adam's sinful separation from God is inherited by his descendants as well.[19] For him, the death that comes to all is not just physical, but more fundamentally spiritual.

5:13–14   Paul next deals with the historical legacy of **sin** and **death**. Sin, he says, was **in the world** before **the law** was given to Israel. Readers have only to skim the

16. According to Gen 2:17, Adam was threatened with death "on the day" (Hebrew *bĕyôm*) that he ate from the forbidden tree, and yet, according to Gen 5:5, he lived to be 930 years old. Genesis thus hints that Adam underwent more than one kind of death—an immediate death that stripped him of the blessings of intimacy with God in the garden, and an eventual death that returned his body to dust. For a perceptive reading of Gen 2–3 along these lines, see R. W. L. Moberly, "Did the Serpent Get It Right?," in *From Eden to Golgotha: Essays in Biblical Theology* (Atlanta: Scholars Press, 1992), 1–27.

17. *2 Baruch* 54.19.

18. For this translation, see the sidebar "With the Result That All Sinned."

19. Andre-Marie Dubarle, OP, *The Biblical Doctrine of Original Sin*, trans. E. M. Stewart (New York: Herder & Herder, 1964), 143–44.

"With the Result That All Sinned"

BIBLICAL BACKGROUND

The meaning of Rom 5:12 hinges on a prepositional phrase translated "inasmuch as" in the NABRE (Greek *eph' hō*). More than a dozen different meanings have been assigned to this expression in the history of biblical and theological scholarship. Ancient Christians often understood it to mean "in whom"[a] or "because of whom,"[b] both phrases referring to the person of Adam. By contrast, a majority of modern scholars hold that Paul uses the phrase as a conjunction meaning "inasmuch as" or "because."[c]

Each of these translations is possible on grammatical grounds, but none succeeds in capturing the subtlety of Paul's logic. Happily, a more satisfying solution has emerged that understands the phrase to mean "with the result that."[d] One can point to several instances of the expression in Hellenistic Greek where this meaning appears certain. Beyond that, this alternative translation clarifies the train of thought in 5:12 and makes it less disjointed. Paul's thesis is not that individuals bring death on themselves but that spiritual death infected the entire human race through natural descent from Adam. The result of this death spreading to all is that all have become godless rebels. This is precisely the point that Paul will make in Rom 5:19 when he states that all were "made sinners" in Adam.

a. E.g., the Latin Vulgate (translated *in quo omnes peccaverunt*), St. Augustine (*Against Two Letters of the Pelagians* 4.7), and St. Thomas Aquinas (*Commentary on Romans* 5.3.419).
b. E.g., St. John Chrysostom (*Homilies on Romans* 10.1) and St. John of Damascus (*Commentary on Romans* 5:12).
c. E.g., Maximilian Zerwick, SJ, *Biblical Greek Illustrated by Examples*, adapted from the Fourth Latin Edition by Joseph Smith, SJ (Rome: Gregorian & Biblical Press, 2011) §127; Murray J. Harris, *Prepositions and Theology in the Greek New Testament* (Grand Rapids: Zondervan, 2012), 139–40; and several contemporary English translations (NABRE, RSV, NRSV, ESV, NIV, JB).
d. For the evidence, see Joseph A. Fitzmyer, "The Consecutive Meaning of ΕΦ' Ω in Romans 5.12," *NTS* 39 (1993): 321–39.

book of Genesis to verify his claim that evildoing was present and thriving in the world in the wake of Adam's disobedience. But then Paul qualifies his remark with a concession: **though sin is not accounted when there is no law**. What does this mean? Clearly he does not mean that God took no notice of human rebellion in the centuries between Adam and Moses; otherwise he would have no way to account for the judgments of God against the wicked generation of the flood (Gen 6–8) and the depraved residents of Sodom and Gomorrah (Gen 19), to cite only two examples.

Paul means that, in the interval between creation and the covenant at Sinai, there was no violation of a divinely revealed commandment. The first man

The Doctrine of Original Sin

LIVING
·TRADITION

Like many doctrines taught by the Catholic Church, the doctrine of original sin is one with a lengthy history of development. Hints and traces of the belief can be found in Scripture and the writings of the earliest Church Fathers. But it was St. Augustine of Hippo in the fifth century who gave it its recognizable form.[a] Medieval scholars such as St. Thomas Aquinas further refined the doctrine but without altering its substance.[b]

The basis for much of this theological discussion was Paul's statement in Rom 5:12. Not surprisingly, when the Council of Trent defined the doctrine of original sin in the sixteenth century, it gave particular attention to this passage. The council fathers censured the idea "that the sin of Adam damaged him alone and not his descendants, and that the holiness and justice received from God, which he lost, he lost for himself alone and not for us; or that, while he was stained by the sin of disobedience, he transmitted only death and bodily pain to the whole human race, but not that sin which is the death of the soul."[c] Propositions such as these, the council said, would contradict the teaching of the Apostle in Rom 5:12.

a. See his twin works *On the Grace of Christ* and *On Original Sin*, both written in 418.
b. See his *Summa Theologiae* I-II.81.1 and *Disputed Questions on Evil* 4.
c. Council of Trent, Session 5, *Decree on Original Sin* 2. Cited from Norman P. Tanner, SJ, *Decrees of the Ecumenical Councils* (Washington, DC: Georgetown University Press, 1990), 2:666.

was bound by the precept given in Gen 2:16–17, and Israel was given over six hundred precepts in the Torah. Between these two historical endpoints, the human race was not guided by a divinely revealed law that was publicly promulgated. Paul therefore suggests that the generations between **Adam** and **Moses** were less culpable for their sins. Not until Israel transgressed the law at Sinai did history witness another sin like Adam's transgression in the garden.

This observation leads Paul to a new insight. If Adam's descendants continued to sin until the time of Moses, yet without their faults being counted as Adam-like transgressions, then how did **death** come to reign throughout the patriarchal period, **even over those who did not sin after the pattern of the trespass of Adam**? If the death of body and soul exercised dominion over these early generations, and imitation of Adam's transgression was not the cause of it, then death must be propagated through natural generation. Think of all the infants and mentally impaired individuals who shared our fallen condition and experienced death without being able to sin as the first man did. With this

Paul and Biblical Typology

Paul is noted for many theological achievements, one of which is an innovative use of the Greek term *typos*, meaning "type." Etymologically, the noun derives from a verb meaning "to strike" and frequently refers to a mark left behind when a solid object impacts a malleable object. A type can be an image that is stamped into a coin or personal insignia pressed into wax or soft clay. The term is used in various ways in the New Testament.[a] For instance, it denotes the "nailmarks" that remained visible on the body of the resurrected Jesus (John 20:25). It also has the extended meaning of a "pattern" or "example" of conduct that others are urged to imitate (Phil 3:17; 2 Thess 3:9; 1 Pet 5:3). In one case, it designates an outline of Christian instruction that guides the faith and life of a baptized believer, perhaps in the form of a creed (Rom 6:17).

But Paul gives the Greek *typos* a unique function in relation to the Bible. In Rom 5:14 as well as in 1 Cor 10:6, he uses the term for a person or event of the Old Testament that foreshadows a greater reality of the New Testament. In Romans, Adam is called a "type" of Christ. There is a correspondence between the two, since both impact the destiny of many by their actions, and yet the effect of Christ's sacrifice far surpasses the effect of Adam's sin. In 1 Corinthians, the miracles of the exodus are seen as "types" of God's saving actions now taking place through the sacraments. The Fathers of the Church would soon follow the Apostle's lead in correlating a myriad of Old Testament types with their New Testament counterparts, called "antitypes."

To make sense of this Christian reading of Scripture, we must realize that Paul is a theologian of the mysteries of God (1 Cor 4:1).[b] The mysteries revealed in the gospel, without being fully penetrable, are nevertheless intelligible. One way of illuminating them is by a theological use of analogy, which promotes a discovery of God's purposes stretching across both Testaments.[c] By applying analogical thinking to the Old Testament, Paul was able to detect recurrent patterns stamped into the structure of salvation history. He discovered that God acts in "typical" ways in bringing about the fulfillment of his plan. Persons, places, events, and institutions in the Scriptures of Israel are thus seen as "types" or analogies of more wonderful things to come in the messianic age. The prophets had already begun to view the †economy of salvation in this way, as Jesus himself did in the Gospels (e.g., Matt 12:6, 41–42; John 3:14). But it was Paul's innovative use of *typos* that gave this approach to Scripture the name "biblical typology."

a. For fuller analysis, see G. W. H. Lampe and K. J. Woollcombe, *Essays on Typology* (London: SCM, 1957); Leonard Goppelt, *TYPOS: The Typological Interpretation of the Old Testament in the New* (Grand Rapids: Eerdmans, 1982); Richard M. Davidson, *Typology in Scripture: A Study of Hermeneutical τύπος Structures* (Berrien Springs, MI: Andrews University, 1981).

b. See especially Jean Paillard, *In Praise of the Inexpressible: Paul's Experience of the Divine Mystery*, trans. Richard J. Erickson (Peabody, MA: Hendrickson, 2003).

c. Noted in Catechism 128–30.

perspective Catholic tradition concurs: no one inherits Adam's personal guilt, but everyone inherits his fallen and mortal nature (Catechism 404).

Finally, the discussion transitions from Adam to Christ. Adam is called a **type of the one who was to come**, a prophetic image of the future Messiah. For the meaning of this, see the sidebar "Paul and Biblical Typology" (p. 85).

Reflection and Application (5:12–14)

Many Catholics find the doctrine of original sin a difficult pill to swallow. It seems to some like a childish belief that sits uncomfortably with our scientific view of the world. It strikes others as patently unjust on God's part, given our individualistic view of the world. As is oftentimes the case, clarifying the Catholic Church's teaching can go a long way toward dispelling misconceptions and easing contemporary discomfort.

Take the alleged childishness of the doctrine. Many of us learned early in our catechesis that original sin is a stain that tarnishes the beauty of every newborn soul. There is nothing wrong with using this language; indeed, the Church has done so effectively for several centuries. And yet, as Catholic theology recognizes, original sin is not an actual stain that defaces the appearance of an immaterial soul. Rather, original sin is a privation of the grace of divine sonship that God intended each of us to have as human beings. He made us to be his children and to live in communion with him. Original sin, then, is not the *presence* of something unseemly that attaches to our souls; rather, it is the *absence* of something wonderful that the Lord willed us to have—the grace that makes us his sons and daughters. Original sin is a gaping hole in the fabric of our nature that we receive from Adam by virtue of our genealogical link with him. It is a void that can be filled only by the grace and life of God.

Likewise, consider the suspicion that original sin casts God in an unflattering light, as though he were a perpetrator of injustice, holding every member of the human race responsible for Adam's transgression. The first man committed sin, and we all share the blame for it, along with the punishment that goes with it. That would indeed be unfair, but it is not what the Church teaches about original sin. Original sin is not a personal fault at all, much less someone else's fault that we are held accountable for.[20] It can be difficult for a world that thinks in strictly individualistic terms to appreciate the bonds that link people together. But sin, as the Bible describes it, is a family affair and not just a personal affair.

20. Catechism 404 teaches: "Original sin is called 'sin' only in an analogical sense; it is a sin 'contracted' and not 'committed'—a state and not an act."

Adam, as the father of the human family, spiritually impoverished himself and his progeny when he turned away from the Lord. Liability for his actions cannot be imputed to his descendants, but the effects of his transgression can still be felt by them. No one blames the children of an irresponsible father who blows all his money gambling. They had nothing to do with his recklessness. Nevertheless, they are consigned to live in poverty and to bear the onerous burdens that come with it.[21] So it is with original sin.

Disgrace in Adam, Divine Grace in Christ (5:15–21)

[15]**But the gift is not like the transgression. For if by that one person's transgression the many died, how much more did the grace of God and the gracious gift of the one person Jesus Christ overflow for the many.** [16]**And the gift is not like the result of the one person's sinning. For after one sin there was the judgment that brought condemnation; but the gift, after many transgressions, brought acquittal.** [17]**For if, by the transgression of one person, death came to reign through that one, how much more will those who receive the abundance of grace and of the gift of justification come to reign in life through the one person Jesus Christ.** [18]**In conclusion, just as through one transgression condemnation came upon all, so through one righteous act acquittal and life came to all.** [19]**For just as through the disobedience of one person the many were made sinners, so through the obedience of one the many will be made righteous.** [20]**The law entered in so that the transgression might increase but, where sin increased, grace overflowed all the more,** [21]**so that, as sin reigned in death, grace also might reign through justification for eternal life through Jesus Christ our Lord.**

OT: Gen 3:1–19; Isa 53:11

NT: 1 Cor 1:30; 15:22, 45–49; 1 John 2:2

Catechism: Christ the new Adam, 411, 532; Christ died for all without exception, 605; Christ transformed death, 1009; Christ the Suffering Servant, 615, 623

Lectionary: 5:17–21: Mass for the Deceased; Commemoration of All the Faithful Departed; 5:12, 17–19: Common of the Blessed Virgin Mary

Paul's objective for the remainder of Rom 5 is to elaborate on the Adamic †typology introduced in 5:14. He aims to sketch out the similarities between Adam and Christ as well as the glaring differences. Both are representative figures whose actions impact the entire human family. Paul draws this comparison by stressing

---

21. A comparison suggested in B. V. Miller, *The Fall of Man and Original Sin* (New York: Macmillan, 1928).

how, in both cases, the deeds of "one" man affect the "many." By way of contrast, he emphasizes that Adam and Jesus made completely opposite choices in relation to God, the former alienating his descendants from God and the latter uniting his disciples with God. Paul's argument proceeds in rabbinic fashion to show "how much more" Christ has done to save us than Adam has done to enslave us. Humanity has gained disproportionately more in Christ than it ever lost in Adam.

5:15   Foremost in Paul's mind is the radical difference between the sin of Adam and the saving obedience of Christ. With emphasis he states in verses 15 and 16 that one is **not like** the other. There is a universe of difference between **the gift** of eternal life that comes through Christ and the dismal legacy of Adam's **transgression**.

Paul also notes how, in both instances, the actions of **one** man rippled out to **the many**. In Semitic parlance the term "many" is typically inclusive, meaning "the multitudes" as distinct from an individual. This explains how Paul, throughout this section, is able to glide back and forth between the terms "all" and "many" without any perceptible difference in meaning.

Thanks to Adam's misdeed, virtually every member of the human family **died**, physically in their bodies and spiritually in their relationship with God. One man determined the lot of all. So it is with **the one person Jesus Christ**. Having made his life a **gracious gift** of sacrifice, he caused **the grace of God** to **overflow for the many**. Jesus, in other words, accomplished a universal redemption that makes possible the salvation of every descendant of Adam.

This is essentially Paul's point. He wants to stress not just the dissimilarity between Adam's sin and Christ's salvation but also the vast disproportion between the two. Both affect the spiritual situation of all, but they are not thereby equivalent. The grace of messianic salvation is effective beyond all comparison. One could imagine the fall of Adam as a pebble plunked into a pond, disturbing the calm of the whole surface of the water. The saving work of Jesus, however, would be more like a boulder hurled into the deep, moving the same body of water but sending out bigger and more powerful waves than any pebble could.

5:16   A similar point is made in the next verse. In the wake of Adam's **one sin**, the Lord's **judgment** fell hard on humanity. It was a sentence of **condemnation** upon every man, woman, and child born of our race (Eph 2:3). Its counterpoint is the divine **acquittal** or justification that comes as a **gift** to those who believe in the Messiah.[22] By means of this gift, the sinful descendants of Adam are "made righteous" (Rom 5:19) in the wake of **many transgressions**.

5:17   Paul also juxtaposes the spiritual **death** unleashed by **the transgression of one person**, Adam, with the spiritual **life** that comes to believers **through** the

---

22. See the sidebar, "Justification," in Rom 3 (pp. 50–51).

mediation of **the one person Jesus Christ**. Here again the gift is declared **much more** efficacious for the fate of the world than the transgression. Interestingly, Paul uses the same verb "reign" (Greek *basileuō*) to express both sides of the comparison. For every person descended from Adam, death **came to reign** as a merciless tyrant who could not be overthrown. But the recipients of **grace** and **justification** will **come to reign** as God's messianic people. Paul's talk of **abundance** brings to mind the teaching of Jesus in the Fourth Gospel: "I came that they may have life, and have it abundantly" (John 10:10 RSV).

In verses 18–19, Paul shows that the actions of Adam and Christ and their   **5:18–19** results are mirror opposites. In Adam's case, **one transgression** brought **condemnation** and death **upon all**; in the Messiah's case, **one righteous act** of **obedience** brings **acquittal** (that is, justification) **and life to all**.

This last statement expresses what Catholic theology calls "the objective redemption." This is the teaching that Jesus Christ made atonement for the sins of the whole world (1 John 2:2), opening the way to salvation for everyone without distinction (Rom 1:16). It is a universal gift, but it remains a gift that must be accepted by faith on an individual basis. If the grace of redemption was conferred automatically, or hereditarily as Adam's sinful condition is, the Apostle would have no reason to evangelize Jews, Greeks, or any others.

Perhaps the most telling antithesis is between being **made sinners** and being **made righteous**. Taken in isolation, references to "condemnation" and "acquittal" could lead us to think that sin and salvation are little more than courtroom decrees. Paul, however, is no theological minimalist. He tunnels more deeply into the mystery. If the sin of Adam separates us from God and inflicts enduring wounds in our human nature, then the salvation of Christ must ultimately repair this damage. It must heal us on the inside, beginning with a real participation in the Messiah's righteousness: "But if Christ is in you, although the body is dead because of sin, the spirit is alive because of righteousness" (8:10). Christ's righteousness dwells in the believer (1 Cor 1:30) precisely because Christ himself dwells in the believer (Gal 2:20)!

It is important to note that Paul alludes in verse 19 to Isaiah's "Song of the Suffering Servant" (Isa 52:13–53:12). Much is mysterious in that ancient passage, but Christians since earliest times have read it as a prophecy of the Messiah's passion. The central figure, identified only as the Lord's Servant, quietly endures rejection and humiliation, finally surrendering himself to violent abuse and death. But, far from this being a tragedy beyond his control, the Servant embraces this fate willingly and pours out his life as an atoning sacrifice for the iniquities of others. Paul seems to have this in mind when he states that **the**

many will be **made righteous** (that is, justified). This is precisely the note that is sounded at the climax of the song, where the Lord announces: "My servant, the just one, shall justify the many, / their iniquity he shall bear" (Isa 53:11). For Paul, Jesus fulfills his role as a new and obedient Adam by following the path of the †Suffering Servant.

5:20–21   The final sentence of Rom 5 ties off the discussion of Adam and Christ. But before Paul states his conclusion, he injects one last thought that reconnects with verse 13. There he said that sin was not accounted in the time between Adam and Moses. Here he says **the law entered in** at the time of Moses **so that transgression might increase**. Few statements have baffled scholars as much as this one. Is God's purpose for the Torah to multiply transgressions? Or is it meant to restrain them so that fewer sins are committed? Paul might be expected to respond "both, in fact." Of course, the law forbids actions that offend God, and in this sense it acts as a moral restraint. But the law also brings greater culpability and a heightened awareness of sin (3:20; 7:13). The law offered guidance to Israel on the path to blessing and life but did not enable Israel to reach this destiny. It exposed the need for salvation without meeting that need. This is one of the ways that the law pointed to Christ (10:4).

Jarring though it is, Paul's statement about the law is quickly overshadowed by his revelation that **grace overflowed all the more**. Again he stresses the disproportionate abundance of Christ's gift over against Adam's ruinous legacy. Speaking in quantitative terms is analogical language, to be sure, yet Paul thinks it an effective way to impress upon readers the surpassing excellence of messianic redemption. When he insists that grace has come in superabundance, he wants us to understand that the obedience of Jesus more than suffices to offset Adam's offense. Christ has paid more than sinful humanity owed in the first place. The value of his obedience was more than enough to cover all our debts of sin. And even beyond that, Christ has made us spiritually rich (2 Cor 8:9)!

Paul concludes with a contrast between the temporary dominion of **sin** and **death** and the unending reign of **justification** and **eternal life** in the Messiah. The former taints the full stretch of human history, but the latter reaches beyond this into the infinite ages of eternity.

Reflection and Application (5:20)

Like many people alive in 2001, I remember exactly where I was on the morning of September 11. Images on live television of human bodies raining down from the upper floors of the World Trade Center amid raging flames and billowing smoke are forever etched in my memory. It was the darkest day of my lifetime. I was so stunned that I hardly remember how I passed many of the hours that day. I had just witnessed the greatest evil I could imagine. What does one do next, I wondered?

One keeps one's commitments. After finishing night prayers with my family, I went, at my appointed time, to the adoration chapel at my parish church. And in my accustomed way I knelt and bowed—and then I raised my head to see Jesus Christ, my Eucharistic Lord, on the altar. At that moment I realized something important: September 11, 2001, was a dark day indeed, but it was not the darkest day in history. This terrorism perpetrated against unsuspecting Americans was heinous, but it was not the worst crime committed by humanity.

The worst crime—our worst crime—was the murder of God, a crime in which Jews and Gentiles conspired, a crime in which every one of us is implicated through the web of our sins. What could be more monstrously evil than torturing and crucifying the innocent Son of the Almighty? And yet God allowed it to happen. Why?

One often hears the cliché that "it's always darkest before dawn," and we can affirm a certain truth in that. But Paul spoke a far greater truth in Rom 5:20–21: "Where sin increased, grace abounded all the more, so that, as sin reigned in death, grace also might reign through righteousness" (RSV). Think about the prophet Elijah urging his opponents to douse his sacrifice with water, not just once, but three times (1 Kings 18:33–37). He allowed himself to be placed at an extreme disadvantage so that God's victory might be all the more evident. Jesus did this to an infinitely greater degree when he died on the cross. And he brought the single greatest good out of the single greatest evil. By the sacrifice of his life he consummated his love for us. He opened a way for us to share in his eternal life.

We will suffer many dark days in the course of our lifetime on earth. But Jesus has empowered us to make an offering of those days, to make them redemptive, to make each and every one of them a day on which his grace abounds all the more.

New Life and Liberation in the Messiah

Romans 6:1–23

Paul continues in Rom 6 to elucidate the doctrine of justification. In earlier chapters he stressed faith as the basis of justification; in chapter 5 he showcased peace and reconciliation with God as essential aspects of justification. Paul now examines the liturgical context of justification as well as the ethical obligations that arise from it. Sacramental transformation leads to moral transformation: in baptism, we are plunged into the saving death of the Messiah, raised to new life in his resurrection, and set on a path toward ongoing sanctification.

Dying and Rising with Christ in Baptism (6:1–4)

---

¹What then shall we say? Shall we persist in sin that grace may abound? Of course not! ²How can we who died to sin yet live in it? ³Or are you unaware that we who were baptized into Christ Jesus were baptized into his death? ⁴We were indeed buried with him through baptism into death, so that, just as Christ was raised from the dead by the glory of the Father, we too might live in newness of life.

OT: Gen 1:9–10; 8:13–14; Exod 14:10–31

NT: Mark 10:38–39; Luke 12:50; 1 Cor 12:13; Gal 3:27; Eph 2:5; Col 2:12

Catechism: baptism—death and resurrection with Christ, 1214, 1220, 1227; baptism—the sacrament of faith, 1226, 1253–54

Lectionary: 6:3–11: Easter Vigil (Years ABC); Consecration of Virgins and Religious Profession; 6:3–5: Conferral of Infant Baptism; 6:3–4, 8–9: Funeral for Baptized Children; 6:2–4, 12–14: Mass for the Laity

Origen of Alexandria on Dying to Sin

LIVING TRADITION

Consider the meaning of living and dying to sin. Just as the person who lives according to the will of God lives to God, so the one who lives according to the will of sin lives to sin. The apostle expresses the same idea in saying, *Do not let sin exercise dominion in your mortal bodies, to make you obey their passions* (Rom 6:12). Thus he shows that obeying the desires of sin is living in sin. If to satisfy the desires of sin is to live to sin, then if we do not satisfy the passions of sin or obey its dictates, we die to sin.[a]

a. *Commentary on Romans* 5.7. Translation adapted from J. Patout Burns Jr., trans. and ed. with Constantine Newman, *Romans: Interpreted by Early Christian Commentators*, The Church's Bible (Grand Rapids: Eerdmans, 2012), 133.

Paul transitions into Rom 6 with a string of rhetorical questions. Clearly he is concerned that his remarks in Rom 5 could lead to mistaken inferences, and he wants to head off potential misunderstandings. His instruction is offered "by way of reminder" (15:15 RSV). That is, Paul assumes that his original readers already have some knowledge of the baptismal catechesis that he reviews in these verses.

Paul opens by asking: **What then shall we say? Shall we persist in sin that** **6:1** **grace may abound?** He wants to prevent a misunderstanding of his statement in 5:20 that sin has called forth a superabundance of grace. The question is how this relates to Christian conduct. Some might wrongly conclude that Paul promotes evildoing, at least implicitly, since this would afford God greater opportunity to exercise his mercy—a charge already leveled against him by certain confused minds, as his comment in 3:8 indicates. Others might mistake his teaching as a license for moral laxity. Paul dispatches both errors with the strenuous **Of** **course not!** Sin may not be considered a stimulus for good. God's grace has flooded the world for the purpose of drowning and obliterating sin; it is hardly meant to encourage wrongdoing as useful to salvation.

When Paul next asks, **How can we who died to sin yet live in it?** he hopes **6:2** readers will recognize this proposition as squarely at odds with the gospel. Reveling in sin makes no sense if believers have been released from sin and its power to dominate their lives. Believers, once tyrannized by sin, have undergone a death to an old way of living that should not be resuscitated. What is dead and buried in the past should stay dead and buried in the past.

Paul assumes that readers are not **unaware** of what he is talking about. He **6:3–4** expects they have had sufficient instruction in the faith to follow his reasoning.

Figure 5. Stone baptismal font in a reconstruction of a church's *bēma* (presbytery) assembled from pieces found at seventeen different sites in Israel (Byzantine period, fourth–sixth century AD).

At the same time, the Apostle recognizes he is addressing a congregation that he has yet to visit in person, and so he reviews basic Christian teaching on baptism and its implications for living. Virtually everything Paul says in the rest of the chapter is premised on the truth of verses 3–4.

The critical point is that Christians **were baptized into Christ Jesus**. Paul uses the preposition "into" to speak of incorporation into Christ. Baptism unites believers with Christ and inserts them into the ecclesial body of Christ, the Church (1 Cor 12:13). Still, membership in the messianic community is not the focus of this statement. Rather, Paul is straining the limits of speech to communicate a mystery of faith that words can only partially convey.

For Paul, baptism into Christ means that recipients have been **baptized into his death** as well as **buried with him** and **raised from the dead**, just as Jesus was.[1] These terse statements call for some explanation. First, Paul views baptism as a symbolic representation of Jesus' death and resurrection. It shows in a tangible way the Christian's participation in these saving events. Death and burial with Christ are signified by an immersion in water; resurrection

1. It is implied throughout Rom 6 that believers undergo a spiritual resurrection in Christ, even though Paul is preoccupied with the new way of life that baptism initiates. See N. T. Wright, *The Resurrection of the Son of God*, Christian Origins and the Question of God 3 (Minneapolis: Fortress, 2003), 251–52.

St. Cyril of Jerusalem on Baptism

We know full well that baptism not only washes away our sins and procures for us the gift of the Holy Spirit, but it is also a representation of the passion of Christ. That is why Paul proclaimed: *Do you not know that all we who have been baptized into Christ Jesus have been baptized into his death? For through baptism we were buried along with him.* . . . For in the case of Christ, death was real, his soul really being separated from his body. His burial, too, was real, for his sacred body was wrapped in clean linen. In his case, it all really happened. In our case, however, there was only a likeness of death and suffering, whereas concerning salvation there was not a likeness but the reality.[a]

a. *Mystagogical Catechesis* 2.6–7. Translation adapted from *The Works of Saint Cyril of Jerusalem*, vol. 2, trans. Leo P. McCauley, SJ, and Anthony A. Stephenson, FC 64 (Washington, DC: Catholic University of America Press, 1970), 165–67.

with Christ is signified by emergence from the water. Second, Paul is clear that baptism is not reducible to a symbolic rite. It is also an efficacious rite—what later Christian theology would come to call a "sacrament." Baptism transfers us from the dominion of sin and death into the realm of the Messiah's risen life. It is **through baptism** that we receive the blessings that flow from the dying and rising of Jesus. Of course, the saving *events* of the Triduum are not repeated in the rite; it is rather the saving *effects* of the Lord's passion that are actualized when the sacrament is administered. The human experience of Jesus descending into death, lying in the tomb, and rising to new life becomes the spiritual experience of all who are baptized in his name. The recipient of baptism undergoes a death to the bondage of sin and is brought to life again by a reception of grace. Third, the efficacy of baptism is indicated by Paul's threefold use of the passive voice, which implies that God is the unseen agent who baptizes, buries, and raises the Christian to new life. Neither the minister of the sacrament nor its recipient could ever hope to produce a spiritual union with the crucified and risen Jesus apart from the hidden action of God working in and through the sacrament.

What is the origin of Paul's baptismal theology? Is relating baptism to death, entombment, and resurrection his own innovation? Or is it a common feature of the earliest apostolic preaching? It is difficult to say for sure. Jesus himself described his approaching passion in Jerusalem as a "baptism" (Mark 10:38–39; Luke 12:50). Likewise, water is a symbol of death as well as a symbol of life in the Semitic mind.[2] The very first verse of the Bible depicts a lifeless world submerged in the primeval waters; from these depths the earth emerges and bursts forth with abundant life (Gen 1:9–10). Later the waters of the flood bring death to a wicked world, only to draw back at God's command so that life can flourish once again (Gen 6–8). The waters of the sea part to give salvation to God's people fleeing from bondage, and then roll back to entomb the pursuing enemy (Exod 14:10–31).[3] These examples indicate that baptism could be viewed as a boundary event between death and new life, between the end of one existence and the beginning of another.

Finally, Paul elucidates the purpose behind our baptismal death and resurrection with Christ. The **Father** raised Jesus to life again **so that** believers **might live in newness of life**. Paul is describing a spiritual resurrection that regenerates a person in grace and makes possible a new way of living. In fact, Paul's primary objective throughout Rom 6 is to stress that God has called us to the pursuit of sanctification and salvation (6:22). The NABRE captures this well by translating the Greek verb *peripateō* as "live," although the term literally means "walk," since walking is a Hebrew idiom for "conducting oneself" in relation to God. In Scripture, a person walks either in the way of wickedness (Ps 1:1; Prov 2:13; Isa 65:2) or in the way of righteousness (Ps 86:11; Prov 8:20; Isa 33:15). Being raised with Jesus means directing all our efforts and choices toward the goal of eternal life, as Paul will make clear in Rom 6:18–22.

But how is such a moral miracle possible, even granting that baptized Christians have received the forgiveness of sins? Readers will have to wait until Rom 8 for the full answer, but Paul leaves a clue here. Only twice in his letters does he use the term "newness"—once in this verse (6:4), and once again in Rom 7:6, where he speaks of serving the Lord "in the newness of the spirit."[4] Read in conjunction, these two passages show that Christians are empowered by the Spirit to accomplish by grace what is beyond the ability of human nature. The indwelling presence of God is the critical factor that makes "newness of life" possible for disciples of Jesus.

2. Joseph Ratzinger / Pope Benedict XVI, *Jesus of Nazareth: From the Baptism in the Jordan to the Transfiguration* (San Francisco: Ignatius, 2007), 15–16.

3. Elsewhere Paul makes an explicit link between the sea-crossing and baptism (1 Cor 10:1–2), just as Peter sees baptism prefigured by the flood (1 Pet 3:20–21). The Church Fathers viewed all three events—the creation, the flood, and the exodus—as prophetic images of baptism. See Jean Daniélou, SJ, *The Bible and the Liturgy* (Notre Dame, IN: University of Notre Dame Press, 1956), 70–98.

4. Apparently the NABRE considers 7:6 a reference to the human spirit rather than the Holy Spirit. Other translations render the expression: "the new life of the Spirit" (RSV, NRSV) or "the new way of the Spirit" (ESV, NIV).

Reflection and Application (6:1–4)

It might seem odd that faith towers over so much of the discussion in Rom 1–5 but then fades into the background in Rom 6, where baptism as the inaugural event of the Christian life dominates. Has Paul left faith behind at this point in the letter? Does he view baptism independently of faith? Negative on both counts. Paul presupposes that a person approaching baptism has been drawn there by the gift of faith. As one scholar reminds us regarding Rom 6:1–4: "The baptized's faith is, of course, taken for granted"; it is "not forgotten, nor denied."[5]

In Paul's theology, faith and baptism are twin instruments of salvation. Both are given by God, and both serve as a means of accomplishing our union with Christ. The faith of the believer and the sacramental action of the Church work in tandem. Faith in Christ becomes *saving* faith precisely when it is exercised in the liturgical setting of baptism, since "it is through baptism that . . . faith takes possession of God's gift."[6] It is there, at the sacred font, that "one believes with the heart and so is justified, and one confesses with the mouth and so is saved" (10:10). It is not without reason, then, that the Catholic Church calls baptism the sacrament of faith (Catechism 1253). She insists on the twin necessities of faith and baptism for our salvation. And in doing so, she merely echoes the voice of the Lord Jesus, who declared before his ascent to heaven: "Whoever believes and is baptized will be saved" (Mark 16:16).

Dead to Sin but Alive to God (6:5–11)

> [5]For if we have grown into union with him through a death like his, we shall also be united with him in the resurrection. [6]We know that our old self was crucified with him, so that our sinful body might be done away with, that we might no longer be in slavery to sin. [7]For a dead person has been absolved from sin. [8]If, then, we have died with Christ, we believe that we shall also live with him. [9]We know that Christ, raised from the dead, dies no more; death no longer has power over him. [10]As to his death, he died to sin once and for all; as to his life, he lives for God. [11]Consequently, you too must think of yourselves as [being] dead to sin and living for God in Christ Jesus.

OT: Ps 130:8; Isa 44:22
NT: 1 Cor 6:11; 15:45–49; Gal 2:19–20; Phil 3:10–11; Col 2:12, 20

5. James D. G. Dunn, *Romans 1–8*, WBC 38a (Nashville: Nelson, 1988), 314.
6. Louis Bouyer, *Dictionary of Theology*, trans. Charles Underhill Quinn (Tournai: Desclée, 1965), 255.

Catechism: baptism—the sacrament of justification, 1266, 1992
Lectionary: 6:3–11: Easter Vigil (Years ABC); Christian Initiation apart from Easter Vigil; 6:3–9: Commemoration of All the Faithful Departed; Mass for the Deceased

In these verses Paul continues to unpack the significance of baptism. The overall thrust of his message is clear, yet the density of his thinking can be challenging. What we as Christians "know" (6:6, 9) is the secure point of reference for what we believe about living with Jesus in the future (6:8) and for how we should think about living for God in the present (6:11).

6:5   Verse 5 expands the definition introduced in verse 3. Being baptized into the "death" of Christ means that **we have grown into union with him through a death like his**. Baptism forges a spiritual bond between Christ and the Christian, making them one. The adjective Paul uses to describe this mystery (Greek *symphytos*—literally, "grown together") alludes to the horticultural practice of grafting a young branch onto the trunk of an established tree, so that the two become organically united.[7] Paul will use this same imagery in Rom 11 to illustrate how believers are grafted into the messianic people of God, represented as an olive tree (11:17–24).

Once this union comes about, the Apostle is confident, **we shall also be united with him in the resurrection**. There is some dispute about whether Paul is referring to the *baptismal* resurrection of the believer (6:4) or the *bodily* resurrection of the believer (8:11). Perhaps he has both in mind, since both are modes of participation in the risen life of Jesus. Together they mark the commencement and completion of a process in which the Father fashions us into the image of his glorified Son (8:29).

6:6   Verse 6 is undoubtedly the trickiest in this section. Everything hinges on what Paul means by **our old self** and **our sinful body**—literally, "our old man" and "the body of sin." At one level, Paul is thinking in individual terms: our old self is the sinful and egocentric person we used to be, the person who lived as an enemy of God (5:10); and the body of sin seems to be something like the person whose life in the body was dominated by a service to sin. Thanks to the grace of baptism, these aspects of our past have been **crucified with** Christ and laid to rest in his tomb.

At another level, Paul is thinking in collective terms. For instance, his remarks in this verse can be read as a continuation of the antithesis between Adam and Christ developed in Rom 5:12–21.[8] Adam and Christ are individuals, to be sure.

---

7. Joseph A. Fitzmyer, SJ, *Romans*, AB 33 (New York: Doubleday, 1993), 435.
8. Robert C. Tannehill, *Dying and Rising with Christ: A Study in Pauline Theology* (Berlin: Töpelmann, 1966), 24–30.

A New Exodus in Christ

Unlike the rest of Romans, chapters 5–8 develop without constant reference to the Scriptures. Only two quotations from the Old Testament appear in these chapters, as compared to the nearly sixty citations that punctuate the rest of the letter. It is tempting to view Rom 5–8 as an interlude in Paul's otherwise intensive engagement with the Bible, but it is a temptation we must resist. As one scholar has said about these chapters: "The biblical story of Israel is still present, guiding the discussion and defining its terms."[a] In other words, Paul is still expounding upon several scriptural themes, but without invoking particular verses to make his point.

Romans 6 should be read in this light. The cluster of images and ideas in this chapter suggests that Paul has in mind the exodus, the most spectacular act of salvation in the Old Testament.[b] The following considerations support this view. (1) Paul tells a story in which believers move from slavery to freedom by passing through water and embarking on a new life of service to God. He wants us to view baptism through the prism of Israel's historic escape from bondage. (2) These parallels are significant when we consider that, in 1 Cor 10:1–2, Paul describes Israel's sea-crossing as a prefiguration of baptism. He even recounts this episode using language reminiscent of his baptismal theology: the Israelites "were baptized into Moses" (1 Cor 10:2), just as Christians "were baptized into Christ" (Rom 6:3). (3) Paul makes the unusual point in Rom 6:4 that Christ was raised to life by "the glory" of the Father. Parallel formulas in the Pauline Letters indicate that he is talking about God's "power" (1 Cor 6:14; 2 Cor 13:4). Then why use "glory" in this passage, and not power? In the biblical account of the exodus, the Lord manifested his glory through his mighty deeds of deliverance (the same Greek term for "glory" appears in the †Septuagint version of Exod 15:7, 11 and 16:7).

Romans 6, then, says that baptism brings about a new deliverance, a new exodus. Instead of national solidarity with Moses in the bonds of an Old Covenant, we have sacramental union with the Messiah in the bonds of a New Covenant. Instead of release from oppression in Egypt, we have freedom from the tyranny of sin that once held us captive. Through baptism, the Lord shows himself the redeemer of his people once again.

a. Frank Thielman, "The Story of Israel and the Theology of Romans 5–8," in *Pauline Theology, Volume III: Romans*, ed. David M. Hay and E. Elizabeth Johnson (Minneapolis: Fortress, 1995), 169–95.
b. N. T. Wright, "New Exodus, New Inheritance: The Narrative Substructure of Romans 3–8," in *Romans and the People of God: Essays in Honor of Gordon D. Fee on the Occasion of His 65th Birthday*, ed. Sven K. Soderlund and N. T. Wright (Grand Rapids: Eerdmans, 1999), 26–35.

But they are also representative figures whose actions affect the whole human family. From this point of view, the old man is none other than the first man, Adam, who came from the earth, in contradistinction to the last man, Jesus Christ, who came from heaven (1 Cor 15:45–48). It is Adam, and our solidarity with him in sin, that was **done away with** when the mortal humanity of Jesus perished on the cross.

The purpose behind the death and discarding of these old relations is **that we might no longer be in slavery to sin**. In our native Adamic condition, we lived under the power of sin (Rom 3:9), unable to please God or submit to his law (8:7–8). But now we have undergone a spiritual liberation in baptism that frees us from the captivity of sin and places us under the merciful lordship of Christ.

6:7   Paul next considers the freedoms of **a dead person**. Physical death releases a person from life's burdensome debts and obligations. The same is true of one who has died with Christ in baptism (6:3). Baptism, like physical death, delivers persons from their burdens: from the guilt of sin and from the power of sin that once dominated their lives.[9] Anyone who has died with the Messiah **has been absolved from sin**. These words ring in harmony with early Christian preaching on baptism as a sacrament of forgiveness (Acts 2:38; 22:16). But there is an even deeper significance to the statement. Paul is literally saying that one who has died with Christ "has been justified from sin." In other words, justification, which Paul typically expounds in connection with faith, is here described as an effect of baptism.

The importance of this cannot be stressed enough. Faith has an indispensable role in conversion. But it is not the sole and exclusive instrument of Christian justification.[10] Baptism also plays an indispensable role, for it joins the believer to Christ and imparts the grace of redemption—which is just another way of talking about justification, about God making us right once again and grafting us into his New Covenant.[11] This is one of the key New Testament passages that inform the Catholic Church's understanding of baptism as the sacrament of justification (Catechism 1992).[12] Other statements of Paul's similarly link justification to baptism (1 Cor 6:11; Gal 3:24–27; Titus 3:4–7). Perceptive non-Catholic scholars also see this: "For Paul faith and baptism are theologically coterminous, and faith is the essence of baptism even as baptism is the public expression of faith. Thus what Paul predicates of faith he can also predicate

---

9. See the sidebar, "The Power of Sin," below (p. 103).

10. See also Reflection and Application on 6:1–4 (p. 97).

11. See also the sidebar, "Justification," in Rom 3 (pp. 50–51).

12. In 1547 the Council of Trent described the sacrament of baptism as "the instrumental cause" of justification (session 6, ch. 7).

of baptism, and vice versa, because together they effect, at least from the perspective of the human response, transfer into Christ and thus participatory justification in him."[13]

Verse 8 is nearly a restatement of verse 5, only here Paul describes our future life with Christ as a tenet of faith. This is something that **we believe: that we shall . . . live with him**. Why? Because **if . . . we have died with Christ**, then we are united with one who is no longer dead. The resurrection of Jesus is the pledge and guarantee of our own share in his risen life, both now (6:11) and on the last day (8:11). **6:8**

Paul now steps back to assess Christ's present situation. Having been **raised from the dead**, he has forever escaped the dominion of death. The crucifixion is evidence that death exacted its toll from Jesus, but the resurrection is evidence that death no longer has a claim over him. His death occurred **once and for all**—meaning that the event was definitive and unrepeatable. Now Jesus **dies no more**. Christ's humanity has irreversibly entered a glorified existence in which he forever **lives for God** his Father. In dying, Jesus conquered the power of sin; in rising, Jesus conquered the power of death. This is something Christians **know** with the certainty of faith. **6:9–10**

From this knowledge Paul draws an important conclusion: Christians should **think** of themselves as having passed with Christ through death, burial, and resurrection, his personal experience being the source of their spiritual experience. Just as Jesus underwent a dying and rising in the body, so we are now **dead to sin** and **living for God** as a result of baptism. And this mind-set is not about sustaining a mental fiction, "as if" believers have passed from death to life. It rests on a real transformation effected through the sacrament, which places us **in Christ Jesus**. **6:11**

Freed from Sin and Slaves to Righteousness (6:12–23)

[12]**Therefore, sin must not reign over your mortal bodies so that you obey their desires. **[13]**And do not present the parts of your bodies to sin as weapons for wickedness, but present yourselves to God as raised from the dead to life and the parts of your bodies to God as weapons for righteousness. **[14]**For sin is not to have any power over you, since you are not under the law but under grace.**

13. Michael J. Gorman, *Inhabiting the Cruciform God: Kenosis, Justification, and Theosis in Paul's Narrative Soteriology* (Grand Rapids: Eerdmans, 2009), 79.

¹⁵**What then? Shall we sin because we are not under the law but under grace? Of course not!** ¹⁶**Do you not know that if you present yourselves to someone as obedient slaves, you are slaves of the one you obey, either of sin, which leads to death, or of obedience, which leads to righteousness?** ¹⁷**But thanks be to God that, although you were once slaves of sin, you have become obedient from the heart to the pattern of teaching to which you were entrusted.** ¹⁸**Freed from sin, you have become slaves of righteousness.** ¹⁹**I am speaking in human terms because of the weakness of your nature. For just as you presented the parts of your bodies as slaves to impurity and to lawlessness for lawlessness, so now present them as slaves to righteousness for sanctification.** ²⁰**For when you were slaves of sin, you were free from righteousness.** ²¹**But what profit did you get then from the things of which you are now ashamed? For the end of those things is death.** ²²**But now that you have been freed from sin and have become slaves of God, the benefit that you have leads to sanctification, and its end is eternal life.** ²³**For the wages of sin is death, but the gift of God is eternal life in Christ Jesus our Lord.**

OT: Ezek 11:19–20; 36:25–27
NT: John 8:34; Rom 4:4–5; 1 Thess 4:3–7; 2 Pet 2:19
Catechism: baptism and the faith of the Church, 197, 1237; freedom and slavery, 1731–33; death as the wages of sin, 1006–9

At the midpoint of Rom 6, Paul switches from exposition to exhortation. From the mystery of baptism he turns to consider the obligations that baptism places on our lives. The controlling metaphor of this section is slavery and freedom. Paul paints a black-or-white picture of the human situation: either one lives in service to sin and remains in spiritual bondage, or one lives in obedience to God and enjoys liberation from sin's captivity. It is a stark either-or: no fence-sitting, no third option.

6:12   **Therefore**, Paul says, **sin must not reign over your mortal bodies**. Christians have undergone a death to sin in baptism, and so our former life of sin must remain permanently deceased. Nevertheless, while baptism delivers us from enslavement to sin, it does not place us beyond the reach of its influence. Free will remains in the Christian. We can still choose to **obey** the unruly **desires** of the body and allow them to control our actions. With this in mind, Paul is adamant that sin's will to dominate must be earnestly and persistently challenged.

6:13   This does not mean that Christians go the way of the †gnostics and renounce the body as evil. It is rather a question of who and what is being served. The

The Power of Sin

BIBLICAL BACKGROUND

Several times in Romans, especially in chapters 6–7, Paul speaks of sin as a power that seeks to gain mastery over human life. In these instances, he is not referring to wrongdoing in the abstract or to acts of disobedience in the concrete. Rather, Paul personifies sin as an impulse to perverse and selfish action that dwells in the fallen descendants of Adam (7:20). Seeming to have a will of its own, sin reigns like a king (6:12) and can be served like a taskmaster (6:13). It arouses forbidden desires (7:8), it deceives (7:11), and it works death in those who yield to its aggressions (7:13). Apart from Christ, all people find themselves "under" sin, subject to its domination (3:9).

Paul teaches that Christ died in order to condemn sin in the flesh (8:3). Believers benefit from this in baptism, which unites them with the crucified Messiah (6:3) and frees them from the enslavement of sin (6:6). Jesus' triumph on the cross means that sin's tyrannical reign over their lives has been broken. Nevertheless, sin is still a force to be reckoned with in the Christian life. Believers are no longer hopelessly victimized by its power, yet they remain exposed to its wiles and are free to submit themselves again to its bondage (6:12–14). This is where "the power of God" announced in the gospel comes into play (1:16). By living in accord with the Spirit, Christians are enabled "to put to death the deeds of the body" inspired by sin (8:13). For Paul, then, the indwelling power of sin is outmatched by the indwelling power of the Spirit (8:2).

parts of the human body can be wielded as **weapons**[14] **for wickedness**, or they can be dedicated to **God** and used as **weapons for righteousness**. Paul touched on this theme earlier when he assembled excerpts from the Bible to demonstrate the universality of sin in Rom 3. Several of these passages singled out bodily members used for perpetrating wickedness (throats, tongues, lips, mouths, feet, eyes: 3:13–18). Here Paul says that the body can also be submitted to the lordship of Christ. Later he will describe this commitment as a form of liturgical service, urging fellow believers to present their "bodies as a living sacrifice, holy and pleasing to God, your spiritual worship" (12:1).

Paul further challenges disciples to offer themselves to God as a people **raised from the dead**. Believers owe a debt of gratitude for their baptismal

---

14. Scholars disagree over the intended reference of the Greek *hopla*, which can bear a generic meaning ("instruments") or a specialized military meaning ("weapons"). The force of the passage is not greatly affected either way, but the context suggests that Paul has the service of slaves in view rather than soldiering. So C. E. B. Cranfield, *The Epistle to the Romans*, ICC (Edinburgh: T&T Clark, 1975), 1:318.

resurrection in Christ. They have been freed from sin's enslavement and raised to the dignity of living in a personal relationship with God. Hence, they have every reason to serve him with earnest desire and thankfulness.

6:14   Paul's main point is that **sin is not to have any power over** the baptized—literally, that sin "shall not exercise lordship over" their lives. Believers have been freed from an old master, sin, and placed under the authority of a new Lord, Jesus Christ.

Christians are **not under the law** but **under grace**. This statement is so compact as to be cryptic (like others in Romans). Paul said that the law brings "consciousness of sin" (3:20), that it "produces wrath" (4:15), and that it "entered in so that transgression might increase" (5:20). Under the law of Moses sin both flourished and came into sharper focus. Instead of being the solution to our problems, the law exposed the shocking extent of our problems. Sinners found themselves under its condemnation but were left without justification.

Christians do not live under the Old Covenant but under the New. Paul describes this as living under "grace" (Greek *charis*). Grace is God's free and unmerited favor, as all scholars recognize, but it is more than just a favorable attitude toward the undeserving. Grace is an objective endowment that God imparts to the baptized.[15] Beginning in classical times and extending through the Hellenistic period, "grace" was understood in nonbiblical writings as something that belongs to the divine realm but is communicable to the human realm as a gift.[16] Recipients of grace were said to be endowed with qualities or abilities that exceeded their natural talents and capacities. Once again Paul has the grace of the Spirit in mind. It is the indwelling power of God that outmuscles the power of sin (8:1–13).

6:15–16   Paul immediately anticipates another question that an objector might raise. **What then?** he asks. **Shall we sin because we are not under the law but under grace?** This is a variation of the question posed in 6:1. Both query whether receiving God's grace is a legitimate pretext for sin, and both are squashed with Paul's signature denial, **Of course not!** Living in God's grace is possible only within God's boundaries. It requires us to renounce dishonorable ways and adopt new ways that bring honor to him. Simply put, freedom *from* sin is not a freedom *to* sin (Gal 5:13).

Paul assumes that readers **know** that **if you present yourselves to someone as obedient slaves, you are slaves of the one you obey.** By definition, a

---

15. That grace is a gift that comes with reciprocal obligations toward the giver, see John M. G. Barclay, "Under Grace: The Christ-Gift and the Construction of a Christian *Habitus*," in *Apocalyptic Paul: Cosmos and Anthropos in Romans 5–8*, ed. Beverly Roberts Gaventa (Waco: Baylor University Press, 2013), 59–76.
16. John Nolland, "Grace as Power," *NovT* 28, no. 1 (1986): 26–31.

bondservant renders obedience to an overlord, and a slave cannot serve more than one master at a time. Likewise in the spiritual life: either one does the bidding of **sin**, or one renders **obedience** to God. And these two different masters lead to opposite destinies, one to **death**, the other to **righteousness**. Death in this passage cannot mean physical death, since the demise of the body comes to saints and sinners alike. Paul means spiritual death, which is linked to the final condemnation of the wicked (Rom 2:8), just as the righteousness that awaits the faithful is linked to the final justification of the faithful (2:13).

Paul, for his part, is encouraged by the Roman Christians. His gratitude wells **6:17** up as he gives **thanks** to **God** that, although the members of this community were **once slaves of sin**, they have been baptized and now render obedience to the Lord **from the heart**. Theirs was a sincere conversion to Christianity.

Moreover, Paul hints that scriptural prophecy is being fulfilled in the imperial capital. Several oracles of the Old Testament envision God transforming the stony and stubborn hearts of his people into responsive and obedient hearts (Deut 30:6; Ezek 11:19–20; 36:25–27). If Paul was thinking of passages such as these, it would explain why he thanks God for the conversion of his readers. More than anything, it was the Lord's work within them that made their adherence to the gospel possible.

Finally, the Romans rendered obedience to God according to **the pattern of teaching** that prevailed in apostolic times. Paul appears to have a specific outline of Christian instruction in mind, but scholars have found it difficult to pin down precisely. The pattern of teaching was most likely a "baptismal creed"[17] or a "succinct baptismal summary of faith."[18] If so, it means the Romans understood baptism as the first step on a lifelong journey, the beginning of a new life that required adherence to Christian doctrine and moral standards going forward. It is the apostolic pattern of discipleship, modeled on Jesus, **to which** baptized believers are **entrusted**.

Paul's stress on obedience is a continuation of his slavery metaphor. The **6:18–19** baptized are liberated **from sin** and its oppression, but only to become **slaves of righteousness**, whose new responsibilities are marked out by the gospel. The Apostle admits to **speaking in human terms** because of the weaknesses of human **nature**—literally, "your flesh." He is striving to explain something fresh and unfamiliar to his readers by comparing it to something that is already familiar to them. Believers in Rome would readily understand a slavery

17. Ernst Käsemann, *Commentary on Romans*, trans. Geoffrey W. Bromiley (Grand Rapids: Eerdmans, 1980), 181.
18. Fitzmyer, *Romans*, 449.

metaphor, since the Roman Empire of the first century was propped up on the backs of roughly twelve million slaves![19] Beyond that, however, Paul's effort to speak "in human terms" is also an effort to speak in practical and realistic terms about life as a baptized Christian. Having explained the *sacramental* mystery (our freedom from sin's slavery), he proceeds to explain the *experiential* reality that faces all who serve Christ as Lord (our fight against sin's desire to reenslave us).

The question is how slavery is *like* Christian discipleship. On the one hand, slavery says something about life before baptism, when we **presented** the members of our **bodies as slaves to impurity** and **lawlessness**. This was indeed a dehumanizing way of life, as Paul pointed out in his tirade against Gentile depravity in 1:18–32. But the focus of Paul's analogy lies elsewhere. The master-slave relationship approximates how one person can exercise an absolute claim over another. Released from sin, Christians belong to a new master, Christ the Lord, whom they are obligated to serve with total obedience. Equally important, Paul is acknowledging that slavery is a highly demanding form of service. He would not have us embark on a life of discipleship with our eyes closed, as though nothing but smooth sailing lies ahead. The grace of the Messiah makes victory over sin possible, but not easy.

Hence, it is the duty of the baptized to **present** their bodily members **as slaves to righteousness** for the purpose of growing in holiness, otherwise known as **sanctification**. Christians are initially sanctified in baptism, as Paul indicates in 1 Cor 6:11; but progress in sanctification is a lifelong responsibility, as Paul indicates here and in other passages, such as 1 Thess 4:3–7.

6:20–22   This brings us to Paul's synopsis of the Christian's spiritual journey. Before baptism, believers were **slaves of sin** and **free from righteousness**. They lived a paradox of being enslaved and free at the same time: sin asserted its will over them in such a way that righteousness could exert no appreciable influence. As it turns out, this was a false liberty that conferred no actual freedoms. Paul therefore asks, **what profit did you get then from the things of which you are now ashamed?** Immorality is supremely unprofitable because, whatever its apparent gains and momentary thrills, it leads to eternal **death**.

Baptized persons are **freed from sin** and made **slaves of God**. This is a liberty that is real and pays enormous dividends. Serving God **leads to** greater and greater degrees of **sanctification** and eventually to **eternal life**. Of the two

19. See S. Scott Bartchy, "Slaves and Slavery in the Roman World," in *The World of the New Testament: Cultural, Social, and Historical Contexts*, ed. Joel B. Green and Lee Martin McDonald (Grand Rapids: Baker Academic, 2013), 169–78.

options, Paul leaves us in no doubt which is genuine freedom and which is the counterfeit version.

The final verse of Rom 6 states the message of the letter in a nutshell. Paul **6:23** has been struggling to clarify the meaning of **death** and **life** and their relation to **sin** and **God**. To be sure, death means the decease and disintegration of the body, just as life means ongoing existence in the body. But Paul has been pushing readers to see that death and life are *theological* realities, not just biological realities. The death paid out as **wages** to the sinner is spiritual and eternal death; it is the definitive demise of a person's relationship with the Lord. Eternal life, by contrast, is a divine **gift** rather than a wage. It is bestowed as a grace, apart from any contractual obligation on God's part to pay out earnings in strict proportion to our efforts. And this gift is found **in Christ Jesus our Lord**, who grants believers a share in his divine and resurrected life even now.

Reflection and Application (6:15–23)

Paul's original readers must have arched an eyebrow the first time they heard Rom 6 read to the congregation. A full half of the chapter appeals to the practice of slavery to explain the responsibilities of Christian living. It is easy to understand why Paul would use this metaphor to speak of our former "slavery to sin." Living a godless life is wretched, pitiable, and oppressive. One who is mastered by sin is enslaved by a power that degrades one's dignity as a human person. That much is clear.

But how can Paul use the same metaphor to explain our "slavery to God"? This seems risky. A reader could draw inferences that are not only mistaken but also unsettling. Yet nothing Paul says in Romans implies that serving the Lord is distasteful, abusive, or inhumane. Nothing he teaches implies that fear of punishment is the principle motive behind Christian obedience.

So what is the rationale behind calling Christians "slaves of righteousness" (6:18) and "slaves of God" (6:22)? Paul's analogy underscores how slaves belong entirely to another. Slaves possess wills of their own, of course, but the will of their lord is supreme. It is to him that slaves must present themselves for prompt and dependable service. At the same time, Paul knows that every analogy limps insofar as similarities stand alongside points of dissimilarity. He simply wants to drive home the point that baptism brings us under the benevolent lordship of Christ. Jesus is the one we must serve with every fiber of our being, every ounce of our energy, every day of our lives.

But there is more. Paul also uses the slavery metaphor to say that the Christian life is difficult. Yielding oneself to the will of another is a formidable task, to say the least. It means constantly overcoming the selfishness of the flesh. There is no point in sugarcoating the reality. Israel, having escaped Egyptian slavery, quickly discovered that serving the Lord was even more demanding on the will than serving Pharaoh, so much so that some yearned for the old days in Egypt (Num 11:4–6). This is a fact we should take to heart in view of Paul's new exodus †typology in Rom 6.[20] Through baptism we too have been freed from serving a heavy-handed master, but our freedom is not for a life of ease. We too must tread a path to the promised land that takes us through a wilderness of trials and temptations and requires a valiant conquest of all the obstacles of sin that stand in the way.

20. See the sidebar "A New Exodus in Christ" (p. 99).

The Law of Moses and the Law of Sin

Romans 7:1–25

If Romans is the most difficult of Paul's Letters, Rom 7 is the most challenging section of the letter to interpret. There are several reasons for this. One is that Paul makes use of analogy to expound an essential truth of the gospel but leaves it to readers to finish connecting the dots. Another is that Paul examines the struggle against sin both through the lens of his theological convictions and in the light of personal experience. More than anything, Rom 7 tackles an extremely complicated subject in a highly compressed way. In a mere handful of verses, Paul attempts to explain how the desires of sin fight against the demands of the law and how this creates a dilemma in the lives of God's people. Ultimately, the problem laid out in Rom 7 is a buildup to the solution to be revealed in Rom 8.

Release from the Law (7:1–6)

¹Are you unaware, brothers (for I am speaking to people who know the law), that the law has jurisdiction over one as long as one lives? ²Thus a married woman is bound by law to her living husband; but if her husband dies, she is released from the law in respect to her husband. ³Consequently, while her husband is alive she will be called an adulteress if she consorts with another man. But if her husband dies she is free from that law, and she is not an adulteress if she consorts with another man.

⁴In the same way, my brothers, you also were put to death to the law through the body of Christ, so that you might belong to another, to the one who was raised from the dead in order that we might bear fruit for

God. [5]For when we were in the flesh, our sinful passions, awakened by the law, worked in our members to bear fruit for death. [6]But now we are released from the law, dead to what held us captive, so that we may serve in the newness of the spirit and not under the obsolete letter.

OT: Isa 54:5–6; 62:5; Jer 3:1; Hosea 3:1–5
NT: Matt 25:1–13; John 3:28–29; Rom 2:29; 1 Cor 7:39; 2 Cor 3:6; Eph 5:23–33; Rev 19:7–8
Catechism: captivity of the law, 1963; marital fidelity and fruitfulness, 2364–67; fruit of the Spirit, 736, 2074

Romans 7 is thematically continuous with Rom 6. Having claimed that Christians have died to the slavery of sin, Paul turns to the related point that Christians have died to the dominion of the law. He announced in 6:14 that believers are "not under the law," but quickly moved on, leaving the remark dangling. The initial verses of Rom 7 finish his thought by stating a general truth about the law (v. 1), by illustrating it with a specific example (vv. 2–3), and by making direct applications to the Christian situation (vv. 4–6).

7:1   Paul begins by stating a truism he expects readers will accept without argument: **the law has jurisdiction over one as long as one lives.** Some argue that Paul is speaking about any law that governs human conduct, but the surrounding context suggests that he has the Mosaic law specifically in mind.[1] And if Paul expects readers to **know** this **law** already, it is because the congregation in Rome was likely born out of the synagogue community, where not only Jews received instruction in the Torah but interested Gentiles could and did as well.[2] At any rate, one can hardly object to the statement that death terminates the binding force of the law over our lives.

7:2–3   To illustrate this point, Paul considers the case of matrimony, where **a married woman is bound by law to her living husband.** Only when death robs a wife of her husband is she **released from the law in respect to her husband.** The marital bond that once united the couple is dissolved by the passing of one of the spouses. However, before that time, **while her husband is alive**, a wife will be **called an adulteress if she consorts with another man.** Paul envisions not a promiscuous woman having an extramarital affair with another man, but a wife who separates from her first husband and marries a second. This is obscured by the NABRE's use of the expression "consorts with," but in fact Paul's Greek mimics a Hebrew idiom for "belonging to a

---

1. The Greek term *nomos*, "law," in 7:1 lacks the article, which could suggest that it is indefinite or qualitative ("law") rather than definite ("the law"). This is unlikely the case, however, and most commentators hold that Paul is concerned with the Mosaic law. A minority of scholars hold that Paul is talking about (1) natural law, (2) Roman law, or (3) law in general.
2. See "Christianity in the Capital" in the introduction (pp. xvii–xx).

Marriage and Covenant in Scripture

Both Testaments, the Old and the New, describe the covenant between God and his people as a marriage. In the Jewish Scriptures, the Lord wedded himself to Israel as a husband marries a bride (Isa 54:5–6; 62:5; Jer 3:1; Hosea 3:1–5). In the Christian Scriptures, the same theme is sounded, only transposed into a new key: Jesus is the divine bridegroom who takes the Church to be his bride (Matt 25:1–13; John 3:28–29; Eph 5:23–33; Rev 19:7). It is hard to imagine a better way of underlining the ideals of the covenant, especially love and lifelong commitment.

In Rom 7:4 Paul uses marriage imagery to describe the individual's relationship with Christ, but he also takes an ecclesial perspective. Baptism certainly unites each and every believer to the Messiah in a profoundly personal and spousal way. Yet Jesus is not the husband of multiple wives. He has only one bride, the Church. He is united to a chosen and cherished people, to the ecclesial community of the baptized.

That Paul is thinking along these lines in Rom 7 is suggested by the context. One should notice how Paul follows an exposition of baptism and freedom from slavery in Rom 6 with an exposition of spiritual marriage in Rom 7. This is the story of the exodus told anew. In the first exodus, the people of Israel passed from slavery to freedom through the waters of the sea in order to be united to the Lord in the conjugal bonds of the Mosaic covenant (Exod 14–24; Ezek 16:8). In the new exodus, the people of God are redeemed from slavery to sin through the waters of baptism, in order to be united in a marital covenant with Jesus, the messianic bridegroom.[a]

a. See the sidebar, "A New Exodus in Christ," in Rom 6 (p. 99).

man" in the bonds of marriage.[3] In other words, Paul is thinking of the early Christian view of marriage, which adhered to the revolutionary teaching of Jesus in disallowing remarriage after divorce as a form of adultery (Mark 10:11–12; Luke 16:18).

The main point is that death brings release from the **law** of marriage. When a woman's **husband dies**, she becomes a widow who is **free** to marry another eligible man without fear of being an **adulteress**. So death marks the end of an old relationship; at the same time, it allows for the formation of an entirely new relationship. The example of the remarried widow illustrates this point simply and effectively.

3. See the use of *ginesthai andri* in the LXX version of Lev 22:12; Deut 24:2; and Hosea 3:3, pointed out by C. E. B. Cranfield, *The Epistle to the Romans*, ICC (Edinburgh: T&T Clark, 1975), 1:333; and Joseph A. Fitzmyer, SJ, *Romans*, AB 33 (New York: Doubleday, 1993), 458.

7:4–5   Complications arise, however, when Paul moves from illustration to application. He wants believers to understand that a "death" has taken place that frees them to embark on a new union with Christ. But as Paul explains it, the Christian plays the role *both* of the husband who dies *and* of the surviving wife who remarries. Believers experience a **death** by their baptism into the death of the Messiah (6:3), whose **body** expired on the cross. In this respect, they are like the husband in verse 2. But the sacrament also unites believers to **another**—namely, to the Lord Jesus, **who was raised from the dead**. In this respect, they are like the wife in verse 2. No doubt the analogy is stretched further than we might expect, but this is because, as one scholar puts it, "Paul is trying in this analogy to express the reality of a unique event in the world, an event which makes it possible for a man to die and yet live. . . . There are no parallels for this experience."[4]

At any rate, believers have been **put to death to the law**. Paul thus identifies the law of our first marriage as the law of Moses, which no longer has jurisdiction over the people of God as it once did. Baptized believers have been freed to serve God in a new and more powerful way, as Paul will intimate in 7:6.

But if the Mosaic law was the law of our first marriage, who is the husband to whom we were formerly joined? The answer is plausibly found in 6:6, where Paul asserts that "our old self" was crucified with Christ. If we allow that Paul associates the old self with our spiritual identity in Adam,[5] then it is our spiritual solidarity with Adam that dies in baptism, freeing us for a bridal union with Christ.[6] Paul prepared us to see this in Rom 5:12–21 when he claimed that justification detaches us from the first Adam, freeing us from the condemnation that he drew upon our race, and joins us to Christ, the new Adam.[7]

Paul develops the application further when he introduces in verses 4–5 an element not expressly mentioned in the analogy of verses 2–3: the fruitfulness of marriage. Before baptism, Christians lived exclusively **in the flesh**,[8] by which Paul means at the behest of **sinful passions** that come with our fallen, Adamic nature and dominate our lives. The Mosaic **law** was there to distinguish good from evil; but instead of calming the rumblings of sin, it **awakened** our sinful and selfish impulses so that our **members** were roused

---

4. Joyce A. Little, "Paul's Use of Analogy: A Structural Analysis of Romans 7:1–6," *CBQ* 46 (1984): 87.
5. See commentary on 6:6.
6. N. T. Wright, *Paul and the Faithfulness of God*, Christian Origins and the Question of God 4 (Minneapolis: Fortress, 2013), 893.
7. For marriage as a fitting way to describe justification, see Michael Waldstein, "The Trinitarian, Spousal, and Ecclesial Logic of Justification," in *Reading Romans with St. Thomas Aquinas*, ed. Matthew Levering and Michael Dauphinais (Washington, DC: Catholic University of America Press, 2012), 274–87.
8. See the sidebar "Life in the Flesh" (p. 123).

Ambrosiaster on "Letter and Spirit"

LIVING TRADITION

Ambrosiaster was an orthodox Christian writer, possibly a presbyter in the church at Rome, who produced a Latin commentary on the Pauline Epistles in the 370s. His actual name is unknown, and for centuries his work was mistakenly attributed to St. Ambrose of Milan. His commentary was widely read and respected in the Christian West during the medieval and Renaissance periods.

> The law of Moses is not called old because it is evil, but because it is out of date and has ceased to function. But the law of the Spirit is the law of faith, because faith is in the mind and is believed in the heart, not calculated by works. . . . The old law was written on tablets of stone, but the law of the Spirit is written spiritually on the tablets of the heart, that it might be eternal, whereas the letter of the old law is consumed with age. There is another way of understanding the law of the Spirit, which is that where the former law restrained evil deeds, this law, which says that we ought not to sin even in our hearts, is called the law of the Spirit, because it makes the whole man spiritual.[a]

a. *Commentary on the Pauline Epistles: Romans* 7:6. Cited from Ambrosiaster, *Commentaries on Romans and 1–2 Corinthians*, trans. Gerald L. Bray, Ancient Christian Texts (Downers Grove, IL: InterVarsity, 2009), 54.

to **bear fruit for death**.[9] Paul basically reiterates here what he said in 6:21, that the shameful actions of our past constitute the "profit" (the Greek *karpos* is literally "fruit") that leads to spiritual death. This is the offspring produced by our marriage to Adam.[10]

Conversely, the purpose of our spousal union with Christ is to **bear fruit for God**. Some suggest that Paul has in mind a fruitful ministry of preaching or evangelization. But looking to what he says in verse 6, he is more likely thinking of "the fruit of the Spirit" (Gal 5:22). These are the manifestations of grace produced in believers who live according to the Spirit. Paul enumerates them in Gal 5:22–23 as "love, joy, peace, patience, kindness, generosity, faithfulness, gentleness, self-control." This is the harvest of offspring produced by one united with Jesus.

To sum up the contrast between the first and second marriage—one by nature (birth in Adam), the other by grace (baptism in Christ)—Paul formulates an antithesis between **letter** and **spirit**, which he uses to differentiate the Old   **7:6**

9. Paul will explain what he means by this in 7:7–12.

10. Biblical terms for "fruit" can designate not only the horticultural produce of a tree or vine or the agricultural harvest of a field but also the offspring of the womb (see Deut 28:11; Luke 1:42).

Covenant from the New (Rom 2:29; 2 Cor 3:6).[11] The letter stands for the Torah, an external law given through Moses that condemns disobedience but offers no inward assistance toward obedience. The gospel has made this an **obsolete** or antiquated way of serving God.[12] Now, with the advent of messianic grace, believers are **released** from its condemnation (Rom 8:1). Christians possess a new law: "the law of the Spirit of life in Christ Jesus" (8:2). The Spirit dwells within and empowers from within, supplying the love (5:5) we need to fulfill the law (13:8–10). It is not a matter, then, of discarding the Torah in messianic times, but of fulfilling it with a new ability that comes from God (8:4).

Defense of the Law (7:7–13)

> [7]What then can we say? That the law is sin? Of course not! Yet I did not know sin except through the law, and I did not know what it is to covet except that the law said, "You shall not covet." [8]But sin, finding an opportunity in the commandment, produced in me every kind of covetousness. Apart from the law sin is dead. [9]I once lived outside the law, but when the commandment came, sin became alive; [10]then I died, and the commandment that was for life turned out to be death for me. [11]For sin, seizing an opportunity in the commandment, deceived me and through it put me to death. [12]So then the law is holy, and the commandment is holy and righteous and good.
>
> [13]Did the good, then, become death for me? Of course not! Sin, in order that it might be shown to be sin, worked death in me through the good, so that sin might become sinful beyond measure through the commandment.

OT: Gen 3:1–6, 13; Exod 20:17; 32:1–6; Lev 18:5; Deut 4:1; 5:21; 30:15–20
NT: Rom 3:20; 5:20; 6:23; 2 Cor 11:3; 1 Tim 2:14
Catechism: awareness of sin through the law, 708; concupiscence, 405

After affirming our release from the law, Paul mounts a defense of the law, lest the law be blamed for the evils of sin. This requires probing into the wounds of our fallen condition, so that sin, identified as a power dwelling within, can be

11. Evidently the NABRE understands this as a reference to the renewed human "spirit." Many, however, understand Paul to mean the "Spirit" of God; see, e.g., Fitzmyer, *Romans*, 460. The same is true of several modern translations, such as the RSV, NRSV, ESV, and NIV, all of which capitalize "Spirit." For a classic study of this contrast, see Bernardin Schneider, OFM, "The Meaning of St. Paul's Antithesis: 'The Letter and the Spirit,'" *CBQ* 15 (1953): 163–207.

12. The expression in Rom 7:6 underlying the NABRE's "not under the obsolete letter" can be literally rendered "not in accord with the oldness of the letter."

exposed as the real culprit behind our inability to fulfill the law as God intends. Paul's language in this section is almost as cryptic as it is clarifying, making it difficult to ascertain his meaning with precision.

Paul begins by raising a question: **What then can we say? That the law is** **7:7** **sin?** If we have been following the thread of Paul's argument closely, we can appreciate why he addresses the issue here. In Rom 6, Paul warned that sin can still exercise "power over" our lives (6:14); here in Rom 7, he uses the same Greek term to indicate that the law has "jurisdiction over" the living (7:1). Likewise, in Rom 6, Paul claimed that Christians have "died" to sin (6:2); in Rom 7, he uses the same Greek term to state that Christians are now "dead" to the law (7:6). Again, in Rom 6, Paul announced that baptized believers have been "freed" from sin (6:18, 22); in Rom 7, he declares them "released" from the law (7:6), just as a widow is made "free" from the law of her deceased husband (7:3).

Given this echo effect, in which sin and the law are described in nearly the same way, it is reasonable to ask whether sin and the law are not one and the same thing. Paul responds with an emphatic denial: **Of course not!** The law is an innocent actor in the drama of salvation history; sin is the real troublemaker.

That said, there is a close relationship between the two, for Paul says, **I did not know sin except through the law**. The Torah, in its capacity as a moral informant, unmasks the ugly reality of sin for what it is—not just wrongdoing that earns a rebuke from one's conscience, but willful rebellion against God and his authority as the lawgiver. Paul touched on this in 3:20, when he announced that "through the law comes consciousness of sin." Paul likewise assumes as background the scenario described in 5:13, that "up to the time of the law, sin was in the world, though sin is not accounted when there is no law."

Now he unpacks the assertion with an example: **I did not know what it is to covet except that the law said, "You shall not covet."** The excerpt is taken from the †Decalogue, specifically from the ninth and tenth commandments, which forbid us to desire another person's spouse or belongings (Exod 20:17; Deut 5:21). It is interesting that Paul should single out the Mosaic prohibitions against coveting, since these disallow not only outward actions, such as adultery or stealing, but also the inward movements of the heart that lead to these sins. Even here, in the hidden center of the person, restraint is required. A knowledge of sin is thus acquired that, even if vaguely perceived in the patriarchal period, is made clear and explicit with the revelation of the Mosaic law.

Recall that, in Paul's mind, **sin** is more than disobedience or transgression. Sin **7:8** is a rebelliousness that dwells in the human heart, a power that Paul personifies throughout Romans because it seems to have a will of its own that fights against our best intentions to serve God.[13] Paul accuses sin of dredging up **every kind of covetousness** in the one who knows that God forbids it. In the words of Origen of Alexandria, the enigma of sin is such that "whatever is forbidden is desired all the more tenaciously."[14] The **commandment** is like the rancher who tries to saddle a wild horse for riding: the very attempt at restraint provokes the animal to rear up in opposition. Not every sin can be accounted for in this way, of course, but many can.

Apart from the law, Paul goes on to say, **sin is dead**. His point is not that sin does not exist without the law. This would contradict his remarks in 2:12 and 5:13. By "dead" the Apostle seems to mean something like "dormant." Sin was present in our fallen race well before the Mosaic law was given to Israel, and yet its true nature and gravity were not fully perceived until that time. Paul thus implies that, before the Torah, "sin did not have the opportunity it needed to assert itself."[15]

7:9–10   Paul next describes the interaction between sin and the law in the form of a story. The critical question here is: Whose story is it? Who is the mysterious **I** (Greek *egō*) that punctuates the discourse of Rom 7 from here to the end of the chapter?

Nearly all interpretations fall into one of two categories. Either Paul is speaking *autobiographically* about his own experience with sin, or Paul is speaking *rhetorically* about the experience of someone else. These options present us with further questions. If autobiographical, is Paul giving his perspective as a youth, as a Pharisee, or as a Christian? If rhetorical, is Paul adopting the standpoint of Adam, of Israel, or of fallen humanity in general?

My own sense is that Paul is telling a story that operates at more than one level. Initially he assumes the role of Israel at Mount Sinai.[16] The narrative in a nutshell is the sequence: **I once lived outside the law, but when the commandment came, sin became alive** and **then I died**. Before arriving at the mountain, the chosen people lived in a relationship with God despite not having a public expression of his law. But when the Torah became known through Moses, things changed. Within weeks Israel rose up in rebellion, bowed before a golden calf idol, and fell from its first grace (Exod 32:1–6).[17] The law, which promised **life**

13. See the sidebar, "The Power of Sin," in Rom 6 (p. 103).

14. *Commentary on Romans* 6.8.6. Translation from Origen, *Commentary on the Epistle to the Romans, Books 6–10*, trans. Thomas P. Scheck, FC 104 (Washington, DC: Catholic University of America Press, 2002), 32.

15. Frank J. Matera, *Romans*, PCNT (Grand Rapids: Baker Academic, 2010), 174.

16. That Paul also speaks autobiographically, see commentary on 7:14–25.

17. Rabbinic tradition viewed the golden calf apostasy as the "original sin" of Israel. See Leivy Smolar and Moshe Aberbach, "The Golden Calf Episode in Postbiblical Literature," *HUCA* 39 (1968): 91–116.

Figure 6. Seventeenth- or eighteenth-century Torah scroll written on leather, displayed at the museum of the synagogue of Casale Monferrato in Piemonte, Italy.

for faithful obedience, brought **death** for flagrant defiance of the Lord and his covenant (Lev 18:5; Deut 4:1; 6:24; 30:15–20).

This scenario best accounts for Paul's exposition in these verses, but it is not the only one. Resonating in the background is an echo of Adam's story. The comment that sin **deceived me** recalls the words Eve said after sharing the forbidden fruit with Adam: "The serpent deceived me, and I ate" (Gen 3:13 ESV). Paul, who is adept at discovering recurrent patterns in salvation history, sees the fall of Adam in the garden reenacted in the fall of Israel at Sinai.[18] Both disobeyed the Lord's **commandment**, with deadly consequences (Gen 3:19; Exod 32:25–28).

Sin is the one that inflicts **death** on would-be servants of God by drawing **7:11** them into disobedience. The divine **commandment** provided **an opportunity** for sin to rouse itself into deadly action, but the commandment is not a criminal accomplice. Paul thus distinguishes between sin as the *cause* of death and the law as the *occasion* of death.

Harkening back to the question posed in 7:7, Paul insists that the law of **7:12** Moses must not be confused with the deceptions of sin. On the contrary, it

18. See Wright, *Paul and the Faithfulness of God*, 894: "Paul tells the story of Israel at Sinai in such a way as to echo the story of Adam in the garden. He explains, in other words, that what happened to Israel when Torah arrived on Mount Sinai was a recapitulation of the primal sin of Adam."

is something **holy and righteous and good**. The Torah is "holy" because it comes from the Lord, who is holy to the highest degree, utterly untouched by the defilements of the world (Isa 6:3). The Torah is also "righteous" because it promotes justice among God's people and uprightness in the covenant (Deut 4:8; 6:25). Finally, it is "good" because it prohibits evil and denounces evil with divine authority. These adjectives apply not only to **the law** in its entirety but to each individual **commandment** therein.

7:13   Paul introduces a final clarification with the question, **Did the good, then, become death for me?**[19] Paul is still speaking about the law, which he just declared "good" (7:12). Now he inquires whether the law bears responsibility for the death that follows violations of it. As expected, his comeback is the emphatic **Of course not!** Paul intimated earlier that **sin**—not the law—ushers death into the world (5:12; 6:23). He has not changed his mind since then. Yet it remains for him to explain what divine purpose the law serves in relation to sin.

He does so by enunciating a twofold purpose behind the law. The first aim of the Torah, he says, was to *expose* sin **in order that it might be shown to be sin**—in other words, to drag sin out of the shadows and expose to the light its perverse character as the creature's revolt against the creator. The second of God's purposes for the Torah was to *exacerbate* the seriousness of evil **so that sin might become sinful beyond measure**. This is one of Paul's more puzzling sayings—the opposite, in fact, of what we expect him to say. Was not the law given to restrain sin and to limit its devastation in our lives? Yes, it was, but this is not the whole story. In the designs of God, sin was allowed to exploit the commandments with lethal effect, bringing **death** to the disobedient **through** what is **good**. In the process, the sinfulness of sin was intensified. Sin was unwittingly making itself a bigger target for the saving intervention of God. As Paul put it in 5:20: "Where sin increased, grace overflowed all the more."

Reflection and Application (7:7–13)

What Paul describes in Rom 7 is nothing less than a spiritual pathology. It is a disorder called "sin" that resides and operates in the mortal flesh of our race. It is something native within our fallen nature that seeks to sabotage our attempts at keeping God's law.

---

19. Modern translations differ in treating v. 13 as the conclusion of the paragraph beginning in v. 7 (JB), as a paragraph in its own right (NIV, NRSV), or as the beginning of the following paragraph (NABRE, RSV, ESV).

Catholic theology recognizes this disorder under the name "concupiscence." By this is meant the sinful disposition we inherit from Adam; it is the result of original sin as well as the cause of actual sin (Catechism 405). Concupiscence is not to be confused with the personal guilt of sin or with specific acts of sin. It is rather our inborn selfishness, that chronic stubbornness that urges us to misuse our free will in sinful ways. It is that inner thirst for pleasure and power and possessions that is never sated. Because of the presence of concupiscence, the very foundation of the moral life is out of balance: we are free to choose sin but hindered in our freedom to choose higher and spiritual goods. Such is the downward inclination of concupiscence that Paul describes under the name "sin" in Rom 7.

Indictment of Sin (7:14–25)

[14]We know that the law is spiritual; but I am carnal, sold into slavery to sin. [15]What I do, I do not understand. For I do not do what I want, but I do what I hate. [16]Now if I do what I do not want, I concur that the law is good. [17]So now it is no longer I who do it, but sin that dwells in me. [18]For I know that good does not dwell in me, that is, in my flesh. The willing is ready at hand, but doing the good is not. [19]For I do not do the good I want, but I do the evil I do not want. [20]Now if [I] do what I do not want, it is no longer I who do it, but sin that dwells in me. [21]So, then, I discover the principle that when I want to do right, evil is at hand. [22]For I take delight in the law of God, in my inner self, [23]but I see in my members another principle at war with the law of my mind, taking me captive to the law of sin that dwells in my members. [24]Miserable one that I am! Who will deliver me from this mortal body? [25]Thanks be to God through Jesus Christ our Lord. Therefore, I myself, with my mind, serve the law of God but, with my flesh, the law of sin.

OT: Pss 19:8–12; 119:1–176
NT: Rom 2:20; Gal 1:13–14; Phil 3:5–6
Catechism: law of God and the law of sin, 2542; concupiscence in the baptized, 1426, 2520

The second half of Rom 7 is a theological analysis of sin within the framework of human experience. At issue is a conundrum that everyone faces in life: we know what we should do, and we often desire to do it, yet we frequently fail to do it. There is a glaring discrepancy between our intentions and our actions, a moral disconnect that the Apostle attributes to the inner workings of sin. This problem gives rise to the sense of helplessness that Paul verbalizes in verse 24 and thus underscores our desperate need for deliverance in Jesus Christ, as indicated in verse 25.

One question typically asked of Rom 7:14–25 is whether Paul is speaking from a Jewish perspective or a Christian perspective. Many scholars accept that the Apostle's words in this section are autobiographical.[20] But is Paul talking about his preconversion experience as a Pharisee or his postconversion experience as a baptized believer?

My own view is that Paul speaks as a Christian to fellow Christians who continue to wrestle with the agitations of sin in their lives. Several considerations support this. (1) It is clear from elsewhere in the New Testament that Paul the Pharisee had a "robust conscience" rather than a tortured conscience.[21] In other words, he experienced nothing like the woeful sense of inadequacy that dominates Rom 7. Quite the opposite. He considered himself "blameless" when it came to "righteousness based on the law" (Phil 3:6). (2) Neither the Old Testament nor early rabbinic literature attests to the kind of agonizing internal conflict that Paul describes in Rom 7. They indicate that obedience is sometimes a struggle, but in these writings the Torah is a cause for delight and celebration, not of a psychological distress hounding those who seek to observe it. It seems, rather, that Paul is examining our sinfulness under the influence of Christian grace, which magnifies the reality of sin and enables him to observe our predicament at a higher resolution than was previously possible. (3) Paul speaks in the past tense in 7:7–13, where he alludes to the disobedience of Adam and Israel, but then he shifts to the present tense in 7:14–25. This supports the hypothesis that, from verse 14 onward, Paul is speaking of a present dilemma facing Christians. It is difficult to square this shift in tenses with an interpretation that reads Paul's words as a flashback to his "former way of life in Judaism" (Gal 1:13). (4) For most of Christian history since the time of St. Augustine of Hippo, theologians have read Rom 7 in relation to Christian experience. In his early writings, Augustine thought that Paul was depicting the struggles of the Jew living "under the law." Later, however, he shifted his position to say that Paul describes the trials of the baptized believer who is "under grace" but continues to experience the residual effects of Adam's fall.[22] St. Thomas Aquinas preferred this solution as well.[23]

---

20. See commentary on 7:9–10.

21. Famously pointed out by Krister Stendahl, "The Apostle Paul and the Introspective Conscience of the West," reprinted in *Paul among Jews and Gentiles and Other Essays* (Philadelphia: Fortress, 1976), 78–96.

22. See Augustine's *Retractations* 1.22 and the detailed study by Thomas F. Martin, *Rhetoric and Exegesis in Augustine's Interpretation of Romans 7:24–25a* (Lewiston, NY: Edwin Mellen, 2001).

23. *Commentary on Romans* 7.3.558. For support from modern scholars, see J. de Waal Dryden, "Revisiting Romans 7: Law, Self, and Spirit," *JSPHL* 5, no. 1 (2015): 129–51; David H. Campbell, "The

This is not to suggest that Rom 7 offers a complete picture of the Christian situation. Not by a long shot. The point is only that believers, having been released from the bondage of sin through baptism, still have to reckon with the mischief of sinful desires. The Christian is still capable of living "according to the flesh" by responding imperfectly to the grace of Christ. For this reason, everything Paul says in this chapter is a preparation for the next, in which he describes the necessity of living "according to the Spirit." One could say that just as the end of Rom 5 presents a problem (sin and death in Adam) that finds its solution in Rom 6 (forgiveness and new life in Christ), so the end of Rom 7 presents a problem (the vexations of the flesh) that finds its solution in Rom 8 (victory in the Spirit).

Paul begins this section with a declaration that **the law is spiritual**. Essentially these words summarize his description of the law in verse 12. The Torah is spiritual because it comes from God, it leads us back to God, and it instructs us how to live in communion with God. It is spiritual in its origin as well as its purpose. The problem, Paul admits to his readers, is that he is **carnal** or "of the flesh."[24] Even the Apostle is beset with the frailties and inclinations to sin of Adam's descendants. **7:14**

Paul also describes himself as **sold into slavery to sin** or "sold under sin." These are shocking words, given that much of Rom 6 was an argument that baptism frees us from the enslaving power of sin (6:17–22)! But this passage assumes the truth of everything Paul said in Rom 6. Baptism delivers us from the guilt of sin as well as its total control over our lives. Yet we the baptized remain in mortal bodies where sin is always trying to regain its mastery. And unless we yield to the Spirit and "put to death the deeds of the body" (8:13), we can submit ourselves to its bondage all over again. Because this is a permanent and inescapable situation that faces everyone—Christians included—Paul can assert that we are "sold" under its influence.

Sin is a confounding riddle of the moral life. Disobedience to the law is not always intelligible to the one guilty of it. Paul admits that he does **not understand** his own actions at times. **For I do not do what I want**, he confesses, **but I do what I hate**. Even the best of us consent to doing things that we know are wrong. **7:15–16**

Identity of ἐγώ in Romans 7:7–25," in *Studia Biblica 1978: III. Papers on Paul and Other New Testament Authors*, ed. E. A. Livingstone, Sixth International Congress on Biblical Studies (Sheffield: JSOT Press, 1980), 57–64; and J. I. Packer, "The 'Wretched Man' Revisited: Another Look at Romans 7:14–25," in *Romans and the People of God: Essays in Honor of Gordon D. Fee on the Occasion of His 65th Birthday*, ed. Sven K. Soderlund and N. T. Wright (Grand Rapids: Eerdmans, 1999), 70–81.

24. See the sidebar "Life in the Flesh" (p. 123).

St. Augustine on Concupiscence in the Baptized

> Was not the apostle Paul baptized? Or had he not been forgiven every sin whether original or personal, either of ignorance or of knowledge? Why, then, did he say such things . . . ? Indeed, this law of sin which is in the members of the body of death, is forgiven by spiritual regenera-tion, yet also remains in the mortal flesh—forgiven indeed, because its guilt is remitted by the sacrament through which the faithful are reborn; but it remains, because it produces desires against which the faithful struggle.[a]

a. *Against Julian* 2.3.5, translation adapted from Augustine, *Against Julian*, trans. Matthew A. Schu-macher, CSC, FC 35 (New York: Fathers of the Church, 1957), 60–61.

There is a thin silver lining in this frustrating scenario: **if I do what I do not want, I concur that the law is good**. To the extent that Paul recognizes evil for what it is and does not genuinely desire it, he remains in partial harmony with God's law. That is, Paul still assents to the Torah as the embodiment of divine "knowledge and truth" (2:20). This is why he can say without flinching, "I myself, with my mind, serve the law of God" (7:25).

7:17–23   Even so, there is a gaping chasm between **willing** and **doing** that Paul traces to an inner conflict between **I** and the **sin that dwells in me**. The person in-structed in the Torah but still living this earthly life is divided against himself, pulled in different directions by two opposing forces vying for control. The Jewish community at Qumran, associated with the Dead Sea Scrolls, explained this struggle in terms of *two spirits* dwelling in man, one truthful and the other perverse.[25] Rabbinic Judaism developed a similar notion of *two impulses* tugging at the heart, one good and one evil.[26] Paul is unique in positioning the "I"—the individual's center of consciousness and decision-making—between *two laws*, the **law of God** and the **law of sin**.

Paul claims to serve the law of God with his **mind** or **inner self**, while his **members** are subject to the indwelling law of sin, resulting in a **war**. The mind that serves God takes **delight** in his commandments, much as the writer of Ps 119, who spoke of them in glowing terms, did. But within his members, Paul discovers **another principle** that takes his will **captive** to the restless cravings of sin. When the Apostle states that **good does not dwell in me, that is, in my**

25. *Community Rule* (1QS 3.18–4.26).
26. See W. D. Davies, *Paul and Rabbinic Judaism* (Philadelphia: Fortress, 1980), 20–27.

Life in the Flesh

Paul speaks often about "the flesh" in Rom 6–8, so it is important to understand what he means by the term. The flesh is not simply the body as distinct from the mind or spirit of a person; and yet, in Paul's conception, it definitely includes the body. It is almost a realm or a state of being. To be "in the flesh" is to exist in a fallen, unregenerate state, beset with weaknesses (6:19) and sinful passions (7:5) that make us unable to please God (8:8). It is to live in a mortal body where sin asserts itself against the will of God (6:12; 7:23) and drags captives into "impurity" and "lawlessness" (6:19). Those who live by the flesh set their minds on the flesh (8:5–6) and cannot submit themselves to God's law (8:7). In a word, life in the flesh is life in solidarity with disobedient Adam.

Paul is clear that baptized Christians are not "in the flesh" (8:9) in the sense of being outside the realm of redemption, for they are "in Christ Jesus" (8:1). The Messiah came in the likeness of our sinful flesh so that, through his death, God might condemn sin in the flesh (8:3). But if Christians are no longer in the flesh, they can still live "according to the flesh" by falling back on the meager resources of their Adamic nature (8:13). Believers still possess bodies where sinful inclinations are at work, and so failure to rely on God's grace can subject them once again to the control of the flesh. Paul thus urges us to live according to the Spirit, by whose power we can overcome the assaults of the flesh, fulfilling the law (8:4) and putting to death the deeds of the body that lead away from eternal life (8:13).

flesh, he affirms the inability of human nature in its fallen state **to do the good** prescribed by the law (as in Rom 8:7–8).

Still, it remains puzzling why Paul repeats the line: **it is no longer I who do it** (7:17, 20). If blame for disobedience is fixed squarely on **sin**, the lawbreaker himself would seem to be acquitted of any wrongdoing. Is Paul ducking responsibility for his transgressions of the law? Certainly not. He is more likely exercising some poetic license to dramatize how sins are committed under duress. In other words, life is not a level playing field for the children of Adam, as though fidelity and infidelity to the Lord require equal effort. On the contrary, the sin that dwells within can have an overpowering effect on the human will, outmuscling even the best of our law-abiding intentions.

The final verses of the chapter are transitional. They sum up the message of **7:24–25** Rom 7 and pivot toward Rom 8. Verse 24 brings Paul's exposition to an impassioned high point: **Miserable one that I am!** he exclaims. **Who will deliver me**

from this mortal body?[27] It is important to recognize this as a cry of distress, not a groan of despair. Paul feels acutely the burdens of his fallen humanity, yet it is not a situation of utter hopelessness, such that Paul fears his cry will go unheeded.

For this reason, he moves quickly from lament to thanksgiving. Answering the question "Who will deliver me?" of verse 24, Paul expresses gratitude **to God through Jesus Christ our Lord** in verse 25. The Lord, in sending his Messiah, has accomplished a deliverance that will bring about a renewal of all things, including "the redemption of our bodies" (8:23). Paul's prayer has already been answered; his problem has already been met with a solution. In the meantime, he is caught in the middle, between serving **the law of God** with the **mind** and **the law of sin** in the **flesh**.

This means, in effect, that Christians straddle the threshold between two ages, the old and the new. At the present stage of salvation history, we possess the flesh of Adam, even as we are filled with the Spirit of Christ. We have come to possess eternal life, even as we inhabit a body that is doomed to perish and that still throbs with sinful desire. Understanding this readies us for Paul's teaching on the Spirit in the next chapter. The indwelling power of the Spirit is precisely what enables us to rise above the turbulence of Rom 7 into the calm and sunny skies of Rom 8.

27. The Greek underlying "this mortal body" is literally "this body of death."

The Law of the Spirit and the Love of God

Romans 8:1–39

All commentators agree that Rom 8 is something special. If Romans is a breathtaking landscape, this chapter is a majestic peak towering above its surroundings. If Romans is a grand symphonic performance, this chapter is a resounding crescendo that touches the soul and moves the listener to tears. Of course, Rom 8 is only the midpoint of the letter, and much that Paul has to say in later chapters is of paramount importance. Still, when we cross over into Rom 8, we enter upon especially hallowed ground.

Paul's focus in this chapter is threefold: the divine work of the *Spirit*, the divine gift of *sonship*, and the divine purpose of *suffering*, each in relation to the practical realities of Christian living. Thus he puts the capstone on everything he said in Rom 5–7. Paul gave us glimpses of these themes in earlier chapters; finally, the time has come to elaborate on them, and to glory in the blessings that God has lavished upon his people.

The Flesh and the Spirit (8:1–13)

¹Hence, now there is no condemnation for those who are in Christ Jesus. ²For the law of the spirit of life in Christ Jesus has freed you from the law of sin and death. ³For what the law, weakened by the flesh, was powerless to do, this God has done: by sending his own Son in the likeness of sinful flesh and for the sake of sin, he condemned sin in the flesh, ⁴so that the righteous decree of the law might be fulfilled in us, who live not according to the flesh but according to the spirit. ⁵For those who live according to

the flesh are concerned with the things of the flesh, but those who live according to the spirit with the things of the spirit. ⁶The concern of the flesh is death, but the concern of the spirit is life and peace. ⁷For the concern of the flesh is hostility toward God; it does not submit to the law of God, nor can it; ⁸and those who are in the flesh cannot please God. ⁹But you are not in the flesh; on the contrary, you are in the spirit, if only the Spirit of God dwells in you. Whoever does not have the Spirit of Christ does not belong to him. ¹⁰But if Christ is in you, although the body is dead because of sin, the spirit is alive because of righteousness. ¹¹If the Spirit of the one who raised Jesus from the dead dwells in you, the one who raised Christ from the dead will give life to your mortal bodies also, through his Spirit that dwells in you. ¹²Consequently, brothers, we are not debtors to the flesh, to live according to the flesh. ¹³For if you live according to the flesh, you will die, but if by the spirit you put to death the deeds of the body, you will live.

OT: Jer 31:31–34; Ezek 36:26–27; 37:1–14

NT: Matt 22:34–40; 2 Cor 5:21; Gal 3:21; 5:16–25; Phil 3:20–21; Heb 11:6

Catechism: law of the Spirit, 972; names of the Spirit, 693; Christ's resurrection and ours, 658, 995; general resurrection, 988–91, 1002–4

Lectionary: 8:1–4: St. Alphonsus Liguori; 8:8–11: 5th Sunday of Lent (Year A); 8:8–17: Pentecost Sunday (Year C)

It is hard to miss that Paul is preoccupied with the Holy Spirit in Rom 8. The Greek term *pneuma* ("Spirit" or "spirit"), which appears only a handful of times in the first half of the letter, now explodes into the foreground. It is used twenty-one times in this chapter alone. The NABRE adopts a minority position by treating most of these as references to the human "spirit." However, I take at least eighteen instances of *pneuma* in Rom 8 as references to the "Spirit" of God, a reading that lines up more closely with other modern translations (RSV, NRSV, ESV, NIV). Only in two verses, 8:10 and 8:16, is it clear that Paul has in mind the human "spirit" instead of the Holy Spirit.

In terms of the letter's unfolding argument, 8:1–13 unpacks the significance of 7:6. Paul explains what it means for Christians to serve the Lord in the "newness" of the Spirit. The Spirit is the presence and power of God in the life of the believer, the animating principle of Christian morality and spirituality. In short, the indwelling of the Spirit makes it possible to live victoriously as a disciple of Jesus Christ.

8:1   Romans 8 begins as a trumpet blast breaking in on the somber tones of Rom 7. The opening word **Hence** indicates that Paul is turning a corner in his argument. The problem of sin manipulating our members is about to find its solution. In fact, the word **now** has something of an †eschatological ring to it, as in 3:21, suggesting that God's plan of salvation has reached a new level of fulfillment.

And what is Paul's triumphant announcement? That there is **no condemnation** for baptized believers, since now they live **in Christ Jesus**. United to God's Messiah, they are delivered from the divine judgment pressing upon sinners. For Israel, this means deliverance from "the ministry of condemnation" worked through the curses of the Mosaic covenant (2 Cor 3:9). For the human family in general, this means deliverance from the "condemnation" imposed on the descendants of Adam in the wake of his disobedience (Rom 5:16, 18).

Paul continues by spelling out a critical component of this new situation: **the law of the spirit of life in Christ Jesus has freed you from the law of sin and death**.[1] Readers of Rom 7 will remember that Paul has been playing on the word "law" (Greek *nomos*, which is also translatable as "principle"). First he uses the term to designate the Mosaic law. But then he speaks of another law or principle that dwells in fallen man and interferes with his intentions to keep the Mosaic law. This is what Catholic theology calls concupiscence; in Pauline terms, it is "the law of sin that dwells in my members" (7:23). In this scenario, the law of sin that works death in the flesh is a hindrance to faithful observance of the law of Moses.

Paul now adds a third dimension to his play on the word *nomos*. Christians are the recipients of a third law or principle: the law of God's life-giving Spirit.[2] If the law of sin brings us into captivity (7:23), the law of the Spirit liberates us from that bondage. Not that the believer is taken out of the flesh and put beyond the reach of sin's influence. That will not take place until our members are glorified and made new with the future resurrection of the body (8:11). But just as the law of sin outmuscles our ability to live by the law of God, so the law of the Spirit gives us the inner strength to prevail over the law of sin and adhere to the law of God.[3] We could say that the third law (the Spirit) enables us to restrain the urges of the second law (concupiscence) in order to fulfill the moral requirements of the first law (the Torah).

8:2

---

1. It is disputed whether the prepositional phrase "in Christ Jesus" should modify the noun "life" (NABRE, RSV) or the verb "set free" (ESV, NIV).

2. On the three laws in Rom 7–8, see Gordon Fee, *God's Empowering Presence: The Holy Spirit in the Letters of Paul* (Peabody, MA: Hendrickson, 1994), 517, 522. St. Thomas Aquinas, *Commentary on Romans* 604, speaks of four laws, the fourth being the natural law or what Paul calls "the law of my mind" (Rom 7:23).

3. Many scholars identify "the law of sin and death" in 8:2 with the law of Moses. This, I think, is to miss Paul's point—namely, that the Spirit enables us to overcome the inner urging toward sin that operates in the flesh. One commentator who sees this clearly is St. John Chrysostom, *Homilies on Romans* 13.

But why does Paul speak of the *law* of the Spirit rather than, say, the power or grace of the Spirit? Most likely he is thinking of the messianic blessings promised in the Old Testament. For instance, in Jeremiah's New Covenant oracle, the Lord announces he will reconstitute the covenant bond between himself and his people in a new way. Unlike the Old Covenant, with its Torah engraved on tablets of stone, God's promise is that "I will place my law within them, and write it upon their hearts" (Jer 31:33). Similarly, the Lord pledges through Ezekiel, "I will put my spirit within you so that you walk in my statutes, observe my ordinances, and keep them" (Ezek 36:27). An indwelling *law* from God, an indwelling *Spirit* from God, and a new ability to render *obedience* to God—this is precisely the cluster of prophetic hopes that are bundled together in the opening verses of Rom 8.[4] Paul is thus claiming that the Messiah has made good on the Lord's promises in the Scriptures.

8:3   Paul then gives the backstory of this grand announcement. It is not enough to insist that the Torah is "holy and righteous and good" (7:12) if the people charged with keeping it are not. The Mosaic **law** proved weak against stubbornly disobedient human **flesh**; as an exterior written code (7:6), the Torah proved **powerless** to eradicate sin from the interior depths of the heart.

God intervened **by sending his own Son**[5] to resolve the problem of sin in a definitive way. The Messiah's mission was to do what the Torah was unable to do—to vanquish the power of sin entrenched in the flesh. And so the Son of God came **in the likeness of sinful flesh**. This is Paul's way of referring to the incarnation, his version of the Johannine proclamation: "The Word became flesh / and made his dwelling among us" (John 1:14). Paul seems to be walking a theological tightrope in order to convey his meaning precisely: he affirms that the Son entered our history as a real man, but without implying that the Son was tainted by our sinfulness. Paul is aware that the Messiah endured the suffering and death that sin inflicts on our mortal humanity, and yet he remains convinced that Christ "did not know sin" (2 Cor 5:21).

Paul adds that God sent the Son **for the sake of sin**, an expression that can have a general meaning ("to deal with sin," NRSV) or a sacrificial meaning ("to be a sin offering," NIV). Most likely Paul intends the sacrificial meaning, given that the same phrase (in Greek) appears numerous times in the †Septuagint to

---

4. For this same expectation in early Jewish writings outside the Bible, see Barry D. Smith, "'Spirit of Holiness' as Eschatological Principle of Obedience," in *Christian Beginnings and the Dead Sea Scrolls*, ed. John J. Collins and Craig A. Evans (Grand Rapids: Baker Academic, 2006), 75–99.

5. Paul here assumes the preexistence of the Son, as for example in Gal 4:4 and Phil 2:6–7.

refer to a "sin offering."[6] Paul thus reiterates that the death of the Messiah was a sacrifice of atonement (as in Rom 3:25).

Paul's main assertion in this verse is that God **condemned sin in the flesh**. He is referring to Christ's crucifixion and its consequences: the Messiah, having assumed our flesh, rendered a sinless obedience to God to the point of suffering death in the flesh (Phil 2:8). And through this act of obedience in the flesh, divine judgment on sin was carried out. Sin remains an active presence in the world, but God, through the faithfulness of his Son, defeated its power and deprived it of any rightful claim over our humanity.[7]

All of this directly addresses the predicament in Rom 7. The Son of God 8:4 made himself an expiatory sacrifice **so that the righteous decree of the law might be fulfilled in us, who live not according to the flesh but according to the spirit**. And what is the righteous decree of the Torah? Not its several hundred commandments considered individually, but the overarching intent of the whole. For Paul, as for Jesus, "love is the fulfillment of the law" (13:10; see Matt 22:34–40). Love for God and others constitutes the primary objective of the law.

Yet the Torah cannot be kept completely or consistently by those who walk according to the flesh, relying on the inadequate resources of our fallen nature. To love as God commands requires an enabling grace that we receive from above. Paul prepared us to see this when he stated earlier that "the love of God has been poured out into our hearts through the holy Spirit that has been given to us" (Rom 5:5). Christians, in other words, have been gifted with a new power to love. Indwelt by the Spirit, they have been strengthened within to do by grace what is beyond the capacity of nature.

The emphasis here is on God's gift, which is why Paul describes Christian fulfillment of the law in the passive voice. Instead of saying "so that we *might fulfill* . . . the law," he words it the other way around: "so that . . . the law *might be fulfilled* in us." This is an instance of what scholars call a divine passive—the passive form of the verb implies that God is the subject of the action. The significance of this in 8:4 is summed up nicely in the words of one exegete: "The verb here is in the passive, so aware is Paul of the fact that while it remains a free act of man, this 'fulfillment' is much more an act of God, of the Spirit who

6. The NABRE has "purification offering" instead of the traditional "sin offering" in the relevant Old Testament passages (except Ps 40:7). Most occurrences of the phrase can be found in Leviticus (e.g., Lev 5:7; 7:37; 9:2) and Numbers (e.g., Num 6:11; 7:16; 15:24).

7. Brendan Byrne, SJ, *Romans*, SP 6 (Collegeville, MN: Liturgical Press, 1996), 243.

St. Augustine on Law and Grace

LIVING TRADITION

The law was given, in order that grace might be sought; grace was given, in order that the law might be fulfilled. Now it was not through any fault of its own that the law was not fulfilled, but by the fault of the carnal mind; and this fault was to be demonstrated by the law, and healed by grace. "For what the law could not do, in that it was weak through the flesh, God, sending his own Son in the likeness of sinful flesh and for sin, condemned sin in the flesh, that the righteousness of the law might be fulfilled in us, who walk not after the flesh, but after the Spirit."[a]

a. *On the Letter and the Spirit* 34. Translation adapted from *Basic Writings of Saint Augustine*, ed. Whitney J. Oates (New York: Random House, 1948), 1:487.

works within man."[8] Without negating the role of human cooperation in the form of moral effort, Paul is stressing that grace is the driving force behind the Christian life.

8:5–6   Paul begins to elaborate on **the flesh** and **the Spirit** as alternative ways of living. The antithesis is sharply drawn and designed to highlight the stark contrast between godly and ungodly behavior.

Paul appears to be indebted to the classical Jewish notion of the "two ways."[9] When a person lives **according to** the flesh or **according to** the Spirit, the individual's thinking and acting are directed and determined by one or the other. Paul has in view both a mind-set and the moral conduct that flows from it. One who walks according to the flesh habitually yields to sinful and selfish desires in the affairs of life; nearly everything he does is guided by human calculation and takes place on a purely human level. Conversely, one who walks according to the Spirit is mindful of living for God and drawing on the strength of his grace; he is not the center of his universe but a humble servant of the Lord.

Ultimately, the ways of the flesh and the Spirit move in opposite directions toward opposite destinies. On the one hand, the **concern of the flesh is death**.[10] Clearly Paul means more by "death" than bodily expiration and corruption. The desires of the flesh lead away from God toward spiritual death. On the other hand, the **concern of the spirit is life and peace**—eternal life and everlasting

8. Stanislaus Lyonnet, SJ, "Christian Freedom and the Law of the Spirit according to St. Paul," in Ignace de la Potterie, SJ, and Stanislaus Lyonnet, SJ, *The Christian Lives by the Spirit*, trans. John Morriss (New York: Alba House, 1971), 160.

9. See the sidebar "The Two Ways," in Curtis Mitch and Edward Sri, *The Gospel of Matthew*, CCSS (Grand Rapids: Baker Academic, 2010), 119.

10. Or "To set the mind on the flesh is death" (RSV).

peace. Paul uses these terms in connection with the final judgment in chapter 2, when he announces that God will give "eternal life" to those who persevere in good works (2:7) along with "glory, honor, and peace" (2:10).

Many suppose that men and woman in their natural condition are basically **8:7–8** good—not perfect, of course, but generally innocent of serious crimes against God and humanity. Paul looks at the world a bit differently. For him, persons **in the flesh**—in a natural, unregenerate state apart from the saving grace of God—**cannot please God**. They may be upstanding citizens who conscientiously pay their taxes, but they remain in a dire predicament of alienation from God. In fact, they are in a position of **hostility toward God** insofar as they live by the flesh. They are heedless of **the law of God** because they are powerless to overcome the downward pull of sin in their lives. This is the desperate plight of all the descendants of Adam (5:12), who are born into the world as "children of wrath" (Eph 2:3).

Paul, however, assures the Roman Christians that they **are not in the flesh**, **8:9–10** which is to say they are not alienated from God (5:10). Having been reconciled to God, they live **in the spirit**. This is Paul's shorthand way of saying that **the Spirit of God dwells in** believers, making them temples of God's presence in the world, and that believers **belong** to Christ, who likewise dwells **in** them.[11]

In fact, 8:9 may be the closest thing we have in Paul's Letters to a definition of what it means to be a Christian.[12] It is more than simply professing an apostolic creed or belonging to an apostolic church. A Christian is one who is indwelt with **the Spirit**. This is the indispensable condition (signaled by the phrase **if only**) for bearing the name of Christ and belonging to Christ. Everything else plays a supporting role. One will notice, too, that the Spirit is associated with **God** and with **Christ**[13] at the same time. A budding theology of the Trinity seems to have left its mark on this section. The Christian lives in relation to Father, Son, and Spirit.[14]

Paul explains the result of this divine indwelling as it pertains to **the body** and **the spirit**, the material and immaterial constituents of the human person (1 Cor 7:34; 1 Thess 5:23). In this life, Christians are suspended between descent from Adam and total conformity to Christ. They have one foot in the realm of Adamic mortality and one in the realm of messianic salvation. Even though **Christ** lives **in** the believer, the body of the believer is still doomed to perish; it

---

11. For the joint mission of the Son and the Spirit in Paul's Letters, see Yves Congar, *I Believe in the Holy Spirit*, trans. David Smith (New York: Crossroad, 1999), 37–39.

12. James D. G. Dunn, *Romans 1–8*, WBC 38a (Nashville: Nelson, 1988), 444.

13. Paul similarly relates the Spirit to Christ in Gal 4:6 and Phil 1:19.

14. Joseph A. Fitzmyer, SJ, *Romans*, AB 33 (New York: Doubleday, 1993), 481.

is still **dead because of sin**. At the same time, the spirit of the believer, endowed with the divine presence, is **alive because of righteousness**. So it is that the Christian is wasting away on the outside but pulsating with the life of God on the inside, as Paul intimates in 2 Cor 4:16.

8:11   Thankfully, our present mortal condition is not permanent. Directing his gaze to the future, Paul reminds readers that **the Spirit** will not fully accomplish his work in believers until the resurrection of the dead.[15] Just as the Holy Spirit imparts life to our spirits in the present (the era of grace, 8:10), so too will he impart life to our bodies in the future (the era of glory, 8:11). Only then will the people of God be fully conformed to the risen Messiah.

Possession of the Spirit thus serves as a down payment toward our final victory over death. But if the Spirit is a *pledge* of bodily resurrection, the Father is the *agent* of bodily resurrection. He is **the one who raised Jesus from the dead**; he is the One who will **give life** to our **mortal bodies**. The resurrection of the Christian is thus patterned after the resurrection of Christ himself. Easter offers us a glimpse of the last day.

Paul further indicates that the Father raises the dead **through his Spirit**.[16] The expression points to an instrumental and accompanying role played by the Spirit, an idea not unique to Paul. Resurrection by the Spirit of God was already a traditional concept before Paul's time. Its clearest articulation can be found in Ezekiel's vision of the valley of dry bones (Ezek 37:1–14), where the prophet looks on as the Lord makes the dead of Israel live again, summoning his people from the grave and reconstituting their bodies by breathing his "spirit" on them (Ezek 37:10). The same idea is echoed in rabbinic theology.[17] Indeed, this is one of the reasons why Christians profess faith in the Holy Spirit as "the Lord, the Giver of life" (Nicene Creed).[18]

8:12–13   Paul concludes his exposition in this section with an exhortation. His appeal is logically related to what precedes (as indicated by **consequently**) and is intended to drive home the point that Christian living is a high-stakes proposition. Even though Spirit-filled believers are no longer "in the flesh," they can still live **according to the flesh**, despite being under no obligation to do so. The grace of the Spirit is resistible, and so a commitment to follow the Spirit's leading must be made continually.

15. The Jewish and Christian doctrine of the general resurrection includes the belief that God will raise the bodies of the righteous and the wicked alike (Dan 12:2; John 5:28–29; Acts 24:15). Paul's concern in Rom 8:11 is with the righteous only.

16. That the Spirit was active in Christ's resurrection is implied in Rom 1:4 (Catechism 695).

17. †Mishnah *Sotah* 9.15.

18. Richard B. Hays, "Spirit, Church, Resurrection: The Third Article of the Creed as Hermeneutical Lens for Reading Romans," *JTI* 5, no. 1 (2011): 35–48.

The choice facing every believer—and notice that Paul makes his appeal personal by speaking directly to readers as **you**—is between life and death, final justification and final condemnation. The one who yields without repentance to the sinful demands of **the flesh** will **die** an eternal death apart from God; but the one who prevails over the urges of **the body** will **live** an eternal life in God's presence. Paul describes the latter as an effort to **put to death the deeds of the body**. Catholic spirituality terms this "mortification" (from the Latin *mortificare*, which is used to translate Paul's Greek *thanatoō*, "put to death"). It is the action taken by Christians to suppress the "law of sin" that seeks to gain mastery over their lives. Paul's use of the present tense of the verb *thanatoō* indicates that mortification requires a continual exertion that extends over time; it is not a once-and-done deal. At the same time, Paul is no †Pelagian who believes that men and women possess the natural willpower to accomplish such a feat without the inward assistance of grace. Believers can successfully mortify the flesh only **by the spirit**—that is, in conscious reliance on God's indwelling presence. Spiritual discipline must be exercised "in the Spirit."

Children of God by Adoption (8:14–17)

14For those who are led by the Spirit of God are children of God. 15For you did not receive a spirit of slavery to fall back into fear, but you received a spirit of adoption, through which we cry, "Abba, Father!" 16The Spirit itself bears witness with our spirit that we are children of God, 17and if children, then heirs, heirs of God and joint heirs with Christ, if only we suffer with him so that we may also be glorified with him.

OT: Deut 14:1; Isa 63:16; Wis 14:3; Sir 23:1

NT: Mark 14:36; John 1:12; Rom 9:4, 26; Gal 4:4–7; Eph 1:5; 1 John 3:1

Catechism: grace of divine sonship, 257, 1996–97; gifts and fruits of the Spirit, 1830–32; divine sonship in the Old Testament, 441; prayer to God as Father, 2777–82

Lectionary: Trinity Sunday (Year B); Confirmation; Anointing of the Sick; 8:8–17: Pentecost Sunday (Year C); 8:14–23: Commemoration of All the Faithful Departed; Mass for the Deceased

Our familial relationship with God is the controlling idea in this next section of Romans. Adoption, sonship, and inheritance are the constituent elements. These are first of all theological concepts harvested from the Scriptures,[19] where the

19. Brendan Byrne, *Sons of God—Seed of Abraham: A Study of the Idea of the Sonship of God of All Christians in Paul against the Jewish Background*, AnBib 83 (Rome: Biblical Institute, 1979).

covenants between God and Israel created ties of legal kinship between them.[20] At the same time, talk of divine adoption must have resonated with readers immersed in Roman society, where adoption signaled entrance into a new family, with all the privileges and duties of household membership attaching thereto.[21] Paul, building on these foundations, describes Christian salvation as adoption into the family of God. An "interchange" has taken place through the Messiah that makes us children of the Father and heirs of his glory.[22] It would be hard to find a purer distillation of Paul's gospel than this.

8:14   To the blessings enumerated in 8:1–13, Paul adds that **the Spirit** places Christians in a new relationship with God. Those who are guided by the Spirit are no longer merely servants of God but **children of God**. The indwelling of the divine Spirit enables them to "share in the divine nature" (2 Pet 1:4). United with the Son of God, believers are raised above their natural standing to the dignity of being sons and daughters of God.[23] By grace they are made participants in Christ's filial relation to the Father. This is a mystery we can only marvel at, just as John did when he wrote, "See what love the Father has bestowed on us that we may be called the children of God. Yet so we are" (1 John 3:1).

Living as God's children means being **led** by the Spirit (Gal 5:18). Children in a natural family are expected to love and honor their parents, and so it is in the family of God. The Spirit gives direction and inspiration from within so that believers can glorify the Father by their actions and choices. This means bearing the fruit of the Spirit (Gal 5:22–23). It means living as God the Son lived, for he too was led on his earthly journey by the Holy Spirit (Luke 4:1). In fact, giving due weight to the immediately preceding verse, it seems that Paul is thinking primarily about the role of the Spirit in enabling us to mortify the deeds of the flesh.[24]

8:15   Paul clarifies the kind of spirit that Christians have received. It is not **a spirit of slavery to fall back into fear**. Slavery and fear are part of being fallen children of Adam "under the law," as Rom 6–7 implies. For a slave, fear was often the strongest motive for obedience to an uncompromising master. In the spirit of

20. Scott W. Hahn, *Kinship by Covenant: A Canonical Approach to the Fulfillment of God's Saving Promises*, AYBRL (New Haven: Yale University Press, 2009).

21. Trevor J. Burke, *Adopted into God's Family: Exploring a Pauline Metaphor*, NSBT 22 (Downers Grove, IL: InterVarsity, 2006).

22. Morna D. Hooker, *From Adam to Christ: Essays on Paul* (New York: Cambridge University Press, 1990), 13–69.

23. For an articulation of this from a Catholic perspective, see Martin W. Schoenberg, OSC, "St. Paul's Notion on the Adoptive Sonship of Christians," *The Thomist* 28 (1964): 51–75.

24. Pointed out by Trevor J. Burke, "Adopted as Sons (ΥΙΟΘΕΣΙΑ): The Missing Piece in Pauline Soteriology," in *Paul: Jew, Greek, and Roman*, ed. Stanley E. Porter (Leiden: Brill, 2008), 259–87.

slavery, people can live only as captives of sin, powerless to escape the fearful prospect of condemnation that goes with it.

But thanks be to God, believers have been given **a spirit of adoption**. Endowed with the Spirit, the sons and daughters of Adam have become the sons and daughters of God in Christ Jesus, the new Adam. The keynote here is the Greek term *huiothesia*, which means "adoption as sons."[25] Although the word rarely occurs in ancient writings, adoption was widely practiced in upper-class Roman culture, where it was typically viewed as a great honor and an enhancement to one's social standing. No doubt Paul would expect readers to understand divine adoption in these terms; yet the real foundation for his thinking on this subject lies in the Old Testament, where the language of divine sonship ("sons of God") appears with frequency and variety. Sometimes angels are called sons of God (Job 38:7; Ps 29:1). Sometimes the Israelites are called sons of God (Deut 14:1; Isa 63:8). Sometimes the kings of Israel from David's line are called sons of God (2 Sam 7:14; Ps 2:7). Sometimes the nation of Israel is collectively designated the son of God (Exod 4:22; Hosea 11:1).

Paul shows himself well aware of this background in Romans. For instance, he correlates the Davidic lineage of Jesus (Rom 1:3) with Jesus' designation as "Son of God" (1:4). He lists "adoption" as the first of many blessings bestowed on Israel (9:4). He reminds readers of God's promises by citing the prophetic words of Hosea 2:1, which announce that the Lord's restored people will be "sons of the living God" (Rom 9:26 RSV). In the New Covenant, divine sonship is most fully embodied in the divine Son, whose relationship to the Father is extended to us as a participatory grace.

Divine adoption also means that Christians have the honor of addressing God as **"Abba, Father!"** whenever they **cry** out to him in prayer. The Aramaic term *Abba* is generally thought to convey a sense of filial intimacy and endearment.[26] This is the way that children, young and old alike, would typically address their father in the home. The early Christians had a special attachment to the word *Abba* (Gal 4:6), which came from the lips of Jesus during his passion (Mark 14:36). The term was almost a one-word prayer of complete abandonment to the Father and his will.

It is true that the nation of Israel addressed the Lord as "Father," but instances of this are rare (Isa 63:16; Wis 14:3; Sir 23:1). What was occasional in Israel became habitual with the Messiah. Invoking God as Father was Jesus' normal

---

25. J. M. Scott, *Adoption as Sons of God: An Exegetical Investigation into the Background of ΥΙΟΘΕΣΙΑ in the Pauline Corpus* (Tübingen: Mohr Siebeck, 1992), 3–57.

26. Fee, *God's Empowering Presence*, 411.

way, the most prominent and distinctive feature of his prayer and speech. Now Christians indwelt with the Spirit have the privilege of making Christ's prayer their own. Believers "can say 'Abba' because they have become sons in the Son."[27]

8:16–17   Certifying our status as **children of God** is the internal testimony of the **Spirit**, who **bears witness** to our filial dignity. Paul seems to be saying that the Spirit conveys to **our spirit** a comforting awareness that we are sons and daughters of the Most High. This is something produced by the ministry of the Spirit within us, and it will prove to have great practical significance in Paul's discussion of Christian suffering in the remainder of Rom 8.

Before that, however, Paul pursues the logic of adoption to its end. **If we are God's children**, then it follows that we are God's **heirs** (the same reasoning appears in Gal 4:6–7). Again, Paul's thinking pivots around the workings of family life. A father's name and estate pass down as an inheritance to his offspring. So too in the family of God, only here the children are called **joint heirs with Christ**. The significance of this remark will emerge as we read on. Since Jesus is the Father's "firstborn" (Rom 8:29), he is the Father's primary heir (Deut 21:27); nevertheless, he shares what the Father bequeaths to him with the rest of the family—his "many" adoptive "brothers" (Rom 8:29). And what is this inheritance? Nothing less than "all things" seen and unseen (8:32 RSV; see Col 1:15–16; Heb 1:2).

Lest readers become too elated by the abundance of promises, Paul attaches a sobering condition: **if only we suffer with him so that we may also be glorified with him**. Notice the sequence: first suffering, then glory. Notice too the negative implication: no suffering, no glory. Surely this is one of the most underrated sayings of Paul. Yet we ignore it to our peril. Christians must first be conformed to the image of Christ crucified; only then can they hope to bear the image of Christ risen again (1 Cor 15:49). The way this plays out in real life is the focus of the verses that follow.

Revelation and Redemption of the Children of God (8:18–27)

> [18]I consider that the sufferings of this present time are as nothing compared with the glory to be revealed for us. [19]For creation awaits with eager expectation the revelation of the children of God; [20]for creation was made subject to futility, not of its own accord but because of the one who subjected it, in hope [21]that creation itself would be set free from slavery to

27. Pope Benedict XVI, *Saint Paul: General Audiences, July 2, 2008–February 4, 2009*, trans. *L'Osservatore Romano* (San Francisco: Ignatius, 2009), 47.

Exodus, Adoption, and Inheritance

BIBLICAL BACKGROUND

It has been said that Paul views Christian salvation as a new exodus patterned on the old exodus of Israel's deliverance from Egypt. This is beyond dispute in passages outside Romans (1 Cor 10:1–11), and a case can be made that the same current flows just beneath the surface of Rom 6–7 and into Rom 8. In Rom 6–7, the leading ideas and images, as well as their sequential placement in Paul's argument, suggest that the Apostle has the exodus story in mind when he speaks of our baptism, of our transference from slavery to freedom, and of our spiritual marriage with the Lord in the bonds of a New Covenant.[a]

This same exodus motif is continued and completed in Rom 8:14–30, where several details converge around the theme like spokes of a wheel. (1) Paul indicates that Christians are *sons of God* by divine *adoption* (8:14–17), calling to mind how Israel was once the captive son of God, rescued from bondage (Exod 4:22; Hosea 11:1) and united to the Lord as sons by covenant (Deut 14:1). Later in Romans Paul uses the same language of "adoption" to describe this blessing on his people (Rom 9:4). (2) Paul contends that believers address God in the Spirit *as Father* (8:16). Interestingly, the fatherhood of God is first made explicit in the Bible in connection with his care for the exodus pilgrims of Israel in the wilderness (Deut 1:30–31; 8:5; 32:6). (3) Paul affirms that the children of God are *led* by the *Spirit* (Rom 8:14). In the †Septuagint, the language of leading describes how the Lord guided Israel out of bondage and through the wilderness (Deut 8:2, 15; 29:4; Josh 24:8). The prophet Isaiah even specifies that Moses and the people were guided by the Spirit of the Lord (Isa 63:11–14). (4) Paul states that believers *groan* amid the tribulations of life as they await *redemption* (Rom 8:23). Here again one thinks of the exodus, especially the passage where God assures Moses that he has heard the "groaning" of his people in Egypt and will act to "redeem" them in a powerful way (Exod 6:5–6). (5) Finally, Paul heartens readers with the promise of being *heirs of God* (Rom 8:17) who hope to receive all things with Christ (8:32). Readers will recall that the completion of the exodus was Israel's possession of the land of Canaan as the "inheritance" of the Lord's people (Deut 4:21 RSV).

The conclusion thus appears sound: a story that begins with passing through water from slavery to freedom, that develops with a nuptial union between the Lord and people, and that culminates with the Lord leading his people to their inheritance—this is not only the epic narrative of the exodus, but it is also the theological narrative of Rom 6–8.[b]

a. See the sidebars "A New Exodus in Christ," in Rom 6 (p. 99), and "Marriage and Covenant in Scripture," in Rom 7 (p. 111).

b. See Sylvia C. Keesmaat, *Paul and His Story: (Re)Interpreting the Exodus Tradition*, JSNTSup (Sheffield: Sheffield Academic, 1999).

corruption and share in the glorious freedom of the children of God. ²²We know that all creation is groaning in labor pains even until now; ²³and not only that, but we ourselves, who have the firstfruits of the Spirit, we also groan within ourselves as we wait for adoption, the redemption of our bodies. ²⁴For in hope we were saved. Now hope that sees for itself is not hope. For who hopes for what one sees? ²⁵But if we hope for what we do not see, we wait with endurance.

²⁶In the same way, the Spirit too comes to the aid of our weakness; for we do not know how to pray as we ought, but the Spirit itself intercedes with inexpressible groanings. ²⁷And the one who searches hearts knows what is the intention of the Spirit, because it intercedes for the holy ones according to God's will.

OT: Gen 3:16–17; 1 Sam 16:7; Ps 8:4–9; Isa 65:17–25; Mic 4:9–10

NT: John 16:21–22; Acts 14:22; Rom 5:1–11; 1 Cor 15:50–57; 2 Cor 4:17; Eph 1:13–14

Catechism: future glory, 1721; destiny of creation, 280, 1046–48; resurrection of the body, 989–91; Christian hope, 1817–21; prayer in the Spirit, 741, 2736, 2766

Lectionary: Anointing of the Sick; 8:22–27: Pentecost Vigil (Years ABC); St. Teresa of Jesus; 8:26–27: Confirmation; 8:26–30: Common of Holy Men and Women

---

The second half of Rom 8 turns to the subject of suffering. Divine adoption is not a ticket to an untroubled life of ease. On the contrary, it means following the path of the crucified Messiah through a world inundated with frustration and pain. Suffering is an inescapable reality; it pervades the entire created order. But more importantly, Paul contends that embracing trials and giving consent to suffering configures us more closely to Christ. It is a mechanism that helps us die to our selfishness and surrender ourselves more completely to the Lord. Suffering, in other words, has real, redemptive significance in the saving designs of God.

Paul also reminds readers that natural afflictions are transitory compared to the eternal light of glory. The day is coming when believers will be raised immortal and glorious, and the whole of God's material creation will be set free from corruption. Until then, the human and nonhuman worlds continue in a state of groaning (8:22–23) and waiting (8:19, 23, 25) until God's purposes are fully accomplished.

8:18   The section opens with a cost-benefit analysis of suffering in relation to **the glory** that God has in store for his children. In Paul's estimation, **the sufferings of this present time are as nothing** compared to the blessings that await the saints beyond this life. The full magnificence of future glory has yet **to be revealed**; even so, Paul is adamant that no amount of pain or grief in this world should deter us from pressing toward this goal. There is simply no equivalence between time and eternity (2 Cor 4:17). Besides, it is the Father's desire to "Christify" his children—that is, to make them more like Christ in his suffering and death, so that they might also share in his resurrection (as stated in Phil 3:10–11).[28]

Verses 19–22 are a curious mixture of theological prose and imaginative   **8:19–22** poetry. Paul personifies **creation** in order to dramatize its predicament, much as the Scriptures of Israel had done (Isa 24:4; Jer 4:28). The nonhuman world—excluding the angels—is compared both to a slave yearning for freedom and to an expectant mother longing to give birth. Paul envisions **the revelation of the children of God** coinciding with a massive renovation of the visible cosmos. The relationship between man and the world is so close that the fate of the one is tied up with the fate of the other. Creation **awaits** the resurrection of the saints **with eager expectation** because it too is destined to share in **the glorious freedom of the children of God**. The scope of messianic salvation thus embraces the entire natural order, which, like sinful humanity, must be rescued from a state of bondage.[29]

Paul's teaching on the state of the material world is deeply indebted to Scripture.[30] His assertion that **creation was made subject to futility**—obstructed in achieving the purposes for which it was made—rests on the foundation of Gen 3:17–19, where God placed the earth under a curse in the wake of Adam's primal transgression (see also *4 Ezra* 7.11). This curse made the world a place of frustration for man, "alien and hostile" to his efforts to exercise dominion over it (Catechism 400). Creation's subjugation was **not of its own accord** or "not by its own choice." God is **the one who subjected** the world in this way, and yet he did so **in hope**—that is, with the plan of one day reversing the sentence and restoring the cosmos to its original state of integrity.

The story of the fall in Genesis is also the quarry from which Paul hews the imagery of **groaning in labor pains**.[31] Eve's experience of the curse in her role as mother is indicated in the Lord's words to her: "I will greatly multiply your pains and your groaning; in pains you will bear children" (Gen 3:16 LXX). Creation, like Eve and Adam, and because of them, is under divine judgment. Paul also appears to be indebted to the prophets, who used the "pangs of childbirth" motif to describe the Lord's people in distress.[32]

---

28. See the detailed analysis by Siu Fung Wu, *Suffering in Romans* (Eugene, OR: Pickwick, 2015).

29. Scripture teaches that "God did not make death" (Wis 1:13), meaning that death was not an original, constituent feature of human existence at creation but a later development that entered human history "by the envy of the devil" (Wis 2:24). See Catechism 400 and 1008.

30. Jewish apocalyptic texts likewise envisioned a restoration of the created world at the consummation of time (*1 Enoch* 51.4–5; *2 Baruch* 29.1–8; *Sibylline Oracles* 3.777–79).

31. D. T. Tsumura, "An OT Background to Rom 8.22," *NTS* 40 (1994): 620–21.

32. Isa 26:16–18; Jer 4:31; Hosea 13:13; Mic 4:9–10.

Latent in the image of birth pangs is the expectation of delivery, of the joy and relief that follow after suffering reaches its greatest intensity. Creation has been laboring **until now**, but when the time for giving birth comes, it will finally know the freedom that comes with new life. That is, it will be **set free from slavery to corruption**.[33] Reconstituted in the glory of God—a concept closely related to immortality in Romans—creation will be delivered from the laws of death and decay. This too is an expectation that Paul derived from the Old Testament, especially Isaiah's visions of a "new heaven" and a "new earth" where toil and strife and death no longer have a place (see Isa 11:6–9; 25:7–9; 65:17–25).

8:23   Paul adds that **we ourselves groan** in unison with creation **as we wait for adoption**. This statement appears to be in tension with 8:14–17, where Paul contends that believers are already the adopted sons and daughters of God because they possess the Holy Spirit. But the tension is more apparent than real. Divine adoption as Paul describes it encompasses two events: baptism and bodily resurrection. It has its beginning in the sacrament and awaits its completion at the end of history. Believers receive the grace of adoption, which imparts life to their spirits (8:10), before their **bodies** are made full beneficiaries of God's **redemption**.

This same distinction between present and future benefits is programmed into Paul's description of **the Spirit** as **the firstfruits**. Here he alludes to the liturgical traditions of Israel. The firstfruits were the first stalks of grain gathered from the spring harvest and taken to the temple in Jerusalem. There they were offered to the Lord in thanksgiving for a successful beginning and in petition for his blessing on the rest of the harvest season. Paul uses this logic of the part in advance of the whole to describe the Spirit as a down payment on the full amount of God's blessings to come. In the wording of Ephesians, the Spirit is given to us as "the first installment of our inheritance" (Eph 1:14).

8:24–25   All of this comes under the rubric of **hope**. For Paul, Christian hope is neither presumption nor wishful thinking about salvation. It is not something **that sees for itself** how things will turn out for believers who are still struggling in the world. We know by *faith* that God's purposes will be fully and finally realized for creation as a whole, but *hope* is our personal confidence that God will make good on his promises to us, provided we uphold our end of the deal (5:1–5). Final salvation is held out before us but is not yet within our grasp. And so we must **wait with endurance** to attain it.

33. That groaning and release from slavery recall the exodus story; see the sidebar "Exodus, Adoption, and Inheritance" (p. 137).

Paul goes on to state that our prayers in the midst of suffering are not only   8:26–27
heard by God; they are also *helped* by God. The **Spirit**, he says, **comes to the
aid of our weakness** by interceding for us with **inexpressible groanings**. The
Spirit adds his voice to the chorus of groans rising up from this valley of tears,
translating our wordless moans and sighs into filial petitions to the Father. Paul
expects readers will find this a comforting thought, since suffering causes great
disturbance in our lives and confuses us about the purpose of our trials so that
we do not know how to pray as we ought. More than that, our feeble understanding of God's ways is such that we desperately need help in the struggle to
pray **according to God's will**.

Despite the challenges to prayer that tribulation forces on the mind, the **one
who searches hearts**—the Father from whom nothing in our lives is hidden
from view—**knows what is the intention of the Spirit**. He hears the distraught
cries of his children with divine clarity, since the Spirit **intercedes for the holy
ones according to God's will**. Perhaps Paul is thinking of our tendency to
pray for what we want rather than seeking from God what we need to grow in
Christian maturity. If so, then the Spirit's ministry must include bringing our
petitions into closer alignment with the Father's plan to save us.

More Than Conquerors in Christ (8:28–39)

[28]We know that all things work for good for those who love God, who
are called according to his purpose. [29]For those he foreknew he also predestined to be conformed to the image of his Son, so that he might be
the firstborn among many brothers. [30]And those he predestined he also
called; and those he called he also justified; and those he justified he also
glorified.

[31]What then shall we say to this? If God is for us, who can be against
us? [32]He who did not spare his own Son but handed him over for us all,
how will he not also give us everything else along with him? [33]Who will
bring a charge against God's chosen ones? It is God who acquits us. [34]Who
will condemn? It is Christ [Jesus] who died, rather, was raised, who also is
at the right hand of God, who indeed intercedes for us. [35]What will separate us from the love of Christ? Will anguish, or distress, or persecution,
or famine, or nakedness, or peril, or the sword? [36]As it is written:

"For your sake we are being slain all the day;
we are looked upon as sheep to be slaughtered."

³⁷**No, in all these things we conquer overwhelmingly through him who loved us. ³⁸For I am convinced that neither death, nor life, nor angels, nor principalities, nor present things, nor future things, nor powers, ³⁹nor height, nor depth, nor any other creature will be able to separate us from the love of God in Christ Jesus our Lord.**

OT: Gen 22:1–18; 50:20; Exod 4:22; Pss 8:6–7; 44:23; 89:28; 110:1; Isa 50:8; 53:7

NT: Rom 5:3–5, 10; 1 Cor 15:20–28; Phil 3:21; Col 1:15–18; Heb 2:6–10; 7:25; 1 John 2:1

Catechism: hope and future glory, 1821, 2016; divine providence, 313–14, 395; God's saving plan, 257, 381; Abraham and the Father, 2572; Jesus as intercessor, 2634

Lectionary: 8:28–30: Common of the Blessed Virgin Mary; 8:28–32: Conferral of Infant Baptism; 8:31b–34: 2nd Sunday of Lent (Year B); 8:31b–39: Sts. Perpetua and Felicity; Common of Martyrs; 8:31b–35, 37–39: Commemoration of All the Faithful Departed; Sacrament of Marriage

This crescendo of Rom 8 expounds the connection between Christian suffering and Christ's love. In times of adversity, it is tempting to think that God is distant, unmoved by our anguish, perhaps showing his disfavor. But in Paul's view, suffering is God's way of sculpting us into the image of his Son. It is the sign of an unbreakable bond of love that unites believers to Christ. As with the crucified Messiah, so with his cruciform people: what looks and feels like defeat is really our greatest triumph.

8:28   Paul appeals to a conviction he has in common with his Christian readers: **We know that all things work for good for those who love God, who are called according to his purpose.**³⁴ God, who is in sovereign control of history, is steering the course of human and cosmic events to a glorious end, in spite of the evil that presently engulfs the world. This is something Paul discovered from contemplating Scripture. One thinks, for example, of the patriarch Joseph, who was betrayed by his brothers but raised up by God to rescue his kin. Addressing his brothers, he explained, "Even though you meant harm to me, God meant it for good, to achieve this present end, the survival of many people" (Gen 50:20). Paul expresses a similar sentiment: the tragedies of life do not fall outside the scope of divine providence. They are part of an orchestrated plan to bring us unforeseen blessing.

The recipients of this good are **those who love God**. Earlier Paul said that Christians are endowed with a new capacity to love the Lord by the inpouring of the Spirit (Rom 5:5). Putting two and two together, we can say that divine providence works **good** for those who live by the Spirit. In fact, the expression "those who love God" is biblical shorthand for "those who are loyal to the Lord and live by his covenant" (see Exod 20:6; Deut 7:9; Josh 22:5). Love for God is

34. Modern translations differ on whether the subject of the verb "work" is "all things" (NABRE, NRSV, ESV) or "God" (RSV, NIV, JB) because ancient manuscripts of Romans attest both readings.

not merely a heartfelt affection; it is also evidenced in the concrete by keeping his commandments (John 15:10).

Paul examines the successive steps of Christian salvation. Both history and **8:29–30** eternity are punctuated by the Lord's gracious initiative on our behalf. First, God **foreknew** a community of believers and **predestined** them for filial adoption in Christ "before the foundation of the world" (Eph 1:4).[35] Foreknowledge, in the language of the Bible, is closely related to God choosing or electing persons for a sacred purpose (Jer 1:5). Predestination involves setting a plan in place to bring those who are chosen to the blessings that God has prepared. These are the actions of God hidden in eternity.

Stepping from eternity into history, Paul speaks of three more events that affect the lives of his people in a decisive way. At some point God **called** us to faith in Jesus Christ. Thereupon he **justified** us by his grace, making us righteous in his sight, and even **glorified** us by infusing his Spirit to dwell within us. It is true that our glorification will not take place in full until our bodies are raised immortal on the last day, but even now glorification is under way. It is a process of transformation that unfolds in a hidden way as the Spirit works to make believers more and more like Christ (see 2 Cor 3:18). So it is that Paul views God's grace at work before history, throughout history, and at the end of history.

The Father's purpose in all this is that we should be **conformed to the image of his Son**. By conformity Paul means that we are destined to "participate in a way of being" that now characterizes the life of the Lord Jesus.[36] In other words, Paul has the general resurrection in view. The glory and honor intended for Adam, who was made *in* the image of God (Gen 1:27), has now been attained by the risen Lord, who *is* the image of God (Col 1:15) and is crowned and elevated over all things (Ps 8:6–7; Heb 2:6–10). Believers are destined to share in this kingly splendor at the resurrection, when Christ "will change our lowly body to conform with his glorified body" (Phil 3:21) in order that we might "bear the image" of the new and heavenly Adam (1 Cor 15:49).

Likewise, God intended that Christ should be **the firstborn among many brothers**. Here again Paul touches on the mystery of divine adoption (as in Rom 8:14–17, 23). When the Father grants us a share in the sonship of Jesus, we become younger brothers and sisters in the family of God. Kinship is extended by grace, and the household of God is enlarged. But since Jesus is the eternal Son of the Father, the dignity of being the firstborn belongs to him.

---

35. For theological considerations concerning predestination, see Reginald Garrigou-Lagrange, OP, *Predestination: The Meaning of Predestination in Scripture and the Church*, trans. Dom Bede Rose, OSB (Rockford, IL: TAN, 1998).

36. Byrne, *Romans*, 272.

But this is only part of the picture. In the biblical tradition the idea of the "firstborn" has significance beyond that of birth order.[37] In the domestic family, the firstborn son was the principal heir of his father, the one granted rights to receive a double portion of his inheritance (Deut 21:15–17). In the larger human family, Adam and Eve are the firstborn children of God, given royal dominion over creation (Gen 1:27; 5:3). Among the nations Israel is the Lord's firstborn son, the people chosen to bring the nations back to God (Exod 4:22). Among heads of state, the Davidic king of Israel was hailed the firstborn son of God, making him a leader among the rulers of the earth (Ps 89:27). For Paul, Jesus embodies all of these firstborn prerogatives in himself. He is the Father's primary heir; he is the new Adam who reclaims the glory and dominion of the old; he is the faithful Israelite who fulfills the national vocation of his people to enlighten the world; and he is the Davidic Messiah who is enthroned over all nations.

8:31   Verse 31 moves us into the rhetorical climax of Rom 8. As in earlier chapters, Paul poses questions to carry along the discussion, but at this point his tone is lyrical rather than polemical. His emotional intensity seems to be dialed to its highest setting.

His lead-in question is twofold: **What then shall we say to this?** And, **If God is for us, who can be against us?** The two questions are interdependent. All that Paul has explained so far in Rom 5–8 indicates that God, being a loving Father, is on the side of his children. Believers cannot reasonably doubt his love or commitment, given what he has already done for them through the joint ministries of the Son and the Spirit. And since no creature is his equal and no worldly power can thwart his purposes, it follows that no one and nothing arrayed against us can hope to rob us of our inheritance in Christ.

8:32   Paul gets at the same thing in verse 32, in which he alludes to one of the most memorable stories in the Bible: the binding and sacrifice of Isaac (Gen 22:1–18). Scripture portrays the event as the supreme test of Abraham's faithfulness. Jewish tradition remembers it as a source of divine blessings for Israel.[38] Paul's reference to this episode is not explicit; he says only that the Father **did not spare** (Greek *ou pheidomai*) **his own Son.** Nearly identical words appear in the †Septuagint, where the Lord commends Abraham because he "did not spare" his "beloved son" Isaac but was willing to offer him in sacrifice (Gen 22:12 LXX).

Paul thus implicitly relates the crucifixion of Jesus to the sacrifice of Isaac. It is a †typology that includes the actions of the Father as well as the Son.

---

37. For an insightful discussion, see Tom Holland, *Contours of Pauline Theology: A Radical New Survey of the Influences on Paul's Biblical Writings* (Ross-shire, UK: Mentor, 1994), 237–86.

38. See, among other works, James Swetnam, SJ, *Jesus and Isaac: A Study of the Epistle to the Hebrews in Light of the Aqedah* (Rome: Biblical Institute, 1981).

Abraham, the loving and faithful father, foreshadows the divine Father, who **handed over** his Son to death **for us all**; Isaac, the only beloved son, prefigures the divine Son as a sacrificial victim. From this Paul reasons that if the Father held nothing back to achieve our salvation, not even his cherished Son, will he not follow through and **give us everything else along with him?**[39] By this Paul means that we are destined to share in the cosmic dominion of Christ, the "heir of all things" (Heb 1:2).

Paul's rhetorical questions continue in rapid succession: **Who will bring a charge against God's chosen ones?** Who in this world could hope to file a charge against the children of God and successfully litigate the case, when the judge who presides is their Father? Readers familiar with the Bible might think specifically of Satan (Hebrew for "accuser") in light of texts such as Zech 3:1–2. Paul, however, keeps the question open-ended as a way of ruling out the possibility absolutely. **8:33–34**

He reinforces the idea with **It is God who acquits** or "justifies," followed by **Who will condemn?** Most commentators read these words as a paraphrase of Isa 50:8, where the prophet announces of the Lord, "He who declares my innocence is near. Who will oppose me?" Again, Paul is looking forward to the last judgment, when God will render his final verdict of justification on the lives of the faithful (as in Rom 2:13). If ever a judicial ruling was deemed incontestable, this would be it.

And just to extinguish every last ember of doubt, Paul adds that **Christ [Jesus] who died** and **was raised** is enthroned as Lord and king **at the right hand of God**—yet another allusion to Scripture, this time to the messianic Ps 110:1. Jesus, the royal Davidic Messiah, uses his position of authority and proximity to the Father to advocate for his younger siblings on earth. In a word, the Son **intercedes for us** in heaven, just as the Spirit intercedes in our hearts (Rom 8:27). Not only is the judge our Father, according to Paul, but also we have the premier defense lawyer in our firstborn brother.

In a sense, Paul's barrage of questions boils down to one: Does anything in this world have the power to **separate us from the love of Christ?** Again, the answer is a thunderous no! Not **anguish, or distress, or persecution, or famine, or nakedness, or peril, or the sword**. These types of suffering bring us to a fuller participation in the Messiah's passion and produce a greater degree of likeness between Christians and Christ. Following in the path of Jesus, who was "like a lamb led to the slaughter" (Isa 53:7), believers too are **looked upon** **8:35–36**

---

39. Perhaps Paul, in raising the issue of inheritance, is still thinking of Christ in terms of Isaac, to whom Abraham "gave everything that he owned" (Gen 25:5).

Bearing Curses Redemptively and Psalm 44

Many find it odd that Paul quotes Ps 44 at the pinnacle of Rom 8. In the midst of a full-on celebration of God's love in Christ, the Apostle cites the words of a communal lament that bemoans the hardships of Israel in exile. In particular, the psalmist puzzles over the suffering of the innocent and pleads for divine deliverance. The chosen people are experiencing the curses of the covenant in the form of deportation and death in a foreign land, and yet the psalmist speaks for those who have *not* been false to the covenant. In other words, he seems to be voicing the frustrations of the faithful †remnant of Israel who suffer in solidarity with the unfaithful masses. Indeed, part of the lesson conveyed in Ps 44 is that suffering cannot always be understood as divine punishment, for many of God's people experience it undeservedly.[a] In this instance, even the pious of Israel are drawn into the afflictions that weigh heavy on the exilic community for its national infidelity.

Paul reads Ps 44 with reference to the Church. Christians are likewise besieged by affliction and looked upon as "sheep to be slaughtered," despite their faithful adherence to the gospel (Rom 8:36). They too are harassed, persecuted, and even put to death for the Lord's sake, yet they have done nothing wrong to provoke such antagonism from the world.[b] This may seem illogical and unjust, but Paul envisions Christians sharing in the passion of Christ. Psalm 44 has been rightly described as "the voice of the church declaring its participation in the cross of Israel's Messiah."[c] Jesus is the Innocent One par excellence, yet he bore the curses of Israel's broken covenant in an act of messianic redemption (Gal 3:13). The disciples of Jesus are called to share the same burden. They too have crosses to bear. In fact, it appears that Paul's list of afflictions in Rom 8:35 deliberately evokes the covenant curses that sin brings on the world: anguish and distress (Deut 28:53, 55, 57 LXX), persecution (Deut 28:25, 29–34), famine (Lev 26:26; Jer 29:18), nakedness (Deut 28:48; Ezek 23:28–29), and the sword (Lev 26:25; Ezek 21:8–9). Paul thereby implies that the suffering faithful are taken up into the mystery of Christ's passion, an event where the curses of the past are turned into blessings for the future. They too experience the curses of pain and death in a redemptive way that brings them into closer conformity with the crucified and risen Messiah.

a. Pointed out by Richard B. Hays, *Echoes of Scripture in the Letters of Paul* (New Haven: Yale University Press, 1989), 60.
b. According to Wu, *Suffering*, 198–206, the psalm is meant to reassure the Christians in Rome of their innocence.
c. Tyler A. Stewart, "The Cry of Victory: A Cruciform Reading of Psalm 44:22 in Romans 8:36," *JSPHL* 3, no. 1 (2013): 45.

by the unbelieving world **as sheep to be slaughtered** (a verbatim quotation from Ps 44:23 LXX).

Paul's conclusion, which caps off not only this chapter but also the whole **8:37–39** of Rom 5–8, is that in **all these things**—meaning "all these sufferings"—**we conquer overwhelmingly**. The very things that afflict us are what make us sharers in Jesus' triumph over sin. And, as always, Paul is quick to clarify that this takes place not by our own power but **through him who loved us**. Thanks to his grace, no circumstance or created power outside ourselves is capable of severing the bond that joins us to the risen Lord.

Finally, to show how **convinced** he is that God's **love** is unconquerable, Paul recites a litany of created entities that mark out the boundaries of human existence and habitation. He puts these forward as potential rather than actual dangers to a permanent participation in Christ. Paul lists the circumstances before and after mortality takes over (**death** and **life**); the unseen host of spiritual beings, whether good or evil (**angels**, **principalities**, and **powers**); the happenings of history at the moment or still to come (**present things** and **future things**); and the spatial extremities of the world, which are traced out by the course of planets and stars climbing to their zenith and then sinking out of sight below the horizon (**height** and **depth**). Nothing in the created universe, in any of its domains or dimensions, can **separate us from the love of God in Christ Jesus our Lord**.

Reflection and Application (8:37–39)

It is not uncommon to hear televangelists and radio preachers appealing to the final lines of Rom 8 to support a doctrine known as "once saved, always saved." This is the non-Catholic belief that a Christian, once he or she accepts Jesus as personal Savior and Lord, is instantly and permanently saved. Believers will continue to struggle with sin, of course, but this does nothing to jeopardize their salvation. Heaven is assured for the true believer.

Not all Protestant communions subscribe to this teaching, but many do. And those who profess an absolute assurance of salvation claim to find it in Rom 8, among other places. The reason is fairly obvious. Nowhere more than in Rom 8 does Paul trumpet the strength of God's love for us. He insists in the most strenuous terms that nothing in heaven or on earth, nothing seen or unseen, can drive a wedge between Christians and Christ. The "once saved, always saved" interpretation sounds plausible, at least when these verses are read in isolation.

But Paul would have us interpret his words in context. If we step back a few verses, we see that his discussion is dominated by the question of suffering. At issue is whether life's most painful experiences give us reason to doubt God's love. When Paul runs down the list of potential threats to our union with Christ, he singles out anguish, distress, persecution, famine, nakedness, and sword (8:35). Nothing is said about apostasy, adultery, immorality, idolatry, debauchery, and the like. In other words, Paul denies *suffering* the power to separate us from Christ, not *sin*. His entire focus is on painful calamities, not personal conduct. Besides, Paul is emphatic in other passages that sin without repentance does in fact pose a threat to obtaining a heavenly inheritance (e.g., Rom 2:5–10; 8:13; 1 Cor 6:9–10; Gal 5:19–21).

This is not to diminish the grandeur of Paul's remarks at the closing of Rom 8. On the contrary, he wants believers to have a bulletproof assurance that God loves them. He wants us to be solidly certain of this fact as a matter of Christian faith, so that nothing the world throws at us will cause us to doubt it.

God's Faithfulness to Israel

Romans 9:1–33

The transition from Rom 8 into the next major section of the letter, Rom 9–11, seems abrupt at first, as if Paul suddenly turns the wheel and begins speeding off in a new direction. Some have viewed these chapters as little more than a tangent sandwiched between the doctrinal instruction of Rom 1–8 and the moral exhortations of Rom 12–16—interesting, but not really part of the logical structure of the letter. Thankfully, this simplistic assessment has fallen out of favor.[1] Since the middle of the twentieth century, scholars have come to see that Rom 9–11 is not only a vital part of the epistle, tied tightly and thematically to the rest of Romans, but is also something of a fireworks finale. It is the final burst of Paul's theological genius lighting up the whole horizon of God's actions in history.

These chapters focus on the place of Israel in the plan of God, which can be seen as the next logical step in Paul's exposition of the gospel in Romans. We have seen in earlier chapters that Paul defends the righteousness of God in justifying Jews and Gentiles on equal terms. But this has placed a question mark beside Israel's special role in salvation history now that the Messiah has come. Does resistance to the gospel among Jews mean that God has rejected his beloved Israel? Does the present dilemma of unbelief, which is simply the latest in a long line of national crises for the chosen people, mean that God has not been faithful to Israel? And what of all the promises in Scripture that God

---

1. Mark Reasoner, "Romans 9–11 Moves from Margin to Center, from Rejection to Salvation: Four Grids for Recent English-Language Exegesis," in *Between Gospel and Election: Explorations in the Interpretation of Romans 9–11*, ed. Florian Wilk and J. Ross Wagner (Tübingen: Mohr Siebeck, 2010), 73–89.

will save and restore the twelve tribes of Israel after centuries of judgment and exile have whittled the nation down to a bare †remnant? These are the pressing matters that Paul takes up in Rom 9–11.

But I would suggest that even more is going on in these chapters. Paul is continuing his theological account of divine sonship from Rom 8 and applying its principles directly to Israel. He declared in chapter 8 that Christians indwelt with the Spirit have received the gift of divine sonship in Jesus Christ (8:15), who is revealed as the "firstborn" among many adopted children in the family of God (8:29). Then, in chapter 9, he notes that first among the blessings bestowed on Israel was the gift of adoptive sonship (9:4). It is not an accident that he is reprising this theme here. Paul wants to show that a right understanding of divine sonship is critical for grasping God's purpose of †election regarding the sons of Israel; divine sonship is properly defined not according to the flesh, by physical descent, but according to the Spirit, by election, promise, and faith. The Father has only one Son by nature, and so sonship among God's people can only be a participation by grace in the divine sonship of Christ the firstborn. This truth enables Paul to show that God's promises to Israel, the sons of the Lord by covenant, could never be tied exclusively to biological lineage. Divine sonship rests on the calling and promises of God (9:6–13). The biblical history of Israel verifies this fact for Paul, who turns to the Scriptures throughout Rom 9–11 to show that "elect" Israel has always been a fraction of the larger family of "ethnic" Israel. The faithfulness of God to Israel is thus demonstrated by his promises reaching fulfillment in a remnant chosen by grace (11:5). It is in that chosen portion of Israel that acceptance of the gospel is found and the divine promise to call forth "children of the living God" is fully realized (9:26).

Besides this theological concern with divine sonship, Rom 9–11 is shaped by its connection with the prophetic expectations of the Old Testament. At the outset of the letter, Paul declares that his gospel fulfills what God "promised previously through his prophets in the holy scriptures" (1:2). The point is significant. Prophecies about the age of messianic fulfillment envision the salvation of Israel alongside the Gentiles, not the rejection of Israel as God's people and their replacement by Gentiles. This is a deeply meaningful hope in the Bible. The majority of the tribes, forming the northern kingdom of Israel, were carried off into captivity by the Assyrians in the eighth century BC, never to return. The handful of tribes that remained, forming the southern kingdom of Judah, were later carried off by the Babylonians in the sixth century BC; of these, only some made it back to the homeland of Judah. Even so, the Lord promised to recover the scattered tribes of Israel and Judah and to reunite them under the kingship of the Davidic

Messiah (Isa 11:11–12; Jer 23:5–6; Ezek 37:15–28; Hosea 3:4–5). Paul sets himself the task in Rom 9–11 of showing how his mission as "the apostle to the Gentiles" (11:13) makes this a reality. It achieves both the salvation of the Gentiles and the restoration of "all Israel" (11:26). For when the nations accept the gospel with the "obedience of faith" (1:5), they place themselves under the lordship of Jesus Christ, the messianic heir of David and restorer of his kingdom (1:3; 15:12).

Finally, it must be noted that Rom 9–11 boasts the highest concentration of Old Testament quotations in any three chapters of Paul's Letters. According to the statistics of one scholar, "nearly 40% of Romans 9–11 is composed of Old Testament quotations . . . and more than half of the Old Testament citations in Romans appear in Romans 9–11, and 66% of all Pauline quotations are found in Romans. That means more than one-third of the Old Testament quotations in the authentic Pauline Letters are found in Romans 9–11."[2] The significance of this must be appreciated at the outset, since careful analysis reveals that Paul's scriptural citations carry the weight of his argument in these chapters.[3] Rarely, if ever, does he reference the Bible merely to add ornamentation to his preaching; and nowhere are his citations mere proof texts buttressing convictions that he has derived through other means. Romans 9–11 is best viewed, then, not simply as Paul's theological reflection on history but as Paul's theological reading of Scripture.

God's Gifts to Israel (9:1–5)

---

[1]I speak the truth in Christ, I do not lie; my conscience joins with the holy Spirit in bearing me witness [2]that I have great sorrow and constant anguish in my heart. [3]For I could wish that I myself were accursed and separated from Christ for the sake of my brothers, my kin according to the flesh. [4]They are Israelites; theirs the adoption, the glory, the covenants, the giving of the law, the worship, and the promises; [5]theirs the patriarchs, and from them, according to the flesh, is the Messiah. God who is over all be blessed forever. Amen.

OT: Gen 12:1–3; Exod 4:22; 19:6; 32:31–32; Lev 1–7; Deut 14:1; Wis 12:21; Jer 31:3

NT: Matt 1:1–17; Rom 1:3; 10:1; 11:1, 29; Gal 1:8–9; Eph 2:12; 1 Tim 2:7

Catechism: the Church and the Jewish people, 839–40; Moses, mediator and intercessor, 2574–77; Jesus, the divine Lord, 449

2. Daniel J.-S. Chae, *Paul as Apostle to the Gentiles: His Apostolic Self-Awareness and Its Influence on the Soteriological Argument in Romans* (Carlisle, UK: Paternoster, 1997), 217–18n18.

3. James W. Aageson, "Scripture and Structure in the Development of the Argument in Romans 9–11," *CBQ* 48 (1986): 265–89.

Romans 9 opens with a strange combination of lament and celebration. Paul wants to assure readers in the strongest terms that he is grieving for Israel. At the same time he speaks admiringly of seven unique gifts entrusted by God to Israel at Mount Sinai. The question is how these two things are related. The blessings enumerated, from adoption to the patriarchs, are those that mark out the chosen people as the nation set apart for the Lord's special purposes. But there is an eighth gift as well—the Messiah—and this is where the problem arises. Paul is pained by the fact that so many of his kinsmen by race have refused this crowning blessing of God to his people (11:20, 23).

9:1–2   The opening verse of Rom 9 is an oath. Paul is adamant that he is speaking **the truth in Christ** and that he does **not lie** about having **great sorrow** and **constant anguish** in his heart. Similar statements found in his other letters suggest that he wants to dispel rumors or suspicions to the contrary (2 Cor 11:31; Gal 1:20; 1 Tim 2:7). It is probable that certain people had taken Paul's evangelization of the Gentiles in the wrong way, as though he had abandoned all hope of bringing his unbelieving brethren to faith in Christ.

But has Paul ceased to be concerned about the salvation of his own people? Not at all. He is deeply grieved by their unbelief, and the internal testimony of his **conscience** is corroborated by the witness of **the holy Spirit**. Paul could not have declared his heartache more strenuously. In the next chapter, he will add that he prays for the "salvation" of his kinsmen (Rom 10:1).

9:3   Paul then reveals the degree of his concern for the covenant people. Not content to stand aside while so many refuse their inheritance, Paul makes the astounding claim: **I could wish that I myself were accursed**[4] **and separated from Christ for the sake of my brothers, my kin according to the flesh**. Most scholars understand this expression to mean: "I would sacrifice my life for my unbelieving kindred if such an act could bring them salvation." There is some question about Paul's exact frame of mind, since the prospect includes separation from the Messiah.[5] Whatever his precise meaning, it is clear that Paul, out of a deep affection for his people, would willingly forfeit his life and union with Christ if this would bring them to conversion.

Paul is talking about bearing the curses of the covenant, a subject that links this chapter closely to the preceding chapter.[6] In 8:35–36 he listed seven traditional curses that believers face in a world that persecutes Christianity. But instead of separating us from Christ, these sufferings conform us to the image

---

4. Paul uses the Greek term *anathema*, meaning "devoted to destruction."
5. Greek *apo tou Christou.*
6. C. Marvin Pate, *Romans*, TTCS (Grand Rapids: Baker Books, 2014), 186.

of Christ, who became "a curse for us" on the cross (Gal 3:13). Here Paul desires to imitate Jesus in the fullest and deepest way possible: to suffer the curses of the covenant in a way that transforms them into a blessing for others. If possible, he would surrender himself to death to bring his kin into the grace of the New Covenant.

Reinforcing this picture, Paul assumes the posture of Moses interceding for Israel at Mount Sinai following the golden calf apostasy (Exod 32–34).[7] Only weeks after receiving the Torah, along with the mission of being the Lord's holy people, Israel forsakes the covenant and bows before an Egyptian idol. This occasions a national crisis in which Moses intercedes before the Lord to mitigate the curses deserved by Israel. Initially God proposes to annihilate his people and to start again by making a great nation from Moses (Exod 32:10). But Moses protests on the grounds that God must remain faithful to his covenant with the patriarchs, even when his people prove unfaithful. So the prophet confesses Israel's sin and puts forward an alternative: "Ah, this people has committed a grave sin in making a god of gold. . . . Now if you would only forgive their sin! But if you will not, then blot me out of the book that you have written" (Exod 32:31–32). If Israel as a whole must be destroyed, then Moses insists on sharing the fate of his people. His is the heart of a godly mediator who identifies so closely with his own that reconciliation with the Lord is pursued no matter the cost to himself.

Paul's remarks in verse 3 are reminiscent of Moses' entreaty at Sinai. He too confronts a crisis of national unfaithfulness; he too would offer to share the fate of his people; he too seeks a path toward mercy and restoration for Israel.

In verse 4, Paul identifies his kindred as the **Israelites**. Readers routinely as-   9:4–5
sume that Paul is talking about "the Jews," but this is imprecise. The two terms are not synonymous. In the Bible and other ancient sources, a "Jew" (Greek *Ioudaios*) is typically a member of the tribe of Judah, a person who resides in the land of Judea, or one who professes the postexilic religion of Judaism.[8] An "Israelite" (Greek *Israēlitēs*), however, is a member of any of the twelve tribes descended from the patriarch Jacob, who was renamed Israel. There is overlap, of course, but "Israelite" is a more encompassing term than "Jew." Members of the tribe of Judah can rightly be called Israelites; but the great majority of Israelites are not Jews in the tribal sense, since the latter are only a fraction of the former.

---

7. Brian Abasciano, *Paul's Use of the Old Testament in Romans 9.1–9*, LNTS 301 (London: T&T Clark, 2005), 45–115.

8. Shaye J. D. Cohen, *The Beginnings of Jewishness: Boundaries, Varieties, Uncertainties*, Hellenistic Culture and Society 31 (Berkeley: University of California Press, 1999); Josephus, *Jewish Antiquities* 11.133, 173.

St. Francis de Sales on Paul's Zeal for His Brethren

LIVING TRADITION

> Saint Paul desired to be filled with ignominy, crucified, cut off, abandoned, and sacrificed for the sin of the Jews so as to bear the curse and punishment they had merited. Therefore, just as our Savior bore the sins of the world, and in such wise was made anathema, sacrificed for sin, and abandoned by his Father, without ceasing to be perpetually the *beloved Son in whom* the Father is *well pleased*, so also the holy apostle truly desired to be anathema, and cut off from his Master so as to be abandoned by him and left to the mercy of the reproaches and punishments due to the Jews. But he never desired to be deprived of the charity and grace of his Lord, from which nothing could ever separate him.[a]

a. *Treatise on the Love of God* 10.16. Translation adapted from St. Francis de Sales, *Treatise on the Love of God*, vol. 2, trans. John K. Ryan (Rockford, IL: TAN, 1974), 189.

Why stress this distinction? Because it represents a master key in the effort to unlock Rom 9–11. In chapters 1–8, Paul used the language of "Jew" or "Jews" nine times as a people distinct from Gentiles, but not once did he make reference to "Israel" or "Israelites." In chapters 9–11, the situation is almost completely reversed: there are only two references to "Jew" and "Jews," and thirteen references to "Israel" and "Israelites." I read this as a clear signal that Paul has broadened his perspective. The Jews are still in the picture, for sure, but Paul is zooming out to include Israel's entire tribal family within the scope of his exposition. The significance of this will become clear as we proceed through Rom 9–11, culminating in Paul's announcement that "all Israel will be saved" (11:26).[9]

At the moment, however, Paul looks back at the founding gifts that made Israel the †elect people of God. These are the blessings received and confirmed at Mount Sinai that marked them out as the Lord's special possession: Israel received a divine **adoption** by covenant in connection with the exodus and Sinai events (Exod 4:22; Hosea 11:1). Israel witnessed the fire and smoke of the Lord's **glory** enveloping Sinai (Exod 19:16–20) and making its dwelling in the tabernacle of Moses (Exod 40:34). Israel is the appointed heir of the divine **covenants** that God made with Abraham (Gen 17:1–14; 22:16–18), Moses

9. See Scott W. Hahn, "'All Israel Will Be Saved': The Restoration of the Twelve Tribes in Romans 9–11," *Letter & Spirit* 10 (2015): 63–104; and James M. Scott, "'And Then All Israel Will Be Saved' (Rom 11:26)," in *Restoration: Old Testament, Jewish, and Christian Perspectives*, ed. James M. Scott (Leiden: Brill, 2001), 489–526.

Figure 7. Mount Sinai (Jebel Musa or Mount Horeb) in the Sinai Peninsula, Egypt.

(Exod 24:7; Deut 28:69), and David (2 Sam 23:5; Ps 89:2–5). At Sinai Israel was entrusted with **the law** (Exod 20:1–17) and its stipulations for sacrificial **worship** (Lev 1–7; 16). Israel inherited the divine **promises** made in ancient times to **the patriarchs**, Abraham, Isaac, and Jacob (Gen 12:1–3; Rom 4:13–22; 11:28; 15:8). Finally, Israel's premier endowment is **the Messiah**, the royal offspring of David **according to the flesh** (Rom 1:3), whose mission is to reign over the whole house of Israel (Luke 1:32–33).

Awed by these blessings, Paul is moved to prayer. The words **God who is over all be blessed forever** seem straightforward enough, but there are questions about what Paul is saying in this verse, since the passage can be punctuated in more than one way. If a period is placed between "Messiah" and "God," as in the NABRE and RSV, then the final words sound like a traditional Jewish benediction affirming the Lord's supremacy over creation. However, if the words "Messiah" and "God" are separated by a comma, as in the NRSV, NJB, ESV, and NIV, then the final benediction asserts the divinity of the Messiah and his lordship over all things. Grammatical considerations alone make it difficult to choose between these options. However, theological considerations[10] tilt the balance in favor of a comma instead of a period, in which case the final line should read: "the Messiah, who is God over all, blessed forever. Amen."[11]

It is true that Paul does not usually speak so bluntly about Christ's deity in his writings, but in this case we can understand why he does. Israel's greatest blessing is the gift of a divine Messiah. Of all the endowments bestowed on

---

10. For instance, Paul is known to interpret prophecies about the Lord God of Israel as speaking about the Messiah. One example appears in Rom 10:13, where Paul cites Joel 3:5 and proceeds to identify Jesus as the divine "Lord" whose name is invoked for salvation.

11. Romans 9:5 has been read in this way since at least the second (St. Irenaeus, *Against Heresies* 3.16.3) and third centuries (Origen of Alexandria, *Commentary on Romans* 7.13.9).

Israel, none surpasses the mystery of God coming in the flesh *as an Israelite* with the mission of saving his people from their sins (Rom 11:26–27; Matt 1:21).

God's Purposes in History (9:6–13)

⁶But it is not that the word of God has failed. For not all who are of Israel are Israel, ⁷nor are they all children of Abraham because they are his descendants; but "It is through Isaac that descendants shall bear your name." ⁸This means that it is not the children of the flesh who are the children of God, but the children of the promise are counted as descendants. ⁹For this is the wording of the promise, "About this time I shall return and Sarah will have a son." ¹⁰And not only that, but also when Rebecca had conceived children by one husband, our father Isaac—¹¹before they had yet been born or had done anything, good or bad, in order that God's elective plan might continue, ¹²not by works but by his call—she was told, "The older shall serve the younger." ¹³As it is written:

> "I loved Jacob
> but hated Esau."

OT: Gen 18:10, 14; 21:12; 25:23; Isa 40:8; 55:1; Mal 1:3
NT: Matt 3:9; Rom 4:13–25; 8:14; 11:5–7; Gal 4:21–31; 1 John 3:1
Catechism: trustworthiness of God's word, 215; call of Abraham, 59–60, 72, 706; Israel, the people of Abraham, 63, 709, 762

Verses 1–5 constitute a preface for the whole of Rom 9–11. In verse 6, Paul sets forth his initial thesis and plunges immediately into exposition. The burden of this next section, which extends from 9:6 to 9:29, is to show that Israel's divided response to the Messiah is nothing out of the ordinary, for Scripture reveals this to be a consistent pattern in biblical history. There has always been a †remnant of Israel alongside the rest of Israel, just as there have always been chosen children of Abraham within the biological lines of descent stemming from Abraham. This remnant plays a special role in God's plan. The reason behind this is the sovereignty of Israel's God, who is free to call whomever he chooses for the fulfillment of his purposes.

9:6 Paul states the thesis he intends to demonstrate: **it is not that the word of God has failed**. His focus is on the divine word going forth from God at critical moments in salvation history. Paul wants to demonstrate that Israel is brought into being by the word of God: just as God created the universe by his word, so God fashioned a people for himself by his word expressed as promise and call.

Making sense of Israel's role begins with understanding God's word. Paul takes a step toward this by introducing a distinction: **not all who are of Israel are Israel**. The *elect* of Israel—those chosen as the bearers and beneficiaries of his promises—exist within the wider circle of *ethnic* Israel. It is true that God favored Israel and set Israel apart from other nations; nevertheless, it is also true that God blessed a chosen portion of Israel in ways not shared by the larger family of Israel. Paul can therefore speak of an †election within an election, a special calling for some Israelites within a national calling of all Israelites. Insofar as the †elect obtain what God has promised, the word of God has not failed (11:5–7).

From assertion Paul moves to demonstration. But before making applica- **9:7–9** tions for the present, and before considering Israel's prospects for the future, Paul steps back to the past. Even in the patriarchal period, prior to the birth of Israel as a nation, God's plan of election was already in progress, made visible in the twists and turns of biblical history.

Paul starts with the figure of Abraham precisely because Israel's election begins with Abraham. Not all, he says, who claim Abraham as their forefather are **children of Abraham** simply **because they are his descendants**. Initially the assertion sounds outlandish, but Paul is adhering strictly to the book of Genesis. Abraham fathered a total of eight sons by three different women (Gen 16:16; 21:2–3; 25:1–2), and yet only one of them—Isaac the son of Sarah—was chosen to mediate the blessings of the Abrahamic covenant to future generations (Gen 17:19–21). Isaac's older brother, Ishmael, was destined to receive blessings as well, but he was passed over in the determination of Abraham's primary heir. Paul substantiates this point by citing Gen 21:12 LXX: **"It is through Isaac that descendants shall bear your name."** Those who **are counted as descendants** of Abraham are not equivalent to the **children of the flesh**, since this would result in Isaac and Ishmael being equally chosen as mediators of the Abrahamic covenant.

Instead, only Isaac and his descendants are selected to be **children of the promise**. By putting it this way, Paul reminds us of the circumstances of Isaac's conception. Much of the drama surrounding the story of Abraham arises from the fact that he and his wife Sarah were elderly and childless. This posed quite a problem in view of God's promise to bless Abraham with an uncountable number of descendants (Gen 13:16; 15:4–5). If the divine plan had depended on the generative potency of the flesh, the promise would never have been fulfilled. Yet what was impossible by nature could still be accomplished by a miracle of grace. And so it was. Fusing together words from Gen 18:10 and 14,

Paul quotes the Lord's promise to Abraham: **"About this time I shall return and Sarah will have a son."** The word of God, expressed in the promise, goes forth to accomplish the will of God—the conception and birth of Isaac, who would become the grandfather of the twelve tribes of Israel.

9:10–13   Moving to the next generation, Paul shows that God made a choice between Jacob and Esau. This time two brothers were born to the same mother, **Rebecca**, who was married to **Isaac**. And just as the Lord chose Isaac over his older brother, Ishmael, so the Lord chose Jacob over his older brother, Esau. This took place **in order that God's elective plan might continue**. It shows that the path of God's grace is never determined solely or even primarily by physical descent. So too it shows that the divine plan of election operates independently of human merit and demerit. Paul draws attention to this latter point by citing Gen 25:23, where the Lord told the pregnant Rebecca regarding her twins, **"The older shall serve the younger."** The crucial point is that Jacob and Esau were still infants in the womb at this point in the story. Neither had **been born** or been capable of doing any **works** that could be judged **good or bad**. The Lord simply selected one over the other to carry his plan forward. So it is that Jacob, despite being the younger of the brothers, was chosen in advance by the **call** of God.

Paul is also making a point about the nations descended from Jacob and Esau, the Israelites and the Edomites. This is why he cites the declaration in Mal 1:3: **"I loved Jacob / but hated Esau."** The passage is talking not about the individuals in Genesis but about the Lord's choice of Israel as his covenant people over the descendants of Esau. The language of loving and hating is used to differentiate between the calling of Israel to national ministry and the noncalling of Edom to this unique role in salvation history.[12] The point is *not* that God despises the Edomites or predestines them for condemnation, as some mistakenly suppose. We can state this with confidence because other passages of the Old Testament indicate that God shows genuine concern for the Edomites (e.g., Deut 23:8; Amos 2:1–3).

Paul is drawn to this passage because it reveals that Israel's divine election springs from divine love. It is a sign of the Lord's special affection to be called as his covenant people. Indeed, for Paul the supreme token of God's love for Jacob is embodied in the Messiah, who was to be born of his family (Rom 9:5). At the same time, Scripture is clear that God selected Israel not simply to be an *object* of his love but to be an *instrument* of his love to the world. No doubt the descendants of Esau are included among the intended recipients of this

---

12. In addition, Malachi employs a Semitic figure of speech in which stark contrasts are used to express differences in degree. Thus, when "hate" is juxtaposed to "love" it means "love less" (as in Luke 14:26).

love, even if they are not called to be a minister of God's plan in the special way that Israel is.

The Freedom to Show Mercy (9:14–18)

[14]What then are we to say? Is there injustice on the part of God? Of course not! [15]For he says to Moses:

> "I will show mercy to whom I will,
> I will take pity on whom I will."

[16]So it depends not upon a person's will or exertion, but upon God, who shows mercy. [17]For the scripture says to Pharaoh, "This is why I have raised you up, to show my power through you that my name may be proclaimed throughout the earth." [18]Consequently, he has mercy upon whom he wills, and he hardens whom he wills.

OT: Exod 9:16; 33:19
NT: Rom 5:8; 11:5–7, 32
Catechism: mercy of God, 210–11, 270; sovereignty of God, 269

Paul continues to trace the thread of salvation history forward. He moves next from Genesis to Exodus (9:14–18), then to the prophets (9:24–29), and then to the time of prophetic fulfillment (9:30–10:21). He frames the discussion as a lively debate between himself and a hypothetical objector, who worries about whether divine †election amounts to divine injustice. Paul counters by insisting on God's freedom to call whomever he wills. Just as the Lord was free to choose Isaac (over Ishmael) and Jacob (over Esau) as founders of Israel, so the Lord was free to show mercy to Israel in the wake of national apostasy. So too, in Paul's day, God exercises his freedom to call some of the descendants of Israel to share in the riches of his mercy. The thesis of 9:6 is thereby supported: the word of God has not failed or proven ineffective but achieves its purpose in the †remnant that God saves.

Like a skilled chess player, Paul anticipates his opponent's next move: **What**   9:14–16
then are we to say? Is there injustice on the part of God? His response is predictably emphatic: **Of course not!** It is unthinkable for anyone formed in the Scriptures to suppose that God could be anything but perfectly just in all his ways. But instead of citing passages from the Bible that assert the Lord's justice in punishing sin, Paul quotes a passage from the book of Exodus that asserts God's freedom to forgive. The context is the renewal of the Sinai covenant immediately

following the golden calf rebellion, a grievous defection from the covenant that imperiled Israel's status as the chosen people of God (Exod 32–34). Despite the debacle at Sinai, Moses convinces the Lord to remain with Israel, to renew his covenant with Israel, and to reaffirm his choice of Israel. In the midst of negotiations the Lord discloses his inner mystery as a gracious and compassionate God, slow to anger and abounding in forgiveness. The passage Paul quotes is Exod 33:19: **"I will show mercy to whom I will, / I will take pity on whom I will."**

It is important to notice the scope of divine freedom this passage implies. Moses is told not simply that God is free to act as he sees fit, but that God is *free to extend mercy to those who are undeserving of it.*[13] The Israelites had just broken the covenant by worshiping an idol; God had every right to unleash the curses of the covenant against his disobedient people in full force. But instead the Lord chose to extend mercy. It is one thing to say that God selected Isaac and Jacob apart from anything that made them worthy of their calling; it is quite another to say that God reaffirmed his commitment to Israel in the face of their sinful unworthiness. The claim that divine election **depends not upon a person's will or exertion, but upon God, who shows mercy** rests securely on the foundation of Scripture.

9:17–18   Paul further examines the mystery of election by citing another divine saying from the exodus period. This time he quotes Exod 9:16, where the Lord addresses **Pharaoh** amid the plagues ravaging Egypt: **"This is why I have raised you up, to show my power through you that my name may be proclaimed throughout the earth."** The point is that even Pharaoh, the arrogant oppressor of Israel, played a pivotal role in the unfolding of salvation history. God had made him the mightiest king of his times, but only to show himself mightier still by breaking Pharaoh's will and redeeming Israel from his hand.

In sum, Paul has shown from the book of Exodus that God **has mercy upon whom he wills, and he hardens whom he wills.** Israel received a wealth of mercy at Sinai, and Pharaoh's heart was hardened to bring about Israel's deliverance from Egypt on a spectacular scale. The question many readers have at this point is what Paul means by "hardens" and why he introduces this concept into a discussion of Israel's calling. At least three points should be made.

First, Paul derives the concept of divine hardening from the story of the ten plagues in Exod 7–12. Several times in these chapters God is said to harden

---

13. See William S. Campbell, "Divergent Images of Paul and His Mission," in *Reading Israel in Romans: Legitimacy and Plausibility of Divergent Interpretations,* ed. Christina Grenholm and Daniel Patte (Harrisburg, PA: Trinity Press International, 2000), 187–211. On p. 202 he states: "God's freedom means that he is not obligated to discard Israel, however unworthy an object of his mercy it may actually be at any particular point in history."

Pharaoh's heart, leaving him unresponsive to Moses' pleas to release the Israelites from bondage. Hardening in this context is clearly a form of divine judgment. Yet we must be careful to interpret this divine action aright. God does *not* harden Pharaoh's heart in the sense that he overrides his free will and causes him to commit sin. Rather, he surrenders Pharaoh to the consequences of his stubborn rebellion. The more a person resists God's will, the more he degrades his own ability to respond to God's will. Divine hardening takes place when God stands back and allows this progression to run its course. Admittedly, Paul does not state explicitly that the hardening of Pharaoh was a divine reaction to the king's defiance. Nevertheless, the book of Exodus reveals that Pharaoh hardened his own heart against the Lord's demands (Exod 7:14, 22; 8:15; 9:7) prior to any mention of God imposing a hardening on him (Exod 9:12; 10:1, 20, 27; 11:10).

Second, divine hardening is not necessarily a prelude to eternal damnation. Paul is asserting God's freedom to pardon sinners in this life, not his freedom to punish sinners in the next life. No doubt the Lord used Pharaoh to advance his plan for Israel, and in the process he brought terrifying judgments on the king and his country. But even the Lord's judgments can have a saving and restorative purpose. The Lord often has to humble the proud through suffering before the proud are ready to humble themselves before the Lord. Divine hardening means that God sets the strong and boastful of the world on a path toward painful humiliation, with the aim that they will come to seek forgiveness. Whether Pharaoh reached this point of repentance is simply unknown to us. The point is that even God's wrath can be exercised with a view to showing his mercy.

Third, Paul alludes to the hardening of Pharaoh in order to set the stage for Rom 11, where he explains that part of Israel is hardened (11:7, 25), while a †remnant of Jews and Gentiles are lavished with mercy and called to salvation in Christ (9:22–24). By drawing attention to the example of Pharaoh, Paul puts his finger on something profoundly relevant to the shape of Christian history. The pattern of God working out his designs by calling some to mercy while hardening others is replicated *within Israel* even now. A remnant of the chosen people is robed in divine mercy, as Israel was at Mount Sinai, while the rest are unresponsive to the gospel, reprising the role of obstinate Pharaoh on the eve of the exodus (11:6–7).

Reflection and Application (9:6–18)

The central section of Rom 9 rehearses the story of Scripture from the patriarchs to the founding of Israel as a nation. It is the story of God selecting some

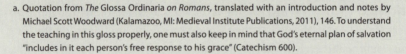

The *Glossa Ordinaria* on Romans 9:18

LIVING TRADITION

The *Glossa Ordinaria* is a collection of marginal annotations included in medieval editions of the Latin Bible that offer continuous commentary on the texts of Scripture, frequently with reference to the Church Fathers.

> *Therefore he has mercy on whom he will.* There is no meriting of mercy, but the sin of the whole condemned lump merits hardening. Nor does God harden by imparting evil, but by not imparting mercy which they do not deserve. He does this by a hidden justice that is beyond human understanding; and the apostle does not explain it but simply marvels: *O the depths of the riches of wisdom!* (Rom. 11:33) *and hardens whom he will.* Not as though he forces anyone to sin, but only that he does not impart the mercy of his justification to some who are sinners, and he is said to harden them because he does not have mercy on them, not because he compels them to sin.[a]

a. Quotation from *The* Glossa Ordinaria *on Romans*, translated with an introduction and notes by Michael Scott Woodward (Kalamazoo, MI: Medieval Institute Publications, 2011), 146. To understand the teaching in this gloss properly, one must also keep in mind that God's eternal plan of salvation "includes in it each person's free response to his grace" (Catechism 600).

for special blessing (Isaac, Jacob, Israel) while passing over others (Ishmael, Esau, Pharaoh). The question many readers have is whether these divine choices are merely arbitrary. One approach is to throw up our hands and confess our ignorance in words that echo the book of Isaiah: "God's ways are not our ways!" (Isa 55:8–9)—which is true. Human minds will never fully comprehend the infinite mysteries of God. But has the Lord simply hidden from us the reasoning behind his choices? I don't think so.

God is teaching us that the ways of nature are not the ways of grace. This is why he passes over the bigger, the stronger, and the older in preference for the smaller, the weaker, and the younger. In a very real sense, the order of redemption is the order of creation turned on its head. Likewise, what is esteemed by the world is of little account to God, and what is despised and forgotten by the world is precious in the eyes of God. Jesus made this point when he warned that "the last will be first, and the first will be last" (Matt 20:16), and also when he said "whoever exalts himself will be humbled; but whoever humbles himself will be exalted" (Matt 23:12). Mary touched on the same theme in her Magnificat, praising God as one who "has thrown down the mighty from their thrones / but lifted up the lowly"; "the hungry he has filled with good things; / the rich he has sent away empty" (Luke 1:52–53).

This gives us a clue to the mystery of election that Paul lays out in Rom 9. The Lord lifts up the humble with his justifying mercy and brings low the prideful with his merciful justice. All are invited to participate in the blessings of salvation, yet each experiences a redemptive reversal that overturns the expectations of the world and underlines the justice and mercy of God. Ultimately God's purpose is to "have mercy upon all" (11:32).

The Potter and the Clay (9:19–29)

[19]You will say to me then, "Why [then] does he still find fault? For who can oppose his will?" [20]But who indeed are you, a human being, to talk back to God? Will what is made say to its maker, "Why have you created me so?" [21]Or does not the potter have a right over the clay, to make out of the same lump one vessel for a noble purpose and another for an ignoble one? [22]What if God, wishing to show his wrath and make known his power, has endured with much patience the vessels of wrath made for destruction? [23]This was to make known the riches of his glory to the vessels of mercy, which he has prepared previously for glory, [24]namely, us whom he has called, not only from the Jews but also from the Gentiles.

[25]As indeed he says in Hosea:

> "Those who were not my people I will call 'my people,'
>   and her who was not beloved I will call 'beloved.'
> [26]And in the very place where it was said to them, 'You are not my people,'
>   there they shall be called children of the living God."

[27]And Isaiah cries out concerning Israel, "Though the number of the Israelites were like the sand of the sea, only a remnant will be saved; [28]for decisively and quickly will the Lord execute sentence upon the earth." [29]And as Isaiah predicted:

> "Unless the Lord of hosts had left us descendants,
>   we would have become like Sodom
>   and have been made like Gomorrah."

OT: Wis 12:12; Sir 33:11–13; Isa 1:9; 10:22–23; 29:16; Hosea 1:9; 2:25
NT: Matt 24:22; Acts 9:15; Rom 2:4; 8:14–17, 29; 11:13–14, 25; Eph 1:5; 2 Tim 2:20
Catechism: sovereignty of God, 269; doctrine of predestination, 600, 1037

9:19–21 To raise the question of divine sovereignty and human free will is to open an enormous can of worms, theologically speaking. So Paul continues in a conversational mode. **You will say to me then, "Why [then] does he still find fault? For who can oppose his will?"** Contrary to the accusations embedded in these questions, Paul never says that God's interventions in Israel's past suppressed the free will of the persons involved or absolved them of moral responsibility. Nevertheless, his one-sided emphasis on divine sovereignty could be taken in the wrong way, as though God treats human beings as mere pawns in a game of his own making. This mistaken inference is not only at odds with the rest of Romans; it is also contradicted by the rest of the Bible.

Still, Paul shows no interest in balancing out his emphasis on divine sovereignty with strong affirmations of human freedom. Instead, he doubles down on the point with two rhetorical questions: **But who indeed are you, a human being, to talk back to God? Will what is made say to its maker, "Why have you created me so?"** Probing the relationship between God's will and human freedom is perfectly legitimate in its place. But Paul's point here is that God is not answerable to human beings. Creatures can claim no right to interrogate the creator about the wisdom of his ways. Audacity of this sort rises from a pride that forgets who God is in relation to the world he has made.

To drive this point home Paul uses the biblical metaphor of **the potter** exercising his authority **over the clay**. The wording of the statement in Romans is closest to Isa 29:16, although other passages such as Isa 45:9 and Jer 18:1–11 come to mind as well. God, like the village potter, turns and shapes the clay as he desires, forming a whole range of vessels from cups to bowls to jars to pitchers and so on. For Paul, as for Isaiah and Jeremiah, **the same lump** represents the people of Israel. Even in dealing with the descendants of Jacob, the divine potter is free to fashion **one vessel for a noble purpose** and **another for an ignoble** purpose. It is absurd to think that the clay on the potter's wheel should speak out in protest against the hands that are shaping it. Human beings are in no position to question God's actions or intentions in dealing with the children of Israel.

9:22–23 Extending the metaphor, Paul depicts Christian Jews and Gentiles as **vessels of mercy** and implicitly portrays unbelievers as **vessels of wrath**. At this point we come face-to-face with some real interpretive difficulties.

First of all, verses 22–23 constitute a grammatically incomplete sentence. Paul begins to formulate a conditional statement with an "if" clause but never follows up with a balancing "then" clause. This makes it hard to determine his complete train of thought since the unstated part of the sentence has to be inferred. Presumably, had Paul finished his sentence, he would have said something like: "Then isn't it within the scope of God's freedom to do so?"

Furthermore, if we read these verses in isolation, or if we fail to appreciate what Paul is driving at, we run the risk of misinterpreting his meaning. It is often said, for instance, that Paul is concerned with the determination of eternal destinies—whether the vessels in question will come to final salvation or final condemnation. At first glance this seems a reasonable way to understand the contrast between **wrath** and **destruction**, on the one hand (9:22), and **mercy** and **glory**, on the other (9:23). Wrath and glory are terms Paul uses elsewhere in connection with the final judgment (2:5–8).[14] Yet Paul is not here concerned with the consignment of destinies. He is setting forth a scenario for the sake of argument in order to defend God against the charge of acting unjustly toward Israel. He is not delivering a prophecy that reveals who will reach heaven and who will go to hell. Rather, the context indicates that Paul is concerned with *God's freedom to assign different roles to different persons in implementing his designs for history.* It is a matter of God choreographing the †election of some and the hardening of others in order to accomplish his plan of redemption. It is within this historical frame of reference that the Lord has a purpose for all the vessels of Israel, noble and ignoble alike.

From here Paul moves into the next stage of his argument. He has shown **9:24** that God poured his mercy on Israel *gathered* at Sinai; he now shows that God's mercy reaches out to Israel *scattered* among the nations. Here too the Lord finds vessels of mercy, a group that Paul calls **us whom he has called**. No doubt "us" refers to the Apostle and his readers in Rome and thus designates Christian disciples. The language of being "called" is the language of election, as it is throughout Rom 9.

Paul specifies that believers in Jesus, who constitute "the elect" of God's new people (11:7), were summoned **not only from the Jews but also from the Gentiles**. That a number of Jews came to faith in the Messiah is clear from the book of Acts, among other places. But what does it mean to say that vessels of mercy were found among the Gentiles? Most commentators suppose that Paul is thinking exclusively of Gentile converts to Christianity. However, the Greek term *ethnē* translates either as "Gentiles" or "nations." This is significant because Paul is about to quote passages from the Old Testament that announce the salvation of Israelite exiles living among the nations.[15] Given this context,

---

14. Paul can also speak of God's wrath and glory experienced in history (see Rom 1:18–32; 8:30).

15. James M. Scott, *Paul and the Nations: The Old Testament and Jewish Background of Paul's Mission to the Nations with Special Reference to the Destination of Galatians*, WUNT 84 (Tübingen: Mohr, 1995), 134.

the "Gentiles" in question appear to include persons of Israelite ancestry who had been scattered among foreign lands for centuries.

9:25–26   Paul moves to demonstrate the assertion in 9:24 by paraphrasing Hosea 2:25 as rendered in the †Septuagint: **"Those who were not my people I will call 'my people,' / and her who was not beloved I will call 'beloved.'"** The prophet foretells not the divine calling of foreigners outside the family of Israel but the Lord's plan to restore the exiled tribes of northern Israel to full covenant status. Scholars routinely say that Paul is applying this prophecy to the conversion of Gentiles rather than in accord with its original meaning. But this, I submit, is to misunderstand Paul. The background of Hosea's prophecy is Assyria's conquest of northern Israel in the eighth century BC, at which time ten of the twelve tribes of Israel were dispersed as captives into distant lands, never to return. Over time these pure-blooded descendants of Jacob blended into the nations of their exile through intermarriage and cultural assimilation, effectively *becoming Gentiles*.

Hosea announces the Lord's plan to "call" members of these gentilized tribes back into covenant communion, making them his "beloved" people once again. This is where Paul comes in. He sees the salvation of the exiled and forgotten tribes of Israel taking place through the Church's mission to evangelize the nations! The same idea is reinforced by another quotation from the same book, this time from Hosea 2:1: **"And in the very place where it was said to them, 'You are not my people,' / there they shall be called children of the living God."** The geographical indicators "there" and "in the very place" must not go unnoticed. If the greater part of Israel is scattered among the nations, then the only way to save these lost descendants of Israel, now indistinguishable from Gentiles, is to take the gospel to the Gentiles. In this way the gift of covenant sonship, which Israel received under Moses (Rom 9:4), can be given anew through the Spirit of the Messiah (8:14–17).

Paul is not squeezing a meaning out of these texts that is alien to the message of Hosea. He is arguing from the standpoint of historical fulfillment.[16] Israel is being saved as the nations are being saved, precisely because the bulk of Israel has long since dissolved into the nations. God has made the impossible possible by reversing a tragedy that appeared to be irreversible, all in fulfillment of his word.

9:27–28   Paul follows with an appeal to **Isaiah**. The text quoted is Isa 10:22–23, although the opening words of the citation come from the Septuagint translation

---

16. Although it is not the usual interpretation, a few scholars are beginning to consider the possibility that Paul may indeed have the original context of the Hosea texts in mind. See, e.g., Jason A. Staples, "What Do the Gentiles Have to Do with 'All Israel'? A Fresh Look at Romans 11:25–27," *JBL* 130, no. 2 (2011): 371–90; and Pablo T. Gadenz, "'The Lord Will Accomplish His Word': Paul's Argumentation and Use of Scripture in Romans 9:24–29," *Letter & Spirit* 2 (2006): 141–58.

of Hosea 2:1. Isaiah speaks to the same crisis addressed by Hosea: the Assyrian invasions, which dismantled the northern kingdom of Israel and dispersed the northern tribes of Israel into foreign captivity. Into these devastating circumstances the prophet injects a message of hope: **"Though the number of the Israelites were like the sand of the sea, only a remnant will be saved; for decisively and quickly will the Lord execute sentence upon the earth."**[17] God will show mercy by saving a "remnant" from the midst of his judgment on the northern tribes. The reader should notice that Isaiah is not speaking about Jews from the tribe of Judah or residents of the southern kingdom of Judah. Rather, God is promising to rescue a †remnant from the larger "house of Jacob" (Isa 10:20).

In Paul's reading of the oracle, verse 27 confirms his thesis in Rom 9:6 of an †elect Israel singled out for blessing within the national family of Israel ("not all who are of Israel are Israel"), just as verse 28 confirms his thesis in 9:6 that God's word never fails to accomplish his will ("it is not the word of God that has failed"). Isaiah declares with prophetic certainty that the Lord will execute his "sentence" (the Greek is *logos*, "word") and will do so "decisively and quickly"— in other words, without fail and without delay.[18]

Paul's final quotation in this section is another prophecy from **Isaiah**. This **9:29** time he turns the spotlight on the southern tribes of Israel by citing the words of Isa 1:9: **"Unless the Lord of hosts had left us descendants, we would have become like Sodom and have been made like Gomorrah."** The passage forms part of Isaiah's opening oracle that addresses "Judah and Jerusalem" (Isa 1:1) at the very end of the eighth century BC, when Assyrian forces devastated much of the land of Judah. Only the inhabitants of Jerusalem were spared, thanks to a miracle of God, leaving them as "the surviving remnant of the house of Judah" (2 Kings 19:30 RSV).

Isaiah calls these survivors "descendants" (the Greek *sperma* means "seed, offspring"). It is this group that experiences God's mercy and ensures that Israel's past and Israel's future are linked by an unbroken line of continuity. Had the Lord

---

17. Several modern translations add the word "only" to the first sentence (9:27), although it does not appear in the Greek text (NABRE, RSV, NRSV, NIV, ESV). Unfortunately, this makes the oracle sound more like a threat than a hopeful promise. See Richard B. Hays, *Echoes of Scripture in the Letters of Paul* (New Haven: Yale University Press, 1989), 68.

18. The NABRE's two adverbs ("decisively and quickly") are used to render two Greek participles ("accomplishing and cutting short") that in turn render a Hebrew expression from Isa 10:22 and 28:22. For a careful discussion proposing the meaning "fulfilling decisively," see Pablo T. Gadenz, *Called from the Jews and from the Gentiles: Pauline Ecclesiology in Romans 9–11* (Tübingen: Mohr Siebeck, 2009), 124–30. Given this background, it is more likely that Isaiah is stressing not the swiftness of judgment to come but the sureness of deliverance for some.

not intervened to save Jerusalem from annihilation, the covenant people would have fared no better than Sodom and Gomorrah. And because the redeemed in this case were Judeans, or Judahites, Paul's statement in Rom 9:24 that God calls some "from the Jews" is verified, just as the preceding quotations from Hosea and Isaiah supported the calling of northern Israelites from "the Gentiles" or "nations."

Reflection and Application (9:22–23)

Over the centuries Rom 9:22–23 has figured prominently in theological discussions of predestination—the belief that God has already decreed the salvation of some since before the foundation of the world. There can be no doubt that the basis for this belief is found in the New Testament, and the Catholic Church has affirmed the doctrine in subsequent centuries.[19] But how predestination is best understood has been debated by theologians, not only across denominational lines but even within the Catholic tradition. Predestination is a mystery of divine sovereignty and human free will. On the one hand, Scripture indicates that God has foreordained some for divine adoption in Christ; on the other, it insists that all have the freedom to choose their own destiny. Both truths are affirmed, but where the two intersect and how they fit together lies beyond the horizon of human understanding in this life.

That said, the Catholic Church has set definite limits to the scope of the doctrine, lest it be misunderstood. One such misunderstanding goes by the name of "double predestination." This is the notion that God not only preselects some for salvation but also foreordains the damnation of others. This formulation of the doctrine, which has gained traction mainly in Calvinist theology since the sixteenth century, is firmly rejected by the Catholic Church (Catechism 1037).

If there is one passage of Scripture that advocates of double predestination appeal to more than any other, it is Rom 9:22–23. This is certainly a difficult text that, in isolation, could *seem* to teach that God fashions some for eternal destruction. But is this what Paul is saying? Are the vessels of wrath hopelessly doomed regardless of the choices they make in life? Not at all, and it is important to understand why.

First, if Paul really believed that non-Christian Israel was infallibly predestined for hell, it would make no sense for him to be praying and working for the salvation of Israel, as he tells us in 10:1 and 11:14. Indeed, Paul would be working and praying in conscious opposition to the will of God.

---

19. See especially the study by Reginald Garrigou-Lagrange, OP, *Predestination: The Meaning of Predestination in Scripture and the Church*, trans. Dom Bede Rose, OSB (Rockford, IL: TAN, 1998).

Second, Paul stated earlier in Romans that God exercises his "patience" toward Israel in order to lead the disobedient to repentance (2:4). Only if they fail to repent will they experience divine "wrath" for disobeying the truth that God has made known to them (2:8). It hardly makes sense for Paul to turn around and insist that "wrath" is the guaranteed destiny of the vessels of Israel that God endures with "patience" (9:22). These assertions are complementary rather than contradictory. In other words, Paul teaches in Rom 2 that the purpose of God's patience is to allow time for repentance, and in Rom 9 that the purpose of God's patience is also to make known his wrath, his power, and his glory.

Third, Paul tells us later in Romans that his unbelieving kinsmen, despite being severed like branches, can still be reattached to the olive tree of God's messianic people. The Lord is fully able to restore them, so long as they do not persist in "unbelief" (11:23). Evidently Paul does not view the hardened members of Israel as trapped in an inescapable situation.

Fourth, the expression "made for destruction" (9:22) sounds at first like predestination to damnation, but these words can and should be understood differently. The Greek indicates that, at the present time, the vessels of wrath are "fit" or "ripe" for divine judgment. In other words, the vessels of wrath are following a course that leads to destruction, but Paul never says that such an outcome is inevitable. It is even possible that Paul means that the vessels of wrath "have prepared themselves" for ruin.[20] These alternative ways of understanding the passage accord better with Paul's metaphor. It is not unusual for a potter to fashion bowls, cups, and jars for menial uses; but no potter turns out clay vessels solely for the purpose of destroying them.

The Stone in Zion (9:30–33)

[30]**What then shall we say? That Gentiles, who did not pursue righteousness, have achieved it, that is, righteousness that comes from faith;** [31]**but that Israel, who pursued the law of righteousness, did not attain to that law?** [32]**Why not? Because they did it not by faith, but as if it could be done by works. They stumbled over the stone that causes stumbling,** [33]**as it is written:**

> **"Behold, I am laying a stone in Zion**
> **that will make people stumble**

20. A point made by St. John Chrysostom, *Homilies on Romans* 16, who takes the Greek *katērtismena* as a middle voice participle rather than a passive voice participle.

> **and a rock that will make them fall,**
> **and whoever believes in him shall not be put to shame."**

OT: Deut 6:25; Isa 8:14; 28:16

NT: Matt 21:42; Rom 8:34; 11:11; 1 Cor 1:23; Gal 4:26; Eph 2:20; 1 Pet 2:4–10

Catechism: gift of righteousness, 1987, 1991; gift and act of faith, 143, 153–55; Christ exalted in heaven, 659–64

The central section of Rom 9–11 begins in 9:30. Having covered Israel's ⁺*election* in the past (9:6–29), Paul now wrestles with Jewish *rejection* of the gospel in the present (9:30–10:21), which prepares him to speak of Israel's *restoration* in the future (11:1–32). This new section opens with a contrast between Israel and the Gentiles couched in the metaphor of a footrace. The irony is that Israel, having stumbled along the way, failed to reach the finish line, while a multitude of Gentiles, coming to faith in the Messiah, arrived at God's appointed goal. Once again, Paul interprets the shape and direction of salvation history with the help of carefully selected texts from the Old Testament.

9:30   Paul's transition to the middle of Rom 9–11 comes in the form of a question: **What then shall we say? That Gentiles, who did not pursue righteousness, have achieved it . . . ?** The implied answer is "Yes, they have." Scores of Gentiles, regardless of their ethnic roots, have now received the **righteousness that comes from faith** in Jesus as Messiah and Lord. As recipients of justification, they have been endowed with the gift of Christ's righteousness (5:17). Noteworthy are the conditions of this bestowal: it has been given to those who were making no effort to acquire it. Paul is underscoring the obvious fact that Gentiles were unconcerned with following the Torah, the law that governed Israel. Nevertheless, since coming to believe in Jesus, these heathen multitudes have received the winner's prize for a race they were not even conscious of running.

9:31–33   Israel's situation is just the reverse. The question of whether **Israel, who pursued the law of righteousness, did not attain to that law** implies that unbelieving Jews, who count themselves members of the larger family of Israel, failed to obtain the object of their striving. As Paul sees it, pursuing righteousness by careful observance of the Torah (Deut 6:25) is a misspent effort if it stops short of embracing the Messiah, who is the goal of the law (Rom 10:4) and embodies God's saving righteousness (1 Cor 1:30). This is why he says they pursued righteousness **not by faith, but as if it could be done by works** of the Mosaic law. The prize eludes their grasp because their pursuit is misdirected.

Paul depicts this situation using the word picture of a runner stumbling **over the stone that causes stumbling**. He derives the image from two prophetic passages, Isa 28:16 and 8:14, which he splices together in a mutually interpreting fashion. The combined texts share the image of a "stone" or "rock" that becomes a blessing for those who believe and a tripping hazard for those who do not: **"Behold, I am laying a stone in Zion / that will make people stumble / and a rock that will make them fall, / and whoever believes in him shall not be put to shame."** Isaiah uses imagery linked with the temple in Jerusalem in order to make a point about the necessity of fearing the Lord and trusting in his plan. In Isa 8, God promises to be a sanctuary of protection for those who fear him but a stumbling stone for those who trust instead in their own ability to provide for the welfare of Israel and Judah through human, political means. Sadly, the Lord proved to be "a rock of stumbling to both houses of Israel" (Isa 8:14 RSV). In Isa 28 the prophet delivers a similar message to the rulers of Judah, who had staked the survival of the southern kingdom on a strategic alliance with Egypt in spite of the Lord's opposition. Instead of trusting in God, the Judean leadership vainly placed hope in their own ability to save themselves from a devastating Assyrian assault by forging a treaty with another powerful nation. The message of both oracles is essentially the same: only trustful reliance on the Lord, the foundation stone of Israel's life and faith, enables his people to escape the shame of national ruin. It is failure to put faith in him that makes the foundation stone a stumbling stone that causes the fall of many in Israel.

Paul is no doubt alert to the historical meaning of these passages. Yet he also detects a messianic meaning in Isaiah's words that is relevant to his own day.[21] The cornerstone in Zion is none other than Jesus Christ, he who was destined for "the fall and rise of many in Israel" (Luke 2:34). Those who stumble over him are those who refuse to believe in him, suggesting that Paul sees an analogy between the stumbling of Israel and Judah in the Old Testament period and the stumbling of unbelieving Jews in the New Testament period. History practically repeats itself as Paul's kindred find the message of a crucified Messiah scandalous (1 Cor 1:23) and instead seek to establish a righteousness of their own based on works of the law (Rom 9:32).

---

21. The Aramaic *Targum of Isaiah* identifies the Zion stone of Isa 28:16 as "a strong king," which is a typical designation for the Messiah in these texts. Paul's reading of the passage is thus in line with a messianic reading of Isaiah attested in early Judaism. This is noted on pp. 564–65 of Craig A. Evans, "Paul and the Hermeneutics of 'True Prophecy': A Study of Romans 9–11," *Bib* 65, no. 4 (1984): 560–70.

Israel's Response to the Gospel

Romans 10:1–21

Paul took occasion in Rom 9 to review the biblical history of Israel from Abraham to the exile. It was a story of God working out his purpose of †election in fidelity to his word. In the latter part of the chapter, Paul moved the discussion from the past into the present. The majority of his own people are resisting the gospel, while Gentiles in large numbers are coming to faith in Jesus. It is this enigma that receives fuller explanation in Rom 10. On the one hand, Paul explains that his people's unbelief is not a failure to hear the gospel but a failure to discern the ultimate aim of the law. On the other hand, he contends that even the disappointing response of the covenant people fits into the larger plan of God, for Moses foretold in Scripture that they would be made jealous by a people outside the covenant. Paul continues to pray for the "salvation" of his kindred (10:1) and to insist that anyone, Gentile or Jew, who calls on the name of the Lord Jesus "will be saved" (10:13).

Christ the End of the Law (10:1–4)

¹Brothers, my heart's desire and prayer to God on their behalf is for salvation. ²I testify with regard to them that they have zeal for God, but it is not discerning. ³For, in their unawareness of the righteousness that comes from God and their attempt to establish their own [righteousness], they did not submit to the righteousness of God. ⁴For Christ is the end of the law for the justification of everyone who has faith.

OT: Num 25:6–13; Deut 6:25; 1 Kings 19:10, 14; 1 Macc 2:24–27, 54, 58; Sir 45:23; 48:2

NT: Acts 21:20; 22:3; Rom 1:16–17; 3:21–26, 31; Gal 1:14; 3:24; Phil 3:6–9

Catechism: prayers of petition and intercession, 2632, 2636; religious zeal, 579; Christ the end of the law, 1953; Christ and the unity of Scripture, 128–30, 134

Romans 10:1–4 builds on the work of 9:30–33. So many of Paul's kinsmen ran after the Torah and its righteousness yet failed to reach either one because, he explains, they overlooked the vital necessity of "faith," supposing the Mosaic covenant could be fulfilled simply by adherence to its prescribed "works." This problem was fully exposed when so many of Paul's countrymen declined to accept Jesus as the Messiah.

10:1 Like Rom 9, Rom 10 begins autobiographically, with Paul disclosing the secrets of his heart. Both openings affirm the depth of his concern for his kindred according to the flesh, and both reveal his **desire** to see their present unbelief give way to future **salvation**. Paul offers continual **prayer to God** for this intention. Later we discover that he labors in the mission field with the hope of saving "some of them" (11:14).

10:2 Part of the irony of Jewish unbelief is its religious motivation. Speaking from his own experience as a Pharisee, Paul can say: **I testify with regard to them that they have zeal for God.** The Jews are passionate about serving the Lord by meticulous observance of the Torah. It is hardly the case that many rejected the Christian message due to a national apathy toward divine revelation. Just the opposite. Israel long prized the virtue of "zeal" throughout its history, all the way up to Paul's day (Acts 21:20; 22:3). Several figures of the Old Testament were admired for their uncompromising zeal, especially Phinehas, the grandson of Aaron (Num 25:6–13); Elijah the prophet (1 Kings 19:10, 14); and Mattathias, the father of Judas Maccabaeus (1 Macc 2:24–27). Zeal was not only the driving force behind pious determinations to keep the Torah;[1] it was also expressed as a commitment to defend the purity of God's people against moral and religious defilement.[2] Zeal in this sense could even inspire violent action against those who brazenly transgressed the Mosaic law. Paul attributes his own persecution of the earliest Christians to this type of zeal (Phil 3:6). Before his stunning reversal on the Damascus road, he viewed the Christian message as a serious threat to Judaism's ancestral faith and life. He was convinced that Jesus and his followers were leading his people astray—away from the covenant, away from the law, away from God.

1. Rightly stressed by Vincent M. Smiles, "The Concept of 'Zeal' in Second-Temple Judaism and Paul's Critique of It in Romans 10:2," *CBQ* 64 (2002): 282–99, although he downplays the extent to which zeal entails a separation from defilement.

2. James D. G. Dunn, *The Theology of Paul the Apostle* (Grand Rapids: Eerdmans, 1998), 346–54.

The fervor of Judaism's most zealous is ultimately misguided, Paul declares. His brethren by race have a zeal that is **not discerning**. By this he means that they are carried off course by an incomplete knowledge of the truth. They are committed to a traditional understanding of Moses and the prophets, but they fail to recognize the fullness of revelation that has come in the Messiah. Consequently, many of their efforts are misspent in chasing a goal that remains elusive.

10:3   Paul says that his unbelieving kindred are unaware **of the righteousness that comes from God**. Righteousness is the gift of membership within the covenant, the grace that transforms sinners into sons and daughters of God.[3] Those preoccupied with pursuing righteousness by careful observance of the Torah (Deut 6:25) were refusing to acknowledge the greater righteousness accomplished by the Messiah (Rom 5:18). It is a fundamental error, according to Paul, to think you can do for yourself what God has already done for you in Christ. Yet the covenant people tried **to establish their own [righteousness]**[4] apart from the free gift of righteousness offered in Jesus (5:17). Inasmuch as many withheld belief in the gospel, Paul can say they **did not submit to the righteousness of God**—that is, they declined to accept the saving work of God in the dying and rising of the Messiah.

10:4   Verse 4 serves as the thesis statement for the unit stretching from 9:30 to 10:21. It sums up for Paul the all-important truth that many among the Jewish people had yet to accept: that **Christ is the end of the law**. Essentially the difference between Judaism and Christianity boils down to this conviction.

That said, Paul's exact meaning is not immediately clear.[5] The critical question is whether Paul is asserting *continuity* between the Torah and Christ or advocating *discontinuity* between the Torah and Christ. Is Jesus the goal and fulfillment of the law? Or does Jesus signal the expiration and termination of the law?

These options depend on the precise meaning of the word "end" (Greek *telos*), which in Greek literature can have a teleological sense ("goal, purpose") as well as a temporal sense ("termination, cessation"). Deciding between these translations is a delicate task, but several reasons point to the teleological sense as Paul's intended meaning. (1) Statistically, use of the noun *telos* to mean goal, aim, or purpose is clearly predominant in ancient secular and biblical texts, whereas the temporal sense is only occasionally attested. (2) Contextually, Paul

---

3. For discussion of "the righteousness of God" in Romans, see commentary on 1:17.

4. In the NABRE, brackets are placed around words or expressions that the editors consider textually uncertain because they appear in some ancient manuscripts but are absent from others.

5. See especially Robert Badenas, *Christ the End of the Law: Romans 10.4 in Pauline Perspective*, JSNTSup 10 (Sheffield: JSOT Press, 1985), to which the commentary that follows is much indebted.

contrasts Israel and the Gentiles in terms of a footrace metaphor (9:30–33). This is significant because *telos* is used in classical texts for what we call the "finish line" of a race.[6] Moreover, Paul twice uses the noun *telos* in 6:21–22, and in both instances he has the outcome of our actions in view, not their discontinuation. (3) Thematically, Paul is concerned throughout the book of Romans to uncover the biblical roots of Christian faith by frequent appeal to the Scriptures. The gospel, he says, was "promised previously" in the Old Testament (1:2) and is "now manifested through the prophetic writings" (16:26). The gospel of Jesus Christ is thus seen as "supporting the law" rather than contradicting it or rendering it obsolete (3:31). (4) Historically, with only a few exceptions, patristic and medieval writers understood Rom 10:4 as a statement about the unity of the Bible revealed in Christ, not about the expiration of some or all of the Mosaic commandments.

Paul's point, then, is that the Torah follows a trajectory that leads to Christ. God's intention for the Mosaic law is fully and finally realized in Jesus the Messiah. Rather than being an end in itself, the law is oriented toward a goal beyond itself. To put it differently, what health is to medicine, Christ is to the Torah—its intended destination, the purpose for which it exists.[7]

The problem, according to Paul, is that his kinsmen by race are unwilling to accept this purpose behind the Torah, even though it leads to **the justification of everyone who has faith**. One senses that Paul is emphasizing the word "everyone" in this statement (as in 10:13), which is his shorthand way of saying "Jews as well as Gentiles." The covenant people, like the newly converted Gentiles, have only to believe in Christ to obtain the object they so zealously pursue. And should they choose to believe, they will come to possess the indwelling Spirit, who makes it possible for believers to fulfill the righteous requirement of the law (8:4) that was once impossible (9:31).[8]

The Righteousness of Faith (10:5–13)

---

[5]**Moses writes about the righteousness that comes from [the] law, "The one who does these things will live by them." [6]But the righteousness that comes from faith says, "Do not say in your heart, 'Who will go up into**

---

6. See entry on *telos* in LSJ, 1772–74.

7. An analogy suggested by St. John Chrysostom, *Homilies on Romans* 17, who compared Christ and the law to physical wellness and the physician's art.

8. Paul W. Meyer, "Romans 10:4 and the 'End' of the Law," in *The Theological Interpretation of Scripture: Classic and Contemporary Readings*, ed. Stephen E. Fowl (Cambridge: Blackwell, 1997), 338–55.

St. Jerome on Christ in Scripture

LIVING TRADITION

I interpret as I should following the command of Christ: *Search the Scriptures* [John 5:39], and *Seek and you shall find* [Luke 11:9]. Christ will not say to me what he said to the Jews: *You erred, not knowing the Scriptures and not knowing the power of God* [Matt 22:29]. For if, as Paul says, Christ is the power of God and the wisdom of God, and if the man who does not know Scripture does not know the power and wisdom of God, then ignorance of Scripture is ignorance of Christ.[a]

a. *Commentary on Isaiah*, preface. Translation from *The Liturgy of the Hours*, vol. 4, Ordinary Time Weeks 18–34 (New York: Catholic Book Publishing, 1975), 1447–48.

heaven?' (that is, to bring Christ down) [7]or 'Who will go down into the abyss?' (that is, to bring Christ up from the dead)." [8]But what does it say?

> "The word is near you,
>> in your mouth and in your heart"

(that is, the word of faith that we preach), [9]for, if you confess with your mouth that Jesus is Lord and believe in your heart that God raised him from the dead, you will be saved. [10]For one believes with the heart and so is justified, and one confesses with the mouth and so is saved. [11]For the scripture says, "No one who believes in him will be put to shame." [12]For there is no distinction between Jew and Greek; the same Lord is Lord of all, enriching all who call upon him. [13]For "everyone who calls on the name of the Lord will be saved."

OT: Lev 18:5; Deut 9:4; 30:12–14; Isa 28:16; Bar 3:29–30; Joel 3:5

NT: Acts 2:21; Rom 3:9, 23, 29; 2 Cor 8:9; Gal 3:24; 1 Pet 2:6

Catechism: calling on the name of Jesus, 432, 2666; Jesus as Lord, 446–51; baptism and profession of faith, 14, 1253–54

Lectionary: 10:8–13: 1st Sunday of Lent (Year C); Presentation of the Creed; 10:9–18: St. Andrew; Mass for the Evangelization of Peoples

Having established that Christ is the goal of the law, Paul considers the implications for Israel's pursuit of the law. He begins by summoning witnesses from the Torah, to which he adds supporting testimony from the prophets. Although this section ranks high among passages in Romans that are difficult to follow in detail, its overall thrust is clear: righteousness is not something one can obtain through mere observance of the law; rather, it comes to those who put faith in Jesus as Lord and call upon him for salvation. Once again, Paul contends that the core of the Christian gospel has been present all along in the Scriptures of Israel.

If Paul is to substantiate his claims about the law, he must first present con-   10:5
vincing evidence from the law. With this in mind, he turns to **Moses**, traditionally identified as the author of Leviticus, who **writes, "The one who does these
things will live by them."** The quotation is from Lev 18:5, which speaks about
the righteousness that comes from [the] law.[9] Moses urges the people of Israel
to observe the commandments of the law rather than imitate the perverted ways
of the Egyptians and the Canaanites. For those who follow the law and adhere
to the covenant, Moses promises the blessing of the covenant—namely, life.
This is significant, since elsewhere in Romans Paul speaks of "righteousness"
and "life" almost as two ways of saying the same thing (1:17; 5:17).[10]

Paul's next witness is a personified theological concept. He is about to quote   10:6–8
again from the law of Moses, only this time he identifies the speaker as **the
righteousness that comes from faith**. Obviously he is exercising some poetic
license to make his point. The "righteousness from faith" is about to speak the
words of Deut 30:12–14.

Yet a problem presents itself immediately. How do verses 6–8 relate to verse
5? At the beginning of verse 6, Paul uses a word (Greek *de*) that can be either
conjunctive ("and") or adversative ("but"). Most modern translations, including the NABRE, opt for the latter and open the sentence with **but** (also RSV,
NRSV, ESV, NIV, JB). Several scholars have raised objections to this rendering.[11]
Grammatically it could go either way. Contextually, however, it seems unlikely
that Paul would pit Moses against Moses, Leviticus against Deuteronomy, and
thus claim that the Torah puts forth two contrary perspectives on the way to
righteousness and life. If that were so, Israel would have scriptural warrant for
pursuing the righteousness of the law by means of works, and yet this is the
very thing that Paul faults them for doing in Rom 9:31–32.

Most likely Paul reads these two passages from the Torah as complementary
texts that build on each other rather than as contrastive texts that represent
two different alternatives. Leviticus 18:5 stresses *that* Israel must keep the law,
and Deut 30:12–14 clarifies *how* Israel is to keep the law. Recall from Rom 9:32
that Paul critiques unbelieving Israelites not for pursuing the law but for the
manner in which they pursue it.

Before expounding the righteousness of faith, Paul adds an important preface
to his remarks. He introduces his main scriptural text, Deut 30:12–14, with a

---

9. Reference to this passage appears elsewhere in Neh 9:29; Ezek 20:11, 13, 21; Gal 3:12.
10. It is likely that Paul arrived at this view by a close reading of the Torah. For example, just as Deut
6:25 states that keeping the commandments leads to "righteousness" (RSV), so Deut 30:15–16 states
that keeping the commandments leads to "life."
11. See the discussion in Badenas, *Christ the End of the Law*, 121–25.

warning: **Do not say in your heart**. These cautionary words come from the Greek version of Deut 8:17 and 9:4. Paul's reason for citing this expression becomes apparent when we look at the original context. In both passages, Moses is warning the Israelites against presumption, against thinking that either their deliverance from Egypt or their acquisition of the promised land was attributable to their righteousness. No, the Lord accomplished these feats in faithfulness to his covenant with the patriarchs (Deut 8:18; 9:5). Paul is reminding his kindred that God's righteousness—and not their own righteousness—is the basis for God's greatest gifts (Rom 10:3).[12]

Then follows the quotation of Deut 30:12–14. Paul does not cite the whole passage but selects key expressions from each verse in succession, interspersing his own interpretive comments among them. Basically, Paul says about the gospel what Deuteronomy says about the law. His rationale for doing so is rooted in the conviction that "Christ is the end of the law," by which he means the goal of the law (Rom 10:4).

In Deut 30:12–14, Moses dismisses any excuses Israel might have for not obeying the Torah. The word of God is not hidden away in some far-off corner of the cosmos, such that one could say, **Who will go up into heaven?** or **Who will go down into the abyss?** in order to retrieve it.[13] Israel, in other words, has no need to traverse great distances, searching high and low, to discover the will of God. The Lord has already made known his Torah and placed it in the midst of his people. Moses thus contends, **The word is near you, / in your mouth and in your heart**. The children of Israel cannot plead ignorance of the word of God, for God has made it fully accessible to them.

For Paul, what is true of the Mosaic law is true of the Messiah, since the law points the way to Christ (Rom 10:4). The gospel is not inaccessible to the Jews or beyond their reach. If the Torah is near, its testimony to Christ is near. If Israel is expected to know and observe the law, the covenant people can be expected to embrace the Messiah. The saving word of God is more accessible than ever: in the incarnation, **Christ** came **down** from the Father; in the resurrection, **Christ** was brought **up from the dead**; in the preaching of the apostles, **the word of faith** has come **near**; and in the Christian confession of faith, the word can be found **in your mouth and in your heart**. So now that the ultimate aim of the law has been revealed, obedience to the law takes a new form. This is what Paul

12. Richard B. Hays, *Echoes of Scripture in the Letters of Paul* (New Haven: Yale University Press, 1989), 78–79.

13. Both the Hebrew Masoretic Text and the Greek LXX formulate this verse as a question about crossing over the sea, not about descending into the abyss. Nevertheless, the sea and the abyss are closely related in Jewish literature.

calls "the obedience of faith" (1:5; 16:26). Believing in Jesus and accepting the gospel is now the way that keeping the law leads to life.[14]

Paul extends his interpretation of Deut 30:14 by relating the terms **mouth**   10:9–10 and **heart** to the believer's confession of faith and the justification that results. He words the pronouncement as a conditional promise: the people of Israel can indeed be **justified** and **saved**—expressions that are basically synonymous for Paul—but only **if** they confess that **Jesus is Lord** and believe that **God raised** Jesus **from the dead**. In putting it this way, Paul underscores that the gospel calls for a response from the whole person, inside and out, from the mind and heart as well as the lips and tongue.

Paul continues to support his thesis in 10:4 ("Christ is the end of the law")   10:11–13 with three additional sentences, each of which begins with **For**. Repetition of this word brings out the logic of the argument, showing that the essence of Paul's gospel is held together by these interlocking assertions.

In verse 11, Paul quotes the †Septuagint translation of Isa 28:16: **"No one who believes in him will be put to shame."** He already quoted this verse in full in Rom 9:33, and the interpretation given there applies here as well. The only difference is that here Paul adjusts the wording slightly (saying "no one who believes" instead of "whoever believes") in order to underscore the universal application of Isaiah's promise. All who put their faith in Jesus, regardless of nationality or ethnicity, will be spared the disgrace of final condemnation.

Verse 12 reinforces this point by stressing that there are no limits on the availability of salvation in Jesus. Several terms in this passage are recycled from earlier chapters. The claim that **there is no distinction between Jew and Greek** in the matter of salvation is one that readers will remember from 3:9 and 3:23, where Paul was adamant that no distinction can be made between Jews and Gentiles in the matter of sin. Likewise, affirming that **the same Lord is Lord of all** is an echo of 3:29, which indicated that God is the God of all nations, not just the God of the Jews.

Verse 13 pulls the discussion together with a quote from the prophet Joel: **"everyone who calls on the name of the Lord will be saved"** (Joel 3:5). The passage is a summons to faith in the God of Israel, who offers salvation to his people. In the Hebrew text of Joel, the "Lord" who saves is Yahweh (the Tetragrammaton †YHWH is used). Paul, however, applies the passage directly to Jesus as Lord, just as Peter did in Acts 2:21, 36. Christian faith believes that Christ is not merely human but the divine Son of God; and beyond that, his

---

14. N. T. Wright, "Romans 9–11 and the 'New Perspective,'" in *Between Gospel and Election*, ed. Florian Wilk and J. Ross Wagner (Tübingen: Mohr Siebeck, 2010), 37–54.

Paul and the Story of Scripture

To modern readers, Paul's reading of Deut 30:12–14 in Rom 10:6–8 may seem highly unusual. The passage is clearly talking about the law, yet the Apostle interprets it in reference to Christ. What suggested to him that these verses have a Christian fulfillment? How do we explain his reasoning?

Paul expects readers to be familiar with the original context of the passage he cites. In this instance he is drawing from a section of Deuteronomy that looks ahead to the future exile and restoration of Israel. In the verses immediately preceding the ones quoted in Romans, Moses prophesies the path Israel will follow. He foresees Israel (1) enjoying the blessings of the covenant, then (2) enduring the curses of the covenant, most notably exile, but in the end (3) experiencing the mercy of God, who rescues his people and renews his covenant by circumcising the hearts of his people, giving them a new ability to love and obey him (Deut 30:1–8).

This prophecy of covenant renewal is precisely what Paul sees fulfilled in Jesus Christ. The Apostle locates himself and his readers in the third and last stage of the story—the time of restoration when God's mercy has the final say.[a] In Rom 9:6–29 Paul traced the story of Israel from the patriarchs to the exodus to the prophets and then to the exile. With the coming of the Messiah, the final corner is turned. Now, at long last, God is acting to restore Israel and to renew his covenant as promised.

That Paul is thinking along these lines is suggested by the whole sweep of Romans. Early in the letter Paul stated that "circumcision is of the heart" (2:29), recalling the vision of Moses in Deut 30. Later he announced that "the love of God has been poured out into our hearts" (Rom 5:5), bringing to mind how Moses foresaw Israel's new ability to love as a gift from God in Deut 30. Likewise Paul declares that Christian love is "the fulfillment of the law" (Rom 13:10) for those who live according to the Spirit (8:4). This too correlates with Moses' prophecy in Deut 30 that God will empower his people by grace to observe his commandments.

The lesson is that Paul's theology is tied to the narrative of the Bible. When he cites a passage of Scripture to make a point, he routinely shows himself attentive to its context—not simply its literary context, but its historical and theological context as well, its place in the grand story of salvation. Indeed, awareness of the stages of God's unfolding plan is one of the keys to unlocking Paul's interpretation of the Bible. To read the Scriptures in light of Christ is to read them not only as a story about Israel in the past but as a living word that speaks to the present and future as well. For Paul, Christ makes sense of the whole of Scripture because the whole of Scripture directs us to Christ.

a. See Wright, "Romans 9–11 and the 'New Perspective,'" 45–47; and Steven R. Coxhead, "Deuteronomy 30:11–14 as a Prophecy of the New Covenant in Christ," *WTJ* 68 (2006): 305–20.

enthronement at the Father's right hand makes him the agent of God's universal lordship over creation. Calling on Jesus as Lord is a plea for the salvation that only God can accomplish in our lives.

Reflection and Application (10:9–13)

It is not uncommon to hear "Bible Christians" quote Rom 10:9–10 to insist that nothing is required for salvation beyond believing in Jesus with your heart and acknowledging him before others. Consequently preachers and evangelists often claim that one can become a Christian virtually anywhere. A person can invite Jesus into his heart while standing in line at the grocery store, while driving to work, while gazing at the night sky, while attending a worship service.

Certainly there is a measure of truth in this. God can move powerfully in our lives at any time or place of his choosing to convict us of sin and to convince us of his love. But Paul seems to have a very specific situation in mind. "Believing" and "confessing" are closely tied to the sacrament of baptism. It is in the liturgical context of Christian initiation that a person's inward conviction of faith is matched by an outward confession of faith in the lordship of Jesus Christ. It is when a believer is "washed" that he or she is "justified in the name of the Lord Jesus Christ" (1 Cor 6:11) and "saved" from past sins (Titus 3:5).

The baptismal setting of believing and confessing is also suggested by Paul's reference to Joel 3:5 ("everyone who calls on the name of the Lord will be saved") in Rom 10:13. This verse was invoked in the first apostolic summons to baptism in Christian history. Peter quotes the prophecy of Joel 3:1–5 to explain the outpouring of the Spirit on the earliest disciples of Jesus on Pentecost. Yet for Peter the passage also has a level of fulfillment that stretches beyond this unique event. Having announced that "everyone shall be saved who calls on the name of the Lord" (Acts 2:21), Peter goes on to identify Jesus as the "Lord" of Joel's prophecy (Acts 2:36) and then urges the crowds to "be baptized, every one of you, in the name of Jesus Christ for the forgiveness of your sins" (Acts 2:38). It is in the administration of baptism that *the name of the Lord is called upon for salvation!*

Israel's Unbelief as Disobedience (10:14–21)

---

¹⁴But how can they call on him in whom they have not believed? And how can they believe in him of whom they have not heard? And how can

they hear without someone to preach? [15]And how can people preach unless they are sent? As it is written, "How beautiful are the feet of those who bring [the] good news!" [16]But not everyone has heeded the good news; for Isaiah says, "Lord, who has believed what was heard from us?" [17]Thus faith comes from what is heard, and what is heard comes through the word of Christ. [18]But I ask, did they not hear? Certainly they did; for

> "Their voice has gone forth to all the earth,
>   and their words to the ends of the world."

[19]But I ask, did not Israel understand? First Moses says:

> "I will make you jealous of those who are not a nation;
>   with a senseless nation I will make you angry."

[20]Then Isaiah speaks boldly and says:

> "I was found [by] those who were not seeking me;
>   I revealed myself to those who were not asking for me."

[21]But regarding Israel he says, "All day long I stretched out my hands to a disobedient and contentious people."

OT: Deut 32:21; Ps 19:5; Isa 52:7; 53:1; 65:1–2
NT: Matt 8:17; Luke 22:37; John 12:38; Acts 8:32–35; 1 Pet 2:21–25
Catechism: Christ the Suffering Servant, 615, 623
Lectionary: 10:9–18: St. Andrew; Mass for the Evangelization of Peoples

In the final section of Rom 10, Paul faults his unbelieving kinsmen for not obeying the gospel. This tragic situation cannot be explained by their ignorance of the Christian message but only by their determined resistance to it. The good news has successfully reached the covenant people, just as it fanned out to the wider world. But Scripture itself foresaw Israel's resistance. Paul's claim in 9:6 that the word of God has not failed is thus vindicated; the real failure lies with the chosen people for refusing to accept their Messiah with the obedience of faith (10:16).

10:14–15   Paul probes the mystery of unbelief with a series of pointed rhetorical questions. In order for people to call upon the Lord for salvation, as advocated in 10:13, a series of conditions must first be met. Paul's kin cannot be expected to **call on him in whom they have not believed**, nor can they be expected to **believe in him of whom they have not heard**. Paul is perfectly willing to admit this in principle. In fact, he even carries the logic one step further, asking, **how can people preach unless they are sent?** All are legitimate concerns to address with respect to the gospel and the Jewish people. Yet, as Paul will make clear in 10:18, all the necessary conditions have been sufficiently met. God has done everything required to afford his people the opportunity to hear and to heed the good news.

To demonstrate this, Paul turns directly to Scripture. His first quotation comes from Isa 52:7: **"How beautiful are the feet of those who bring [the] good news!"** Isaiah delights in the prospect of a herald or messenger bringing glad tidings to Zion and announcing that its redemption is at hand. Scholars often read the oracle as an announcement of the end of the Babylonian captivity and the homecoming of exiled Jews in the sixth century BC. Paul perceives a deeper level of fulfillment that corresponds to the announcement of messianic redemption. He even makes a slight adjustment to the wording in order to include all "those" (plural) who carry God's word to his people.[15] Paul wants us to see that Isaiah's prophecy is ultimately fulfilled in the apostles taking the gospel to the world as missionaries.

But despite the apostolic witness to Jesus as Lord, **not everyone** among the people of Israel **heeded the good news**. The gospel challenges the Lord's people to embrace the Messiah with "the obedience of faith" (1:5; 16:26). Yet many refused the invitation. This is not only a disappointing fact of history; it is also something prophetically indicated in the Bible. To make this point, Paul turns to the opening line of **Isaiah** 53, where the prophet asks with dismay: **"Lord, who has believed what was heard from us?"** Paul draws our attention to Isa 53:1 for at least two reasons.

10:16–17

First, the prophet foresees a message of glad tidings falling on deaf ears. Heralds have gone out to proclaim peace and salvation (Isa 52:7), yet their proclamation is met with disbelief among the covenant people. The quotation reinforces Paul's contention that "hearing" is a necessary precondition for "believing" (Rom 10:14)—**Thus faith comes from what is heard**.

Second, Paul's use of Isa 53:1 tells us not only about the reception of the message but also about its content. What is the report that is going out that many find hard to accept? It is the startling news of the Lord's †Suffering Servant, an innocent figure who is despised and abused by his own people and eventually put to death. The prophet learns that God willed this fate for his Servant, who was offering his life as a sacrifice for the sins of others. Paul's citation of Isa 53:1 has the effect of evoking the whole story line of Isa 53. Paul could assume

---

15. Beyond the fact that Paul wishes to include the apostles and other ministers of the Word within the scope of the prophecy, the change from singular to plural may also be influenced by his follow-up citation of Isa 53:1, which tells of a message "heard from us."

his readers were already familiar with Isa 53 since the passage was universally read as a prophecy of the Messiah's passion and death in early Christianity.[16] So too for Paul: Isaiah's oracle is an expression of **the word of Christ**—a message *about* Christ proclaimed in the Scriptures of Israel.

10:18   Lest readers struggle to follow his reasoning, Paul poses the critical question concerning Israel: **did they not hear?** If the gospel never reached his people, then their nonacceptance of the Messiah is both explained and excused. But this is not the case. Paul insists that **they did** hear the summons to salvation in Christ.

Again he buttresses his claim with the words of Scripture, this time with Ps 19:5: **"Their voice has gone forth to all the earth, / and their words to the ends of the world."** Few of Paul's Old Testament citations are as obscure as this one. The *wording* of the passage seems to address his concern well enough, but the *context* of the passage seems entirely unrelated to the subject at hand. Psalm 19 falls into two main parts: the first half marvels at the glory of God revealed through the grandeur of the skies (Ps 19:2–7), while the second half celebrates the glory of God revealed in the Torah (Ps 19:8–15). How Ps 19:5 relates to the worldwide diffusion of the gospel is certainly not obvious.

Some scholars hold that Paul is borrowing the language of Scripture without regard for its original context, as a way of giving his own assertions a familiar ring.[17] I find this unlikely, since Paul typically attends to the context of his Old Testament citations. Perhaps we can say that Paul is arguing from analogy, comparing the extension of God's natural revelation throughout the world to the extension of God's saving revelation throughout the world. Just as the glory of God reaches all through the silent witness of the heavens, so the glory of God in Christ reaches all through the missionary witness of the Church. Understood in this way, the premise that Israel had occasion to hear the good news is not so much demonstrated as reiterated.

10:19–21   Paul anticipates a final objection: **did not Israel understand?** Is it possible that those who identify as Israel failed to comprehend the good news and its implications? Rather than address the question from the standpoint of his own missionary experience, Paul seeks insight from the law and the prophets. In verse 19 he invokes the words of **Moses**, and in verses 20–21 he turns to the testimony of **Isaiah**.

The first quotation comes from the Song of Moses, a poem that surveys the turbulent history of Israel's relationship with the Lord (Deut 32:1–43). This

16. Matt 8:17; Luke 22:37; John 12:38; Acts 8:32–35; 1 Pet 2:21–25.
17. William Sanday and Arthur C. Headlam, *A Critical and Exegetical Commentary on the Epistle to the Romans*, ICC, 5th ed. (Edinburgh: T&T Clark, 1902), 289.

whole passage had a major influence on Paul's thinking about the shape of salvation history. In fact, Deut 32 is one of the most frequently cited chapters of the Old Testament in Paul's Letters.[18]

The verse in question reads, **"I will make you jealous of those who are not a nation; / with a senseless nation I will make you angry."** The speaker is the Lord, who promises to bring judgment on Israel for its idolatry and apostasy during the wilderness period. His just punishment will closely correspond to the crimes of his people: just as Israel provoked the Lord to jealousy with idols ("no gods"), so the Lord will provoke Israel to jealousy with Gentiles ("no nation"). In other words, God will cause his own people to feel the pain that comes with betrayal, to experience the anger and bitterness that arises from offended love.

For Paul, whatever manifestations this judgment may have taken in the centuries since Moses, there is a genuine fulfillment of Deuteronomy taking shape in his own day. Acceptance of the gospel among the Gentiles signals that God is lavishing affection on "those who are not a nation." God is pouring out his grace beyond the covenantal borders of Israel, and this is provoking a jealous reaction among Jewish nonbelievers. Indeed, as Paul will explain in Rom 11:11, 14, God intends to use this judgment to good effect, drawing the covenant people to himself by stirring them to imitate the faith of the Gentiles.

The next quotation comes from the †Septuagint translation of Isa 65:1–2 and stands as one of the harshest of Paul's prophetic indictments against Israel. In the original context, both verses appear to speak of Israel. Paul, however, cleaves the passage in two and applies the first verse to believing Gentiles (Rom 10:20) and the second verse to unbelieving Israelites (10:21). The passage indicates that the Lord (the "I" speaking in the oracle) reaches out to everyone and yet encounters a divided response. Of those who accept his initiative, he states with satisfaction, **"I was found [by] those who were not seeking me; / I revealed myself to those who were not asking for me."** But over those who snubbed his welcoming gestures, the Lord laments with disappointment, **"All day long I stretched out my hands to a disobedient and contentious people."** It is true that Paul does not come out and identify the receptive group as Gentiles, but his description of Gentiles as those "who did not pursue righteousness" in 9:30 makes this all but certain. Conversely, Paul interprets the following verse as a statement **regarding Israel** and its opposition to the word of the Lord in the gospel.

So, if Isaiah was speaking of Israel, what justifies Paul's double reading of these verses? I propose that it is the dispersed and assimilated condition of Israel in

---

18. Paul cites Deut 32 also in Rom 12:19 and 15:10.

the first century AD. Readers will recall from Paul's reference to Hosea 2:1 and 25 back in Rom 9:25–26 that, following centuries of exile among the nations, a majority of the Israelite tribes assimilated into the nations, effectively becoming Gentiles. They had been cut off from the covenant and over time ceased to be identifiable as the Lord's †elect people. In Paul's estimation, then, Isaiah must have foreseen the *restoration* of long-forgotten Israelites, now indistinguishable from Gentiles, as well as the stubborn *resistance* of those who continued to identify as Israel.

Perhaps the parable of the prodigal son in Luke 15:11–32 best illustrates what Paul is getting at. The father in the parable welcomes home his runaway son who has squandered his inheritance and defiled himself far from home, while the otherwise faithful son, who oversaw the family estate, puts up a fuss at the celebration surrounding his brother's return. It is not a question of the father transferring his affection from one son to the other. It is a question of reaching out to both and being heeded by only one.

God's Mercy for All

Romans 11:1–36

By this point in the argument of Rom 9–11, Paul has set forth his case that God is faithful to his word (ch. 9) even when Israel is not (ch. 10). Now he charges out of the final turn into the homestretch, pursuing the question of Israel's ultimate fate (ch. 11). He maintains that God's love for his covenant people endures (11:28), so much so that "all Israel will be saved" (11:26). How this will come about is a mystery that leaves Paul in awe. It involves God hardening a part of Israel, opening a door of salvation for the nations, and in the process wooing the entire family of Israel back into his arms. In the end, Israel and the Gentiles stand together in a single family of faith, boasting not of themselves but owing everything to the mercy of God.

Paul and the Remnant (11:1–10)

¹I ask, then, has God rejected his people? Of course not! For I too am an Israelite, a descendant of Abraham, of the tribe of Benjamin. ²God has not rejected his people whom he foreknew. Do you not know what the scripture says about Elijah, how he pleads with God against Israel? ³"Lord, they have killed your prophets, they have torn down your altars, and I alone am left, and they are seeking my life." ⁴But what is God's response to him? "I have left for myself seven thousand men who have not knelt to Baal." ⁵So also at the present time there is a remnant, chosen by grace. ⁶But if by grace, it is no longer because of works; otherwise grace would no longer

be grace. ⁷What then? What Israel was seeking it did not attain, but the elect attained it; the rest were hardened, ⁸as it is written:

> "God gave them a spirit of deep sleep,
>   eyes that should not see,
>   and ears that should not hear,
>   down to this very day."

⁹And David says:

> "Let their table become a snare and a trap,
>   a stumbling block and a retribution for them;
> ¹⁰let their eyes grow dim so that they may not see,
>   and keep their backs bent forever."

OT: Deut 29:3; 1 Sam 12:22; 1 Kings 19:10, 14, 18; Pss 69:23–24; 94:14; Isa 29:10
NT: Mark 4:11–12; 2 Cor 11:22; Gal 2:16; Phil 3:5
Catechism: Elijah and the prophets, 2582–84, 2595; grace of faith, 153, 162

11:1   The chapter begins with a critical question: **has God rejected his people?** The end of Rom 10 depicted a bleak situation for Israel, with the law and the prophets describing a nation that was jealous, angry, disobedient, and contentious (10:19–21). Yet for one schooled in the Jewish Scriptures, the thought of God casting Israel aside is unthinkable. Paul's spring-loaded retort **Of course not!** slams the door on any notion that God has backed out of the covenant or disowned his people.

Paul forwards himself as living proof of God's unremitting faithfulness to Israel. **I too am an Israelite**, he says, **a descendant of Abraham**. If it is true that "not everyone has heeded the good news" (10:16), it is also true that not everyone among his kin has rejected it. Paul and virtually all the earliest disciples of Jesus were descendants of Abraham, Isaac, and Jacob. In these very first believers, the faithful mercy of God toward Israel is both embodied and confirmed.

Notice that Paul rounds off his résumé with mention of **the tribe of Benjamin**. That he should be aware of his tribal affiliation is not surprising. The tribes of Judah, Benjamin, and Levi, comprising the main elements of the southern kingdom of Judah in the preexilic period, retained their identity into the first century AD, despite their captivity in Babylon and the dispersion of Jewish communities across the ancient world. However, this was not the lot of their sibling tribes who once formed the northern kingdom of Israel. In their case, the Assyrian deportations of the eighth century BC thrust them into permanent exile, so that over time the northern tribes assimilated into the populations of the Gentile world and became lost to history as identifiable Israelites (Isa 27:13).[1] Why is this background significant? Because it shows us that Paul is thinking of the *tribal structure* of Israel as a nation descended from the twelve sons of the patriarch Jacob.[2] It is vital to keep this perspective in mind as we advance toward Paul's announcement that "all Israel will be saved" (Rom 11:26).

In answering his opening question, Paul enunciates the thesis statement **11:2–4** of the chapter: **God has not rejected his people whom he foreknew.** Now as always, the faithfulness of God toward Israel surmounts every obstacle, even the faithlessness of Israel toward God (3:3–4).

Paul derives this confident assertion from two passages of the Old Testament, 1 Sam 12:22 and Ps 94:14, both of which categorically dismiss the possibility that God would forsake Israel. Both are formulated as denials, and yet both function as positive affirmations of Israel's †election. Particularly suited to Paul's concern is the first passage, which is part of Samuel's final prophetic speech to Israel (1 Sam 12:1–25). Samuel urges the people to adhere to the covenant and assures them of God's lasting commitment to Israel, even in the face of the nation's most recent failure in faith—demanding a king other than the Lord to rule over them (1 Sam 8:4–9). This defection from God's plan notwithstanding, Samuel insists that "the LORD will not abandon his people" (1 Sam 12:22).

Paul finds additional support in the account of **Elijah** pleading with the Lord **against Israel**. Elijah had been hiding on Mount Horeb from the murderous rage of Queen Jezebel, who slaughtered the Lord's prophets and swore to bring death to Elijah as well (1 Kings 19:1–8). When the Lord asks why Elijah is hiding on the mountain, the prophet sighs: **"Lord, they have killed your prophets, they have torn down your altars, and I alone am left, and they are seeking my life"** (1 Kings 19:10, 14). As far as the prophet could see, he was the last man standing, the only person left in Israel still faithful to the Lord. But God exposes his limited vision: **"I have left for myself seven thousand men who**

---

1. According to the Old Testament, the stragglers of the northern Israelites who never went into Assyrian exile retained an awareness of their tribal lineage, at least for a time (2 Chron 30:10–11). But evidence from later times preserves precious few references to individuals descended from one of the northern tribes of Israel (see Tob 1:1; Luke 2:36). Likewise, Josephus, in his account of the end of the Babylonian exile, tallies the number of returnees from Judah, Benjamin, and Levi, while noting that others joined the group who claimed to be "Israelites" but who could not verify their genealogies (*Jewish Antiquities* 11.69–70; see Ezra 2:59). The ancient Jewish document *Testament of Asher* 7.6 specifies that the northern Israelites, once scattered among foreign nations, would no longer remember their ancestral tribe or mother tongue.

2. James M. Scott, "'And Then All Israel Will Be Saved' (Rom 11:26)," in *Restoration: Old Testament, Jewish, and Christian Perspectives*, ed. James M. Scott (Leiden: Brill, 2001), 489–526. See also commentary on 9:4–5.

have not knelt to Baal" (1 Kings 19:18).[3] Elijah might have thought that *he* was preserving a †remnant in Israel. But it was God's mercy that accomplished it entirely apart from Elijah's notice.

For Paul, the Elijah episode is layered with significance. (1) Typologically, it points to a recurring pattern in salvation history. The crisis of faith in Paul's day mirrors the crisis of faith in Elijah's day. At both times Israel resists the Lord and his plan on a national scale, with only a few remaining faithful. (2) Pastorally, Paul wants to caution readers lest they conclude as Elijah did that the Israel of faith has dwindled to nothing. True, the Jewish people are resisting the gospel in startling numbers, but God always preserves some in the shelter of his mercy. Consequently, the work of Christian evangelization must go on with confidence that the Lord wants to continue his saving work among the covenant people. (3) Contextually, it is striking that the remnant unknown to Elijah was a throng of the faithful from northern Israel, from among the very tribes that were considered lost in Paul's day. Since Elijah's ministry was conducted in the northern kingdom, the reader is prepared to see that the salvation of "all Israel" in Rom 11:26 will include the northern tribes. (4) Rhetorically, Paul adopts what scholars designate a "hermeneutic of prophetic criticism." In other words, he assumes the role of a prophet who confronts and critiques Israel from within. He draws on his nation's sacred traditions to challenge those who presume that God is unconditionally obligated to bless Israel, even in times of national rebellion.[4] True prophets insist that God is obligated to enforce the covenant by activating its sanctions on disobedience. The effect of this prophetic critique is that "the comparison between Israel of Paul's day with the Israel of Elijah's day would have been deeply resented" by Jewish opponents of the gospel because it implies that "Israel is in a state of apostasy."[5]

11:5–6 Paul next makes explicit what was implicit in the foregoing: Elijah faced a situation in the eighth century that anticipates **the present time**. Then as now, there exists **a remnant** of the covenant people still in God's favor. The remnant concept has a long history in ancient literature, undergoing its fullest development in the prophetic books of Scripture.[6] It comes into play in times of

---

3. Baal was the storm and fertility god of Canaanite religion. He was the Lord's chief rival and competitor for devotion among the Israelites during Elijah's ministry in the eighth century BC.

4. Craig A. Evans, "Paul and the Prophets: Prophetic Criticism in the Epistle to the Romans (with special reference to Romans 9–11)," in *Romans and the People of God: Essays in Honor of Gordon D. Fee on the Occasion of His 65th Birthday*, ed. Sven K. Soderlund and N. T. Wright (Grand Rapids: Eerdmans, 1999), 115–28.

5. Evans, "Paul and the Prophets," 126.

6. For the early history of the idea, with careful attention given to the Elijah episode, see Gerhard F. Hasel, *The Remnant: The History and Theology of the Remnant Idea from Genesis to Isaiah*, 2nd ed.

national catastrophe or apostasy, when the majority of Israel is swept away by foreign armies or pagan cults, leaving behind a distressingly small group that survives or remains loyal to the Lord. In theological terms, the existence of a remnant indicates that God's judgment on Israel is limited by his mercy. Lest Israel come to nothing and the Lord default on his promises, God intervenes to preserve some who will continue in his blessings.

Paul is well aware of this, which is why he defines the remnant as a community **chosen by grace**. †Election is an act of sheer gratuity on God's part. One is not given a place among the remnant **because of works**. If that were so, **grace would no longer be grace**. In Paul's day, the grace of election is the grace to believe in Jesus as Messiah and Lord.

In verse 7 Paul pauses to summarize the progress of his argument thus far. **11:7** The question **What then?** is his verbal prompt, and his answer takes the form of three assertions.

First, he says that **Israel** as a whole **did not attain** what it sought. These cryptic words are decipherable in view of 9:30–31, where Paul said that the unbelievers of Israel never arrived at the "righteousness that comes from faith" because of their misguided attempt to earn righteousness for themselves by observance of the Torah.

Second, Paul qualifies his prior assertion with another: **but the elect attained it**. By coming to faith in Jesus, a †remnant of Israel has come to possess the saving righteousness of the Messiah, while those withholding assent to the gospel have not.

Third, Paul accounts for Israel's unsuccessful pursuit of righteousness by revealing that **the rest were hardened**. In other words, besides faulting Israel for an incomplete knowledge of the truth (10:2–3), Paul attributes Israel's failure to believe to an act of divine discipline.[7]

Paul thus draws a line through the midst of Israel. Part of Israel constitutes the "remnant" who have come to salvation in Christ, while part of Israel comprises the "rest" who presently stand under judgment. Such is the result of Israel's divided response to the gospel. But far from being an isolated event, rejecting Jesus is the culmination of a pattern of unfaithfulness that stretches over the whole history of the covenant people. Most commentators, with an eye toward 11:25–26, are concerned with the question of when Israel's hardening will *end*. But no less important is the question of when Israel's hardening *began*, for what

---

(Berrien Springs, MI: Andrews University, 1974). For a summary of its later development, see Roland de Vaux, OP, "'The Remnant of Israel' according to the Prophets," in *The Bible and the Ancient Near East*, trans. Damian McHugh (New York: Doubleday, 1971), 15–30.

7. For this concept, see commentary on 9:18.

is true of unbelieving Israel in the present is equally true of unfaithful Israel in the past. Recall that Paul first spoke of divine hardening in his review of the exodus, where the Lord hardened the heart of Pharaoh (9:16–18). So likewise, as the following quotations from Scripture demonstrate, Israel experienced a hardening by God on many occasions, extending from the exodus period all the way to the exile.

11:8–10   Paul explains Israel's hardening by invoking the triple witness of Scripture. He draws passages from the law, the prophets, and the Psalms, which together represent the three primary divisions of the Jewish Bible (Luke 24:44). In classic rabbinic fashion, he draws together several verses that share a common word, a technique known as *gezerah shawah*. In this instance, the catchword is "eyes." The Apostle capitalizes on this term to show that the Old Testament defines hardening as spiritual blindness.

Following the formula **as it is written,** Paul offers a paraphrase of Deut 29:3, stating positively what was originally expressed negatively: **God gave them . . . / eyes that should not see, / and ears that should not hear, / down to this very day**. These are the words of Moses spoken before Israel crossed into the land of Canaan. As part of his farewell address, Moses chides the people of Israel for witnessing the wonders of God's power in the exodus while failing to appreciate the blessings they had received. Because the people redeemed from bondage kept straying from the covenant in their hearts, the grace of spiritual understanding was withheld from them. Theirs was a generation blindfolded by the Lord's just judgment.

Into this quotation Paul inserts an expression from the prophets. The phrase **a spirit of deep sleep** comes from Isa 29:10, where Isaiah pronounces doom on wicked Jerusalem (poetically called "Ariel" in Isa 29:1). His message is that God has closed the eyes of Judah's prophets and leaders, those on whom the nation relies for direction. The rebellious people of God were left to fly blind into a storm of divine reckoning.

The third Old Testament citation is from Ps 69:23–24, traditionally attributed to **David**. This is not a prophecy, strictly speaking, but an imprecatory prayer in which the king invokes divine judgment on his enemies, probably those in Israel who oppose his rule and harass those who are loyal to him. **Let their table become a snare and a trap,** he pleads, **a stumbling block and a retribution for them**. Then David adds the line that links up with the first two citations: **let their eyes grow dim so that they may not see, / and keep their backs bent forever**. Chilling words indeed from "the sweet psalmist of Israel" (2 Sam 23:1 RSV).

Behind Paul's reading of this psalm is the early Christian conviction that Jesus is the Davidic Messiah, the anointed one descended from David's line who is destined to reign as David's Lord (Matt 22:41–46; Luke 1:31–33; Rom 1:3–4; 15:12). In unison with this tradition, Paul hears the voice of Christ speaking through the voice of David. For him the psalm anticipates the opposition of the hardened part of Israel to the Davidic Messiah.[8]

Together these excerpts from Scripture suggest that Israel's blindness is both "divinely imposed *and* humanly deserved."[9] Unbelieving Israel stands at the intersection of divine judgment and national rebellion. Both sides of the equation are affirmed as true in a way that retains an element of mystery.

Apostleship to the Gentiles (11:11–16)

---

[11]Hence I ask, did they stumble so as to fall? Of course not! But through their transgression salvation has come to the Gentiles, so as to make them jealous. [12]Now if their transgression is enrichment for the world, and if their diminished number is enrichment for the Gentiles, how much more their full number.

[13]Now I am speaking to you Gentiles. Inasmuch then as I am the apostle to the Gentiles, I glory in my ministry [14]in order to make my race jealous and thus save some of them. [15]For if their rejection is the reconciliation of the world, what will their acceptance be but life from the dead? [16]If the firstfruits are holy, so is the whole batch of dough; and if the root is holy, so are the branches.

OT: Num 15:17–21; Deut 32:21; Ezek 37:1–14
NT: Acts 9:15; Rom 10:19; 16:5; 1 Cor 16:15; Gal 1:15–16; James 1:18
Catechism: resurrection of the dead, 992, 1038

In this transitional section Paul makes two points that prepare for the high point of the chapter. First, he hammers in another secure point of reference. Just as he vigorously denied that God has rejected Israel (11:1), so now he denies that Israel has fallen without hope of recovery (11:11). Second, Paul addresses the Gentile Christians in Rome directly. His aim, continuing into the next section, is to remind the Gentiles of their place in the plan of God, a plan in which Israel still has priority status.

8. C. Marvin Pate, *Romans*, TTCS (Grand Rapids: Baker Books, 2014), 212.
9. Frank J. Matera, *Romans*, PCNT (Grand Rapids: Baker Academic, 2010), 259, emphasis original.

11:11   Paul asks about the hardened part of Israel: **did they stumble so as to fall?**
Commentators concur that Paul is resuming the footrace metaphor deployed in
9:30–33. There the point is that Israel tripped and stumbled over the Messiah;
here the question is whether Israel has been knocked out of the race entirely.
To this the Apostle responds: **Of course not!** Israel may have struck an obstacle
on the track, but Paul remains confident that his people are still able to regain
their footing and reach the finish line.

Beyond that, Paul contends that God is using Israel's stumbling to good effect, since **through their transgression**[10] **salvation has come to the Gentiles**.
Israel's failing has created an opportunity for other nations to enter into a saving
relationship with the Lord. This was frequently Paul's missionary experience:
several times in the book of Acts we see him, when faced with determined
Jewish opposition, pivoting away from the synagogue to begin preaching to
Gentiles (Acts 13:45–46; 14:1–7; 18:1–6; 28:17–28). This is no doubt part of the
picture. But I would suggest that Paul is also thinking about Israel's historical
unfaithfulness. Israel long ago transgressed the word of God, and as a result
found itself scattered far and wide among the nations. From this standpoint
as well, Israel's dispersion among the Gentiles worked for the benefit of the
Gentiles. With so many families and tribes of Israel lost to history, thoroughly
dissolved into the bloodlines and cultures of other nations, God must reach
out to save the nations in order to honor his pledge to restore all Israel. In my
view, this is a vital part of the mystery soon to be revealed in Rom 11:25–26.

Finally, Paul claims that salvation has come to the Gentiles **so as to make**
Israel **jealous**. This divine purpose was revealed in Deut 32:21, which he already
quoted in Rom 10:19. There we learned that God would use people *outside* the
covenant (Gentiles) to provoke the people *of* the covenant (Israel) to jealousy.
The dynamic is akin to a love triangle. When a woman learns that her beloved
has diverted his affections to another, she experiences the anger and jealousy of
offended love. But there is another side to jealousy. The Greek verb *parazēloō* can
mean not only "provoke to jealous anger" but also "inspire to emulation."[11] The
offended lover wants to win her beloved back, so she takes the steps necessary
to recover what her rival has stolen away. The Lord wants Israel to experience
the angst of seeing his mercy shown to the Gentiles, but only so that Israel will

---

10. Modern translations differ over the translation of the Greek *to autōn paraptōma* in this context.
In addition to "their transgression" (NABRE, NIV), one also finds "their trespass" (RSV, ESV), "their
stumbling" (NRSV), and "their fall" (JB). Scholars have likewise proposed "their misstep" in view of
the running metaphor.

11. Richard H. Bell, *Provoked to Jealousy: The Origin and Purpose of the Jealousy Motif in Romans
9–11*, WUNT 63 (Tübingen: Mohr, 1993).

be aroused to reclaim its birthright. Israel, he hopes, will be moved to emulate the Gentiles by coming to faith in Jesus.

Building on verse 11, Paul formulates an argument that reasons from the **11:12** lesser to the greater. If Israel's stumbling brings benefits to the Gentiles, then readers should consider **how much more** benefit will come to the world with Israel's full restoration in the Messiah. For the Gentiles, salvation is spiritual **enrichment** on a grand scale, and this came about because of his kinsmen's **transgression** of God's word in the gospel. But just imagine, Paul says, what riches will be lavished on the world if the **full number** of the people and tribes of Israel, currently reduced to a **diminished number**, should embrace the good news.

In the next several verses, Paul addresses the Christian **Gentiles** in Rome **11:13–14** directly to caution them against drawing false conclusions about the saving work of God on their behalf.

His pastoral counsel begins with an undisputed fact: **I am the apostle to the Gentiles**. Everyone knows that Paul was commissioned by Jesus to carry his gospel to the nations (Gal 1:15–16). This is his unique mandate.

But it is not the case that Paul's missionary assignment entails a disregard for Israel. Christians often forget that Paul was tasked with bringing Jesus' name "before the Gentiles and kings *and the sons of Israel*" (Acts 9:15 RSV, emphasis added). Announcing the good news of salvation to Israel, dispersed far and wide among the nations, was part of his job description from the outset.

Paul's apostleship must be understood in light of this clarification. Far from avoiding any evangelistic responsibility toward Israel, he declares, **I glory in my ministry in order to make my race**[12] **jealous and thus save some of them.** In other words, Paul fulfills his ministry for the express purpose of reclaiming at least some of his unbelieving brethren for Christ. It is a matter of bringing the gospel to all nations, *including* Israel. Indeed, by reaping a harvest of conversions among the Gentiles, Paul hopes to provoke his kinsmen to a jealous emulation of Gentile faith. There is divine irony in this reversal: in biblical history, it is precisely Israel's weakness for imitating the nations and their religious cults that landed the covenant people in exile among them. Now, at long last, God has made it safe for Israel to emulate the Gentiles in their embrace of the gospel. No longer an occasion for judgment, imitation of the nations has been made a path to salvation.

---

12. Literally, "my flesh," which is shorthand for "my kin according to the flesh" (Rom 9:3). Translations such as the RSV and ESV render the phrase "my fellow Jews," even though the term "Jews" does not appear in the Greek.

11:15   As in verse 12, Paul reasons from a given assumption to a greater reality. God's hardening of part of Israel has made possible **the reconciliation of the world**. Readers already know from Rom 5 that Paul understands reconciliation to mean the "peace with God" (5:1) that is brought about "through the death of his Son" (5:10). The opportunity for this was created by widespread **rejection** of the gospel among his countrymen.

But notice that Paul holds out hope for their **acceptance** of the gospel. As he is about to point out, his people can still attain messianic salvation "if they do not remain in unbelief" (11:23). When his kin come to embrace Jesus, they will experience **life from the dead**. Similar language used earlier in Romans suggests to some that Paul has in mind a *baptismal* resurrection that occurs when believers receive a sacramental infusion of Christ's risen life (6:4, 13). Others maintain that Paul envisions the *bodily* resurrection of believers from Israel on the last day, an †eschatological event also touched on earlier in Romans (8:11). I think it probable that Paul had both of these saving events in mind.

Paul's expectation of Israel's national resurrection is likely connected with Ezekiel's prophetic vision in Ezek 37:1–14. This is part of a collection of prophecies in Ezek 36–37 that announce the Lord's plan to reunify the whole tribal family of Israel divided by exile. The prophet sees a valley strewn with the bones of a slain army, only to witness them reassembling and receiving new life from the Spirit of God. Sin led to the covenantal death of Israel among the nations. God intends to reverse the tragedies that left his people scattered and lifeless.

11:16   The final verse in this section enables Paul to segue into what follows. It consists of two metaphors, one liturgical and one horticultural. Both operate on the principle that the holiness of a part extends to the whole. Despite illustrating the same principle, these metaphors appear to speak about two different things.

Paul first speaks of the **firstfruits** taken from a **whole batch of dough**. If the former is **holy**, he reasons, then so is the latter. The imagery comes from Num 15:17–21, where Moses instructs the Israelites to offer a single cake from the first batch of meal harvested in the first year of Israel's residency in the promised land. By making this an offering to the Lord, the rest of the year's harvest is sanctified for eating by the people. In all likelihood, Paul means by "firstfruits" the †remnant of Israel, the initial harvest of the gospel among the covenant people (Rom 11:5).[13] He uses this language elsewhere to designate the first Christian disciples of a given region (16:5; 1 Cor 16:15; 2 Thess 2:13). On this interpretation, the ingathering of a holy *remnant* of Israel offers hope for an ingathering of the *rest* of Israel.

---

13. Some commentators take the "firstfruits" to represent the patriarchs.

The second metaphor depicts the **root** of an olive tree (Rom 11:17–24) in organic union with its **branches**. Again, if the former is **holy**, then so is the latter. Paul relies on common knowledge as well as knowledge of passages of the Bible that describe Israel as a people of the Lord's planting. Paul is thinking of Abraham and the patriarchs (the root) in relation to the nation that springs from them (the branches). This idea is not explicitly stated in Scripture, but other Jewish writings refer to Abraham as the "root" of Israel.[14] It is remarkable how Paul begins the argument of Rom 9–11 with Abraham (9:6), how he traces his own ancestry back to Abraham (11:1), and how he ends his exposition on the note that Israel remains beloved "because of the patriarchs" (11:28).[15] Israel's holy origin is the basis for its hopes of national restoration.[16]

The Olive Tree of Israel (11:17–24)

[17]**But if some of the branches were broken off, and you, a wild olive shoot, were grafted in their place and have come to share in the rich root of the olive tree,** [18]**do not boast against the branches. If you do boast, consider that you do not support the root; the root supports you.** [19]**Indeed you will say, "Branches were broken off so that I might be grafted in."** [20]**That is so. They were broken off because of unbelief, but you are there because of faith. So do not become haughty, but stand in awe.** [21]**For if God did not spare the natural branches, [perhaps] he will not spare you either.** [22]**See, then, the kindness and severity of God: severity toward those who fell, but God's kindness to you, provided you remain in his kindness; otherwise you too will be cut off.** [23]**And they also, if they do not remain in unbelief, will be grafted in, for God is able to graft them in again.** [24]**For if you were cut from what is by nature a wild olive tree, and grafted, contrary to nature, into a cultivated one, how much more will they who belong to it by nature be grafted back into their own olive tree.**

OT: Jer 11:16–17; Hosea 14:7; Zech 14:3, 14
NT: Luke 13:6–9; John 15:1–8; Rom 10:16–17; 15:27
Catechism: Church as olive tree, 755; Church's relationship with Israel, 60, 839; grace of faith, 153, 162

14. *1 Enoch* 93.8; Philo of Alexandria, *Who Is the Heir of Divine Things* 279; see also *Jubilees* 16.26; 21.24.
15. Paul's metaphor might also be viewed as Davidic as well as Abrahamic. The Messiah, coming from David's royal line, appears in biblical and Jewish texts as a "branch" or "shoot" (Jer 23:5; 33:15; 4QFlorilegium 1.11) that sprouts from either the "roots" of Jesse (Isa 11:1) or the "root" of Judah (*Testament of Judah* 24.4–6). Beyond this, an olive tree is a fitting image for an "anointed one" inasmuch as the oil used for sacred purposes in Israel was typically pressed from olives (see Zech 4:1–14).
16. Pablo T. Gadenz, *Called from the Jews and from the Gentiles: Pauline Ecclesiology in Romans 9–11* (Tübingen: Mohr Siebeck, 2009), 265.

Here we have Paul's famous olive tree analogy. He introduced it briefly in 11:16; now he develops it in detail. The tree is a visual representation of the messianic people of God, having natural branches (believing Israelites), engrafted branches (believing Gentiles), and excised branches (unbelieving Israelites). The orchard farmer (God) tends the tree with a view to harvesting its yield. Pastorally, Paul uses this imagery to address the danger of Gentile boasting, just as earlier in the letter he spoke to the hazard of Jewish boasting (3:27–30). Theologically, Paul develops a traditional image of Israel into an ecclesial image of the Christian community.[17] He does this not to suggest that the latter supplants the former in the holy purposes of God but to affirm the continuity of the Old Covenant and the New. It is difficult to imagine a more effective way of showing how believers from Israel and the nations alike are fused into a single family of faith.

11:17–18　In the Mediterranean region, olive growers developed grafting techniques to reinvigorate older trees. They would attach shoots from a **wild olive** shrub to the mature trunk of a cultivated **olive tree** by making incisions or boring holes for the new sprig.[18] Paul invites readers to picture a tree with **some** of its natural **branches** sawn off, and shoots snipped from an untended olive shrub **grafted in** among the remaining branches. Once attached, the wild grafts draw their sustenance from the **rich root** of the cultivated **olive tree**.

The Apostle, using the singular pronoun **you**, warns the Gentile believer not to **boast** over the natural **branches** that have been lopped off. No Christian is to find satisfaction in the judgment of unbelieving Israel, nor is he to take pride in his own situation.[19] After all, the branches do not support the root; rather, **the root supports** the branches. Theologically speaking, Gentile believers stand in a dependent relationship to Israel, not a superior one. They have not received grace independently of Israel; rather, they **have come to share** in the graces entrusted to Israel (15:27).

11:19–22　In verse 19 Paul reverts to the †diatribe style we have seen intermittently throughout Romans. He anticipates the assertion of a Gentile objector: **"Branches were broken off so that I might be grafted in."** This is a fact that Paul does not

---

17. For Israel as an olive tree, see Jer 11:16–17; Hosea 14:7; Babylonian Talmud *Menahot* 53b.

18. Columella, *De Re Rustica* 5.9.16. For discussion, see A. G. Baxter and J. A. Ziesler, "Paul and Arboriculture: Romans 11.17–24," *JSNT* 24 (1985): 25–32. The reverse procedure is also attested in ancient sources, e.g., Theophrastus, *De Causis Plantarum* 1.6.10. For discussion, see Philip F. Esler, "Ancient Oleiculture and Ethnic Differentiation: The Meaning of the Olive-Tree Image in Romans 11," *JSNT* 26, no. 1 (2003): 103–24.

19. Several intellectual elites of the Roman world openly despised the Jewish people and poked fun at their ancestral traditions. It is not unlikely, then, even apart from the issue of Jewish unbelief, that some of the earliest Gentile converts continued to carry the baggage of this cultural prejudice, at least for a time. If so, then Paul must have been anxious to tamp down both ethnic and religious snobbery against Israel in Rome.

© Baker Publishing Group

Figure 8. Ancient olive trees at the Church of All Nations on the Mount of Olives, the traditional site of the garden of Gethsemane.

dispute; however, he clarifies it. The olive tree of Israel has been partly dismembered, but this is **because of** the **unbelief** of select branches, just as wild Gentile shoots have been grafted onto the stock **because of** their **faith** in Christ.

Paul's point is that Gentiles must **not become haughty, but stand in awe**. God's grace should not become an occasion for pride any more than God's judgment should be treated lightly. **For if God did not spare the natural branches**, he may **not spare** the wild grafts **either**. The analogy thus confronts readers with God's **kindness and severity**, terms that approximate what later theology calls God's "mercy" and "justice."[20] Believers should be humbled in the face of divine mercy as well as reverential in the face of divine justice. Why? God's **severity** is exercised by severing unbelieving branches from the tree, while his **kindness** is exercised by adding others. The reminder for Gentiles, then, is that grafts remain attached to the trunk only if they continue in faith, humility, and the fear of the Lord. Should they fail in this regard, they **too** will experience the judgment of being **cut off**.

Paul completes his analogy on a hopeful note. Having established that God **11:23–24** has not rejected Israel (11:2), and that his people have not stumbled into a fall

---

20. Joseph A. Fitzmyer, SJ, *Romans*, AB 33 (New York: Doubleday, 1993), 616.

(11:11), Paul addresses the question: What is to be the fate of unbelieving Israel, the severed branches lying on the ground beneath the tree? There is still hope for them, Paul insists, **if they do not remain in unbelief**. Faith is once again the deciding factor, the difference between justification and condemnation. The option for faith always remains a possibility in this life, as does the option for unbelief. God, for his part, **is able to graft** the fallen branches **in again**. Readers know this because "the power of God for the salvation of everyone who believes" is made available in the gospel (1:16).

In essence, Paul is saying that Israel's hardening is not irreversible. His reasoning arises directly from the analogy: if the cuttings of a **wild olive tree** can be **grafted** into the trunk of **a cultivated one**, then native branches can **much more** readily be **grafted back into their own olive tree**. Gentiles are joined to the trunk **contrary to nature**, inasmuch as ingrafting is an artificial procedure. Israelites, however, belong to the tree **by nature**. The blessings of the covenant rightfully belong to them as the inheritance of a firstborn son among the family of nations (Exod 4:22).

Reflection and Application (11:17–24)

Many Christians embrace a misconception that the Church is a replacement for Israel in the plan of God. This perspective is often designated "supersessionism"— the view that the New Covenant supersedes the Old in such a way that God's arrangements with Israel have now been canceled. One can acknowledge that certain precepts and rites of the Mosaic law have given way to the teachings and institutions of Christ. But this is not at issue. The question is whether God has divorced his first wife, the covenant community of Israel, and pledged himself to a new one, the messianic community of Christians.

Closer attention to Rom 11 and to Paul's olive tree analogy in particular might have helped to prevent this mistaken conclusion. Nowhere is it clearer in the New Testament that the Lord is not finished with Israel in fulfilling his purposes. Simply put, Paul does not advocate a *theology of replacement* in which Gentile believers take the place of a disinherited Israel as the new people of God. If that were the case, we would expect him to portray God abandoning his cultivated tree and domesticating a wild one instead. But this is not how the analogy depicts God's relationship with Israel and the Gentiles. Paul advocates a *theology of incorporation* in which Gentiles are given access to the rich sap that runs through Israel from root to branch. They are made fellow sharers in Israel's relationship with God, not replacements who acquire something that was stripped away from Israel. Paul may be said to summarize this perspective when he states in Rom 15:27 that "the Gentiles have come to share in their spiritual blessings." In the final analysis, the olive tree analogy is not about Israel being left behind in the forward march of salvation history; it is about the Gentiles being promoted to participate with Israel in the privilege of being God's people.

The Mystery of Israel's Salvation (11:25–32)

²⁵I do not want you to be unaware of this mystery, brothers, so that you will not become wise [in] your own estimation: a hardening has come upon Israel in part, until the full number of the Gentiles comes in, ²⁶and thus all Israel will be saved, as it is written:

"The deliverer will come out of Zion,
   he will turn away godlessness from Jacob;
²⁷and this is my covenant with them
   when I take away their sins."

²⁸In respect to the gospel, they are enemies on your account; but in respect to election, they are beloved because of the patriarchs. ²⁹For the gifts and the call of God are irrevocable.

³⁰Just as you once disobeyed God but have now received mercy because of their disobedience, ³¹so they have now disobeyed in order that, by virtue of the mercy shown to you, they too may [now] receive mercy. ³²For God delivered all to disobedience, that he might have mercy upon all.

OT: Gen 48:19; Isa 2:2–3; 27:9; 59:20–21; Jer 31:31–34
NT: Luke 21:24; Acts 26:7; Rom 11:7; 16:25–26; 1 Cor 15:51; Eph 3:4–6; Rev 7:4–8
Catechism: Israel's unbelief, 591; Israel and the return of the Messiah, 674, 840; God's love for Israel, 218–19; God's mercy, 1037, 1846, 2040

It is fair to say that everything so far discussed in Rom 9–11 has been a buildup to this point. Finally, in verse 25, Paul draws back the curtain to reveal the "mystery" of how God is working to restore Israel through the redemption of the nations. In a way that was unforeseen, the salvation of Israel is accomplished, not simply *after* the salvation of the Gentiles, or exclusively *alongside* the salvation of the Gentiles, but also *in and through* the salvation of the Gentiles. In Paul's understanding, this is God's answer to the prophetic expectation that

Israel, divided and scattered by centuries of exile, would be reinstated in the blessings of the covenant.

11:25–27   Paul transitions into this section with words of solemn import: **I do not want you to be unaware . . . brothers**. This is a disclosure formula that he uses to summon the full attention of his readers (e.g., 1 Cor 10:1; 2 Cor 1:8; 1 Thess 4:13). In this instance, Paul wants to make Gentile Christians aware of a **mystery** concerning Israel. The Greek *mystērion*, at least in the biblical writings, means far more than "secret information" whispered to a privileged few. A mystery is a truth about God and his ways that was once hidden but is now made known, often through a personal revelation (as in Eph 3:3) in connection with biblical revelation (as in Rom 16:25–26). It has to do with a concealed purpose underlying the divine plan of salvation stretching across centuries.

But before divulging this mystery, Paul adds a word about his reason for doing so. He is making Israel's salvation known **so that** Gentile Christians **will not become wise** in their **own estimation**. This is now the third time, following 11:18 and 11:20, that he makes an appeal for humility in order to keep a lid on Gentile conceit.

Now the mystery itself is set forth: **a hardening has come upon Israel in part, until the full number of the Gentiles comes in, and thus all Israel will be saved**. Few passages in the New Testament are as densely packed as this one. Every component of the statement requires attention. Perhaps the best way to proceed is to break it down into manageable units and then see how they work together.

First, Paul reiterates a point made in 11:7 regarding Israel's divine **hardening**. There he stated that a spiritual blindness has taken hold of unbelieving Israel ("the rest"), with only a †remnant of Israel accepting the gospel ("the elect"). Here too Paul specifies that God's hardening affects not the whole of Israel but only **Israel in part**.[21]

Second, Paul considers the duration of Israel's present hardening. It will last **until the full number of the Gentiles comes in**. The surface meaning of this seems clear enough: Israel's hardening will remain so long as the Gentile mission of the Church is under way. The gospel must first be "preached to all nations" (Mark 13:10) so that all who believe in Jesus Christ among the nations may be grafted into the community of the New Covenant. Scholars have long suspected that "the full number of the Gentiles" has its background in the Old

---

21. Scholars debate whether the phrase "in part" (*apo merous*) modifies "Israel," "a hardening," or "has come." The NABRE ("Israel in part") is one of the more likely translations, along with the RSV, NRSV ("part of Israel") and the JB ("one section of Israel"). Less likely renderings are offered in the NIV ("a hardening in part") and the ESV ("a partial hardening").

Testament. For example, it has been argued that Paul has in mind the Table of Nations tradition in Gen 10, where the world outside Israel is divided into seventy nations, these making up the total number of the Gentiles.[22] Others hold that Paul is thinking of Isaiah's visions of the nations streaming into Zion with gifts of their wealth (Isa 60:4–7; 61:6; 66:12).[23] An even better solution, recently put forward, is that Paul is evoking Gen 48:19, where Jacob prophesies to Ephraim that his descendants will become "the fullness of the nations."[24] The implications of this allusion are staggering. In my view, Paul considers exiled Israel—particularly the northern tribes that never returned from the Assyrian dispersions of the eighth century BC—as indistinguishable from the Gentile nations that absorbed them.[25] The descendants of these Israelites have *become* Gentiles. This is not only a fact of history; it is also something foreseen in the Scriptures. In Jacob's blessing on Ephraim (a name frequently given to the whole northern kingdom of Israel in Scripture), the family of Israel is destined to become not only a great nation, but eventually a multitude of nations! In the words of one scholar: "By citing this prophecy at the climax of his argument, Paul has placed his cards on the table in grand style: the Gentiles now receiving the Spirit are the fulfillment of Jacob's prophecy—they are Ephraim's seed, they are Israel, restored through the new covenant."[26]

Third, having identified the intertextual allusion to Gen 48:19 and considered its import, we are ready for Paul's punch line: "and thus all Israel will be saved." Despite being the mystery revealed, this line has been a mystery in its own right to countless readers of Romans through the ages. Interpretations of the statement vary widely, owing to different understandings of what Paul means by "thus" and "all Israel."

The adverb **thus** (Greek *houtōs*) could be taken to describe either the *manner* of Israel's salvation ("in this way") or the *timing* of Israel's salvation ("afterward"). Strictly speaking, both are viable possibilities.[27] Nevertheless, Paul is most likely

---

22. James M. Scott, *Paul and the Nations: The Old Testament and Jewish Background of Paul's Mission to the Nations with Special Reference to the Destination of Galatians*, WUNT 84 (Tübingen: Mohr Siebeck, 1995), 127.

23. Roger D. Aus, "Paul's Travel Plans to Spain and the 'Full Number of the Gentiles' of Rom XI 25," *NovT* 21, no. 3 (1979): 232–62.

24. Jason A. Staples, "What Do the Gentiles Have to Do with 'All Israel'? A Fresh Look at Romans 11:25–27," *JBL* 130 (2011): 371–90; see also Staples, "Reconstructing Israel: Restoration Eschatology in Early Judaism and Paul's Gentile Mission" (PhD diss., University of North Carolina, 2016).

25. See commentary on 9:25–26; 11:1; and 11:2–4.

26. Staples, "What Do the Gentiles?," 387.

27. For the temporal meaning, see Scott, "And Then All Israel," 490–92, 527; and Pieter W. van der Horst, "'Only Then Will All Israel Be Saved': A Short Note on the Meaning of *kai houtōs* in Romans 11:26," *JBL* 119, no. 3 (2000): 521–25.

"All Israel" in Romans 11:26

No discussion of Rom 9–11 can avoid wrestling with Paul's declaration that "all Israel will be saved" (11:26). Who, precisely, is "all Israel"? According to some, Paul is talking about "all ethnic Israelites"—that is, the Jews. According to others, he has in mind "all the elect of ethnic Israel"—that is, Jewish Christians. Still others take him to mean "God's new Israel, the church of Jews and Gentiles."[a]

What is often lacking in attempts to define this term is a careful study of its biblical background.[b] After all, Paul is using a phrase that appears roughly 150 times in the Hebrew Bible. One can speak of some flexibility of meaning, and yet a dominant meaning can hardly be missed. The breakdown is roughly as follows. (1) Sometimes "all Israel" denotes the northern tribes of Israel that broke away from the royal house of David and formed the northern kingdom of Israel as distinct from the southern kingdom of Judah (1 Kings 12:20). (2) A few times "all Israel" refers to a surviving part of the tribal nation, such as the returnees from exile dwelling in Judah in the postexilic period (Ezra 2:70). Most of these were from the southern tribes of Judah, Benjamin, and Levi, but a few northern tribes were represented as well (1 Chron 9:3). (3) In the vast majority of cases, however, the phrase "all Israel" is equivalent to *all twelve tribes of Israel*. It is most often a collective term for the entire tribal family descended from the patriarch Jacob, either assembled together or represented by their leaders.[c]

There is every reason to suppose, then, that Paul means by "all Israel" what the Old Testament usually means by "all Israel"—the whole family of Jacob, whose twelve sons gave their names to the twelve tribes of Israel. It is an expression that is collective and representative. Understood in this way, the salvation of "all Israel" definitely includes "all Jews" but has a scope and significance that reaches far beyond them.[d]

a. For a survey of different positions, see Christopher Zoccali, "'And So All Israel Will Be Saved': Competing Interpretations of Romans 11.26 in Pauline Scholarship," *JSNT* 30, no. 3 (2008), 289–318.
b. One notable exception is Scott, "And Then All Israel," 498–515.
c. E.g., Exod 18:25; Deut 1:1; Josh 8:33; 2 Sam 8:15; 1 Kings 8:65; 1 Chron 9:1; 2 Chron 1:2; Tob 1:6.
d. See commentary on 9:4.

speaking about the manner of Israel's salvation.[28] This is certainly the default meaning of *houtōs* elsewhere in Paul's writings.[29]

28. Fitzmyer, *Romans*, 622–23; N. T. Wright, "The Letter to the Romans," in *The New Interpreter's Bible*, ed. Leander E. Keck (Nashville: Abingdon, 2002), 10:690–91.
29. Paul could have put a temporal meaning beyond dispute by using other Greek terms such as *tote* or *epeita*, both of which may be translated "then" or "thereafter."

What difference does this make? A great deal, I would contend. To the extent that Paul is concerned with a timeline of events, he envisions the salvation of "all Israel" taking place at the same time as that of the Gentiles. It is a simultaneous process rather than a subsequent event. But even this falls wide of Paul's main purpose. The essence of the mystery is that Israel comes to salvation precisely *by means of* the Gentiles coming to salvation. If the great majority of Israel, historically speaking, has disappeared into the landscape of the nations, then God must save the nations in order to save all Israel.

Now we come to the remaining piece of the puzzle: the promise that all Israel **will be saved**. This claim itself is not the mystery revealed, since Paul is simply echoing one of the grandest hopes of Old Testament †eschatology—the expectation that God will act to restore all the tribes of Israel in the Messiah. Centuries of exile had left the tribal family of Jacob scattered and divided among the nations, but God announced through the prophets that he would restore Israel in his mercy, forgiving the sins of his people and reuniting the two houses of Israel and Judah once again. This prophetic vision is widely attested in the Old Testament,[30] and often appears in connection with the salvation of the nations (Isa 49:6; 60:3–4; 66:19–20) and the coming of a royal Davidic Messiah.[31] The same hope is evidenced in ancient Jewish writings[32] outside the Bible and elsewhere in the New Testament.[33]

The real marrow of the mystery is *how* this takes place. On the one hand, although some scholars have argued otherwise, Paul expects Israel to be saved by accepting Jesus. Salvation is found in embracing the gospel, which is "the power of God for the salvation of everyone who believes: for Jew first, and then Greek" (Rom 1:16). It requires a confession of faith in Jesus as Lord (10:9–13). Paul hopes that his apostolic efforts will help to "save" some of his unbelieving kin (11:14). On the other hand, Paul understands that the *in*gathering of the Gentiles includes and coincides with the *re*gathering of Israel.[34] It is a classic case of felling two birds with one stone: God blesses and saves all the nations, as promised to Abraham (Gen 22:16–18), and in doing so he saves and restores

---

30. Tob 13:3–5; Sir 48:10; Isa 43:5–6; Jer 3:18; 50:17–20; Zech 8:13.

31. Isa 11:1–14; Jer 23:5–6; Ezek 37:15–28; Hosea 2:1–3:5.

32. *Psalms of Solomon* 17.28, 44–49; *4 Ezra* 13.39–48; *2 Baruch* 78.4–7; *Testament of Simeon* 7.1–3; *Testament of Benjamin* 9.2; 10.11; †Mishnah *Sanhedrin* 10.1. Hope for the salvation of tribal Israel is also implicit in the Dead Sea Scrolls, on which see John S. Bergsma, "Qumran and the Concept of Pan-Israelite Restoration," *Letter & Spirit* 8 (2013): 145–59. See also S. Pines, "Notes on the Twelve Tribes in Qumran, Early Christianity and Jewish Tradition," in *Messiah and Christos: Studies in the Jewish Origins of Christianity, Presented to David Flusser on the Occasion of His Seventy-Fifth Birthday*, ed. Ithamar Gruenwald, Shaul Shaked, and Gedaliahu G. Stroumsa (Tübingen: Mohr Siebeck, 1991), 151–54.

33. Matt 19:28; Acts 26:7; James 1:1; Rev 7:4–8; 21:10–14.

34. Argued by Staples, "What Do the Gentiles?"

all the tribes of Israel lost among them, as promised through the prophets. *This is the mystery of Israel's salvation set before us in Rom 11.*

Paul is rarely content to make such assertions without support. He reaches for two citations from the Old Testament to substantiate his claim. In verse 26 and the first half of verse 27, Paul quotes Isa 59:20–21 in a form similar to the †Septuagint: **The deliverer will come out of**[35] **Zion, / he will turn away godlessness from Jacob; / and this is my covenant with them**. This passage is part of the preface to Isa 60, one of the great oracles of restoration in the book of Isaiah. The prophet envisions caravans of foreigners, along with the sons and daughters of Israel, streaming back to the Lord from afar. In the second half of verse 27, Paul excerpts a line from Isa 27:9: **when I take away their sins**, referring to the †expiation of Israel's guilt at this time.

Paul's deployment of these texts from Isaiah calls for comment, as they confirm what he means by "all Israel will be saved" (Rom 11:26). (1) Both oracles are "Jacob" oracles—that is, both have in view the tribal family of Israel as a whole, and neither is restricted in its focus to the Jews. In fact, both set the stage for Israel's exiles to return from their dispersion throughout the Middle East, not least from Assyria (Isa 27:12–13). (2) Likewise, both oracles are best understood as "New Covenant" oracles. These passages envision situations that align not with the end of history but with the dawning of messianic times. The "deliverer" is Jesus Christ, whose gospel of forgiveness radiates out to the world from "Zion"—that is, from Jerusalem (Luke 24:47). Paul sees his own ministry following this trajectory, so that by the time he sends his Letter to the Romans, he can claim that his gospel has spread "from Jerusalem all the way around to Illyricum" (Rom 15:19). Furthermore, the "covenant" that brings a definitive expiation of "sins" is the covenant sealed in the blood of the crucified Messiah, which Paul described in 3:24–26. Knowledgeable readers of the Bible will notice further that Isaiah's prophecy is similar in wording to Jeremiah's famous revelation about the New Covenant (Jer 31:33–34).[36] (3) Given the foregoing, I would contend that Paul interprets these passages from Isaiah in reference to the first coming of Christ rather than his second coming.[37] It is in the Church's proclamation of the gospel that Israel is to find its salvation. This needs to be

---

35. The Septuagint says the deliverer comes "for the sake of" Zion rather than "out of" Zion. The difference between the LXX and Paul's rendition is significant, although not fully understood. For a range of considerations, see Christopher D. Stanley, "'The Redeemer Will Come *ek Siōn*': Romans 11.26–27 Revisited," in *Paul and the Scriptures of Israel*, ed. Craig A. Evans and James A. Sanders, JSNTSup 83 (Sheffield: JSOT Press, 1993), 118–42; also J. R. Daniel Kirk, "Why Does the Deliverer Come *ek Siōn* (Romans 11.26)?," *JSNT* 33, no. 1 (2010): 81–99.

36. This is Jer 38:33–34 in the LXX. See Wright, "Letter to the Romans," 691–93.

37. Brendan Byrne, SJ, *Romans*, SP 6 (Collegeville, MN: Liturgical Press, 1996), 355.

said since Rom 11:26–27 is frequently considered a prophecy of the return of Christ in glory on the last day. Now, it is reasonable to expect that the Lord's second coming will bring the process of Israel's salvation to its triumphant completion, but we should not conclude from this that it does not get under way until then (see Catechism 674). Paul is focused throughout Rom 11 on salvation coming to Israel in the present, not simply in the future.[38]

Unbelieving Israel thus finds itself in a bizarre predicament. The covenant **11:28–29** people are caught between the **gospel** and the gift of **election**. In relation to the former, they are **enemies** whose rejection of the Messiah has worked out for the benefit of the Gentiles (11:11). In relation to the latter, they remain a **beloved** people on account of **the patriarchs** and the covenant God made with them (Acts 3:25–26).

Recalling the discussion in Rom 5, it is likely that Paul uses the word "enemies" in the sense of "not yet reconciled to God" through his Son. This is the status of everyone who shares the sinful human condition and has not yet been justified in Christ (5:10). Still, being members of the chosen people, they remain in the Lord's "everlasting love" for Israel (Jer 31:3 RSV). Israel is still the object of God's affection and still has a priority claim on salvation (Rom 1:16) because, Paul says, **the gifts and the call of God are irrevocable**. God will never back out on Israel or withdraw the blessings bestowed on them, such as those listed in 3:1–2 and 9:4–5.

Paul's reasoning is based on the logic of the covenant. In the biblical view, covenants create families by establishing bonds of kinship that endure through time. This means that a covenant can never be revoked, only enforced. Faithful partners joined in covenant can expect to enjoy its blessings, while an unfaithful partner faces the prospect of its curses. Paul can thus describe Israel from two different vantage points. Because God's love for Israel endures, the covenant with Israel endures. But because the covenant with Israel has been renewed through the Messiah, and many have refused to be a part of it, the disciplinary sanctions of the covenant are put into effect. So it is that unbelieving Israel is "hardened" (11:7) and "beloved" (11:28) at the same time.

Finally Paul draws together the main threads of his theological exposition. **11:30–32** What he says here constitutes a summary not only of Rom 9–11 but of everything covered in Rom 1–11. Distilled to its essence, the story of the world's salvation is a story of human **disobedience** overcome by divine **mercy**. It is the story of the covenant people (**they**) no less than the Gentiles (**you**). The Gentiles **once**

---

38. Ben L. Merkle, "Romans 11 and the Future of Ethnic Israel," *JETS* 43, no. 4 (2000): 709–21 (especially 713–14).

lived in defiance of **God** but have **now** received forgiveness in Christ. Likewise, Paul's kinsmen by race have **now** failed to obey the gospel (10:16) in order that God's compassion on the nations might stir them to a jealous desire for the same, both **now** and in time to come (11:13–14).

At the end of the day, everything is grace. **For God delivered all to disobedience, that he might have mercy upon all**. Neither Gentile nor Jew has ground for boasting. Just as all peoples "have sinned" (3:23), so all "are justified freely by his grace through the redemption in Christ Jesus" (3:24). Paul could not have chosen a more fitting note for the conclusion of his doctrinal argument in Romans.

Reflection and Application (11:25–27)

Catholic exegesis of Rom 11:25–27 developed along various lines through the centuries. For the sake of convenience, we may call the two main approaches the *ecclesial* reading and the †*eschatological* reading.[39] The ecclesial reading, identified mainly with St. Augustine, contends that "all Israel" is a reference to the Church, whose membership includes Jews as well as Gentiles and whose salvation takes place throughout the course of Christian history. The eschatological reading, identified with St. John Chrysostom and others, maintains that "all Israel" is the world community of Jews, who will be saved by a mass conversion to Christ at the end of time.

Obviously these traditional readings cannot be reconciled in all respects. However, both have interpretive strengths that may be harnessed and synthesized. The ecclesial view is right to observe that Paul has the community of Christians from all nations in view in Rom 11 and that salvation reaches them in every age of the Church's pilgrimage on earth. This is central to the message conveyed by Paul's olive tree analogy in 11:17–24. At the same time, it is perfectly reasonable to expect that a surge of Jewish conversions will occur before the glorious return of Jesus. There is no reason to doubt that the grace of messianic faith will break through to the Jewish people before the end. Every aspect of salvation history has been timed and arranged so that the Lord "might have mercy upon all" (11:32). And, as argued in the commentary above, the scope of "all Israel" definitely includes the Jews, even if the term is not restricted to them.

The salvation of all Israel, then, is best understood as a continuous process that stretches to the very end. The salvation of a †*remnant* of Israel in the first

---

39. See Peter Gorday, *Principles of Patristic Exegesis: Romans 9–11 in Origen, John Chrysostom, and Augustine*, Studies in the Bible and Early Christianity 4 (New York: Edwin Mellen, 1983).

century was the beginning phase; the salvation of Israel continues as individuals hear the summons of the gospel throughout the world and throughout history; and there is hope for the future that even more among the people of Israel will step forward to embrace the Messiah appointed for them.

Final Hymn and Doxology (11:33–36)

³³Oh, the depth of the riches and wisdom and knowledge of God! How inscrutable are his judgments, and how unsearchable his ways!

³⁴"For who has known the mind of the Lord
    or who has been his counselor?"
³⁵"Or who has given him anything
    that he may be repaid?"

³⁶For from him and through him and for him are all things. To him be glory forever. Amen.

OT: Job 41:3; Isa 40:13; 55:8–9; Jer 23:18
NT: Rom 16:27; 1 Cor 2:9–16; Col 1:16; 2:2–3
Catechism: prayer of praise, 2639, 2649; doxology, 2641

Romans 11 nears its end with Paul bursting into praise. Call it a hymn, call it **11:33** a lyrical poem; either way, the Apostle marvels at the genius and generosity of God that shines through the "mystery" revealed in 11:25–26 and the "mercy" promised to all in 11:32. **Oh, the depth of the riches and wisdom and knowledge of God!** The divine wisdom cannot be searched to the bottom. Only the Spirit can fathom the limitless reaches of God's infinite mind (1 Cor 2:10). Even when God's purposes become visible through his macromanagement of salvation history, human understanding falls woefully short of adequate comprehension. And so Paul continues with reference to God's actions: **How inscrutable are his judgments, and how unsearchable his ways!**

To these exclamations Paul adds two rhetorical questions drawn from Scrip- **11:34–35** ture. The first approximates the †Septuagint version of Isa 40:13: **For who has known the mind of the Lord / or who has been his counselor?** The implied answer, of course, is "No one." The second question is generally considered an excerpt from Job 41:3, perhaps rendered directly from the Hebrew: **Or who has given him anything / that he may be repaid?** Again, the expected answer is "No one." Paul has drawn together two passages that put the Lord in a category all his own. God is transcendent in knowledge over all his creatures, and he is

in debt to none of them. Everything the human person knows and possesses
has been freely and bountifully given from above.

11:36   The closing line of the chapter continues in the spirit of prayer, this time as
a doxology that extols the divine **glory** (Greek *doxa*). Paul, speaking of God as
him, acknowledges that **all things** in the cosmos come **from** him and exist **for**
him. The third phrase, **through him**, seems particularly suited to describe the
Son, who is the divine mediator of creation (1 Cor 8:6; Col 1:16). Paul closes the
doctrinal portion of Romans with the words **To him be glory forever. Amen.**
A similar doxology will conclude the letter as a whole (16:27).

A New Way of Worship and Life in Christ

Romans 12:1–21

The last major section of Romans stretches from 12:1 to 15:13. Its opening marks a shift from theological exposition to pastoral exhortation. Paul typically structures his letters this way. First he informs readers of what God has done for them in the Messiah, unpacking the substance of Christian *belief*, and then he encourages them in their responsibilities toward God, setting forth the standards of Christian *behavior*. Both parts of the letter work in tandem; neither can be isolated from the other.

Ultimately this seamless continuity between faith and life is a defining feature of the covenant. Because baptized believers take on a new identity as children of God, they also take on new obligations of living in covenant with God as their Father. Earlier Paul designated the filial duty of Christians as "the obedience of faith" (1:5) and characterized it as walking "according to the spirit" (8:4). Now he translates these statements into specific principles for living in the family of God. Throughout the chapter Paul addresses the challenges confronting Christians in ancient Rome. But since he writes as an inspired apostle, his teaching retains its relevance for the Church today.

An Offering of Body and Mind (12:1–2)

[1]I urge you therefore, brothers, by the mercies of God, to offer your bodies as a living sacrifice, holy and pleasing to God, your spiritual worship. [2]Do not conform yourselves to this age but be transformed by the renewal of

211

**your mind, that you may discern what is the will of God, what is good and
pleasing and perfect.**

OT: Exod 34:6; Tob 4:11; Pss 51:19; 141:2; Sir 35:1–9

NT: Rom 8:13; 1 Cor 6:20; 2 Cor 3:18; Eph 4:23; Col 3:10; 1 Pet 2:4–5

Catechism: moral life as spiritual worship, 2031; common priesthood of believers, 1141, 1546;
discerning God's will, 2520, 2826

Lectionary: 12:1–13: Consecration of Virgins and Religious Profession; Mass for the Laity; 12:1–2,
9–18: Sacrament of Marriage

Paul's opening appeal serves as a preface to the pastoral counsel that follows
in Rom 12–15. For the Apostle, liturgy and life form a unity. Christians are
called to serve the Lord in all circumstances, so that every action is a sacrifice
that renders homage to God, and every thought is conformed to the knowledge of his will. Paul envisions nothing less than a total transformation of the
believer—now made possible by the mercies of God.

12:1 Romans 12 begins with a nod toward Rom 1–11. Paul is transitioning from
doctrinal matters to practical concerns, and he wants readers to sense the deep
connection that binds them together. The word **therefore** joins the two sections. It shows that what follows is grounded on everything that came before.

Paul addresses his readers as **brothers**. This may strike us as unremarkable,
perhaps because we have become overfamiliar with the kinship language that
pervades the New Testament. Yet Paul is reiterating a revolutionary truth of
the gospel: that Christians are recipients of the grace of divine rebirth and
adoption. Union with Christ makes us sons and daughters of the Father (8:14),
younger siblings of Jesus the firstborn (8:29), and therefore spiritual siblings of
one another. This is all through God's **mercies**. The plural suggests that Paul is
thinking of the Lord's abundant compassion, a concept expressed in Hebrew by
the plural term *rahamim* (2 Sam 24:14; Ps 51:3; Isa 63:15). Taken together, these
terms imply that Paul's practical instruction rests on the theological instruction
presented in earlier chapters.

From this transition Paul moves immediately into exhortation. He calls for
Christians **to offer** their **bodies** as a **sacrifice** to God. This passage is weighted
with meaning, so we do well to linger and ponder its implications.

First, the passage shows that Paul's vision of Christian living is *incarnational*.[1] The sacrifice in view consists of "bodies" offered to the Lord as a
form of divine worship.[2] Essentially the rest of Rom 12–15 shows what this

1. Robert J. Daly, SJ, *The Origins of the Christian Doctrine of Sacrifice* (Philadelphia: Fortress, 1978), 64.
2. The Greek *sōma* is translated "body." However, scholars often point out that it refers to the whole
embodied person, who is spiritual as well as physical. This explanation does not diminish the corporeal

looks like in everyday life. More specifically, Paul encourages temperance, chastity, and other types of bodily self-control under this appeal.[3] These represent ways that disciples can "put to death the deeds of the body" (8:13) and "glorify God" with their bodies (1 Cor 6:20). Paul is not reducing sacrifice to a mere symbol of how Christians conduct themselves in a spiritual way. Sacrifice is an outward action that engages the whole person, body and soul.

Second, the passage shows that Paul's vision of Christian living is *liturgical*. He is extending the responsibilities of Christian worship to the whole of our life in this physical world. Personal devotion and morality are inwardly connected with divine worship. When the Messiah offered himself in the body as the definitive offering that surpasses all others (Rom 3:25; Eph 5:2), he radically transformed sacrifice. Christians are challenged in turn to conform themselves to the Messiah (Rom 8:29) and his sacrificial death (Phil 3:10). For Paul, this is achieved when baptized believers, who share in the priestly dignity of Christ, offer their trials and sufferings in the body as a holy oblation to the Lord.[4] The Christian who fulfills Paul's injunction renders homage to God both as a sacrificing priest and as a sacrificial victim.

Third, the passage shows that Paul's vision of Christian living is *ecclesial*. This will become clear as we work through the rest of the chapter, but already in the opening verse we have a hint of it. Paul pleads with the Romans to offer their "bodies" (plural) as a "sacrifice" (singular).[5] This detail suggests he envisions not a series of unconnected, individual acts but a collective effort of the Christian community to glorify the Lord in union with one another. Paul does not privatize our service to God in the body. Instead, he calls for a sacrificial, communal commitment from the Church.

To this initial entreaty Paul adds layers of significance by qualifying the noun "sacrifice" three times over. Disciples are bidden to offer sacrifices that are **living**, **holy**, and **pleasing** to God. With the expression "living" Paul contrasts the ancient practice of animal sacrifice with the new mode of Christian

---

aspect of the sacrifice but clarifies that Paul wants believers to put their whole selves into the service of God.

3. In addition to the moral dimension of sacrifice, Paul also uses sacrificial language to describe acts of martyrdom (Phil 2:17) and material generosity (Phil 4:18).

4. Readers should be aware that Catholicism makes an essential distinction between the "common priesthood" of the baptized and the "ministerial priesthood" of those who receive Holy Orders (Catechism 1141, 1547).

5. Pointed out by, e.g., Richard B. Hays, *Echoes of Scripture in the Letters of Paul* (New Haven: Yale University Press, 1989), 206n58. Theologically, it is also true that the "bodies" (plural) of the faithful are united to the one "sacrifice" (singular) of Christ's paschal mystery as this is re-presented in the Eucharist (see Catechism 2031).

"Your Spiritual Worship"

In Rom 12:1 Paul calls the practice of Christian sacrifice our "spiritual worship," in Greek, *logikē latreia*. The expression appears to have been coined by the Apostle, and from him it was taken up into Christian theology and liturgy.[a] Since all agree that *latreia* here denotes the "worship" of the covenant people, discussions of Rom 12:1 typically focus on the adjective *logikē*. And since this term never appears in the Greek Old Testament, scholars have had to venture outside the Bible to get a satisfactory sense of its meaning. The word had currency among ancient Greek philosophers, especially the Stoics, who used it to describe what is "rational" or "reasonable" as distinct from the operations of the world of beasts.[b] In the writings of Hellenistic Judaism, the archangels of heaven are said to serve as priests before the throne of God, presenting him with a "rational" and bloodless offering.[c] Philo of Alexandria, speaking of human worship, holds that God accords more value to the purity of the offerer's "rational" spirit than to the number of sacrifices he or she brings to the temple.[d] Texts such as these suggest that Paul understands "spiritual worship" as something that corresponds to our nature as intelligent beings: rightly ordered and rightly conducted by persons who are created for spiritual communion with God. And yet the practice of Christian sacrifice is not spiritual as opposed to physical, inward as opposed to outward. It arises from the spiritual faculties of mind and will, but it is expressed through the body. It flows from the inside out, so that the whole person—spirit, soul, and body—is engaged in divine worship.

a. For how later Christian tradition connected Rom 12:1 with Christ and the Eucharist, see Jeremy Driscoll, OSB, "Worship in the Spirit of the *Logos*: Romans 12:1–2 and the Source and Summit of Christian Life," *Letter & Spirit* 5 (2009): 77–101.

b. Arrian, *Epictetus* 1.16.20.

c. *Testament of Levi* 3.6.

d. *Special Laws* 1.277.

sacrifice. Obviously animal sacrifice means death for the victim, making the offering a brief, one-time event. Christian sacrifice is a dying that takes place in the midst of living, a dying that unfolds over time rather than ending in a single action. By "holy" Paul means set apart for a sacred purpose. When the body is made a sacrifice, it passes from the profane world into the service of God. And by "pleasing" Paul indicates that God finds the oblation of the faithful acceptable rather than objectionable. These taken together are the **spiritual worship** expected of believers.

Paul continues his exhortation with a prohibition: **Do not conform your-** 12:2
selves to this age.[6] He is cautioning readers against succumbing to the pressures
of the prevailing culture. Conformity with the world, which frequently sets
itself in opposition to God, can lead to moral and spiritual corruption. People
ordinarily want to fit in and be accepted by others. But the gospel challenges
believers to be different, to resist the spirit of the times.

And resistance means holding off the assaults of "this age." Here Paul is
using the language of Jewish †eschatology, which often divided history into two
phases: "this age" and "the age to come."[7] The first is the age dominated by sin
and suffering and strife; the second is the age of messianic fulfillment, a time
of unprecedented peace and mercy. Jesus speaks in these terms in the Gospels
(e.g., Matt 12:32); other New Testament passages do as well (e.g., Eph 1:21).
For Paul, Christians live in the *overlap* of the ages, the transitional time when
"the present evil age" (Gal 1:4) continues alongside the messianic age of grace.
The old age remains a burden and a threat, even as the blessings of the new
age are pouring into the lives of believers. Christians are part of Christ's "new
creation" (2 Cor 5:17), while remaining planted in the old creation, which is
still "groaning in labor pains" (Rom 8:22).

Paul calls believers to **be transformed** by a **renewal** of the **mind**. The Christian whose mind is transformed takes on "the mind of Christ" (1 Cor 2:16).
He or she begins to view and evaluate all things in light of the gospel. But how
does this take place? It is first and foremost God's grace that begins to heal our
worldly ways of thinking. Yet we have a part to play as well. Our ongoing formation in the faith is one way we cooperate in this renewal process, especially
by regular reading and meditation on the word of God in prayerful dialogue
with the Lord. This transformation also requires disciples to live by the power
of the Spirit, who enables the children of God to set their minds on the things
of the Spirit (Rom 8:5).

The purpose of this renewal, Paul says, is **that you may discern . . . the will of**
God. If the will of God is unknowable, then the human family is adrift on a sea
without shores, with no way to discover life's ultimate meaning. But Scripture
insists that God has revealed his will and made known his plan for the world in
many and various ways, most completely in his Son (Heb 1:1–2). It follows that
Christians are greatly advantaged when it comes to discernment. Jesus' example,

---

6. Modern translations differ in wording this command because the Greek verb may be read as
middle voice or passive voice. Taken as middle voice, it is rendered "conform yourselves" (NABRE),
"model yourselves" (JB), or simply "conform" (NIV). Taken as passive voice, it is usually rendered "be
conformed" (RSV, NRSV, ESV).

7. E.g., *4 Ezra* 7.113; *2 Baruch* 15.8; †Mishnah *Avot* 2.7.

reinforced by his teaching, shows us what a human life in perfect alignment with the Father's will looks like. Add to this the inward leading of the Spirit, and believers are fully equipped to ascertain **what is good and pleasing and perfect**.

Paul is saying, in other words, that grace assists our knowing, just as it empowers our doing. It helps us to recognize as "good" what is noble and upright in God's eyes. It guides us along the path that is "pleasing" to the Lord, bringing him delight. Ultimately it leads us to what is "perfect," and perfection is the goal of Christian existence. It is realized when human love and generosity reflect the love and generosity of the Father (Matt 5:43–48).

Reflection and Application (12:1–2)

The richness of Rom 12:1–2 can be savored even in isolation. Yet Paul would have us read it in the broader context of Romans. These verses connect with the larger story that Paul narrates in the first major part of the letter. Careful readers will notice that the depiction of *Christian* worship in Rom 12:1–2 stands in glaring contrast to the *corrupted* worship of humanity presented in Rom 1:18–32.[8] In fact, they are polar opposites.

This is brought out by a number of antithetical parallels between the two chapters. The effect is to make Rom 12 an inverted image of Rom 1. (1) Christian worship is directed to God the creator, whereas the religions of the ancient world reverenced idols made in the image "of mortal man or of birds or of four-legged animals or of snakes" (1:23). (2) The worship offered by believers is rational, whereas those who venerate idols "became vain in their reasoning" (1:21). (3) Christian worship calls for a sacrificial offering of the body to God, whereas pagan worship leads devotees to the "degradation of their bodies" (1:24). (4) By the grace of gospel truth, the mind of the Christian is renewed over time; but by a thankless rejection of God's truth, the impious mind becomes "senseless" and "darkened" (1:21). (5) The renewed mind is equipped to discern the will of God, whereas the darkened mind opposes the decrees of God (1:32). (6) True worship flows out into a rightly ordered life (12:3–21), whereas a false and disordered worship begets all manner of moral deviancy (1:25–32).

Paul's gospel announces a total renovation of worship. The grace of Christ is redeeming our worship and realigning our minds with the Father's will. The

8. Noted by, e.g., James D. G. Dunn, *Romans 9–16*, WBC 38b (Nashville: Nelson, 1988), 708; and Michael Thompson, *Clothed with Christ: The Example and Teaching of Jesus in Romans 12:1–15:13*, JSNTSup 59 (Sheffield: JSOT Press, 1991), 81–83, both of whom rely on C. Evans, "Roman 12:1–2: The True Worship," in *Dimensions de la vie chrétienne (Rom 12–13)*, ed. Lorenzo de Lorenzi (Rome: Abbaye de S. Paul, 1979), 7–33.

world gone mad depicted in Rom 1 has been returned to sanity in Rom 12. The mercies of God have set matters right once again.

The Body of Christ (12:3–8)

³**For by the grace given to me I tell everyone among you not to think of himself more highly than one ought to think, but to think soberly, each according to the measure of faith that God has apportioned. ⁴For as in one body we have many parts, and all the parts do not have the same function, ⁵so we, though many, are one body in Christ and individually parts of one another. ⁶Since we have gifts that differ according to the grace given to us, let us exercise them: if prophecy, in proportion to the faith; ⁷if ministry, in ministering; if one is a teacher, in teaching; ⁸if one exhorts, in exhortation; if one contributes, in generosity; if one is over others, with diligence; if one does acts of mercy, with cheerfulness.**

OT: Isa 11:1–3; Joel 3:1–4

NT: 1 Cor 12:12–31; Eph 4:7–16; Phil 2:3–4; Col 1:18; 1 Pet 4:10

Catechism: analogy of faith, 114; virtue of temperance, 1809; charisms of the Spirit, 951, 2003–4; body of Christ, 789–91

Lectionary: 12:3–13: St. Charles Borromeo; Common of Pastors; Mass for the Promotion of Charity; 12:4–8: Conferral of Holy Orders

Paul continues to discuss the mind's renewal. He attributes his authority to speak   **12:3** on this topic to **the grace given** to him—something he does several times in his letters.[9] Right away in the opening salutation of Romans, he presented himself as one who received "the grace of apostleship" from the Lord (1:5).

This grace authorizes him, among other things, to instruct the congregation in the proper use of the mind. The reader is thus warned **not to think of himself more highly than one ought to think**. Arrogance is an unbecoming attitude among the Lord's disciples, and yet temptations to pride are real. It is all too easy to become forgetful of our human weaknesses and to develop an inflated sense of self-importance. To what extent this was a problem in the Roman church is uncertain, but one will recall that Paul censured those who look down with smug condescension on the unbelievers of Israel (11:20, 25).

Since the best way to conquer vice is to cultivate the opposing virtue, Paul admonishes believers **to think soberly**—to stay levelheaded and to think sensibly about themselves in relation to God and others; to keep their thoughts within

9. Rom 15:15; 1 Cor 3:10; Gal 2:9; Eph 3:2.

the bounds of reality, without either rearing up in pride or shrinking back in false humility. Interestingly, the verb Paul uses for "think soberly" is related to a Greek noun that means "temperance" or "self-control." Temperance is one of the four cardinal virtues enumerated in classical philosophy and endorsed in Hellenistic Judaism.[10] It is the virtue of moderation that keeps the tendencies of our fallen nature in balance and ensures that life is lived within reasonable limits (Catechism 1809).

This is exactly what Paul is applying to the Christian mind in verse 3, except that he adds an important qualification: sober thinking is to be done **according to the measure of faith that God has apportioned**. Faith, in Paul's theology, is a gift that enables us to believe in the gospel (Phil 1:29). Thereafter it furnishes the believer with a reliable point of reference for thinking with hardheaded sobriety.

12:4–5   In the next two verses Paul segues into one of his most familiar analogies: the Church as the body of Christ. The analogy is not unique to Paul, since several thinkers in classical antiquity compared the city-state to a human body, giving birth to the concept of the "body politic."[11] The metaphor proved to be valuable precisely because it was multidimensional. By means of a single image, one could explain the unity, diversity, and interdependency of a whole society. Paul found it helpful for expounding his theology of the Church for the same reason.

The Church, he states, is **one body** made up of **many parts** that **do not have the same function**. Like the human body, the Christian community is a complex organism with a variety of distinct members, each performing a different vital activity. Moreover, its multiple functions work together toward a single overall purpose—namely, the well-being of the whole body. Paul invokes this analogy to prepare readers for a discussion of spiritual gifts in verses 6–8.

Readers should pause over Paul's remark that believers are **one body in Christ**. The individuals who constitute the **we** of the Church, **though many**, are united by something far more profound than legal citizenship in an earthly state. The ecclesial body of Christ is constituted by a *sacramental* union of believers with the Messiah's glorified humanity (Catechism 790). Paul is not explicit on this point in Romans, but he tells us in 1 Corinthians that individuals become living members of Christ's body through baptism and the Eucharist. In one text he says, "in one Spirit we were all baptized into one body" (1 Cor 12:13); in another he explains, "The bread that we break, is it not a participation in the body of Christ? Because the loaf of bread is one, we, though many, are one body, for we all partake of the one loaf" (1 Cor 10:16–17). So far as Paul is concerned,

10. Plato, *Phaedo* 69c; Wis 8:7; *4 Maccabees* 1.18.
11. For two examples, see Plato, *Republic* 462c–d; and Livy, *Roman History* 2.32.

the body of Christ is not reducible to a metaphor. It is a metaphysical reality brought about through the liturgical actions of the Church.[12] So real is our union with Christ and the Spirit that we become **individually parts of one another**. This is the mystery that theologians call "the communion of the saints."

Here we learn the pastoral reason why Paul describes the Christian com-   **12:6–8** munity as an integrated body. If believers are to exercise the sober-mindedness called for in 12:3, they must look beyond themselves to consider the needs and gifts of their fellow disciples. All members of the body of Christ are indispensable. One sign of this is the spiritual **gifts** that believers have received from the Lord. These "charisms" (Greek *charismata*) are gifts of "grace" (Greek *charis*) that are given to Christians to strengthen the Church from within and to move the body of Christ toward a greater collective maturity in its witness to world (Eph 4:13). Elsewhere Paul describes the spiritual or charismatic gifts as manifestations of the Holy Spirit operating in the lives of the faithful (1 Cor 12:7).

Readers should be aware of several things about these gifts. First, Paul explains that they **differ according to the grace given to** each individual. Every believer is endowed in some way, but not all are endowed in the same way. Second, Paul urges believers to **exercise them** as God intends (see 1 Pet 4:10). Third, as the following list indicates, the spiritual gifts are gifts of service by which we minister to others, especially to fellow Christians.[13]

Among the myriad gifts that enrich the Church, Paul confines himself to seven in Romans. Perhaps the number seven is meant to represent all the many charisms animating the body of Christ.[14] However that may be, it is certain that the Apostle offers only a sampling of the Spirit's endowments. We know this because he presents a more extensive inventory in 1 Cor 12:4–31.

Heading the list of spiritual gifts is **prophecy**. Persons gifted with prophecy are inspired to deliver words of exhortation to the assembled church. In 1 Cor 12:28, Paul insists that prophets rank just below apostles; in 1 Cor 14:1–33, he specifies that prophets build up the local church with intelligible words of instruction, encouragement, and revelation. Here we learn that prophecy must be exercised **in proportion to the faith**.[15] Alleged prophetic claims must be

---

12. For theological reflection on this mystery, see Louis Bouyer, *The Church of God: Body of Christ and Temple of the Spirit*, trans. Charles Underhill Quinn (San Francisco: Ignatius, 2011), 293–327.

13. For the ongoing importance of these gifts in the life of the Church, see the sidebar "Vatican II on Charisms," in George T. Montague, SM, *First Corinthians*, CCSS (Grand Rapids: Baker Academic, 2011), 208.

14. Joseph A. Fitzmyer, SJ, *Romans*, AB 33 (New York: Doubleday, 1993), 647.

15. The Greek is literally "according to *the analogy of faith*," an expression that later theology would come to use in different ways, most commonly for "the coherence of the truths of faith among themselves and within the whole plan of Revelation" (Catechism 114).

measured against the deposit of gospel truth entrusted to the Church (1 Tim 6:20–21). Paul hints at such a discernment process for charismatic prophecy in 1 Cor 14:29.

Ministry is a gift of practical service to others of the church community, particularly widows, orphans, and the elderly. **Teaching** equips some to catechize fellow believers with particular clarity. **Exhortation** is the gift of encouraging others and motivating them to live the gospel with heroic fidelity. The charism of **generosity** prompts persons to make liberal use of financial resources to assist the needy and to advance the mission of the Church by their patronage.

Paul next addresses the person who is **over others**—literally, "the one who stands in front." Presumably he means the gift of community leadership,[16] although the circumstances in which the charism is exercised are not specified. The seventh gift inspires **acts of mercy**. Paul probably has in mind a ministry of compassion that reaches out to the hungry, the sick, the dying, the imprisoned, and so forth (Matt 25:35–40). None of these gifts is the same as another, yet all aim at promoting the welfare of the whole Christian community.

The Primacy of Love and Peace (12:9–21)

[9]Let love be sincere; hate what is evil, hold on to what is good; [10]love one another with mutual affection; anticipate one another in showing honor. [11]Do not grow slack in zeal, be fervent in spirit, serve the Lord. [12]Rejoice in hope, endure in affliction, persevere in prayer. [13]Contribute to the needs of the holy ones, exercise hospitality. [14]Bless those who persecute [you], bless and do not curse them. [15]Rejoice with those who rejoice, weep with those who weep. [16]Have the same regard for one another; do not be haughty but associate with the lowly; do not be wise in your own estimation. [17]Do not repay anyone evil for evil; be concerned for what is noble in the sight of all. [18]If possible, on your part, live at peace with all. [19]Beloved, do not look for revenge but leave room for the wrath; for it is written, "Vengeance in mine, I will repay, says the Lord." [20]Rather, "if your enemy is hungry, feed him; if he is thirsty, give him something to drink; for by doing so you will heap burning coals upon his head." [21]Do not be conquered by evil but conquer evil with good.

OT: Lev 19:18; Deut 32:35; Prov 3:7; 25:21–22; Sir 7:34; Amos 5:15
NT: Matt 5:9, 44; Luke 6:27–28; 2 Cor 6:6; Heb 12:14; 13:1–2

16. Modern translations try to capture this with renderings such as "the leader" (NRSV), "the one who leads" (ESV), and "the officials" (JB). It is unclear what rationale underlies "he who gives aid" (RSV).

Catechism: apostolic catechesis, 1971; joy in hope, 1820; the call to bless, 1669; promoting peace, 2302–6
Lectionary: 12:3–13: St. Charles Borromeo; Common of Pastors; Mass for the Promotion of Charity; 12:9–16: Visitation of the Blessed Virgin Mary; 12:9–16b: Mass for Refugees and Exiles

In the final section of Rom 12, Paul strings together a collection of moral maxims that emphasize the pursuit of love (12:9–13) and peace (12:14–21). These goals govern Christians' interactions with others, whether members of the community of believers or not. Paul's instructions are guided partly by the counsels of the Old Testament and partly by the words and example of Jesus.

Verse 9 hangs like a banner over everything that follows. The highest obligation incumbent on God's people is the duty to exercise **love**, by which Paul means a selfless, sacrificial love (Greek *agapē*). This is the lifeblood of the moral and spiritual life. It means willing and doing what is best for another no matter the cost. Christian living, by definition, unfolds in a pattern of "faith working through love" (Gal 5:6). **12:9–10**

Paul specifies, however, that Christian charity must be **sincere**—not hypocritical, not just for outward show. It must be genuine (2 Cor 6:6). Christians should **hate what is evil** in the sight of God. As for **what is good**, this should be prized and clutched firmly. Paul sounds much like the prophet Amos, who proclaimed to his own generation, "Hate evil and love good" (Amos 5:15).

Paul reiterates the appeal to **love one another with mutual**, or "brotherly," **affection**; he is talking about charity between fellow disciples. He will address the proper Christian response to enemies and strangers in just a few verses (Rom 12:14–21). Here he gives spiritual direction on relationships between brothers and sisters in the family of faith, challenging them to **anticipate one another in showing honor**. There is some dispute about the precise meaning of this statement; Paul may be stirring up some "holy competition" in the Roman church.[17] If there is to be any rivalry in the Church of God, it is to be shown in eagerness to honor others more than ourselves (1 Pet 2:17).

The next two verses address the same topic using the same basic structure. Both deal with the spiritual life, and both hit the reader with a rapid one-two-three combination of punches. **12:11–12**

Paul speaks first of the intensity of religious commitment, warning readers against growing **slack in zeal,** and urging them to be **fervent in spirit**.[18]

---

17. Paul's meaning is captured slightly better with the translation "Outdo one another in showing honor" (RSV, NRSV, ESV).

18. The NABRE, JB, NRSV, ESV, and NIV all take this statement in reference to the human spirit (as in Acts 18:25, where Apollos shows an "ardent spirit"). The RSV, which reads, "be aglow with the Spirit," sees a reference to the Holy Spirit inspiring fervor in the believer (perhaps by analogy with 1 Thess 5:19).

Christianity is not a sport for weekend warriors. It demands a dedication and consistency that makes time for God and summons the energy to do his will even when difficult. In a word, the model disciple is eager to **serve the Lord** in season and out.

In the second passage Paul implores the Romans to find joy in the Christian **hope** of salvation, to remain steadfast in times of **affliction**, and to persist in a life of **prayer**. Hope and endurance were already featured in Paul's earlier discussions, especially in 5:3–5 and 8:18–25. The matter of prayer, specifically in relation to Christian suffering, was taken up in 8:26–27, with emphasis on the Spirit's role as our helper and intercessor. Here Paul emphasizes the Christian's role in sustaining a lifelong dialogue with the Lord. He does this in his other writings as well, as when he presses believers to "pray without ceasing" (1 Thess 5:17) and to make their requests known to God "in everything" (Phil 4:6). Ultimately, constancy in prayer is a teaching that goes back to Jesus (Luke 18:1–8).

12:13   To these sayings on love Paul attaches two more exhortations. In the first he commends generosity. **Contribute to the needs of the holy ones,** he says, urging Christians to support fellow believers in times of financial hardship. Paul sets the example for this type of giving even as he writes Romans. He is currently leading a campaign to collect donations from his congregations in the mission field to provide some relief to the impoverished church in Jerusalem (15:25–27).

In the second exhortation Paul calls on believers to show kindness to travelers and strangers, primarily but "not exclusively" fellow Christians, by exercising **hospitality**. This is a duty that ranks high among Christianity's most esteemed social virtues.[19]

12:14   Verse 14 marks a shift from love to peace, which is why several modern translations indent the line as the beginning of a new paragraph (JB, RSV, NRSV, ESV, NIV). **Bless those who persecute [you],** Paul enjoins readers; **bless and do not curse them**. Of all the verses in Rom 12, none is more obviously derived from the teaching of Jesus than this one.[20] The saying has some affinity with Matt 5:44, but a closer parallel is Luke 6:28, where Jesus, instructing his disciples how to respond to hatred, urges them to "bless those who curse you." Obviously the saying in the Gospel differs a bit from Paul's. But the point of both passages is exactly the same: Christians facing abuse, verbal or otherwise, are not to react in kind, but to invoke the blessings of God on the offender. Nor should it pass unnoticed how utterly unique this teaching is. Humanly

19. 1 Tim 3:2; 5:10; Titus 1:8; Heb 13:2; 1 Pet 4:9.
20. See especially Thompson, *Clothed with Christ*, 96–105.

speaking, performing an act of kindness in exchange for a blistering insult is counterintuitive, to say the least. And yet this is one of those revolutionary demands of gospel morality that make Christians stand out. It is most perfectly exemplified in Jesus himself, who invoked the Father's forgiveness on those who crucified him (Luke 23:34).

Encouraging Christian solidarity follows naturally from Paul's discussion **12:15–16** of the Church as the body of Christ (12:4–5). If all are joined together as one in the Lord, then all are affected, for good or ill, as one. Together the body of Christ celebrates its victories, and together it mourns its losses and failures. Paul makes this point with a double command: **Rejoice with those who rejoice, weep with those who weep**. The combination is unique to Paul, but the second command is not. It is strikingly similar to a wisdom saying in Sir 7:34: "Do not avoid those who weep, / but mourn with those who mourn." What Sirach states as a general precept Paul applies to life in the Christian community.

He calls readers to have **the same regard for one another**, an appeal that is sharpened by the specific injunction: **do not be haughty but associate with the lowly**. It is likely the Roman Christians found this difficult. The whole of Roman society, from top to bottom, was a tiered system of class distinctions based on birth, wealth, and circumstance. No one immersed in this culture would dream of having the same regard for an aristocrat and a slave, as if the two stood on an equal footing. Paul works to overcome this social code in the name of the gospel. The social rankings that run through society are to have no place in the Church.

The concluding words of verse 16, **do not be wise in your own estimation**, place the capstone on Paul's periodic calls for humility in Romans (e.g., 11:20, 25; 12:3). They read like a paraphrase of yet another Old Testament passage, Prov 3:7, which counsels, "Do not be wise in your own eyes."

The following cluster of verses takes up the subject of revenge. Paul forbids **12:17–20** that a Christian should **repay anyone evil for evil**—perhaps another echo of the words of Jesus (Matt 5:38–39). Instead, believers are to concern themselves with **what is noble in the sight of all**. Now if "all" means "all humanity," then Paul is acknowledging that Christianity shares at least some common ground with the moral sensibilities of the world. It is in this broad context of relations with non-Christians that disciples should strive to **live at peace with all**, to the extent that this is **possible** (Heb 12:14).

Likewise, believers are not to exact **revenge** on those who wrong them but are to **leave room for the wrath** of God. Readers will recall that wrath is one of Paul's preferred terms for God's †eschatological judgment on sin. It will not be

St. John Chrysostom on Rejoicing and Weeping

LIVING TRADITION

To rejoice with those who are rejoicing requires a soul with a deeper grasp of the faith than to weep with those who are weeping. For nature itself moves us to weep, and no one can remain unmoved and dry-eyed when another is in trouble. But rejoicing requires a really noble soul not only in order to avoid jealousy when another enjoys success but even to find pleasure in the good fortune of the other. For this reason, Paul puts rejoicing first. Nothing so binds love together as sharing another's joy and sorrow. Do not then be slow to sympathize, even if the terrible situation is not a threat to you. For you ought to take upon yourself your neighbor's tribulations. So, join in with another's tears to raise their low spirits; join in with another's joy to make their good cheer strike deep roots. You will firmly establish love and serve yourself as well as your neighbor: you make yourself merciful through weeping, and you purify yourself of jealousy and envy through sharing the pleasure.[a]

a. St. John Chrysostom, *Homilies on Romans* 22.1. Translation slightly adapted from J. Patout Burns Jr., trans. and ed. with Constantine Newman, *Romans: Interpreted by Early Christian Commentators*, The Church's Bible (Grand Rapids: Eerdmans, 2012), 308.

manifest in full measure before the final judgment, but it is no less certain for that reason. Paul grounds his appeal in Scripture by citing the divine declaration in Deut 32:35: **"Vengeance is mine, I will repay, says the Lord."**[21] Paul considers this truth just as relevant to the Church as it was to Israel of old. Retribution for personal offenses is God's business, not ours.

Paul again quotes from Scripture: **"If your enemy is hungry, feed him; if he is thirsty, give him something to drink; for by doing so you will heap burning coals upon his head."** The passage is from Prov 25:21–22 as worded in the †Septuagint, and its meaning is difficult to decipher. It could be read as saying that acts of kindness toward an enemy ensure that God will bring searing judgment on him. This would support Paul's appeal to leave the avenging of personal wrongs to God. However, Jesus directs us to love our enemies, and wishing our enemies ill at the final judgment seems incongruous with the Lord's teaching (Matt 5:44). Hence others interpret the coals as a burning experience of shame that can lead an enemy to repentance. Understood in this way, showing kindness toward an adversary is another way of following Paul's counsel in Rom 12:14 that Christians should bless their persecutors rather than curse them.

21. Paul's quotation reproduces neither the Hebrew nor the Greek version of this passage, but is closer to the wording preserved in the Aramaic *Targum Neofiti*.

The final verse ties all the strands of the chapter together. **Do not be con-** 12:21
quered by evil but conquer evil with good is Paul's exclamation point. Christians are "more than conquerors" in Christ (8:37 RSV), and their lives must be a witness to this fact. Avenging oneself perpetuates rather than halts the spread of evil in the world. It does not solve the problem—it worsens it. The people of God are victorious in doing good, loving, and living at peace with all.

Faithful Citizenship and Fulfillment of the Law

Romans 13:1–14

Paul continues in Rom 13 to offer practical instruction on Christian living. The connection between Rom 12 and 13 is very close. In 12:9–21 Paul outlined the believer's responsibility to love sincerely and to leave the avenging of personal wrongs to the Lord. He takes up the same themes in chapter 13, but now he moves beyond the confines of private life into the public arena. Private justice for personal injuries is not an option for disciples of Jesus. However, it *is* the business of God, who not only keeps account for the final judgment, but who also confers on legitimate government the authority to punish criminal behavior.[1] In view of this arrangement, Christians must submit to civil authorities and their laws (13:1–7), just as they submit to God and his laws by the exercise of love (13:8–10). Paul finishes the chapter with an appeal to Christians to live in the daylight of gospel morality amid the darkness of a sinful world (13:11–14).

Submission to Ruling Authorities (13:1–7)

[1]Let every person be subordinate to the higher authorities, for there is no authority except from God, and those that exist have been established by God. [2]Therefore, whoever resists authority opposes what God has

1. See N. T. Wright, "The Letter to the Romans," in *The New Interpreter's Bible*, ed. Leander E. Keck (Nashville: Abingdon, 2002), 10:718.

appointed, and those who oppose it will bring judgment upon themselves.
[3]For rulers are not a cause of fear to good conduct, but to evil. Do you
wish to have no fear of authority? Then do what is good and you will receive approval from it, [4]for it is a servant of God for your good. But if you
do evil, be afraid, for it does not bear the sword without purpose; it is the
servant of God to inflict wrath on the evildoer. [5]Therefore, it is necessary
to be subject not only because of the wrath but also because of conscience.
[6]This is why you also pay taxes, for the authorities are ministers of God,
devoting themselves to this very thing. [7]Pay to all their dues, taxes to
whom taxes are due, toll to whom toll is due, respect to whom respect is
due, honor to whom honor is due.

OT: Prov 24:21; Eccles 8:2; Wis 6:1–11; Dan 2:21
NT: Luke 20:20–26; John 19:11; 1 Tim 2:1–4; Titus 3:1; 1 Pet 2:13–17
Catechism: Christians and civil authorities, 2234–46; capital punishment, 2267; tax evasion, 2409

Paul contends that exemplary Christians ought to be exemplary citizens. There
is no antithesis per se between gospel and government, so believers have no
grounds for being either indifferent to political authority or social anarchists.
In fact, the authority of human government is derived from God, which means
that submitting to public officials is part of our service to God. It is true that
Paul does not specify a Christian course of action to be taken when political
authorities overstep their bounds. But a tight cluster of seven verses hardly
suffices as a complete statement on the relationship between Christianity and
secular power. Paul is speaking in general terms only. He assumes for the sake
of argument that rulers will act in the interest of the public good.[2]

13:1   Paul's directive is blunt and to the point: **Let every person be subordinate
to the higher authorities**. The expression "every person" is given a certain
emphasis: Paul is addressing Christian readers as individuals. Each and every
disciple is expected to submit to legitimate authority. Secular rulers have a legitimate, though not absolute, claim on our honor and obedience that, at least
in principle, is not in competition with the Christian confession that Jesus is
Lord of every nation (10:12).[3]

The reason is spelled out in the words **there is no authority except from
God, and those that exist have been established by God**. Civil government is
not a product of human ingenuity. It is a divine institution with a divine origin.
God ordered the world in this way. He intends that human society operate according to this hierarchical arrangement.

2. Joseph A. Fitzmyer, SJ, *Romans*, AB 33 (New York: Doubleday, 1993), 665.
3. For similar statements to this effect, see Titus 3:1; 1 Pet 2:13–17; *Martyrdom of Polycarp* 10.2.

Figure 9. Roman bust of Nero from the Julian Basilica at Corinth, circa AD 60.

Paul is touching on a truth already contemplated in Judaism. It is clear from the Old Testament that God wields the sovereign power to raise up kings and to remove them (Dan 2:21), to plant nations as well as to pluck them up (Jer 1:10). God uses earthly empires and potentates, good and evil alike, as instruments to accomplish his purposes in history (Isa 10:5–19; 45:1–6). The book of Wisdom even affirms that world rulers are given dominion "by the Lord" and are therefore answerable to him for governing with justice and equity (Wis 6:1–11). Paul stands squarely within this theological tradition.

Furthermore, when Paul asserts that rulers receive authority from God, he means that civil governance is a sacred stewardship. It is a privilege that comes with hefty responsibilities toward the One who bestows it. Likewise, when he contends that authorities are established by God, he does not mean that God endorses particular officeholders or models of government, such as the Roman imperial system of the first century.[4] It is nothing short of remarkable—not to mention a measure of how much Paul means what he says—that he should counsel believers to obey their government officials during the reign of Nero (AD 54–68), the Caesar when Romans was being written. Even though Nero had not yet become openly hostile toward Christians, he was by all accounts one of the most disturbed and depraved men ever to hold this high office.[5] Only a few years after Paul sent this letter, a fire swept through the city of Rome (AD 64). Nero used it as an excuse to

4. Vatican II, *Gaudium et Spes* (*Pastoral Constitution on the Church in the Modern World*) 74, clarifies that civil authority as such is divinely ordained, while citizens are responsible for choosing specific political structures and candidates.

5. See especially Suetonius, *The Twelve Caesars* 6.

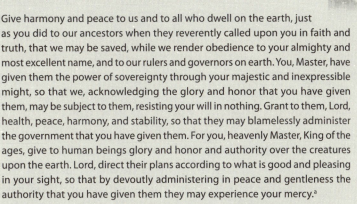

An Ancient Prayer for Earthly Rulers

LIVING
TRADITION

Christianity's relationship to secular government has been contemplated since the earliest days of the Church. Jesus spoke to the question of paying taxes to Caesar (Matt 22:15–22), and both Peter and Paul addressed the duty of civil submission and honoring the emperor (Rom 13:1–7; 1 Pet 2:17). Another voice from the first century is St. Clement of Rome, who gives a beautiful prayer for secular rulers in his letter to the Corinthians:

> Give harmony and peace to us and to all who dwell on the earth, just as you did to our ancestors when they reverently called upon you in faith and truth, that we may be saved, while we render obedience to your almighty and most excellent name, and to our rulers and governors on earth. You, Master, have given them the power of sovereignty through your majestic and inexpressible might, so that we, acknowledging the glory and honor that you have given them, may be subject to them, resisting your will in nothing. Grant to them, Lord, health, peace, harmony, and stability, so that they may blamelessly administer the government that you have given them. For you, heavenly Master, King of the ages, give to human beings glory and honor and authority over the creatures upon the earth. Lord, direct their plans according to what is good and pleasing in your sight, so that by devoutly administering in peace and gentleness the authority that you have given them they may experience your mercy.[a]

a. *1 Clement* 60.4–61.2. Translation from *The Apostolic Fathers: Greek Texts and English Translations*, 3rd ed., ed. and trans. Michael W. Holmes (Grand Rapids: Baker Academic, 2007), 127.

instigate a savage persecution of the Roman church, the first and one of the worst of its kind.[6]

Assuming the truth of verse 1, it follows that **whoever resists authority opposes what God has appointed**. Rebellion against ruling authority is a form of rebellion against almighty God, and to oppose the Lord's will is to sin against him. This is what Paul wants readers to internalize. Persons who **oppose** rightful civil authority **bring judgment upon themselves**—certainly criminal justice administered by civic magistrates, but also, and more to Paul's point, divine judgment.

13:2

Paul next considers the purpose of civil authority. Lawful government exists to promote peace and justice in society and to punish wrongdoing whenever necessary. The implication is that **rulers are not a cause of fear to good conduct, but to evil**. In this sense **fear of authority** incentivizes submission

13:3–4

6. For an ancient description, see Tacitus, *Annals of Imperial Rome* 15.44.

to rulers and compliance with their laws. If an individual chooses to **do what is good**, he or she is living on agreeable terms with the powers that be. Paul even expects that exemplary citizens **will receive approval** from their rulers. Perhaps he is thinking of financial benefactors who contribute to the welfare of the community and receive public recognition from local officials.

At any rate, citizens who choose to **do evil** should **be afraid** of government authorities, for earthly rulers do **not bear the sword without purpose**. The question here is, what does Paul mean by "the sword"? According to some, it symbolizes the power of government to enforce its laws by punishing infractions. According to others, it signals the government's right to use military force to maintain public order. According to others still—and this seems the most likely interpretation—the sword represents the authority of civil government to inflict capital punishment on a society's most dangerous criminal delinquents.[7] In this reading, governing authorities are authorized by God to take lethal action against persons who pose a serious threat to the safety and stability of the community.[8] Secular government's right to administer the death penalty has been generally acknowledged in the Catholic Church's bimillennial tradition.[9]

Paul makes some remarkable *theological* statements about the relation of civil authority to God. On the one hand, he states that the secular ruler, whether that ruler realizes it or not, is a **servant of God** (Greek *theou diakonos*). Normally this language is used for persons who perform religious actions to meet the needs of others. The Greek term for "servant" is the basis for the English word "deacon" (Phil 1:1 RSV). Paul actually refers to Jesus himself as a "servant" later in Rom 15:8! Evidently the Apostle does not separate the world into sealed compartments, secular and spiritual. For him "the earth and its fullness are the Lord's" (1 Cor 10:26, citing Ps 24:1). All live under the lordship of God and participate in his governance of the world—even secular rulers who are unaware of it.

The same secular rulers are commissioned by the Lord **to inflict wrath on the evildoer**. Paul is saying more than the obvious fact that government acts

---

7. Paul acknowledges this right in Acts 25:11.

8. It may be that Paul, by invoking the image of a sword, has in mind the Roman provincial law known as the *ius gladii*, "the right of the sword." It is unclear, however, if this could apply to citizens outside the military. See A. N. Sherwin-White, *Roman Society and Roman Law in the New Testament* (London: Oxford University Press, 1963), 8–11.

9. The Catechism affirms this while adding that today there is far less need to resort to the death penalty, given the enhanced ability of modern societies to neutralize criminal threats to the public (Catechism 2267). In the words of John Paul II: "[Punishment] ought not go to the extreme of executing the offender except in cases of absolute necessity: in other words, when it would not be possible otherwise to defend society. Today however, as a result of steady improvements in the organization of the penal system, such cases are very rare, if not practically non-existent" (Encyclical Letter *Evangelium Vitae* [*The Gospel of Life*] 56).

as a restraint on the bad behavior of citizens. The key term is "wrath," by which Paul means "the wrath of God" (as in, e.g., Rom 1:18; 2:5; 4:15). Recall that in 12:19 he cautioned believers not to avenge themselves on individuals who have caused personal injury, but to leave room for God's wrath to set matters right. Here we learn of one way that God accomplishes this: through government law enforcement.[10] Public authorities act as God's servants in the administration of justice in the temporal sphere.

Verse 5 reveals the takeaway point of Paul's argument: **Therefore**, he says,   13:5
it is necessary for Christians **to be subject** to secular authority. He gives two reasons for this, one practical, the other moral. First, he urges submission to civil power **because of the wrath**. One reason citizens avoid criminal misconduct is their desire to avoid the penal consequences. Second, submission to civil power is required of believers **because of conscience**. Because believers possess an inner awareness of right and wrong, and because they are now informed of the way that God's authority operates in the public domain, they cannot hope to defy the divine will with impunity. The conscience will issue its own guilty verdict, which is an echo of a judgment rendered by God.

Paul reiterates the point made in verse 4 that civic rulers act as **ministers**   13:6
of God (Greek *leitourgoi theou*). The term for "minister" is most often used in Scripture for cultic functionaries, such as priests, who either assist or preside over liturgical worship. It is precisely in this sense that Paul will designate himself a "minister of Christ Jesus . . . in performing the priestly service of the gospel" (15:16).

So again Paul makes the point that government does not operate in a strictly nonreligious way. Officials involved in public service, by **devoting themselves** to the collection of taxes, also perform a divine service. **This is why** believers **also pay taxes** levied by duly constituted authorities. In supporting the political order, they are contributing to a political form of service to God. By the same token, failure to render what is owed to authorities, whether by tax evasion or tax rebellion, is a failure in one's duty toward God. An awareness of this fact explains why a century after Paul penned Romans, St. Justin Martyr observed that Christians strive to pay their taxes "more readily than all people."[11]

---

10. In the words of one commentator: "The specific contextual trigger for Paul's teaching about government and its role in this world may have been 12:19. Forbidding the Christian from taking vengeance and allowing God to exercise this right in the last judgment might lead one to think that God was letting evildoers have their way in this world. Not so, says Paul in 13:1–7" (Douglas J. Moo, *The Epistle to the Romans*, NICNT [Grand Rapids: Eerdmans, 1996], 792).

11. *First Apology* 17.

13:7   Submission to secular rulers translates into paying **to all their dues**. This language implies that believers are debtors in relation to government authorities; their payment of taxes is an obligation of justice and not merely a goodwill offering.

Paul breaks this general mandate into four obligations, two financial and two social. Believers are to pay **taxes to whom taxes are due** and **toll to whom toll is due**. The distinction here is between "direct taxes" and "indirect taxes." The direct tax[12] was the annual payment of tribute to Caesar by his subjects, roughly analogous to an income tax (Luke 20:22; Josephus, *Jewish War* 2.403). The indirect tax,[13] being more like a sales tax, consisted of various fees and tariffs attached to the flow of goods and services in the Roman Empire (1 Macc 11:35; Josephus, *Jewish Antiquities* 12.141). It goes without saying that Paul's readers in the capital would have been quite familiar with the Roman system of revenue collection.

Beyond this, several scholars hold that Paul's maxim in Rom 13:7 seems to be indebted to the saying of Jesus preserved in the synoptic Gospels: "Repay to Caesar what belongs to Caesar and to God what belongs to God" (Mark 12:17; see Matt 22:21; Luke 20:25).[14] It is difficult to imagine that the Christian community in Rome would not have called this teaching to mind, living as they did in Caesar's backyard. Either way, we know that the Christian obligation to pay taxes was not a Pauline innovation. It had already been validated by the express words of Jesus.

Paul adds that believers must give **respect to whom respect is due** as well as **honor to whom honor is due**. By respect he means "reverential fear." It requires that citizens recognize that civil servants hold superior rank in the political realm; they should be ready to comply with their demands. Paul has already encouraged his readers to "outdo one another in showing honor" (Rom 12:10 RSV). Now he commends this as a Christian attitude toward secular authority, much as Peter would later urge the faithful to honor "all," including "the king" (1 Pet 2:17).

Reflection and Application (13:1–7)

Many Christians cringe when Paul speaks in such sweeping terms about civil submission in Rom 13:1–7. This is because he attaches no qualifications to his

12. Greek *phoros*.
13. Greek *telos*.
14. For a discussion of the evidence, see Michael Thompson, *Clothed with Christ: The Example and Teaching of Jesus in Romans 12:1–15:13*, JSNTSup 59 (Sheffield: JSOT Press, 1991), 111–20.

injunction to "be subordinate" to higher authorities. He only insists that a failure to do so equals "opposing" God. It almost sounds as though Paul demands unconditional obedience to secular rulers and their laws. This hardly seems like an acceptable option for Christians, given the corruption of government leaders and institutions throughout history. One need only think of the totalitarian regimes of the twentieth century to consider how far persons in power can go in perpetrating evil.

But is this what Paul means? Does he advocate a submission that knows no limits? Not at all. It is true that Paul never broaches the subject of civil disobedience in explicit terms. Nevertheless, what he *does* say implies its legitimacy in certain situations.

Consider that Paul declares ruling authority a sacred trust from God. From this premise we can infer that government power has definite boundaries, for the simple reason that God has established definite boundaries for human conduct in general. When authority figures venture beyond these acceptable limits—commanding what God forbids or forbidding what God commands—they are no longer acting with God's authority. When they trample on human rights or interfere with the practice of the faith, they are no longer acting with God's authority. In such cases, we can speak of raw political assertion, but not of divinely authorized mandates. A ten-foot-long diving board will only support your weight ten feet out over the water. Step beyond the board, and it no longer supports you. Should government rulers take this fateful step, Christians are bound to "obey God rather than men" (Acts 5:29).[15]

Readers will not be surprised to learn that Rom 13:1–7 has had a profound impact on the development of Christian political thought.[16] This is especially so in discussions about the relationship between church and state. The plain fact, however, is that Paul makes no effort to delineate separate spheres of jurisdiction proper to civil and ecclesiastical authorities. Distinguishing between the temporal and spiritual orders and clarifying their respective domains would become necessary in later centuries. But Paul's concern in Rom 13 is with the individual Christian and the ethics of citizenship.

Closer to Paul's concern is the question of how submission to authority can effect a transformation of society from within. In other words, Christians are called not to subvert the sociopolitical order but to sanctify it. They are to

15. The Catechism clarifies that Christians have not only a right to protest injustices of the state but even a duty (Catechism 2238). See also John Paul II, Encyclical Letter *Evangelium Vitae* (*The Gospel of Life*) 73–74.
16. See, e.g., Victor Manuel Morales Vásquez, *Contours of a Biblical Reception History: Studies in the Rezeptionsgeschichte of Romans 13.1–7* (Göttingen: Vandenhoeck & Ruprecht, 2012).

promote the betterment of society by paying their taxes, yes, but also by bring-ing its leaders to faith and its laws into alignment with the gospel.[17] In this way Christians can become the leaven that Jesus spoke about in Matt 13:33, slowly advancing the kingdom of heaven on earth. According to one of the most beautiful insights from the Apostolic Fathers, believers are to the world what the soul is to the body—its invisible principle of life, dispersed throughout the world, but not of the world.[18]

Love as Fulfillment of the Law (13:8–10)

[8]**Owe nothing to anyone, except to love one another; for the one who loves another has fulfilled the law. [9]The commandments, "You shall not commit adultery; you shall not kill; you shall not steal; you shall not covet," and whatever other commandment there may be, are summed up in this saying, [namely] "You shall love your neighbor as yourself." [10]Love does no evil to the neighbor; hence, love is a fulfillment of the law.**

OT: Exod 20:13–15, 17; Lev 19:18; Deut 5:17–19, 21

NT: Matt 19:16–19; 22:39–40; Rom 5:5; 8:4; 1 Cor 7:19; Gal 5:14; James 2:8

Catechism: charity and the commandments, 1824; greatest commandments, 2055, 2196; love infused by the Spirit, 1972

Paul speaks about the primacy of love in the Christian life. His progression of thought is quite logical. The language of duty in verse 7 is carried over into verse 8 to make a point about the greatest of our religious duties. If rendering taxes and obedience to secular authorities is the discharge of a debt, how much more is the believer obligated to fulfill the law of God. And supreme among all the divine precepts is the law of love.

13:8   Paul opens with the counsel that readers should **owe nothing to anyone**. In what ways he intended readers to apply this directive is not explicit. It can plausibly be taken as a warning against racking up unnecessary financial debts. Christians (and others) are unwise to borrow and spend beyond their means, as this is poor stewardship of the resources that God has entrusted to each. Paul's teaching is a call to avoid the burdens of debt insofar as possible and to make every reasonable effort to climb out of debt if and when it is incurred.

---

17. Noted in St. John Chrysostom's *Homilies on Romans* 23. Likewise, James D. G. Dunn, *Theology of the Apostle Paul* (Grand Rapids: Eerdmans, 1998), 680, contends that faithful Christian citizenship could have been viewed by Paul as a "missionary strategy" commending the gospel to persons of good will.
    18. *Epistle to Diognetus* 6.1–4.

The Apostle does make one exception to this rule, however, since the debt we have **to love one another** always remains outstanding and is never paid in full. Everyone we encounter, inside or outside the family of faith, is entitled to our charity. And, of course, for Paul love has everything to do with practical service and bearing one another's burdens; it has nothing at all to do with sappy sentimentalism. Readers can get a sense of what he means by reading the lyrical description of love in 1 Cor 13:4–13.

Paul adds that **the one who loves another has fulfilled the law**. This is remarkable. The verb "fulfill"[19] means "to satisfy what is required" or "to accomplish in full." But to appreciate the significance of Paul's statement, remember that the Torah presents 613 prescriptive and prohibitive commandments touching on all aspects of Israel's life, worship, and social organization. Underlying this great diversity of precepts is an essential unity of purpose: to teach God's people how to love. Consequently, Paul can say that love for another meets and exceeds the requirements of them all.

Paul quotes the sixth, fifth, seventh, and ninth **commandments** of the †Decalogue to reinforce the point. **"You shall not commit adultery; you shall not kill; you shall not steal; you shall not covet"** (Exod 20:13–15, 17).[20] In short, these are the laws that apply to our neighbor, not our obligations to God. And since there are numerous other laws in the Torah that fall into this category, Paul is quick to include **whatever other commandment there may be**. The focus of his interest is mainly on the moral commandments of Moses, but he is not excluding the liturgical and juridical precepts that stand alongside them. Love is the fulfillment of the entire law of Moses.

All the commandments **are summed up** in a passage from the book of Leviticus: **"You shall love your neighbor as yourself"** (Lev 19:18). When taken in the aggregate, they all add up to this single imperative, which epitomizes the full range of the Mosaic law's religious instruction. Paul makes the same point in Gal 5:14, when he contends that "the whole law is fulfilled in one statement, namely, 'You shall love your neighbor as yourself.'" James calls it "the royal law" of the kingdom of God (James 2:8).[21]

Paul thus underscores the continuity between the Old Covenant and the New. Both the law and the gospel direct God's people to the same goal. This

13:9

---

19. Greek *plēroō*.

20. Paul follows the sequence of commandments as it appears in the Septuagint version of Deut 5:17–21. This order (listing "adultery" before "killing") is not represented in the Hebrew text of either Exodus or Deuteronomy.

21. That a single principle underlies all the commandments was also considered in rabbinic Judaism. See E. P. Sanders, *Paul and Palestinian Judaism* (Philadelphia: Fortress, 1977), 112–14.

vocation to love explains, in turn, why the commandments of the Decalogue, revered for centuries as the pillars of the moral life for the community of Israel, remain standing obligations for the Christian community to this day (Matt 19:16–19; 1 Cor 7:19).

13:10   The climactic verse in this section adds another element to the definition of love, which Paul says **does no evil to the neighbor**. Christian charity disallows all sinful actions in the realm of personal relationships, actions that would do physical, spiritual, emotional, or financial harm to another. In its fullest and purest expression, love is always sincere (12:9) and always looks for opportunities to "conquer evil with good" (12:21). When disciples learn to love others selflessly and sacrificially, they achieve the overarching aim of all God's commandments. So it is that **love is a fulfillment of the law**.

It is important to remember Paul's vision of the law's fulfillment. The Church adheres to the same Decalogue that was laid upon Israel, yet its observance of that law is new and different. Paul already addressed this issue earlier. The most important passage is 8:4, where he says that the Holy Spirit indwells believers "so that the righteous decree of the law might be fulfilled in us." The use of the verb "fulfill" twice in 13:8–10 is no coincidence. Reading these passages in light of one another indicates that Christian fulfillment of the law is made possible by the grace of the Spirit within.[22] Obedience to the commandments is no longer dependent on sheer human effort; believers benefit from a spiritual form of "assisted living" in which the willpower to do what God commands is supplied from above. And how does this relate to the requirement of love? As Paul stated earlier, the love we need to fulfill the law "has been poured out into our hearts through the holy Spirit that has been given to us" (5:5).

Reflection and Application (13:8–10)

Paul's teaching in the latter chapters of Romans often echoes the teaching of Jesus in the Gospels. His remarks in 13:8–10 are a prime example of this. Here he puts an emphasis on love that was characteristic of Jesus in his discussions of the law.

The Gospel of Matthew brings this out clearly. Jesus fields a question from a rich young man on how to gain eternal life. He answers by citing several commandments of the Decalogue alongside Lev 19:18, which mandates loving your neighbor as yourself (Matt 19:16–19). This is precisely what Paul

22. Paula Fredriksen, "Paul's Letter to the Romans, the Ten Commandments, and Pagan 'Justification by Faith,'" *JBL* 133, no. 4 (2014): 801–8.

does in Rom 13. In another passage, Jesus is asked which commandment in the law is the greatest. This time he responds by quoting the †Shema, which outlines Israel's duty to love the Lord wholeheartedly, and then by citing the law of loving one's neighbor from Lev 19:18 (Matt 22:36–39). On top of these Jesus adds an interpretive comment: "The whole law and the prophets depend on these two commandments" (Matt 22:40). This is basically what Paul does in Rom 13.[23]

Jesus and Paul are on the same page when it comes to Christian morality. Both see the commandment to "love your neighbor" towering over the vast landscape of moral laws codified in the Torah. Both teach that love is the thing God wants most in our relationships with others. Paul, it turns out, is not the innovator and maverick he is sometimes made out to be. He is simply a zealous disciple who has internalized the teaching of his master.

Putting on Christ (13:11–14)

> [11]And do this because you know the time; it is the hour now for you to awake from sleep. For our salvation is nearer now than when we first believed; [12]the night is advanced, the day is at hand. Let us then throw off the works of darkness [and] put on the armor of light; [13]let us conduct ourselves properly as in the day, not in orgies and drunkenness, not in promiscuity and licentiousness, not in rivalry and jealousy. [14]But put on the Lord Jesus Christ, and make no provision for the desires of the flesh.

OT: Isa 9:1–6
NT: Mark 13:33–37; Gal 3:27; Eph 5:8–16; 6:11–17; 1 Thess 5:1–11
Catechism: clothed with Christ in baptism, 1227, 1243; baptism and chastity, 2348
Lectionary: 1st Sunday of Advent (Year A)

The final appeal of Rom 13 brings ethics and †eschatology together. Paul summons believers to wakefulness in the midst of a world that revels in sin. He achieves this through the imagery of darkness followed by dawn, which represent "this age" (12:2) yielding to the "glory to be revealed" (8:18). Nighttime is about to give way to full daylight, so disciples must rouse themselves from slumber and attend to their Christian duties while the opportunity remains. It seems likely that Jesus' resurrection before daybreak on Easter morning stands behind Paul's thinking in these verses.[24]

23. For discussion of the parallels, see Thompson, *Clothed with Christ*, 132–40.
24. Wright, "Letter to the Romans," 728.

237

13:11 Verse 11 begins with Paul reminding readers of something they already know—that **the time** and **the hour** has come to **awake from sleep**. The night of our sinful past is far spent, and the dawn of future salvation approaches. Paul urges believers to be metaphorical "early risers" from a world still living in the shadows of rebellion against God.

Christians live in the transitional period between the black of night and the bright light of morning.[25] Salvation is already experienced in part, since believers have been united with Jesus in baptism (6:3) and adopted as children of God in the Spirit (8:14–16). Yet we await the completion that will come with "the redemption of our bodies" (8:23). This is why Paul speaks of **salvation** drawing **nearer now than when we first believed**. Saving grace has already poured into our lives, but God's work in us is not yet fully accomplished.

13:12–13 Paul's †eschatological perspective adds a sense of urgency to his moral exhortations. Since **the night is advanced** and **the day is at hand,** he can view the Christian life as a time of eager expectation. But since the gloom of the present age has yet to dissipate, it remains a time of temptation and risk for God's people. For this reason Paul urges readers to **throw off the works of darkness**, by which he means "the works of the flesh" (Gal 5:19–21). These are the sins and lusts of our fallen nature that typically thrive under the cover of darkness. Paul imagines them as a garment of filthy practices that must be removed and discarded.

In its place believers are to **put on the armor of light** as protection against spiritual dangers. The term for armor[26] denotes all the battle gear worn by a foot soldier, body armor as well as weaponry. Christians, rising before dawn, are admonished to suit up for the struggle with the gifts that God has generously given them, gifts that enable them to behave **properly as in the day**. Paul does not say so here, but similar passages suggest that the "armor of light" indicates such things as faith, hope, love, truth, righteousness, and a knowledge of the word of God (Eph 6:14–17; 1 Thess 5:8).

Paul singles out specific forms of misconduct he wants readers to avoid. Christians are to have no part in **orgies and drunkenness**; they must steer clear of all **promiscuity and licentiousness** as well as **rivalry and jealousy**. These are the foul fruits of abandoning self-control in the areas of sex, alcohol, and personal relationships. The Roman world, like the world today, could be wildly uninhibited in committing sins of sexual perversion; Paul would have believers offer their bodies as a sacrifice to God (Rom 12:1). The Romans, like

25. See commentary on 12:2.
26. Greek *hopla*.

Origen of Alexandria on "Putting on Christ"

LIVING
TRADITION

We have said that Christ is at the same time wisdom, righteousness, sanctification, truth, and all the virtues. Assuredly the one who has received these is said to have put on Christ. For if Christ is all these things, the one who has them necessarily has Christ as well. Now the one who possesses these things makes no provision for the flesh, with its lusts. The apostle practices his customary moderation; he does not forbid provision for the flesh to be made through all things. For certainly it must be provided with necessities. But with respect to pleasures and excesses and every kind of lust, provision is to be absolutely excluded.[a]

a. Origen of Alexandria, *Commentary on Romans* 9.34. Quotation adapted from Origen, *Commentary on the Epistle to the Romans: Books 6–10*, trans. Thomas P. Scheck, FC (Washington, DC: Catholic University of America Press, 2002), 233.

people today, could be utterly indulgent in intoxicating drink; Paul would have believers lead alert and sober lives (1 Thess 5:6). Romans could be ruthlessly competitive and bitterly covetous of what others possessed; Paul would have Christians live at peace with all (Rom 12:18), even rejoicing alongside others who have cause to rejoice (12:15).

Paul implores readers to **put on the Lord Jesus Christ, and make no provision for the desires of the flesh**. A case could be made that this passage summarizes the totality of Paul's moral counsel in the New Testament. Indeed, this verse became famous for jolting St. Augustine of Hippo out of spiritual despondency in the fourth century.[27]

13:14

Again Paul pictures the Christian getting up before sunrise and putting on his or her armor for the battles of the day. Only this time he identifies the warrior's sturdy equipment as the Lord Jesus himself. Readers familiar with the Pauline Letters will recall his teaching in Galatians that all those "who were baptized into Christ" have been "clothed . . . with Christ" (Gal 3:27). This beautiful description seems to have given rise to the ancient liturgical practice of vesting newly baptized believers in white garments, symbolizing their spiritual purity in Christ.[28] Here a connection is made not with the event of baptism itself but with the lifelong duty that baptism places on the Christian. Each and every day believers must renew their commitment to living by the gospel.

27. See St. Augustine, *Confessions* 8.29.
28. See Jean Daniélou, SJ, *The Bible and the Liturgy* (Notre Dame, IN: University of Notre Dame Press, 1956), 49–53.

The unbelieving world, after all, still lives by the desires of the flesh—those base and selfish biddings of our fallen nature. Paul is concerned to put us on guard against these things. His words "make no provision" suggest that he advocates devising personal strategies that will help us to avoid sin and its near occasions.

The Weak and the Strong in Rome

Romans 14:1–23

The final segment of Paul's pastoral teaching in Romans covers 14:1–15:13. Parts of this extended section are clear, while other parts are quite challenging to interpret. Reading through these verses is like listening to one side of a phone conversation. Paul and the Roman Christians are aware of the problems that have called forth his counsel.[1] But modern readers must fill in gaps by piecing together clues from the unfolding discussion.

Paul is seeking a charitable resolution to disagreements in Rome regarding Jewish food restrictions and feast days. His focus is on the pastoral fallout of the controversy, most notably the disruption of fellowship taking place in the Roman church. The congregation was split into two groups, whom Paul calls "the weak" and "the strong."[2] Both sides hold firm convictions about their views, and he grants that both are concerned to honor the Lord by their actions.

Identifying the issues that divide these factions is relatively straightforward, even if questions remain. Paul describes the weak as persons who abstain from meat and wine (14:2, 21) and follow a calendar that regards some days as more important than others (14:5). The strong, by contrast, are persons who embrace an unrestricted diet (14:2) and make no distinction between one day and another (14:5). Basically, the weak are committed to following a traditional Jewish way of life, while the strong believe that Judaism's ritual observances are nonissues for Christians. Does this mean the weak and the strong are Jewish and

1. For detailed analysis, see Mark Reasoner, *The Strong and the Weak: Romans 14:1–15:13 in Context*, SNTSMS 103 (Cambridge: Cambridge University Press, 1999).
2. The names appear in 14:1 and 15:1 respectively.

Gentile Christians, respectively? Broadly speaking, yes, but strictly speaking, no. It is likely the two groups are ethnically weighted, the weak being mostly Jewish believers and the strong being mostly Gentile believers.[3] Nevertheless, the matter is not so cut-and-dried. On the one hand, ancient sources tell us that a fair number of Gentiles adopted Jewish practices in the New Testament period; on the other, Paul counts himself among the strong (15:1) despite his Israelite pedigree (11:1).

One of the most curious features of this section of Romans is the paradox of Paul's own position. Theologically, he shares the conviction of the strong that no food is "unclean in itself" (14:14). Pastorally, however, Paul comes to the defense of the weak by admonishing the strong not to assert their Christian freedoms to the detriment of the weak (14:15). In addition, because the weak and the strong are critical of one another (14:3), he makes a plea for mutual respect and acceptance (15:7).

Romans 14:1–15:13 is Paul's effort to foster unity in the Roman church without imposing uniformity in nonessential matters. He achieves this by an application of the law of love enunciated in 13:8–10. The call of Christian charity is a call to loving concern for all the members of the body of Christ. The strong are urged to love the weak by using their strength to build up the weak (14:19). By sacrificing their freedom to eat certain foods and to forego the observance of certain days, they remove obstacles that could otherwise make their weaker brothers and sisters stumble in conscience (14:20–21). The weak, for their part, are called to abstain from passing judgment on the strong (14:13) and to avoid reducing the kingdom of God to matters of food and drink (14:17). In short, all believers, weak and strong alike, are expected to walk "in accord with love" (14:15).

Welcoming the Weak (14:1–12)

¹Welcome anyone who is weak in faith, but not for disputes over opinions. ²One person believes that one may eat anything, while the weak person eats only vegetables. ³The one who eats must not despise the one who abstains, and the one who abstains must not pass judgment on the one who eats; for God has welcomed him. ⁴Who are you to pass judgment on someone else's servant? Before his own master he stands or falls. And he will be upheld, for the Lord is able to make him stand. ⁵[For] one person

3. See Douglas J. Moo, *The Epistle to the Romans*, NICNT (Grand Rapids: Eerdmans, 1996), 829–31.

considers one day more important than another, while another person
considers all days alike. Let everyone be fully persuaded in his own mind.
⁶Whoever observes the day, observes it for the Lord. Also whoever eats,
eats for the Lord, since he gives thanks to God; while whoever abstains,
abstains for the Lord and gives thanks to God. ⁷None of us lives for oneself, and no one dies for oneself. ⁸For if we live, we live for the Lord, and
if we die, we die for the Lord; so then, whether we live or die, we are the
Lord's. ⁹For this is why Christ died and came to life, that he might be Lord
of both the dead and the living. ¹⁰Why then do you judge your brother? Or
you, why do you look down on your brother? For we shall all stand before
the judgment seat of God; ¹¹for it is written:

> "As I live, says the Lord, every knee shall bend before me,
>   and every tongue shall give praise to God."

¹²So [then] each of us shall give an account of himself [to God].

OT: Lev 23:1–44; Isa 45:23; 49:18

NT: 1 Cor 4:3–5; 8:8–13; 2 Cor 5:10; Phil 2:10–11; Col 2:16; 1 Tim 4:3–5

Catechism: sabbath observance, 345–48, 2171; prayer of thanksgiving, 2637–38; prayer of praise, 2639, 2649; Christ our judge, 678–79; last judgment, 1038–41

Lectionary: 14:7–9: Funeral for Baptized Children; 14:7–9, 10c–12: Commemoration for All the Faithful Departed; Mass for the Deceased; Mass for the Grace of a Happy Death

---

Paul's discussion of Christian conduct continues. He notes theological differences dividing the weak and the strong, but he does not evaluate them—his
first order of business is to help the two sides respect one another again.
When a father hears that his children are quarreling, his first thought is not
to resolve the question of who's right and who's wrong. Initially he intervenes
to calm the storm; then he takes up the task of sorting out the conflict. This
is more or less Paul's approach in Rom 14. He calls for a ceasefire of the criticisms passing between the weak and the strong (14:1–12). Only then does
he address the issues in dispute and lay down some ground rules for family
harmony (14:13–23).

Paul urges the strong in Rome to **welcome anyone who is weak in faith**.   14:1
He is calling the strong to receive the weak into full family communion. The
weak believer, after all, is a "brother" in Christ (14:10, 13, 15, 21). What Paul
expected this acceptance to look like is not specified. However, since the Christian community in Rome consisted of a network of house churches (16:1–16),
it seems likely that Paul is asking the strong to take the lead in showing hospitality. Perhaps he is urging the strong to invite the weak to participate in their
worship and in other activities such as communal meals. The extent to which

the Roman house churches had contact with one another is unknown, but apparently some were unwelcoming toward members of others.

Unfortunately, Paul never clarifies what he means by "weak in faith." The phrase is often taken to mean "having an immature faith," and this is probably near the mark. To their credit, the weak believe in Jesus the Messiah and have come to know the power of his salvation (1:16).[4] But apparently they have yet to accept the full implications of their Christian freedom in relation to Jewish ritual practices. In this matter, the weak need to grow stronger in faith, much as Abraham did in his day (4:19–20 RSV).

Paul adds a qualification to his opening appeal: **but not for disputes over opinions**. He wants to ease tensions between Roman believers, not aggravate them. Personal interaction and fellowship should be times of unity, not disunity. This cannot be realized if hospitality opens the door to haggling over differences.

14:2–3 The strong Christian **believes that one may eat anything**. For him, there is nothing in the ordinary diet that is banned from consumption. But the **weak** Christian lives by a different standard. For religious reasons he **eats only vegetables**. Since vegetarianism is not a traditional feature of either biblical or postbiblical Judaism, there is a question about why the weak avoided meat. It may have been difficult to obtain kosher foods in Rome, thus making a meatless diet the safest course.[5] Local butchers may not have been trusted to process meat in accord with Jewish requirements, putting buyers at risk of eating blood in violation of the Torah's blood prohibition laws (Gen 9:4; Lev 17:10–12). In Greek and Roman antiquity, meat was typically offered in sacrifice to idols before being sold in the marketplace. The question could thus be raised whether consumption of meats implicated one in idolatry.[6]

Whatever the motive behind the abstinence of the weak,[7] Paul's purpose is not to work out a menu of acceptable foods for the faithful. Instead, he is anxious to resolve a more serious problem—Christians ceasing to walk in "love" (Rom 14:15) by passing judgment on fellow Christians (14:4, 10, 13). Addressing the strong, Paul insists that **one who eats must not despise the one who abstains**. The wording of the prohibition suggests the strong had adopted a disdainful, condescending attitude toward the weak. Then, addressing the weak,

4. For a thought-provoking attempt to demonstrate that the weak are Jewish nonbelievers from the synagogue community in Rome, see Mark D. Nanos, *The Mystery of Romans: The Jewish Context of Paul's Letter* (Minneapolis: Fortress, 1996), 85–165. But see Robert A. J. Gagnon, "Why the 'Weak' at Rome Cannot Be Non-Christian Jews," *CBQ* 62 (2000): 64–82.

5. The laws defining clean and unclean foods are found in Lev 11 and Deut 14.

6. This is precisely the issue Paul deals with in 1 Cor 8–10.

7. For further discussion, see the sidebar "Diet in the Jewish Diaspora" (pp. 254–55).

Paul directs that **one who abstains must not pass judgment on the one who eats**. It is one thing if the weak are unwilling to give up Jewish dietary customs deeply rooted in Israel's religious past. It is quite another, however, if the weak become openly critical of the strong and judge their eating habits to fall short of a fervent commitment to God.

Paul bases this double appeal on the action of **God**. Since both strong and weak believers have been **welcomed** into the messianic community, the members of that community are expected to do the same for one another. Patterning themselves after the God of mercy and love, they must "welcome one another" for reconciliation and fellowship (15:7).

In the next verse Paul reverts to his familiar conversational mode. His opening question has the force of an indictment: **Who are you to pass judgment on someone else's servant?** Ordinarily, servants of the same household stand on an equal footing; they do not answer to one another for their actions but to the **master** of the house. The master's approval or disapproval is all that matters. When a servant **stands** at a performance review, he receives commendation; when he **falls**, he is verbally reprimanded and likely punished. The lesson for the weak and the strong is clear: a servant has no authority to pass judgment on a fellow servant. Only the Lord possesses this authority.[8]   **14:4**

Paul expresses confidence that the weak as well as the strong **will be upheld** by **the Lord** at the time of their review. This hope is probably related to the Apostle's recognition that the actions of both parties spring from a desire to serve the Lord in gratitude (14:6). Paul connects this vindication with the general resurrection, at least implicitly.[9] The Greek term for "resurrection" means "standing up." Hence, the Lord's ability **to make** the believer **stand** may be said to evoke this future expectation.

Paul then introduces a second bone of contention. The weak believer **considers one day more important than another**, while the strong believer **considers all days alike**. Again the opposing positions are set forth, and again the dividing line between them is formed by Jewish traditions. Without going into detail, Paul hints that the weak follow the rhythms of Judaism's liturgical calendar, in which every sabbath is set apart for worship and rest, just as every year is punctuated with sacred festivals commemorating the great events of salvation history (Lev 23:1–44). The strong make no distinction between days, meaning that they do not observe the Torah's festal calendar.   **14:5–6**

---

8. Paul's analogy works because the same Greek term, *kyrios*, means "master" as well as "Lord."
9. Pointed out by N. T. Wright, "The Letter to the Romans," in *The New Interpreter's Bible*, ed. Leander E. Keck (Nashville: Abingdon, 2002), 10:736.

One might have expected Paul to intervene at this point to address the issue of holy days and seasons. But again, as in Rom 14:2–3, his attention remains fixed on community harmony rather than questions of ritual practice. **Let everyone be fully persuaded in his own mind** is his appeal. One thing readers must *not* do is act under the pressure of doubt, since "whatever is not from faith is sin" (14:23). Paul is confident, however, that the weak and the strong act with the same purpose in mind. If the weak brother **observes** a sacred **day**, he **observes it for the Lord**. Likewise, if he **abstains** from meat, he **abstains for the Lord and gives thanks to God** for the opportunity to serve him in this way. For Paul, this is no different than a strong believer who **eats** anything he chooses **for the Lord**. He commends both groups insofar as both are animated by the same religious motive.

14:7–9   Paul puts the controversy into proper perspective. The gospel directs that **none of us lives for oneself** and **no one dies for oneself**. Life in the Lord urges us to think beyond the small package of our personal wants and concerns. Earlier in the letter Paul made reference to the communion of saints, saying that believers in the body of Christ are "individually parts of one another" (12:5). Now he draws out the implication of this teaching by saying that Christians have a responsibility to serve one another and to act in the best interests of their brothers and sisters. Even more, it is our task as disciples to **live for the Lord** and **die for the Lord**. Whatever the stage of our pilgrimage, whether we are living or dying, **we are the Lord's**. Paul is urging believers to be servants of the Lord's will rather than servants of their own.

Paul next explains the reason we belong to the Lord: **this is why Christ died and came to life, that he might be Lord of both the dead and the living**. First, we should note that Paul uses the term "Lord" as a title for the risen Jesus. The significance of this will become clear in verse 11. Second, according to the New Testament, Jesus acquired this universal lordship by his death and resurrection (Matt 28:18–20; Acts 2:36). His humiliation on the cross was the prelude to his exaltation as the incarnate Lord of all (Phil 2:6–11). This is why Paul states elsewhere that Christ "died for all, so that those who live might no longer live for themselves but for him who for their sake died and was raised" (2 Cor 5:15). Third, Christian morality finds its ultimate reference point in Christ's own conduct. This anticipates the discussion in Rom 15, where Paul reasons that if Jesus did not live and die simply to "please himself" (15:3), then believers have strong incentive to live unselfishly in this world and not to please themselves (15:1).

14:10   Paul invokes the final judgment to induce the weak and the strong to put their differences aside in view of God's final reckoning. From the perspective of the last day, the importance of special diets and special days simply melts away. Far more important is the peril that faces Christians who pass judgment on one another. **Why then do you judge your brother? Or you, why do you look down on your brother?** These questions address the weak and the strong respectively, echoing the words that Paul used in 14:3 to forbid judging and despising a fellow believer. Moreover, the Apostle is getting more direct and personal with his readers, addressing them as individuals (the "you" in both questions is singular and emphatic). Each believer must refrain from criticizing others and from harboring condescending attitudes toward them.

Paul offers the sober reminder that **we shall all stand before the judgment seat of God**. Everyone will be tried impartially before God's tribunal and receive the Lord's verdict, whether it be the "glory, honor, and immortality" of final justification (2:7) or the "wrath and fury" of final condemnation (2:8). Giving serious thought to this future event can bring wisdom to our moral deliberations in the present.

The judgment about which Paul speaks is foreseen in Scripture. He employs **14:11** his standard quotation formula **for it is written**, followed by an excerpt from the prophet Isaiah. The initial words of the oracle, **As I live, says the Lord**, signals occasions in the Old Testament when God swears an oath in his own name (e.g., Isa 49:18). The rest of the passage follows the †Septuagint translation of Isa 45:23, where the Lord pledges that **every knee shall bend before me, / and every tongue shall give praise to God**. This passage provides a glimpse of the day of judgment, when the God of Israel will reveal himself as the God of all nations. On this fateful day everyone will bow in worship before the divine judge and acknowledge his majesty. The wicked who seethe with anger against the Lord will experience "shame," while Israel's chosen ones will have "vindication and glory" (Isa 45:24–25).

This much is evident. But Paul makes a surprising move that speaks volumes about his understanding of Jesus. Recall that in verses 3–9 Paul designates the Father as "God" and Jesus as "Lord." Now he adduces an oracle from Isaiah that differentiates between "the Lord," who speaks in the first person, and "God," who is spoken about in the third person.[10] Paul, under the influence of divine grace, hears the voice of Christ speaking in the prophecy. He sees the Messiah as the agent of God's universal judgment over the world.

Some modern commentators resist the idea that Paul sees Jesus at the center of Isaiah's vision, but there is little compelling reason to do so. Paul's

---

10. Noted by J. Ross Wagner, *Heralds of the Good News: Isaiah and Paul in Concert in the Letter to the Romans*, NovTSup 101 (Leiden: Brill, 2002), 336–40.

remark that "we shall all stand before the judgment seat of God" in Rom 14:10 is practically a restatement of his teaching in 2 Corinthians, where he says that "we must all appear before the judgment seat of Christ" (2 Cor 5:10). Clearly there is no competition between these two expectations in Paul's mind. Likewise, scholars agree that Isa 45:23 is the primary biblical text behind the Christ hymn in Phil 2:10–11, where Paul affirms that "every knee should bend . . . / and every tongue confess that / Jesus Christ is Lord, / to the glory of God the Father." Here too the lowly servant Jesus is identified as the sovereign Lord of Isaiah's oracle. Other passages affirm the same basic truth: that Jesus is appointed by the Father to judge the living and the dead (John 5:26–27; Acts 10:42). Saul the Pharisee may not have read Isaiah in this way, but Paul the apostle certainly did.

14:12   That said, the role that Jesus plays in the judgment scene of Isa 45:23 is not Paul's main assertion. His goal remains reconciling the weak and the strong by impressing upon them a sense of accountability for their actions toward one another. How do we know this? Because Paul's sole interpretive comment on the passage is an application of its moral lesson: the faithful must remember that **each of us shall give an account of himself** before the divine tribunal. Believers are thereby urged to think twice before pronouncing judgment on fellow believers.

Loving the Weak (14:13–23)

> [13]Then let us no longer judge one another, but rather resolve never to put a stumbling block or hindrance in the way of a brother. [14]I know and am convinced in the Lord Jesus that nothing is unclean in itself; still, it is unclean for someone who thinks it unclean. [15]If your brother is being hurt by what you eat, your conduct is no longer in accord with love. Do not because of your food destroy him for whom Christ died. [16]So do not let your good be reviled. [17]For the kingdom of God is not a matter of food and drink, but of righteousness, peace, and joy in the holy Spirit; [18]whoever serves Christ in this way is pleasing to God and approved by others. [19]Let us then pursue what leads to peace and to building up one another. [20]For the sake of food, do not destroy the work of God. Everything is indeed clean, but it is wrong for anyone to become a stumbling block by eating; [21]it is good not to eat meat or drink wine or do anything that causes your brother to stumble. [22]Keep the faith [that] you have to yourself in the presence of God; blessed is the one who does not condemn himself for what he approves. [23]But whoever has doubts is

condemned if he eats, because this is not from faith; for whatever is not from faith is sin.

OT: Tob 1:10–11; Jdt 12:1–19; Dan 1:8–16; 10:3

NT: Matt 7:1–2; Mark 7:15–23; Acts 10:9–16; Rom 13:8–10; 1 Cor 8:8–13

Catechism: Jesus and Jewish dietary laws, 582; new law of freedom, 1972; scandal, 2284; charity and conscience, 1789; faith and doubt, 2088

The second half of Rom 14 turns on a crucial distinction between objective reality and subjective conscience. Paul acknowledges that the strong are correct on objective grounds: no food is inherently unclean or forbidden for consumption. However, they are not for this reason to exercise their liberty by eating whatever they please. The weak remain convinced, subjectively speaking, that some foods are legally unclean. Paul therefore urges the strong to accommodate themselves to the weak by following Jewish dietary customs while dining in their company, lest the weak be scandalized and their faith harmed. From this specific situation in the Roman church a general principle arises: the exercise of Christian freedom is a failure of Christian love if doing so proves injurious to another.

Paul summarizes his pastoral message thus far: **let us no longer judge one another**. The "us" of this exhortation is inclusive of the weak and the strong. Instead of exchanging criticisms, the two groups must **resolve never to put a stumbling block or hindrance in the way of a brother**. With these words Paul shifts to confront the problem of scandal.   **14:13**

Paul is concerned that Christians who insist on their freedoms will cause harm to fellow Christians (14:16). By acting selfishly and irresponsibly, one believer can position himself as a "stumbling block" in the path of another, causing him to trip and fall, spiritually speaking. Likewise, one believer can make himself a "hindrance" that tempts or entices another to act against his conscience—not because either the weak or the strong are making sinful choices about options on a menu, but because *even the appearance of wrongdoing* can scandalize another. If avoiding scandal means avoiding certain foods in certain situations, then so be it. That is the course to be taken.

Paul next comments on his own position: **I know and am convinced . . . that nothing is unclean in itself**. Judaism's dietary customs are part of an old order that is passing away. The legal distinction between "clean" and "unclean" foods, while historically a central feature of the Mosaic covenant, is no longer an operative distinction in the New Covenant. Paul declares himself fully persuaded of this fact **in the Lord Jesus**.   **14:14**

What precisely Paul means by "in the Lord Jesus" is left unexplained. Perhaps he means that Jesus enlightened him inwardly through the Spirit. Another possibility is that Paul derived his certainty about the cleanness of all foods from the divine revelation given to the apostle Peter in the book of Acts. Acts 10:9–16 relates a vision that Peter experiences on his rooftop, in which a voice from heaven instructs him three times to slaughter and eat any animal he wishes, even those traditionally forbidden for Jewish consumption. To this Peter instinctively replies, "No, Lord; for I have never eaten anything that is common or unclean" (Acts 10:14 RSV). Years of following the dietary practices of the Mosaic law could not be overcome in a moment. Still, the response from heaven was decisive and firm: "What God has cleansed, you must not call common" (Acts 10:15 RSV).

At one level, then, Peter's vision was a revelation about a new development in God's plan that makes the dietary restrictions of the Mosaic covenant passé. History has reached a point where God has cleansed the foods that were formerly considered unclean. A solid case can be made that Paul's conviction that "nothing is unclean" rests squarely on this revelation.

But Peter's vision, while it concerns a question of food, is more immediately concerned with fostering unity between Jews and Gentiles. The primary purpose of the vision was to show Peter—and through him the Church—that God is now intent upon cleansing the Gentiles and bringing them into the covenant. In Mosaic times, God separated Israel from the nations, just as he separated clean animals from unclean. But now, in messianic times, God is bringing Israel and the nations together into a single family of faith. This is the point that Peter comes to understand and explains to the Gentile household of Cornelius: "You yourselves know how unlawful it is for a Jew to associate with or to visit with any one of another nation; but God has shown me that I should not call any man common or unclean" (Acts 10:28 RSV). Later, at the Jerusalem Council, Peter looks back on the conversion of Cornelius and his household as an event in which the Lord "cleansed" the hearts of these believing Gentiles by giving them the Holy Spirit (Acts 15:9 RSV). Is it simply a coincidence that Paul in Rom 14 is promoting fellowship between two groups, one marked by Jewish apprehensions over food (the weak) and the other by a Gentile openness to all foods (the strong)? It seems unlikely.

Paul adds an important proviso here: **still, it is unclean for someone who thinks it unclean**. His reasoning here is subtle. The point is not what happens to food in the hands of the weak, but what happens to the weak when they see certain foods in the hands of the strong. Rather than a culinary description, Paul proposes a pastoral prescription applicable to both strong and weak, but probably addressed mainly to the strong. Our life of faith must be defined

The Council of Florence on Jewish Food Restrictions

LIVING TRADITION

In 1442 the ecumenical Council of Florence defined the distinction between Christianity and Judaism on matters of food. It addressed itself to two issues specifically. First, the council clarified that the Mosaic dietary laws that distinguish between clean and unclean foods ceased to be binding with the coming of Christ and could no longer be viewed or adhered to as necessary for salvation. Second, the council dealt with the apostolic decree in Acts 15:23–29, which forbade Gentile Christians to eat meat sacrificed to idols as well as meat from animals not drained of their blood. According to Florence, the apostolic decree was a temporary ban on foods that Jews considered illegal or religiously offensive. The prohibition was designed to foster unity and fellowship between Jewish and Gentile believers in the early Church. Now that the pastoral situation that gave rise to the decree has passed away, so has the binding force of the decree. Since Paul seeks to unify believers in Rome by accommodating those who think some foods are "unclean" and who also avoid eating "meat," the words of this fifteenth-century council are worth quoting in full.

> The Catholic Church firmly believes, professes, and preaches that every creature of God is good and nothing is to be rejected if it is received with thanksgiving (1 Tim 4:4) because according to the word of the Lord not what goes into the mouth defiles a person (Matt 15:11) and because the difference in the Mosaic law between clean and unclean foods belongs to ceremonial practices that have passed away and lost their efficacy with the coming of the gospel. It also declares that the apostolic prohibition to abstain from what has been sacrificed to idols and from blood and from what is strangled (Acts 15:29) was suited to that time when a single Church was rising from Jews and Gentiles, who had previously lived with different ceremonies and customs. This was so that the Gentiles should have some observances in common with Jews and occasion would be offered of coming together in one worship and faith in God and a cause of dissension might be removed, since by ancient custom blood and strangled things seemed abominable to Jews, Gentiles could be thought to be returning to idolatry if they ate sacrificial food. As soon as the Christian religion was promulgated to the point that no Jew according to the flesh appeared within it, but all who were joining the Church were sharing in the same rites and ceremonies of the gospel, believing that to the pure all things are pure (Titus 1:15): since the cause of this apostolic prohibition ceased, so its effect also ceased.[a]

a. Quotation adapted from Heinrich Denzinger, *Compendium of Creeds, Definitions, and Declarations on Matters of Faith and Morals*, ed. Peter Hünermann, 43rd edition (San Francisco: Ignatius, 2012), §1350, p. 348.

by the truth of God's love. As the Lord bears patiently with our weakness, so we must do the same for others. Objectively, nothing edible is intrinsically defiling; but subjectively, the weak do not (yet) see it that way. So the strong must act according to love and not put the weak at risk of acting against their conscience, which *is* a sin.

14:15   Paul is quick to caution his readers. **If your brother is being hurt by what you eat, your conduct is no longer in accord with love**. The Mosaic commandment "You shall love your neighbor as yourself," which Paul holds up as the overriding aim of all Christian living (13:8–10), is draped over the whole Roman controversy. Even our liberty in Christ is subordinate to the law of love. This principle translates concretely into the exhortation: **Do not because of your food destroy him for whom Christ died**. Paul's decision to use the verb "destroy" is an indicator of how seriously he views the problem of scandal. It is dangerous enough to cause the spiritual ruin of the weak.

14:16–18   Paul's next concern is to relate his admonitions to the subject of Christian witness. Scandal is not only a danger for those within the believing community; it is also a danger for the unbelieving world observing from the outside. Aware of this, Paul urges: **do not let your good be reviled**.[11] In this case, the one who reviles is the urban population of Rome. Should disputes over food and drink descend into serious quarreling among Christians, the gospel itself will come into disrepute in the wider society.

This prompts Paul to formulate an antithetical definition of **the kingdom of God**,[12] one that couples an affirmation with a denial. On the negative side, the kingdom established in the Messiah is not reducible to issues of **food and drink**. On the positive side, the kingdom is essentially a matter of **righteousness, peace, and joy**—spiritual gifts that God lavishes on believers through the ministry of the **Spirit**. Now, in Paul's theology, "righteousness" is the grace of justification imparted to the Christian (5:17), "peace" is the reconciliation that reunites the fallen human family with the Father (5:1), and "joy" is the inner delight in God's goodness that blossoms in the heart of believers indwelt by the Spirit (Gal 5:22). These are the signature signs of the kingdom made present in the Christian community.

Hence Paul continues: **whoever serves Christ in this way is pleasing to God and approved by others**. Paul assures readers of a twofold benefit. God takes

11. By the expression "your good," Paul appears to mean "the Christian freedom to partake of all foods." See Joseph A. Fitzmyer, SJ, *Romans*, AB 33 (New York: Doubleday, 1993), 697.

12. It is sometimes alleged that the kingdom of God is a peripheral concern for Paul, despite being the dominant theme of Jesus' teaching in the Gospels. It is true that Paul speaks only occasionally of the kingdom in explicit terms; nevertheless, as one scholar states it, "the underlying reality of the kingdom plays a central role in Paul's thought" (Frank J. Matera, *Romans*, PCNT [Grand Rapids: Baker Academic, 2010], 317).

pleasure in those who allow his gifts to impact their lives, on the one hand, and the Church gives positive witness to the world, on the other.

The point deduced from this definition of the kingdom comes as an exhor- **14:19** tation to action: **Let us then pursue what leads to peace.** If all that Paul says about the kingdom of God is true, then both the weak and the strong have a clear target to shoot at. Together they must take meaningful steps to create a community of interpersonal harmony and love. Certainly this means preventing scandal. But it also means **building up** the family of faith by strengthening all the members' faith and commitment to the Lord. Perhaps Paul is thinking here of the Church as a temple of the Holy Spirit (1 Cor 3:16). Disciples participate in its construction, adorning and strengthening the edifice by building up one another in love (1 Cor 3:9–15; 8:1).

This brings Paul back around to where he started in this section. Verses **14:20–21** 20–21 are a restatement of verses 13–14 in reverse order. The strong Christian must be careful to **not destroy the work of God**, specifically as it relates to weak Christians. Even if the strong are theologically correct in thinking that all foods are **clean**, charity declares it **wrong for anyone to become a stumbling block by eating** foods that another deems unclean. Relinquishing freedom is sometimes necessary to bring benefit to others. Thus Paul considers it **good not to eat meat or drink wine or do anything that causes your brother to stumble**. (On the question of abstinence from meat and wine, see the sidebar "Diet in the Jewish Diaspora," pp. 254–55.)

The next-to-last verse of Rom 14 is the injunction: **Keep the faith [that]** **14:22** **you have to yourself in the presence of God**. It sounds at first as though Paul advocates privatizing religion. But that is not his intention. The key to interpreting the passage is to recognize that "faith" in this context approximates what we would call "conviction." Thus, because the weak and the strong hold opposite convictions about foods and feast days, despite having a common faith in Jesus, Paul advises them to keep their differences under wraps. The practice of the Christian faith is indeed a public thing; it is something for which the Roman church was widely known and admired (1:8). However, when there is a divergence of views, opinions about nonessential matters are best kept to oneself.

Immediately following the injunction is a beatitude: **blessed is the one who does not condemn himself for what he approves**. By this Paul means that having strong convictions is a commendable thing in itself. At least it is more praiseworthy than being unsure of where you stand when action is called for. Wavering and bending under the weight of social pressure is a danger that Paul would have the faithful avoid. Indeed, this is the subject of the chapter's final verse.

Diet in the Jewish Diaspora

BIBLICAL
BACKGROUND

Readers have often puzzled over Paul's description of the weak in Rom 14. These are Christians who seem to disagree with the propositions that "nothing is unclean" (14:14) and that everything edible "is indeed clean" (14:20). Clearly the weak adhere to Jewish dietary laws that distinguish between acceptable and unacceptable foods as defined by the Mosaic law. But Paul points out that the weak also confine themselves to eating "vegetables" (14:2) and abstain from consuming "meat" and "wine" (14:21). The rationale for this behavior is not entirely clear. The Torah nowhere mandates a meatless diet for Israel, nor does it forbid the drinking of wine. So why do we find a group of predominantly Jewish Christians conducting themselves in this way in first-century Rome?

Historical sources indicate that abstinence from meat and wine became an expression of religious piety in the Jewish †Diaspora.[a] Following the collapse of the monarchies of Israel and Judah in the Old Testament period, vast numbers of God's people found themselves living as exiles among the nations. There they faced considerable pressure to assimilate into the heathen cultures that surrounded them. Many succumbed to the pressure, but others resisted. Typically this resistance meant drawing a line of separation between the covenant people and the Gentiles, not only in terms of morality and worship but also in matters of food and drink. For instance, several sources tell us that Jews were strongly discouraged from eating with Gentiles.[b] Other sources make the point that Jews could maintain their religious separation by refusing to eat Gentile foods, especially meat and wine. Daniel presents us with a clear example of this. He and his companions living in exile requested exemption from eating the rich foods and wines of Babylon, opting instead to eat only

continued on next page

14:23   The conclusion to Rom 14 addresses the danger that doubt or lack of conviction poses for the food controversy in Rome. Up to this point, everything is pretty much black and white. There is no indication that either the weak or the strong are ready to abandon their settled convictions. But what if some are tempted to compromise under the stress of circumstances? This is something Paul will not accept, and so he warns that **whoever has doubts is condemned if he eats, because this is not from faith**. To act against your convictions is to act against your conscience.[13] When this line is crossed, offenders place themselves under judgment (Catechism 1790).

The basis for Paul's ruling is the principle that **whatever is not from faith is sin**. Taken in isolation, these words sound like a general maxim that applies

13. St. Thomas Aquinas relates Paul's words to violations of conscience in *Summa Theologiae* I-II.19.5.

vegetables (Dan 1:8–16). Likewise, Tobit preserved his commitment to God intact by refusing to eat the food of the Gentiles while living in Nineveh (Tob 1:10–11). Queen Esther confesses in prayer that she never ate from the table of the Persian court nor accepted any wine, as this was used in libations to the Persian gods (Esther C:28 = 14:17 RSVCE). Judith, though living in the land of Israel, also declined the food and wine offered to her by the pagan general Holofernes, lest it cause scandal among her people (Jdt 12:1–19).

The Bible's conscientious objectors seem to have inspired other Jews to refrain from taking meat and wine as an ascetical discipline, including the Therapeutae sect in Egypt[c] as well as Jewish Christians such as James, the brother of the Lord.[d] The Jewish historian Flavius Josephus gives an account of priests imprisoned in Rome, not long after Paul wrote his Epistle to the Romans, who would not eat anything except figs and nuts.[e]

Abstinence from meat and wine thus became an expression of Jewish piety as well as a practical way to preserve Jewish identity in a Gentile context. The weak in Rome appear to stand in the same stream of tradition by consciously imitating those biblical figures who had separated themselves from Gentile food and drink. Living in the epicenter of the heathen world, they took a firm stance against assimilation at table. What Babylon was for Daniel, Nineveh was for Tobit, and Persia was for Esther, Rome had become for a group of Jewish-minded Christians intent on following the dietary customs of Israel's most heroic saints.

a. See Gary Steven Shogren, "'Is the Kingdom of God about Eating and Drinking or Isn't It?' (Romans 14:17)," *NovT* 42, no. 3 (2000): 238–56; and James D. G. Dunn, *Romans 9–16*, WBC 38b (Nashville: Nelson, 1988), 800.

b. *Jubilees* 22.16; *3 Maccabees* 3.4; Acts 10:28; 11:3; Gal 2:11–14.

c. Philo of Alexandria, *On the Contemplative Life* 73.

d. Eusebius, *Ecclesiastical History* 2.23.5.

e. Josephus, *Life* 14.

in all circumstances. Some interpreters, such as St. Augustine of Hippo, understood it in this way and thus concluded that nonbelievers, lacking faith in God, are incapable of conducting themselves without sinning in the process.[14] Others, such as St. John Chrysostom, maintained that Paul was speaking directly to the situation in Rome in an effort to dissuade believers from acting contrary to their personal convictions about food.[15] Most modern scholars side with Chrysostom and understand Paul to say that Christians must guard against judging one another (14:3), scandalizing one another (14:13), giving poor witness to the world (14:16), and transgressing their consciences (14:23).

14. Augustine, *Against Julian* 4.32.

15. John Chrysostom, *Homilies on Romans* 26.23.

It remains only for Paul to bring his appeal to the weak and the strong to a climax in 15:1–13.

Reflection and Application (14:1–23)

It is significant that Paul addresses this letter "to all the beloved of God in Rome" (1:7). It suggests that one of his aims is to convince believers of how much God loves them. This can be measured by the extent to which the Lord has gone to save us, as Paul points out in 5:7–8, where he acknowledges that "only with difficulty does one die for a just person," and yet "God proves his love for us in that while we were still sinners Christ died for us." Throughout the book of Romans, the gospel is about nothing if not the love of God.

In the latter section of the letter, chapters 12–16, Paul makes a pastoral application of the supreme mystery of God's love to the Christian life, showing us that our supreme duty is to love—as we have been loved. This is a call to nothing less than the imitation of God (theomimesis): for us to become like God, we must love as God loves. We must embody the love of Christ. And this love, Paul insists, must be "sincere" (12:9) and filled with genuine "affection" (12:10). Indeed, such love is the one outstanding debt that we owe to everyone (13:8).

This is exactly what Paul is getting at in Rom 14. He warns the weak and the strong that "if your brother is being hurt by what you eat, your conduct is no longer in accord with love" (14:15). What does he mean? If we are to embody God's love-in-action, then we must be willing to love others by bearing with their weaknesses, as the Lord has done with us. We should strive to love and support others, especially those who are weak in faith, rather than please ourselves. When we love in this way, we participate—and enter—more deeply into God's life, and make the gospel of God's love more visible—and more believable—to the world that Christ died to save.

Paul's Final Appeal and Future Plans

Romans 15:1–33

Romans 15 is not the final chapter of the letter, yet it finalizes the bulk of Paul's instruction to the Roman church. In four steps the Apostle brings closure: (1) In verses 1–6, he completes his exhortations to the strong and the weak begun in Rom 14. (2) In verses 7–13, he concludes the moral and pastoral catechesis that began back in Rom 12. (3) In verses 14–21, he discourses on the aims and accomplishments of his priestly ministry. (4) In verses 22–33, he reveals his tentative plans to visit the Romans in person and solicits their help in taking the gospel to Spain.

Oneness in Christ (15:1–6)

[1]We who are strong ought to put up with the failings of the weak and not to please ourselves; [2]let each of us please our neighbor for the good, for building up. [3]For Christ did not please himself; but, as it is written, "The insults of those who insult you fall upon me." [4]For whatever was written previously was written for our instruction, that by endurance and by the encouragement of the scriptures we might have hope. [5]May the God of endurance and encouragement grant you to think in harmony with one another, in keeping with Christ Jesus, [6]that with one accord you may with one voice glorify the God and Father of our Lord Jesus Christ.

OT: Ps 69:10; 1 Macc 12:9
NT: Rom 5:1–5; 1 Cor 10:11; Gal 6:2; 2 Tim 3:16

Catechism: Jesus our model, 520; Christians and the Old Testament, 121–23; hope and prayer, 2657; Jesus the Davidic Messiah, 436–39

Lectionary: 15:4–9: 2nd Sunday of Advent (Year A); 15:1b–3a, 5–7, 13: Sacrament of Marriage

The first two units of chapter 15 form a double conclusion to the main body of Romans, each following the same format. Both commence with an apostolic exhortation (15:1–2, 7), both point to the figure of Jesus as the exemplar of Christian conduct (15:3, 7–9), both invoke the teaching of Scripture to validate the Apostle's claims (15:3, 9–12), and both end with a prayer for the Roman community (15:5–6, 13).

15:1–2   Paul's address to the weak and the strong in Rom 14 carries over into the initial verses of Rom 15, making for an imperceptible transition between these chapters.[1] Paul is not shifting his focus away from the problem of disharmony in the Roman church. He is about to make his strongest appeal for unity.

He begins by informing the **strong** (believers who understand that freedom in Christ means freedom from Jewish dietary and festal obligations) of their ethical responsibility toward the **weak** (believers who remain attached to these Mosaic traditions).[2] In a nutshell, the strong **ought to put up with the failings** of their brothers and sisters. Unfortunately, the NABRE's translation "put up with" puts a decidedly negative spin on Paul's words here. The text is not mistranslated per se, but the verb[3] can also mean "bear" in the positive sense of "shoulder a burden" on another's behalf, as in Gal 6:2. I am inclined to understand Paul this way. He is urging the strong in Rome to come alongside the weak and be a means of support for them. Patient endurance of inconvenience is part of the picture, but assuming the role of a servant is the central concern. Paul may have in mind specific Gospel passages that use the same language to describe Jesus bearing the burden of his cross (John 19:17) as well as disciples bearing their own crosses in imitation of him (Luke 14:27).[4]

But what exactly are the strong asked to bear? Again, the NABRE can give the wrong impression. The term translated "failings" is literally "weaknesses." Paul is not suggesting that the customary practices of Judaism are actually sins to be tolerated and left uncorrected. Rather, the weaknesses of the weak are their scruples of conscience, their doubts and apprehensions about living out

---

1. The chapter and verse divisions we know today were not part of the original Bible. Segmenting the text into chapters was an innovation of Stephen Langton, who inserted regular divisions into the Latin Vulgate in the early thirteenth century.

2. For more on the identity of these two groups, see commentary on Rom 14.

3. Greek *bastazō*.

4. Michael Thompson, *Clothed with Christ: The Example and Teaching of Jesus in Romans 12:1–15:13*, JSNTSup 59 (Sheffield: JSOT Press, 1991), 210.

of step with the Torah's ritual demands. It is in these matters that the strong are to show patience and understanding.

As a general rule, the strong are instructed **not to please** themselves by insisting on the exercise of legitimate freedoms at the expense of the weak. The Christian life is not about looking out for ourselves or putting our own interests first. Believers are called to a higher standard, to a service of others that is sacrificial and self-forgetful. Hence Paul adds: **let each of us please our neighbor for the good, for building up**. Edification of all members of Christ's body is the goal, and that is a good that requires making the concerns of fellow believers our own (Rom 12:15).

Notably, the language of obligation in verse 1 is coupled with a reference to one's neighbor in verse 2. Back in 13:8 Paul stated that a disciple's highest obligation is "to love one another" in fulfillment of the commandment: "You shall love your neighbor as yourself" (13:9, quoting Lev 19:18). For the strong, love of neighbor means building up the weak in whatever ways are necessary to prevent scandal and to strengthen their commitment to the gospel.

Paul ties his exhortation to the moral example of Jesus. Because **Christ did** **15:3** **not please himself**, he reasons—on the assumption that readers are acquainted with the story of Jesus—the strong are to pattern their actions after the Messiah, who "did not come to be served but to serve and to give his life as a ransom for many" (Mark 10:45).

Paul then makes a curious move. Instead of referring to the events of the passion or to another familiar incident in Christ's life, he quotes a verse from the hymnal of ancient Israel. He employs his usual formula, **as it is written**, and then cites a line from Ps 69:10 as it appears in the †Septuagint: **"The insults of those who insult you fall upon me."** This is one of several passages in the New Testament that call on Ps 69 to explain Jesus' solidarity with the Father (John 2:17) as well as his betrayal and suffering at the hands of others (Mark 15:23, 36; John 15:25; Acts 1:20). The thing to notice is that Paul, like other apostolic writers, regards Jesus as the *speaker* of the psalm, even though it is a lament attributed to King David.[5] Paul stands arm in arm with the early Church in identifying Jesus Christ as "the true subject of the Psalms."[6] The presupposition behind this interpretation is that Jesus is the messianic heir of David (Luke 1:32), and so David's personal travails prefigure the trials awaiting the Davidic

---

5. Richard B. Hays, "Christ Prays the Psalms: Israel's Psalter as Matrix of Early Christology," in *The Conversion of the Imagination: Paul as Interpreter of Israel's Scriptures* (Grand Rapids: Eerdmans, 2007), 101–18.

6. Pope Benedict XVI, *Jesus of Nazareth: Holy Week, from the Entrance into Jerusalem to the Resurrection* (San Francisco: Ignatius, 2011), 67.

Messiah. Even more, the impetus for this new way of reading the Psalms can be traced back to Jesus, who identified himself with the suffering "I" of two other lament psalms attributed to David, Pss 22 and 31, amid the agony of his crucifixion (Mark 15:34; Luke 23:46).[7] All three of these psalms follow a similar plotline: the psalmist finds himself in personal distress, betrayed even by his kin, and so he cries out in desperation for help, confident that one who waits on the Lord will not be disappointed or ashamed. In earliest Christianity, this was a template for understanding the paschal mystery of Christ's passion and resurrection, the supreme instance of tribulation giving way to triumph, thanks to the saving intervention of God.

Pastorally speaking, Ps 69 serves Paul's purpose by reminding the strong of the afflictions that pressed hard on the Messiah for his devotion to God and his work. Perhaps this reminder is needed because the strong, if they adapt their ways to the customs of the weak, risk exposing themselves to the ridicule of a Roman society that frequently voiced its contempt for Jewish practices.

15:4   To this Scripture reference Paul adds a general remark about the purpose of Scripture in the Christian life. He states that **whatever was written previously was written for our instruction**. The expression "whatever" is Pauline shorthand for "everything written under divine inspiration as found in the Old Testament." The Scriptures of Israel have a permanent relevance for the people of God. The Bible is a document from the distant past, to be sure, but more importantly it comes to us from eternity. It is a living word spoken by the living God, intended to train all generations in righteousness (2 Tim 3:16) and caution them against the dangers of sin (1 Cor 10:11). Here Paul showcases **the encouragement** that believers have in **the scriptures**. His words sound like an echo of 1 Macc 12:9, where Jonathan, speaking as the high priest of Israel, says in a diplomatic letter to the Spartans: "We have for our encouragement the sacred books that are in our possession."

Paul also states that Scripture's purpose is to promote **endurance** through trials leading to a confident **hope** in heavenly glory (as in Rom 5:1–5). God's children can find wisdom in the Bible's proverbs and parables, suitable words for prayer and praise in its psalms and hymns, and reassurance through its stories of a Father who always keeps his promises. These blessings come through a prayerful reading of Scripture precisely because Scripture comes from God. Moreover, it is no accident that Paul relates endurance, encouragement, and

---

7. Pope Benedict XVI, *Jesus of Nazareth: Holy Week*, 146, also discusses the implications of this for the Church's prayer: "In the early Church, Jesus was immediately hailed as the new David, the real David, and so the Psalms could be recited in a new way—yet without discontinuity—as prayer in communion with Jesus Christ."

Vatican II on the Old Testament

LIVING TRADITION

The economy of the Old Testament was designed above all to prepare for the coming of Christ, the universal redeemer, and of the messianic kingdom, to announce this coming by prophecy, and to indicate its meaning by various types. For the books of the Old Testament, in accordance with the state of the human race before the time of salvation established by Christ, disclose both an understanding of God and the human person and the ways in which God who is just and merciful deals with human beings. These books, even though they contain what is only incomplete and provisional, nevertheless demonstrate God's true way of instructing. Consequently, Christians should accept with devotion these books, for they give expression to a vivid sense of God; they contain lofty teachings about God and sound wisdom on human life, as well as a wonderful treasury of prayers; and in them the mystery of our salvation is present in a hidden way.[a]

a. *Dei Verbum* (*Dogmatic Constitution on Divine Revelation*) 15. Quotation adapted from *The Scripture Documents: An Anthology of Official Catholic Teachings*, ed. and trans. Dean P. Béchard (Collegeville, MN: Liturgical Press, 2002), 26.

hope to the purposes of the sacred text. He immediately follows by praying that the Roman congregation will receive grace from "the God of endurance and encouragement" (15:5) who is also "the God of hope" (15:13). In Paul's view, God is the source of all the benefits that flow into the world through his inspired word.

In the next two verses Paul offers a prayer wish on behalf of readers: **May** **15:5–6** **the God of endurance and encouragement grant you to think in harmony with one another, that with one accord you may with one voice glorify the God and Father of our Lord Jesus Christ.** These words are a petition for unity between the weak and the strong in Rome. And the unity Paul has in view is interior as well as exterior, an agreement of minds matched by a oneness of voice. Thinking in harmony is not reaching perfect agreement on all matters whatsoever. It has more the sense of being on the same page when it comes to the essentials of faith and life. Disagreements over opinions, such as those discussed in Rom 14, are not to get in the way of this concord. So too, glorifying the Father with one voice refers to worshiping him as a unified family participating together in a common liturgy.[8] This is precisely the vision that Paul will present in 15:7–13. Finally, Paul asks God to "grant"

8. James D. G. Dunn, *Romans 9–16*, WBC 38b (Nashville: Nelson, 1988), 841.

this unity to the Christians in Rome. The implication is that grace must be given if believers are to rise above their differences and sing the Lord's praises in holy unison.

Welcoming All in Christ (15:7–13)

⁷Welcome one another, then, as Christ welcomed you, for the glory of God. ⁸For I say that Christ became a minister of the circumcised to show God's truthfulness, to confirm the promises to the patriarchs, ⁹but so that the Gentiles might glorify God for his mercy. As it is written:

> "Therefore, I will praise you among the Gentiles
> and sing praises to your name."

¹⁰And again it says:

> "Rejoice, O Gentiles, with his people."

¹¹And again:

> "Praise the Lord, all you Gentiles,
> and let all the peoples praise him."

¹²And again Isaiah says:

> "The root of Jesse shall come,
> raised up to rule the Gentiles;
> in him shall the Gentiles hope."

¹³May the God of hope fill you with all joy and peace in believing, so that you may abound in hope by the power of the holy Spirit.

OT: Deut 32:43; Pss 18:50; 117:1; Isa 11:10
NT: Luke 1:31–33; Rom 1:1–5; Rev 5:5; 22:16
Catechism: Jesus our model, 520; Jesus the Davidic Messiah, 436–39
Lectionary: 15:4–9: 2nd Sunday of Advent (Year A); 15:1b–3a, 5–7, 13: Sacrament of Marriage

15:7 **Welcome one another** is a restatement of 14:1, only this time Paul accents the need for *mutual* reception between the weak and the strong. He again reveals that Christ is the foundation of his ethics. Believers in Rome are to accept and embrace one another **as Christ welcomed** each of them **for the glory of God**. Disciples must not shut one another out over differences of opinion. After all, the Messiah, whose actions are the standard of all Christian conduct, gave his life in sacrifice to gather all—the weak no less than the strong, the Gentiles no less than the Jews—into the communion of God's family.

Paul's words in verses 8–9a are somewhat tricky to translate and interpret. **15:8–9a** He has expressed himself so compactly that commentators have been forced to work out different proposals for capturing the gist of his message. I favor a solution that contends that **Christ became a minister** to two groups of people in order to accomplish two main objectives.[9] He came as a servant to the Jews, here called **the circumcised**, to **confirm the promises to the patriarchs**; likewise, he came as a servant to **the Gentiles** that he **might glorify God**.[10] The Messiah's ministry to the chosen people is a ministry of fulfillment. The many pledges that God made to the people of Israel have been carried out in the Messiah, from the exaltation of David's royal heir (1:3–4) to the circumcision of the heart (2:28–29) to the justification of believers (4:1–12) to the outpouring of the Spirit (8:1–17) to the restoration of the exiled tribes among the nations (chs. 9–11)—all are being realized through Jesus Christ in the New Covenant. The Gentiles too are beneficiaries of the blessings promised to Israel, thanks to the welcoming grace of Christ, who brings glory to God by leading all nations in a chorus of praise to the heavenly Father.

To certify these claims about Jesus' role in salvation history, Paul links to-   **15:9b** gether a chain of Old Testament passages from the Torah (15:10), the prophets (15:12), and the Psalms (15:9, 11), together representing the three main divisions of the Hebrew Bible (Luke 24:44). In classic rabbinic fashion, Paul singles out four citations that share a common catchword: the term in Greek is *ethnē*, which means "Gentiles" or "nations."

The first quotation comes verbatim from Ps 18:50 as it reads in the †Septuagint: **Therefore, I will praise you among the Gentiles / and sing praises to your name**. Psalm 18 is a hymn of thanksgiving that celebrates how God delivered Israel's anointed king from his enemies (Ps 18:49), thereby showing mercy to David and his descendants (Ps 18:51). Not only that, God established David as "head over nations" (Ps 18:44), alluding to the fact that David subdued several Gentile peoples and made them servants of his kingdom (2 Sam 8:1–14). For Paul, however, Jesus is the speaker of the psalm, just as he was the subject of Ps 69 a few verses earlier.[11] The Messiah is a new and greater David summoning the nations not to the obedience of political servitude but to "the obedience of

---

9. See J. Ross Wagner, "The Christ, Servant of Jew and Gentile: A Fresh Approach to Romans 15:8–9," *JBL* 116, no. 3 (1997): 473–85.

10. The NABRE takes "the Gentiles" to be the subject of the verb "glorify" in v. 9. The reading followed here understands "Christ" as the one who glorifies God.

11. See commentary on 15:3.

The Truth and Mercy of God

In Rom 15:8–9, Paul states that Jesus Christ became a minister on behalf of the "truthfulness" and "mercy" of God—in Greek, on behalf of his *alētheia* and *eleos*. These are significant theological terms from the Old Testament. In fact, when the two stand in close proximity in the †Septuagint, they typically represent the Hebrew word pair *hesed* ("mercy, loyalty, love") and *emet* ("truth, fidelity, faithfulness").[a] *Hesed* and *emet* epitomize the Lord's greatest covenant virtues on display throughout the course of salvation history. First appearing in Exod 34:6 as divine "love and fidelity," they reveal something about the inner mystery of God as expressed in the name "Yahweh."[b] He is a Father whose commitment to his children overcomes every obstacle to communion and blessing. Israel was accustomed to celebrate the Lord's mercy and truth as the lifeline of its national existence.[c]

Paul no doubt has this in mind in Rom 15:8–9. He presents Jesus as the one who embodies the Lord's covenant faithfulness and mercy. God's truthfulness is seen clearly in relation to Israel, to whom he made promises that have now been fulfilled in the Messiah; and God's mercy is seen clearly in relation to the Gentiles, who have now been drawn into a covenant relationship with God by an outpouring of divine compassion. Paul's portrait of Jesus as the incarnation of God's truth and mercy nicely encapsulates the whole message of Romans.

a. The NABRE translates these Hebrew terms differently in different passages, e.g., "mercy/truth," "mercy/faithfulness," or "mercy/fidelity."
b. Catechism 214.
c. Pss 25:10; 40:11; 61:8; 117:2; see Tob 3:2.

faith" (Rom 1:5). In exercising this spiritual kingship over the Gentiles, Jesus sings the Father's praises in the midst of a multinational assembly taught to worship the one true God.

15:10   Paul's second quotation reproduces a line from Deut 32:43, again as it appears in the Septuagint: **Rejoice, O Gentiles, with his people.**[12] The invitation forms part of the triumphant conclusion of the Song of Moses, a poetic recital of Israel's early history that also envisions Israel's distant future. Looking ahead to the †eschatological time, Moses summons other nations to join with the people of Israel in praising the God of Israel. It is a picture of the entire human family forming a joyous and unified assembly of worship. This is the "one voice" rising to the Father that Paul had in mind in Rom 15:6.

12. The Hebrew text of Deuteronomy does not include this injunction. However, the Aramaic paraphrase of this passage in *Targum Neofiti* does include a call for the nations to give praise.

The third quotation comes from Ps 117:2: **Praise the Lord, all you Gentiles, /** **15:11**
and let all the peoples praise him. Again we hear a universal call to worship
ringing out from the heart of Israel. Psalm 117 is part of a collection of psalms
that were sung at Israel's annual liturgical feasts. Even in Old Testament times
the Gentiles were encouraged to lift their voices in praise of the God of Israel,
whose blessings reached out beyond Israel through the sacred institutions of
the covenant, most notably the temple (1 Kings 8:41–43). In messianic times
the Gentiles have even more reason for thanks and praise, now that Christ has
made them full and equal heirs of eternal life.

Paul's fourth and final quotation is the capstone, theologically speaking, **15:12**
of the biblical texts strung together in 15:9–12. It is a passage from the Septuagint version of Isa 11:10: **The root of Jesse shall come, / raised up to rule**
the Gentiles; / in him shall the Gentiles hope. Paul must have known this
prophecy well since it played a prominent role in defining the messianic expectations of early Judaism.[13] For **Isaiah**, the image of a "shoot" rising from
the stump of Jesse is a sign of hope for Israel in the aftermath of judgment (Isa
11:1). It indicates that God's covenant of kingship with David remains intact,
despite the historical tragedies that chastise the covenant people, especially
the double exile of Israel and Judah. When the royal scion of David comes,
anointed with the Spirit of the Lord (Isa 11:2), he will be the agent of Israel's
restoration as well as the gatherer of distant nations who will come under his
rule (Isa 11:12–16).

Paul, like his contemporaries, reads this oracle as a messianic prophecy.
The Davidic scion has come in Jesus of Nazareth, and now peoples from every
nation are professing allegiance to him as Messiah and Lord.[14] His kingship is
extending over the world not by force of arms but by a voluntary submission
of Gentiles who place their "hope" for salvation in him. Besides this obvious
point—the inclusion of all nations in messianic redemption[15]—it seems that
Paul's conclusion to the main body of Romans is designed to reconnect with
the introduction to the letter.[16] Paul began the epistle by exalting Jesus as the
royal descendant of David whose gospel, promised long ago in the Scriptures

13. For the Jewish hope in a Davidic Messiah, see John J. Collins, *The Scepter and the Star: Messianism in Light of the Dead Sea Scrolls*, 2nd ed. (Grand Rapids: Eerdmans, 2010), 52–78.
14. I concur with Hays, "Christ Prays the Psalms," 117, who says: "The Davidic messiahship of Jesus is a significant aspect of Pauline Christology, at least at the presuppositional level. This is most clearly evident in Romans. Critical studies of Pauline Christology have seriously underestimated the importance of this element of Paul's thought about Jesus."
15. For additional discussion, see the sidebar, "Among All the Gentiles," in Rom 1 (p. 6).
16. For the links between Paul's introduction and conclusion to Romans, see Christopher G. Whitsett, "Son of God, Seed of David: Paul's Messianic Exegesis in Romans 1:3–4," *JBL* 119, no. 4 (2000): 661–81.

of Israel, beckons all nations to the obedience of faith (Rom 1:1–7). These are precisely the points being made again in 15:12. In fact, Paul probably sees a hint of Christ's resurrection, also featured in the introduction, in the prospect of Jesse's root being "raised up" to rule the Gentiles.

15:13   Paul ends his many chapters of theological and pastoral instruction, stretching all the way back to 1:18, with a prayer wish for his Roman addressees: **May the God of hope fill you with all joy and peace in believing, so that you may abound in hope by the power of the holy Spirit.** The gifts that Paul desires for them are the gifts of the kingdom of God as delineated in 14:17: "righteousness, peace, and joy in the holy Spirit." To possess these is to live under the beneficent reign of Christ, in whom the nations put their hope (15:12), for God is the source of this supernatural hope, just as the Spirit makes it abound in the hearts of believers. If the Christians in Rome can follow the example of Jesus and make full use of God's gifts to overcome their differences, they will participate in the fulfillment of the Scriptures, with the Davidic Messiah leading Israel and all the nations in a majestic chorus of praise.

The Priestly Service of the Gospel (15:14–21)

[14]I myself am convinced about you, my brothers, that you yourselves are full of goodness, filled with all knowledge, and able to admonish one another. [15]But I have written to you rather boldly in some respects to remind you, because of the grace given me by God [16]to be a minister of Christ Jesus to the Gentiles in performing the priestly service of the gospel of God, so that the offering up of the Gentiles may be acceptable, sanctified by the holy Spirit. [17]In Christ Jesus, then, I have reason to boast in what pertains to God. [18]For I will not dare to speak of anything except what Christ has accomplished through me to lead the Gentiles to obedience by word and deed, [19]by the power of signs and wonders, by the power of the Spirit [of God], so that from Jerusalem all the way around to Illyricum I have finished preaching the gospel of Christ. [20]Thus I aspire to proclaim the gospel not where Christ has already been named, so that I do not build on another's foundation, [21]but as it is written:

"Those who have never been told of him shall see,
    and those who have never heard of him shall understand."

OT: Isa 52:15; 66:18–20

NT: Acts 9:15; 15:12; Rom 1:5; 16:26; 1 Cor 3:10–11; 2 Cor 12:12; Heb 2:4

Catechism: evangelization as liturgy, 1070; the gift of miracles, 2003; Jesus the Suffering Servant, 615, 623

Romans 15:14 brings us to the formal conclusion of Romans, the longest in any of Paul's Letters. The final section of a Hellenistic epistle was often reserved for items of personal business between the writer and the recipients, and so it is here. Paul applauds the Roman believers for their progress in the faith and describes his letter as a bold reminder of things they already know something about. More importantly, he explains how the epistle fits into the aims of his evangelistic mission among the nations. A backward glance at 1:8–15 will show that Paul is putting a frame around the letter by reiterating some of his opening remarks.

Paul begins with a word of commendation. **I myself am convinced about**   **15:14** **you**, he says, addressing readers as **brothers** in Christ, **that you yourselves are full of goodness, filled with all knowledge, and able to admonish one another**. Evidently, based on what he has learned from others, Paul regards the Roman congregation as relatively mature, spiritually speaking. Reports have persuaded him that believers in the capital are generous and honest in their dealings with one another; likewise, they have a commendable grasp of the Christian faith. Paul even pays the compliment of saying that some disciples are sufficiently formed to provide guidance and loving correction to erring members among them.

Nevertheless, despite the spiritual maturity of the Roman believers, they still   **15:15** have room for growth. This is one of the reasons Paul decided to write Romans. It was to **remind** this admired congregation of the foundations and implications of the gospel. And if in places Paul has expressed himself **rather boldly**, it is **because of the grace** of apostleship given to him **by God**. Presumably he felt it necessary to point this out, lest his effort to instruct a church he had not personally founded seem presumptuous and self-assertive.

Paul pauses in verse 16 to touch on the mission entrusted to him. Since   **15:16** his encounter with the risen Messiah on the road to Damascus, Paul has been working as **a minister of Christ Jesus to the Gentiles** (Acts 9:15). His whole identity is now expressed in the title "the apostle to the Gentiles" (Rom 11:13).

Interestingly, Rom 15:16 is the one place in Paul's Letters where his apostolic activity is described as that of a priest. Paul's labor for **the gospel of God** is the performance of a **priestly service** (Greek *hierourgeō*) ordered to **the offering up of the Gentiles**. This gift of Gentile converts is rendered **acceptable** as a sacrifice through the action of **the holy Spirit**, who sanctifies even heathen nonbelievers who come to faith in Jesus by transferring them to the realm of divine holiness.[17]

Paul is alluding in this passage to Isa 66:18–20, the most conspicuous Old Testament text to unite the themes of missionary outreach and priestly sacrifice.[18] The prophet, speaking in the name of the Lord, announces a future time of blessing that encompasses both Israel and the Gentiles:

> I am coming to gather all nations and tongues; they shall come and see my glory. I will place a sign among them; from them I will send survivors to the nations: to Tarshish, Put and Lud, Mosoch, Tubal and Javan, to the distant coastlands which have never heard of my fame, or seen my glory; and they shall proclaim my glory among the nations. They shall bring all your kin from all the nations as an offering to the LORD, on horses and in chariots, in carts, upon mules and dromedaries, to Jerusalem, my holy mountain, says the LORD, just as the Israelites bring their grain offering in a clean vessel to the house of the LORD.

The points of contact between this oracle and Paul's words in verse 16 are obvious. The God of Israel announces his plan to send out "survivors"—that is, the †remnant of his people—as heralds of his glory among nations who never heard of him. In this way the scattered children of Israel will be reunited and the Gentiles will be gathered in. This grand event is likened to a "grain offering" presented to the Lord in the Jerusalem temple. In ancient Israel, of course, all such offerings are made through the mediation of a priest.

15:17–18   Paul gives a **reason to boast in what pertains to God**. He cannot take credit for the success of the gospel or the sanctification of the Gentiles taking place through his ministry. **Christ** is the one who makes his labor bear fruit. And so Paul insists: **I will not dare to speak of anything except what Christ has accomplished through me**. He is merely an instrument in the hand of God. God fulfills his purposes through Paul's obedience to this task, in this case leading **the Gentiles to obedience by word and deed** (also noted in 1:5).

15:19   One way that Christ prospers Paul's efforts is **by the power of signs and wonders**. This is a reference to miracles that accompanied Paul's preaching and gave added incentive—what Catholic theology calls "motives of

---

17. That Paul sees himself as a priestly mediator and counterpart to Moses, who consecrated Israel as God's holy people at Sinai, see Sarah Whittle, *Covenant Renewal and the Consecration of the Gentiles in Romans*, SNTSMS 161 (Cambridge: Cambridge University Press, 2015), 165–85.

18. See Roger Aus, "Paul's Travel Plans to Spain and 'The Full Number of the Gentiles' of Rom XI 25," *NovT* 21, no. 3 (1979): 232–62.

Figure 10. Map of the Mediterranean world from Jerusalem to Spain.

credibility"—for nonbelievers to embrace the Christian message.[19] Paul offers no examples in his letters of how **the Spirit** worked powerfully in conjunction with his proclamation, lest this be mistaken for bragging. But the book of Acts gives a sense of what this must have looked like—for example, healings and exorcisms through his word (Acts 14:10), his personal belongings (19:11–12), and his hands (28:8); raising the dead (20:7–12); and sustaining a lethal injury unharmed (28:3–6).

By the time Paul sent Romans, around AD 57, he could claim to have **finished preaching the gospel of Christ** throughout the northeastern quadrant of the Mediterranean world. He carried the gospel **from Jerusalem all the way around to Illyricum**, which means from the mother church of Christianity in Israel to the coastlands of the Adriatic Sea northwest of Greece (apparently reached in Acts 20:1–3). The point is not that he presented every single person in these lands with a personal invitation to believe in the gospel, but that he and his coworkers were able to establish believing communities all along this route that could continue the work of reaching the rest.

Paul declares, **I aspire to proclaim the gospel not where Christ has already** 15:20–21 **been named, so that I do not build on another's foundation**. In other words, he sees himself as a missionary pioneer whose task is to carry the gospel into the unevangelized frontier. Places where Christ has already been named are places

19. Douglas J. Moo, *The Epistle to the Romans*, NICNT (Grand Rapids: Eerdmans, 1996), 893, offers a helpful observation: "'Signs and wonders' is standard biblical phraseology for miracles, the former term connoting the purpose of the miracle and the latter its marvelous and unusual character."

where Christian faith has already taken root—places where Christ is already acknowledged as Lord and his name is invoked for salvation (10:9–13). To build on foundations laid by another is to encroach on the missionary assignments of others, and Paul is not called to take this approach (2 Cor 10:13–16).

However, it is obvious that Paul is enunciating a general rule that admits of exceptions. Otherwise he would have no business writing to the Romans! Christ had already been named in the imperial capital, quite apart from Paul's efforts. The churches in Rome rest on a foundation laid by others.[20]

If verse 20 specifies what Paul's policy is *not*, then verse 21 clarifies what it *is*. Here the Apostle makes use of the prophetic words of Scripture. Leading in with his usual formula, **as it is written**, Paul quotes Isa 52:15 in close agreement with the †Septuagint version: **Those who have never been told of him shall see, / and those who have never heard of him shall understand**. In its original context, this passage says something about the destination of the good news as well as its content. Both aspects are wrapped up in the pronouns of the oracle: "those" who have never seen or heard are the nations beyond Israel and their rulers, while "him" is a reference to the †Servant of the Lord. In Paul's reading, Isaiah announces the Gentile mission of the Church, its effort to evangelize all the nations. But what is the message that goes out to them? It is the startling news set forth in the fourth Servant Song, which extends from Isa 52:13 to 53:12. It is the message of the suffering Messiah, an innocent figure abused and abandoned by his own but whose death makes atonement for human iniquity. Paul does not have to spell this out explicitly, because the Christian vision of Jesus as the Suffering Servant of Isaiah was universally shared in the ancient Church. So even though the identification of Christ with Isaiah's Servant "remains unarticulated, it lingers behind the text as a virtually unavoidable implication of Paul's larger reading of Isaiah."[21] And just as Jesus fulfills the role of the Lord's Servant, so Paul sees himself as a living fulfillment of the same prophecy insofar as he takes the good news to nations unaware of it.

Reflection and Application (15:16)

The Catholic Church is often criticized for claiming that its ministers are priests. One reason given for this criticism is that the New Testament reserves the term "priest" for Jesus Christ, whom the book of Hebrews extols as the high priest of

20. See "Christianity in the Capital" in the introduction (pp. xvii–xx).
21. Noted by J. Ross Wagner, *Heralds of the Good News: Isaiah and Paul in Concert in the Letter to the Romans*, NovTSup 101 (Leiden: Brill, 2002), 335.

the New Covenant (Heb 8:1–6). Practically all other instances of the term in Scripture refer to the Levitical priests of the Old Covenant—that is, the descendants of Aaron who offered sacrifice in the sanctuaries of Israel. Other titles such as "bishop" and "presbyter" are given to Christian ministers in the New Testament, but never "priest." Restricting ourselves to this one consideration, we would indeed be hard-pressed to account for Catholicism's belief in a ministerial priesthood.

But the matter is not as straightforward as that. To say that Jesus is our high priest does not preclude the existence of other priests who participate in his ministry in a subordinate and derivative way. Jesus also claimed to be the good shepherd of his Father's flock (John 10:14), yet he invites the apostles and their successors to collaborate with him as lesser shepherds ordained to serve the spiritual needs of his sheep (e.g., John 21:15–17; 1 Pet 5:1–4). If the pastorate of bishops and presbyters is not in competition with the ministry of Christ the chief shepherd, then a Christian ministerial priesthood does not necessarily encroach on the unique prerogative of Christ the high priest.

Furthermore, in Rom 15:16 Paul describes his apostolic ministry of spreading the gospel in priestly terms. In fact, he calls himself a "minister" of Christ to the nations. The Greek term for "minister," *leitourgos*, is typically used for ministers who perform public acts of liturgical service. In the Hellenistic period, *leitourgos* often refers to a priest of Israel who performs sacred services in the Jerusalem temple. One finds this usage in biblical passages (Sir 7:30; Isa 61:6 LXX) as well as nonbiblical Jewish writings roughly contemporary with Paul.[22] Since Paul immediately speaks of his "priestly service" of presenting the Gentiles as an acceptable "offering," it can hardly be doubted that he thinks of his apostolic ministry in priestly terms. Granted, nothing is said in this context about celebrating the Eucharist or administering other sacraments, but this is to miss the forest for the trees. A priest is a sacred mediator who helps to bring about a covenant communion between God and man. This is accomplished in a myriad of ways, not the least of which is evangelizing unbelievers and bringing them to worship and praise the one true God. Because the Apostle performs this sacrificial service among the nations, he is rightly called a priest.

Jerusalem, Then Rome, Then Spain (15:22–33)

---

[22]That is why I have so often been prevented from coming to you. [23]But now, since I no longer have any opportunity in these regions and since I

22. E.g., Philo of Alexandria, *Life of Moses* 2.94; *Letter of Aristeas* 95; *Testament of Levi* 2.10.

have desired to come to you for many years, [24]I hope to see you in passing as I go to Spain and to be sent on my way there by you, after I have enjoyed being with you for a time. [25]Now, however, I am going to Jerusalem to minister to the holy ones. [26]For Macedonia and Achaia have decided to make some contribution for the poor among the holy ones in Jerusalem; [27]they decided to do it, and in fact they are indebted to them, for if the Gentiles have come to share in their spiritual blessings, they ought also to serve them in material blessings. [28]So when I have completed this and safely handed over this contribution to them, I shall set out by way of you to Spain; [29]and I know that in coming to you I shall come in the fullness of Christ's blessing.

[30]I urge you, [brothers,] by our Lord Jesus Christ and by the love of the Spirit, to join me in the struggle by your prayers to God on my behalf, [31]that I may be delivered from the disobedient in Judea, and that my ministry for Jerusalem may be acceptable to the holy ones, [32]so that I may come to you with joy by the will of God and be refreshed together with you. [33]The God of peace be with all of you. Amen.

OT: Tob 4:7; Sir 7:10; Isa 66:18–20
NT: Luke 12:33; Acts 19:21; Rom 1:8–15; 1 Cor 16:1–4; 2 Cor 8–9
Catechism: love and almsgiving for the poor, 2443–48; intercessory prayer, 2634–36

Romans 15 draws to a close with Paul discussing his upcoming travel plans. He is getting ready to set out for Jerusalem with a relief offering for the poor Christians in Judea. If all goes well there, he hopes to sail across the Mediterranean to visit the house churches in Rome in person for the first time. Then, after a short stopover in Italy, Paul intends to launch the next phase of his missionary work by taking the gospel westward to Spain.

15:22–23 Paul's opening line is logically connected with the preceding paragraph. The reason **why** he has **so often been prevented from coming** to Rome, as indicated in verses 18–21, is that he has been busily sowing the gospel and harvesting its fruits among "the rest of the Gentiles" in the eastern Roman world (1:13). **But now** he considers this phase of his mission to be complete. He **no longer** has **any opportunity in these regions** to preach Jesus Christ among those unacquainted with him. Besides, he harbors a deep personal longing to visit the letter's recipients, saying, **I have desired to come to you for many years**.

15:24 Paul adds, **I hope to see you in passing as I go to Spain**. At this point we might ask: Why Spain? Why not head south from Jerusalem into Africa or eastward into Mesopotamia? Why follow the northwesterly curve from Jerusalem to Illyricum, as stated in 15:19, and then continue west to the Iberian Peninsula?

Obviously, Paul considers Spain a missionary frontier, a place where the gospel is still unknown. But is it also possible that his missionary aspirations are motivated by theological concerns? There is reason to think that Paul's itinerary is guided by Isa 66:19, to which he alluded in Rom 15:16. According to Isaiah, the heralds of God's glory will follow a path that begins at his holy mountain in Jerusalem and stretches out to the western limits of the known world.[23] The Lord himself declares, "I will send survivors to the nations: to Tarshish, Put and Lud, Mosoch, Tubal and Javan, to the distant coastlands which have never heard of my fame, or seen my glory; and they shall proclaim my glory among the nations" (Isa 66:19). In the first century Tarshish was identified as Paul's birthplace of Tarsus in Cilicia, Asia Minor.[24] Put and Lud (called Phoud and Loud in the †Septuagint) were also located in Asia Minor.[25] Mosoch was located in Asia Minor as well, it being a reference either to Mysia or to a people otherwise known as the Phrygians.[26] Tubal too was situated in Asia Minor, either in Cappadocia or Bithynia.[27] Javan is the biblical term for the Greeks (Zech 9:13). Finally, the faraway "coasts" or "islands" marked the western extremity of the world (Sir 47:16). The coincidence between this map and the geographical scope of Paul's mission field is remarkable. It suggests Paul adopted a missionary itinerary that extended from Jerusalem to the Atlantic coast of Spain for a very particular reason: because it would bring Isaiah's vision to fulfillment.[28]

At any rate, Paul voices his desire to fellowship with the Roman Christians while passing through the capital to his ultimate destination. Putting the matter like this is not meant as a slight to his readers, as if Paul was only interested in a courtesy call. His remarks in Rom 1:11–12 indicate otherwise. Paul wants the Romans to partner with him in evangelizing Spain. When he wishes out loud **to be sent on my way there by you**, he is asking the Roman community to provide whatever logistical and financial support is necessary for making this next missionary adventure a success. After Paul has **enjoyed** staying with the congregation **for a time**, he will need provisions for the journey along with the help of their prayers (15:30).

At present, however, Paul is poised to go **to Jerusalem to minister to the**   **15:25–27** **holy ones**—that is, to bring some relief to the impoverished Christians in Judea.

---

23. See Rainer Riesner, *Paul's Early Period: Chronology, Mission Strategy, Theology*, trans. Doug Stott (Grand Rapids: Eerdmans, 1998), 241–53.

24. Josephus, *Jewish Antiquities* 1.127.

25. Jdt 2:23. Another possibility is that Put refers to Libya in north Africa.

26. Herodotus, *Histories* 1.14.

27. Josephus, *Jewish Antiquities* 13.421; 18.97.

28. The New Testament never indicates whether Paul fulfilled the aspiration to reach the furthest limit of the west, but St. Clement of Rome, writing in the first century, claims that he did (*1 Clement* 5.5–7).

For some time now he has been taking up a large **contribution for the poor** believers in Palestine. Among the Gentile churches who donated to this charitable fund, he mentions those in **Macedonia and Achaia,** two Roman provinces stretching over northern and southern Greece respectively. Again, the rationale behind Paul's effort is not just practical but theological. He reasons that Christians who are **Gentiles** are **indebted** to the community of Jewish believers since they **have come to share in their spiritual blessings.** This is an abstract way of communicating what Paul stated in a concrete way when he described believing Gentiles as wild olive branches grafted onto the olive tree of believing Israel (11:17–24). Far from advocating a supersessionist theology that supposes God abandoned Israel and transferred his affections to a predominantly Gentile Church, Paul argues the other way around. Gentiles who believe in Jesus, the Jewish Messiah, **ought** not only to love and admire and pray for their Jewish brethren but **also to serve them in material blessings.** In this way a spiritual debt is discharged by a material gift of alms.

15:28–29   **So,** Paul continues, **when I have completed this** charitable work **and safely handed over this contribution to them, I shall set out by way of you to Spain.** The word "safely" hints at what verse 31 states explicitly—namely, that Paul is anxious about his upcoming reception in Jerusalem and the designs that Jewish unbelievers may have when he gets there.

Despite this looming unknown, Paul keeps a positive tone when speaking about his travel plans to Rome. Whatever opposition may await him in Jerusalem, he is sure **that in coming to** Rome he will **come in the fullness of Christ's blessing.** This did not materialize quite as Paul envisioned it. He did indeed come to Rome after delivering his collection in Judea, but as a prisoner awaiting trial before Caesar's tribunal (the dramatic story of Acts 21–28).

15:30–32   Because Paul is a wanted man in the eyes of **the disobedient in Judea,** he urges the Romans to **join** in **the struggle** by their **prayers to God.** He desires that intercession be made for his deliverance from non-Christian adversaries. He also hopes that his offering will be found **acceptable** to the **holy ones** in need in **Jerusalem.** The purpose of soliciting their prayers is, in his own words, **that I may come to you with joy by the will of God and be refreshed together with you.** This has been his goal from the beginning: that he and the believers in Rome "may be mutually encouraged by one another's faith" (1:12).

15:33   The chapter ends with a short prayer: **The God of peace be with all of you. Amen.** Paul had a fondness for describing God in these terms.[29] The God of peace is the God who grants peace to his people. A glance back over the letter

29. Rom 16:20; 1 Cor 14:33; 2 Cor 13:11; 1 Thess 5:23.

shows that the term "peace" has a particular richness in Romans. More than a generic "absence of conflict," peace is the gift of spiritual reconciliation and communion that comes from God the Father and the Lord Jesus Christ (1:7). Peace with God is one of the benefits of our justification in Christ (5:1) as well as one of the benefits that come from setting the mind on the things of the Spirit (8:6). Peace is a sign of the kingdom of God (14:17) and ultimately awaits the saints in eternal glory (2:10).

The Conclusion to Romans

Romans 16:1–27

Chapter 16 serves as an appendix to the main body of the letter. Scholars sometimes argue that it is not an authentic part of the text of Romans, on the grounds that surviving manuscripts of the book display significant variations in the ending of the letter. Some conjecture that Romans may have had only fourteen or fifteen chapters instead of the full sixteen we have today. Early Christian writers such as Irenaeus, Cyprian, and Tertullian never refer to these final two chapters. The oldest papyrus text of Romans thus far discovered places the concluding doxology, now appearing in 16:25–27, immediately after 15:33, raising suspicions that the bulk of chapter 16 might be an independent composition that became attached to Romans at a later time. A popular hypothesis regards chapter 16 as a separate letter of commendation for Phoebe originally sent to the church at Ephesus.

Despite these modern doubts, the originality of all sixteen chapters of Romans has been established with confidence.[1] No scholar disputes that shorter versions of the letter circulated in antiquity, but this can be explained without calling the authenticity of its final chapter into question. For instance, an abridged version of Romans that preserved the substance of the letter intact but omitted its personalized ending would be more amenable to liturgical use than the unabridged text. Similarly, information specific to Paul's business with the community in Rome might be excluded from copies of the letter that were

---

1. See H. Gamble Jr., *The Textual History of the Letter to the Romans* (Grand Rapids: Eerdmans, 1997). For a concise summary and assessment of the issues, see Joseph A. Fitzmyer, SJ, *Romans*, AB 33 (New York: Doubleday, 1993), 44–67.

made for the instruction of other churches. Romans, after all, has a powerful message relevant to the whole Church, even if its closing remarks have no direct bearing on the lives of believers outside first-century Rome.

Besides this, Rom 16 includes several standard features that appear in Paul's other letter conclusions. The Apostle greets the recipients who are known to him by name, he directs them to exchange a holy kiss, he offers assurances of God's benevolence, and he prays for an outpouring of grace on them. The ending of Romans also sounds a thematic note that ties the epistle together. Mirroring the opening of the letter, Paul fashions its closing around the guiding purpose of his ministry, which is to bring about "the obedience of faith" in Jesus Christ among all nations (1:5; 16:26).

Commendation for Phoebe and Paul's Greetings (16:1–16)

¹I commend to you Phoebe our sister, who is [also] a minister of the church at Cenchreae, ²that you may receive her in the Lord in a manner worthy of the holy ones, and help her in whatever she may need from you, for she has been a benefactor to many and to me as well.

³Greet Prisca and Aquila, my co-workers in Christ Jesus, ⁴who risked their necks for my life, to whom not only I am grateful but also all the churches of the Gentiles; ⁵greet also the church at their house. Greet my beloved Epaenetus, who was the firstfruits in Asia for Christ. ⁶Greet Mary, who has worked hard for you. ⁷Greet Andronicus and Junia, my relatives and my fellow prisoners; they are prominent among the apostles and they were in Christ before me. ⁸Greet Ampliatus, my beloved in the Lord. ⁹Greet Urbanus, our co-worker in Christ, and my beloved Stachys. ¹⁰Greet Apelles, who is approved in Christ. Greet those who belong to the family of Aristobulus. ¹¹Greet my relative Herodion. Greet those in the Lord who belong to the family of Narcissus. ¹²Greet those workers in the Lord, Tryphaena and Tryphosa. Greet the beloved Persis, who has worked hard in the Lord. ¹³Greet Rufus, chosen in the Lord, and his mother and mine. ¹⁴Greet Asyncritus, Phlegon, Hermes, Patrobas, Hermas, and the brothers who are with them. ¹⁵Greet Philologus, Julia, Nereus and his sister, and Olympas, and all the holy ones who are with them. ¹⁶Greet one another with a holy kiss. All the churches of Christ greet you.

OT: Exod 15:20
NT: Mark 15:21; Rom 11:16; Acts 2:46; 18:1–3; 1 Cor 16:15, 19–20; 1 Thess 5:26
Catechism: particular churches and the universal Church, 832–35

The lion's share of Rom 16 is taken up with matters of personal business. First, Paul asks readers to welcome Phoebe, a woman from Corinth, presumably because she is responsible for delivering Paul's Epistle to the Romans in person. Second, Paul offers greetings to two dozen individuals presumed to be in Rome at the time of writing. Phoebe is thus furnished with a list of Christian contacts in the city on whom she can rely for her needs. Third, Paul is preparing the way for his own arrival in the capital. By singling out so many believers for mention—the longest list of greetings found in any New Testament letter—he seeks to build rapport with a network of churches he has never seen face-to-face. Of the twenty-four persons directly addressed, some have Greek names, others have Latin names, and a few either have Hebrew names or reference is made to their Jewish identity. Clearly the Roman community to which Paul writes is ethnically diverse, a family of God's people from Israel and the nations alike.[2]

16:1–2   Paul provides a recommendation for a woman named **Phoebe**. She is a **sister in the faith** and was probably the carrier of the present epistle from Corinth to Rome. To use a modern analogy, vouching for Phoebe is like Paul attaching a personal reference to her application for employment. Since he trusts and endorses her, the Romans can confidently **receive her** with open arms. A snub against Phoebe would amount to a snub against Paul.

Besides being a professing Christian, Phoebe is a respected **minister of the church at Cenchreae**. Cenchreae is the eastern port of Corinth in southern Greece and a prominent trade link between the Greek Peninsula and the eastern Mediterranean. A majority of scholars accept that Paul is writing Romans from Corinth. Less certain is what Paul means by the word "minister," *diakonos* in Greek. Sometimes Paul uses the term in the general or nonspecific sense of a "servant" (Rom 15:8; 2 Cor 11:23). Other times he uses it to designate a member of the pastorate, specifically an officeholder in the Church that would come to be called a "deacon" (Phil 1:1; 1 Tim 3:8, 12). On still another occasion Paul reckons "ministry" (Greek *diakonia*) among the charismatic gifts of the Spirit that animate the body of Christ, the gift of ministry being the charism that inspires believers to offer practical assistance to persons in need (Rom 12:7). Unfortunately, we know too little about Phoebe to state with confidence whether she was a "deaconess" who exercised a specific pastoral ministry in the Church or simply stood out for her generous service to others.[3]

---

2. See "The Christian Community in Rome" in the introduction (pp. xx–xxii).

3. The Ecumenical Council of Nicaea stated in AD 325 that a "deaconess" exercises a lay ministry rather than an ordained ministry (Canon 19).

Paul urges the Romans to receive Phoebe **in a manner worthy of the holy ones**—that is, with all the warmth of Christian hospitality they can muster. He would also have them **help her in whatever she may need,** because **she has been a benefactor to many,** including to Paul himself. This language suggests that Phoebe is a patroness—a woman of high standing and wealth who used her resources to better the lives of others. Paul's logic is that one as charitable as Phoebe deserves an outpouring of generosity in return.

Next follows a litany of greetings from Paul to individual Christians in Rome. **16:3–5a** Some are already known to the Apostle, while others must have featured in reports that were passed along to him.

Heading the list are two of Paul's dearest friends, **Prisca and Aquila** (the "Priscilla and Aquila" of Acts). He first met this Jewish Christian couple in Corinth after the emperor Claudius expelled the Jews living in Rome in AD 49 (Acts 18:1–3). Being knowledgeable teachers of the faith (Acts 18:26), they soon became collaborators or **co-workers** with Paul in the service of the gospel, initially in Corinth and later in Ephesus (Acts 18:18–19). Apparently Prisca and Aquila returned to Rome by the mid-50s, where they became host to a **church in their house,** much as they had done in Ephesus (1 Cor 16:19). In the earliest Christian centuries believers gathered in private homes because they owned no public buildings in which to assemble for prayer and liturgy (Acts 2:46; 12:12; Col 4:15; Philem 2).

Paul adds that he is **grateful** for Prisca and Aquila, as are **all the churches of the Gentiles** on whose behalf he speaks. Why? Because this faithful husband and wife **risked their necks** to save Paul's **life**. Perhaps this occurred during the riot in Ephesus described in Acts 19:23–40, or perhaps the incident has gone unmentioned in the New Testament. Either way, Paul is paying a high compliment to the couple's depth of devotion.

Next the Apostle greets **Epaenetus**. Nothing further is known of the man **16:5b–6** except that Paul describes him as **the firstfruits in Asia for Christ**, by which he means that Epaenetus was the first convert to Christianity in the Roman province of Asia (modern western Turkey).[4] So too, **Mary, who has worked hard** among the Roman believers, is otherwise unknown. She is probably a Jewish Christian woman since her name is a Greek form of the Hebrew "Miriam," the name of Moses' sister (Exod 15:20).

The next greeting goes out to a certain **Andronicus and Junia**. Andronicus **16:7** is a Greek name but one sometimes borne by Jewish men of the time.[5] There

4. Paul is using the cultic language of consecrating a harvest of crops to God. See commentary on 11:16.

5. Josephus, *Jewish Antiquities* 13.75.

is some ambiguity about the name "Junia." Depending on how the Greek is accented, it could be either a man's name (JB, RSV, NIV) or a woman's (NABRE, NRSV, ESV). Overall, the weight of the evidence favors the feminine Junia, in which case Paul is probably addressing another married couple.

Paul tells us four things about these individuals. First, Andronicus and Junia are his **relatives**, by which he means fellow Jews. Second, they are **fellow prisoners**. This could mean either that they were imprisoned *with* Paul at a certain point, or that *like* Paul they spent time in jail for spreading the faith. Third, they **are prominent among the apostles**. The question here is whether Andronicus and Junia are themselves apostles or whether Paul means they are favorably esteemed by the Lord's apostles. Both are possible on grammatical and historical grounds. It is good to keep in mind that the word "apostle" had a broader application in the earliest days of the Church than the modern reader may realize. Jesus, of course, commissioned twelve apostles to be the heralds of God's kingdom to all nations (Luke 6:12–16). But local churches also sent emissaries on special assignments, and these individuals were likewise called "apostles" (2 Cor 8:23; Phil 2:25; *Didache* 11.3–6). Scholars typically favor this broader meaning of the term in the present verse. Finally, Andronicus and Junia **were in Christ before** Paul, whose conversion took place in the mid-30s. Possibly they were among the Roman pilgrims who attended the feast of Pentecost in Jerusalem in AD 30 and returned home as Christians (Acts 2:5–11, 41).

16:8–10   Paul's greetings continue with addresses to four men: **Ampliatus**, **Urbanus**, **Stachys**, and **Apelles**, each of whom is mentioned with a short, admiring remark. Unfortunately history preserves no further information about these figures. Roman sources indicate that the first three names were common among slaves, and the fourth is a Greek name attested among Jews. But whether this information tells us something about the background of the individuals in question is uncertain.

The adjoined greeting for **those who belong to the family of Aristobulus** is a little different. In this case Paul is addressing the Christian members of a household, which in the Roman world included all the dependents of the family father—his wife, his children, his slaves, and anyone else living under his roof. Since Aristobulus, who bears a common Greek name, is not actually greeted, he may be a nonbeliever or no longer living. One intriguing suggestion is that this man is Aristobulus, the grandson of Herod the Great, who resided in Rome and was known to rub shoulders with the emperor Claudius.[6] This Aristobulus died a few years before Paul wrote Romans.

6. Josephus, *Jewish Antiquities* 20.12; *Jewish War* 2.221.

A possible link between Aristobulus and the aristocratic family of Herod   16:11–12
could also explain Paul's greeting to a Jewish believer named **Herodion.** But
since nothing more is known of this person, the link must remain conjectural.

Greetings for another household follows, this one for **those in the Lord who
belong to the family of Narcissus.** Again the head of the household, Narcissus,
receives no actual greeting, indicating that he may not have been a Christian
or even alive at this point. It is worth noting that a man of this name served as
a slave under the emperor Claudius but was driven to suicide by threats from
Nero's mother, Agrippina, a few years before Romans was written.[7]

Paul next singles out for mention three hardworking women. It is a good
bet that the first two, **Tryphaena** and **Tryphosa,** are sisters. The third, **Persis,**
bears a Greek name common among slaves. Their labor for the Lord is highly
regarded but not specified.

Of all the names listed in Rom 16, one of the most discussed is **Rufus,** whom   16:13
Paul says is **chosen in the Lord.** Why so? Some have sought to link him with
Simon of Cyrene, the man who helped Jesus to carry his cross, identified in
Mark's Gospel as "the father of Alexander and Rufus" (Mark 15:21). Admittedly,
this is a thin thread of evidence, especially since Rufus was a fairly common
Latin name. However, since tradition places the composition of Mark's Gospel
in Rome in the middle of the first century, the hypothesis has merit. Mark ap-
pears to mention these brothers in passing as persons familiar to his original
readers. Were Alexander and Rufus members of the Christian community in
Rome? Quite possibly. The parallel passages about Simon's service to Jesus in
Matt 27:32 and Luke 23:26 make no mention of his sons.

Paul also reserves a greeting for Rufus's **mother,** with whom he must have
developed a close relationship at some point. By saying that she is also **mine,**
the Apostle expresses his heartfelt regard for this motherly figure in his life.

The following individuals—**Asyncritus, Phlegon, Hermes, Patrobas,** and   16:14–15
Hermas—along with **the brothers who are with them,** apparently belonged
to the same house church in Rome. According to ancient sources, these names
were often borne by slaves and former slaves.

Something similar appears likely for the next group: **Philologus, Julia,
Nereus and his sister, and Olympas, and all the holy ones who are with
them.** One suspects this is another house church, the hosts being a married
couple (Philologus and Julia) with children (Nereus and his sister) and possibly
a household servant (Olympas). Paul greets them as believers associated with
a company of fellow Christians.

---

7. Tacitus, *Annals of Imperial Rome* 11.1.

16:16   Paul ends this section with a final injunction: **Greet one another with a holy kiss.** Judging from the New Testament, this was a widely established custom in the early Church.[8] The sign of affection exchanged between believers is "holy" because it expresses love—love not between romantic partners but among brothers and sisters in the spiritual family of faith. Also, keeping in mind that Paul's Letters were read aloud in the context of community worship, we see the beginnings of a liturgical tradition known as "the kiss of peace,"[9] which lives on today, typically in the form of a handshake or similar

Figure 11. Fragment of P[49] containing Rom 16:14–23.

gesture (see the sidebar "St. Justin Martyr on the Kiss of Peace in the Eucharistic Liturgy"). Finally, greetings are conveyed to the Roman Christians not only from Paul but from **all the churches of Christ** under his care.

Reflection and Application (16:3–15)

From a certain point of view, the greetings that often appear at the end of Paul's Letters are among the least inspiring parts of Scripture, right up there with biblical genealogies. Name follows name in a list of persons who are totally unknown to us and long since deceased. Is it possible to derive a lesson applicable to Christian living from these humdrum passages of the Bible?

I believe it is. These greetings show us that Christian ministry must always be an investment in people. Ours is not a religion restricted to ideas and abstract

8. 1 Cor 16:20; 2 Cor 13:12; 1 Thess 5:26; 1 Pet 5:14.
9. The expression appears in Hippolytus, *On the Apostolic Tradition* 4.1; and Tertullian, *On Prayer* 18.

St. Justin Martyr on the Kiss of Peace in the Eucharistic Liturgy

LIVING TRADITION

But we, after thus baptizing the one who has been convinced and has assented, lead him to those who are called brethren, where they are assembled; and we offer prayers in common for ourselves and for the one who has been illuminated and for all others everywhere, that we may be accounted worthy, having learned the truth, by our deeds also to be found good citizens and guardians of what is commanded, so that we may receive eternal salvation. Having ended the prayers we greet one another with a kiss. Then there is brought to the Ruler of the Brethren bread and a cup of water and [a cup] of wine mixed with water, and taking them he sends up praise and glory to the Father of the Universe through the name of the Son and of the Holy Spirit, and offers thanksgiving at some length for our being accounted worthy to receive these things from Him.[a]

a. *1 Apology* 65. Translation adapted from St. Justin Martyr, *The First and Second Apologies*, trans. Leslie W. Barnard, ACW 56 (Mahwah, NJ: Paulist Press, 1997), 70.

dogmas that have minimal connection to life. Christianity is a religion of the Word incarnate. The Son of God became consubstantial with us in order to reach us in the depths of our human need. His disciples can do no less when it comes to being his witnesses in the world. Ministry, in other words, is an incarnational activity. It requires a spirit of real compassion that attends to real needs. Evangelization, youth ministry, and other pastoral activities have as much to do with building personal relationships as with anything else. Even some of the finest preaching and teaching can fall on deaf ears when a personal connection is lacking. Ministry tends to be most fruitful when we give ourselves to others along with our message.

This is something that comes to mind when I read the greetings that Paul sends to the Christians in Rome. Behind many of these names is the face of a friend known to Paul. Behind others is a believer who must have been greatly encouraged to be singled out for mention by the apostle to the Gentiles. Few figures have had an impact on the history of the world quite like Paul, and this in part is because of his loving attention to people.

A Warning from Paul, Greetings from Corinth (16:17–23)

[17]I urge you, brothers, to watch out for those who create dissensions and obstacles, in opposition to the teaching that you learned; avoid them.

¹⁸**For such people do not serve our Lord Christ but their own appetites, and by fair and flattering speech they deceive the hearts of the innocent.** ¹⁹**For while your obedience is known to all, so that I rejoice over you, I want you to be wise as to what is good, and simple as to what is evil;** ²⁰**then the God of peace will quickly crush Satan under your feet. The grace of our Lord Jesus be with you.**

²¹**Timothy, my co-worker, greets you; so do Lucius and Jason and Sosipater, my relatives.** ²²**I, Tertius, the writer of this letter, greet you in the Lord.** ²³**Gaius, who is host to me and to the whole church, greets you. Erastus, the city treasurer, and our brother Quartus greet you.** [²⁴]

OT: Gen 2:16–17; 3:15; Wis 2:24
NT: Matt 10:16; John 8:44; Rom 15:33; 2 Cor 11:14–15; Gal 5:20; Phil 3:19; Rev 12:9
Catechism: disunity in the Church, 817; the Protoevangelium, 410–11

Readers often feel that verses 17–20 come out of nowhere. Paul seemed to be drawing the letter to a close in verses 1–16, but now he launches abruptly into a warning against those who would lead the Roman Christians astray. One suspects the idea occurred to Paul at the last minute and that he wanted to make sure he included these admonitions in the letter before sending it off. Hence his words take on a serious tone for a few lines. Verses 21–23, which round off this unit, convey greetings to the Romans from Paul's companions in Corinth.

16:17–18   This is the only passage in the letter where Paul puts readers on guard against troublemakers from outside the Roman community. He warns them **to watch out for those who create dissensions and obstacles, in opposition to the teaching that you learned; avoid them**. He has in mind people who claim the name "Christian" but tear at the unity of the Church and place stumbling blocks in the path of the faithful. For Paul, divisions and scandals arise within the community when believers live according to the flesh (Gal 5:20). Most likely he is concerned that Judaizers—Jewish Christians who wrongly insist that Gentiles who embrace the gospel must follow the ritual laws of the Torah, beginning with circumcision—will make their way to Rome. Paul had to contend with this threat in other letters such as 2 Corinthians, Galatians, and Philippians. Whatever the precise identity of these misguided teachers, the Romans must keep a lookout for anyone who contradicts the teaching of the apostles. Furthermore, they must keep their distance should persons of this description appear on their doorstep.

Paul then exposes the motives of these dividers and scandalizers: **such people do not serve our Lord Christ but their own appetites**—literally, "their own stomach." Despite appearances of piety, these agitators serve their own selfish interests, be it a hunger for money, notoriety, influence, or whatever. And their usual method involves a display of **fair and flattering speech**. Paul's concern is that **innocent** believers will be taken in by these smooth talkers and their **hearts** led astray from a pure commitment to Christ (see 2 Cor 11:3).

Paul carries the admonition further in verse 19, now balancing his words of caution with words of reassurance. He has not forgotten that the faith and **obedi-ence** of the Romans is **known** and admired by **all** the churches of the Christian world (Rom 1:8). This is something that causes him to **rejoice**. Nevertheless, the dangers of deception and disunity are real, even in a community that is spiritually mature (15:14). Paul desires to insulate his audience from the threat, saying, **I want you to be wise as to what is good, and simple as to what is evil**. **16:19**

In the language of Scripture, good and evil encompasses "truth and error" as well as "right and wrong." Paul wants the Romans to align both their minds and their wills with the gospel. Being wise means discerning the truth and rejecting falsehood; and being innocent means choosing the right path in pref-erence to wrongdoing. Jesus spoke similar words when instructing his disciples about the dangers awaiting them in the mission field: "Behold, I send you out as sheep in the midst of wolves; so be wise as serpents and innocent as doves" (Matt 10:16 RSV).[10]

Confident the Romans will heed this warning, Paul promises them God's de-liverance from the schemes of the Evil One: **the God of peace will quickly crush Satan under your feet**.[11] Like an enemy combatant defeated on the battlefield, the devil will find himself pressed down under the feet of God's people (see Josh 10:24–25). However, since natural human resources are woefully inadequate for subduing the prince of darkness, Paul can only describe this as God's doing rather than our own. There can be no victory over Satan apart from Christ and the strength he supplies. Hence the prayer that follows: **The grace of our Lord Jesus be with you**. Grace is the indispensable factor in this equation. It is the help we need for Paul's promise to become a reality in everyday life. **16:20**

Paul resumes the business of sending greetings to the believers in Rome. Un-like the personal greetings in verses 3–15, those in verses 21–23 are intended for the whole congregation and come from individuals who are present with Paul as he dictates the letter. Eight men send their best to Christians in the capital. **16:21–23**

The first is Paul's **co-worker** named **Timothy**. We know from elsewhere in the New Testament that Timothy was the son of a Greek father and a Jewish Christian

---

10. Douglas J. Moo, *The Epistle to the Romans*, NICNT (Grand Rapids: Eerdmans, 1996), 932, considers Paul's words a probable allusion to this saying of Jesus.

11. For the expression "God of peace," see commentary on 15:33.

Genesis 3:15 and the Church

Scholars rightly detect in Rom 16:20 an allusion to Gen 3:15, a passage known in Christian tradition as the *Protoevangelium* (Latin for "first announcement of the gospel"). This verse, coming right after the fall of Adam and Eve, gives us the first indication in Scripture that God has a plan to bring judgment on the serpent and to rid the world of evil. Confronting the serpent, God foretells his future doom: "I will put enmity between you and the woman, and between your offspring and her offspring; he shall bruise your head, and you shall bruise his heel" (Gen 3:15 ESV). Not only will the serpent remain locked in a struggle with the offspring of Eve; he will also finally suffer defeat when the heel of her offspring stomps on his head, crushing him underfoot.

Paul makes a pastoral application of this prophecy in Romans that falls in line with Jewish and Christian tradition. He assumes as common knowledge that the deceiving serpent in Genesis was really "the devil" in disguise (Wis 2:24). Also, in concert with the †eschatological hopes of Judaism, he anticipates the final demise of the devil, variously named in ancient texts as Satan, Mastema, Azazel, the angel of darkness, and so forth.[a] Both of these beliefs are taken up into Christian theology (Rev 12:9; 20:7–10).

The question is how to identify the offspring of Eve. Ancient Jewish writings offer more than one interpretation. Among these is a messianic reading that sees the offspring of Eve as a conquering Messiah.[b] There is also a communal reading that identifies Eve's offspring as God's covenant people treading down the devil and fellow spirits of evil.[c] Again, both interpretations are attested in early Christian writings.[d]

For Paul, these two ways of understanding Gen 3:15 are not contradictory but complementary, since the Messiah and his messianic community are united as one. Paul has made this abundantly clear in Romans. The Church is the living body of Christ (Rom 12:4–5), the community baptized into Christ (6:3), the sons and daughters indwelt by the Spirit of Christ (8:9). It is precisely and only because the faithful are united with Christ that they can conquer overwhelmingly through Christ (8:37). We can distinguish between Paul's Christology and his ecclesiology, his doctrine of Christ and his doctrine of the Church, but we can never separate them. Holding them together is oftentimes the key to understanding Paul's interpretation of the Old Testament, as in Rom 16:20.

a. *Jubilees* 10.8–11; 23.29; 1QS 3.20–22; 1QM 17.5; *Testament of Moses* 10.1.

b. *Palestinian Targum* on Gen 3:15.

c. *Testament of Simeon* 6.6; *Testament of Levi* 18.12; *Testament of Zebulon* 9.8. It is important to realize that the noun "offspring" in Hebrew can be *singular*, referring to an individual, as well as *collective*, referring to a group. This is why the NABRE, in its translation of Gen 3:15, refers to the woman's offspring as "they."

d. Rev 12:17; St. Irenaeus, *Against Heresies* 3.23.7.

mother named Eunice, who formed him in the teaching of the Scriptures (Acts 16:1–3; 2 Tim 1:5; 3:15). Despite his being a young man, Paul recruited Timothy as a member of his missionary team and eventually ordained him (1 Tim 4:14; 2 Tim 1:6). He is named as a cosender of several Pauline Epistles (e.g., 2 Cor 1:1; Phil 1:1; 1 Thess 1:1). Some years later, Paul stationed Timothy in Ephesus to shepherd the church in that region (1 Tim 1:1–3). While serving in this capacity, he received two New Testament letters from Paul: 1 and 2 Timothy.

The next three to send greetings are **Lucius, Jason**, and **Sosipater**, identified as Jewish **relatives** of Paul. All three names are borne by Christians in the book of Acts: a Lucius of Cyrene (Acts 13:1), a Jason of Thessalonica (Acts 17:5–9), and a Sopater of Beroea (Acts 20:4). The Lucius mentioned in Romans is of uncertain identity, but the Jason and Sosipater who send greetings here are probably the Jason and Sopater of Acts.

The fifth person to offer greetings is **Tertius**, who identifies himself as **the writer of this letter**. The statement comes as a surprise to modern readers, who reasonably assumed that Paul had the pen in hand all along (Rom 1:1). But according to ancient convention, the sender of a letter was not always the scribe who wrote in down. So it is here. The Letter to the Romans was written by Tertius under Paul's direction and probably at his dictation.

The sixth individual to send greetings is **Gaius**, with whom Paul is presently staying in Corinth. Presumably this is the Corinthian man whom Paul baptized, according to 1 Cor 1:14. Gaius's generosity as **host** to **the whole church** suggests that he opened his home as a gathering place for community liturgy and fellowship.

The seventh and eighth to send greetings are named **Erastus** and **Quartus**. Paul tells us that Quartus is a fellow Christian **brother**, but beyond that nothing further is known about him. Erastus, however, is the name of a civic official in Corinth, acting as **the city treasurer** at this time. Interestingly, archaeologists have uncovered a first-century Latin inscription that states that Erastus personally financed the installation of a paved square in the city of Corinth. It is possible this man is the associate of Paul mentioned here and in Acts 19:22 and 2 Tim 4:20, but it is difficult to be certain.

Finally, the NABRE omits verse 24, placing the verse number in brackets because it is absent from the most reliable manuscripts of Romans.

Concluding Doxology (16:25–27)

[²⁵Now to him who can strengthen you, according to my gospel and the proclamation of Jesus Christ, according to the revelation of the mystery kept secret for long ages [26]but now manifested through the prophetic writings and, according to the command of the eternal God, made known to all nations to bring about the obedience of faith, [27]to the only wise God, through Jesus Christ be glory forever and ever. Amen.]

OT: Dan 2:18–19, 27–30, 47
NT: Mark 4:11; Rom 1:1–5; 11:25–27, 33–36; 15:18; 1 Cor 15:51–55; Eph 1:9–10; 3:4–6
Catechism: obedience of faith, 143, 2087; prayer of praise, 2639, 2649; doxology, 2641
Lectionary: 4th Sunday of Advent (Year B)

Romans concludes with a doxology of praise, ascribing glory to "the only wise God" (16:27). The NABRE places these final three verses in brackets because their originality is uncertain. In early manuscripts of Romans, the doxology is either missing entirely, appears twice, comes after 14:23, comes after 15:33, or comes after 16:23. So too it has a distinct style that leads some scholars to doubt that Paul actually wrote it.[12]

Regardless of its origin, the doxology is a canonical portion of Scripture that fits nicely into the larger letter. One could say that the final three verses complete the circle of Romans by connecting the end of the letter with its beginning. In both instances, the focus rests squarely on the gospel of Jesus Christ—the gospel that Paul preaches, the gospel made known through the Scriptures of Israel, the gospel that summons all nations to the obedience of faith.

16:25–26   The final unit is a closing prayer. Having addressed the Roman community at length, Paul turns to address the heavenly Father, **who can strengthen** believers with all that is needed to grow in the life of faith. Perhaps he is thinking specifically of the spiritual gifts entrusted to him for encouraging others in the faith (1:11–12). The strength that God supplies is linked with Paul's **gospel and the proclamation of Jesus Christ**, wherein lies the power of salvation for all who believe (1:16).

Paul's gospel is defined as **the revelation** or unveiling of **the mystery**. Despite the nonreligious connotations of the word "mystery" in our day, the Greek term *mystērion* was commonplace among the religious conceptions of the world in which Paul and his readers lived. In the Bible, the idea is first found in the book of Daniel, which uses an equivalent term (Aramaic *raz*) to designate God's hidden plan for the triumphant arrival of his kingdom in history. This mystery is encoded in the images and story line of a dream given to King Nebuchadnezzar of Babylon, and its meaning was decipherable only through a divine revelation given to the prophet Daniel (Dan 2:1–49). Similarly, Palestinian Jewish writings

12. For considerations that favor its authenticity as Paul's own prayer, see Moo, *Epistle to the Romans*, 936–38.

such as the Dead Sea Scrolls discourse about the "mysteries" of God in terms of his hidden ways and plans (1QM 14.14) as well as the hidden meanings he has placed in the Scriptures (1QpHab 7.5; 1QS 3.23).[13]

Paul uses this traditional Jewish language to articulate the Christian message.[14] For him, the mystery is made known in the person of Jesus Christ and his work of redemption (1 Cor 2:1–2; Col 2:2–3). It encompasses the restoration of Israel (Rom 11:25–26), the salvation of the Gentiles as heirs of grace alongside the Jews (Eph 3:3–6), the bodily resurrection and glorification of the faithful (1 Cor 15:51–55), and ultimately God's intention to place all creation under the headship of the Lord Jesus (Eph 1:9–10).

So it is that the "mystery" of God's plan was **kept secret for long ages but** is **now manifested** in messianic times. The adverb "now" is small in size but great in importance. It shows that Paul sees himself living at the high point of salvation history, the age in which the mystery long concealed is finally revealed. In the coming of the Messiah we have the climactic disclosure of God's designs for drawing the world back into his arms.

Still, it is curious that Paul should see this revelation coming **through the prophetic writings**—that is, through "the law and the prophets" of the Old Testament (Rom 3:21). These inspired texts already existed for "long ages" and yet the mystery was "kept secret" within them. The assumption behind Paul's assertion is that the Scriptures of Israel have layers and dimensions of meaning beyond what our natural powers of observation can detect. The Old Testament is a collection of holy books that announce the gospel beforehand, as Paul insists in 1:1–4, and yet its witness to the mystery of God's plan in Christ unfolds slowly in incremental stages. Sometimes it is only when you reach your destination that you come to understand fully the directions that got you there. Paul thus seems to imply here what he states openly in 2 Cor 3:12–18—namely, that the Hebrew Scriptures remain opaque to those who do not believe in Christ. When a person comes to faith in Jesus, however, the Spirit removes a veil from the mind to reveal the Bible's patterns of redemption converging on a dying and rising Messiah. The point is not that nothing can be known about God from reading the Old Testament as a non-Christian, only that becoming a Christian gives the believer new eyes for seeing how Jesus embodies the faithfulness and mercy of God toward all.

And this accords with **the command of the eternal God**. Some take this as a reference to the eternal decree of salvation conceived in the mind of God before

---

13. For a classic study of this background, see Raymond E. Brown, *The Semitic Background of the Term "Mystery" in the New Testament*, FBBS 21 (Philadelphia: Fortress, 1968).

14. See Markus Bockmuehl, *Revelation and Mystery in Ancient Judaism and Pauline Christianity* (Grand Rapids: Eerdmans, 1997).

the dawn of creation but only recently come to light in Christ. Others find in these words a reference to Paul's commission as an apostle, obligating him to make the gospel known **to all nations** and thus **to bring about the obedience of faith**[15] among "Gentiles and kings and the sons of Israel" (Acts 9:15 RSV).

16:27   The last line of the letter is the doxology proper, since it ascribes **glory** (Greek *doxa*) **to the only wise God**. Fundamental to all of Paul's teaching in Romans is the monotheistic belief that "God is one" (3:30), a belief that Christianity derives from the Jewish Scriptures, along with the conviction that God has a "depth of . . . wisdom" that leaves the mind in speechless awe (11:33). There is no more fitting response to God than praise, both now and **forever**. And this is offered **through** the mediation of **Jesus Christ**, who is seated at the right hand of the Father (8:34). **Amen.**

---

15. For this important expression in Romans, see commentary on 1:5.

Suggested Resources

From the Christian Tradition

Bray, Gerald, ed. *Romans*. Ancient Christian Commentary on Scripture 6. Downers Grove, IL: InterVarsity, 2005. Short selections from the Church Fathers and other early Christian writers on nearly every passage of Romans.

Burns, J. Patout, Jr., trans. and ed. with Constantine Newman. *Romans: Interpreted by Early Christian Commentators*. The Church's Bible. Grand Rapids: Eerdmans, 2012. Long selections from the Church Fathers and other early Christian writers on nearly every passage of Romans.

Landes, Paula Fredrickson, trans. *Augustine on Romans: Propositions from the Epistle to the Romans, Unfinished Commentary on the Epistle to the Romans*. Texts and Translations 23, Early Christian Literature Series 6. Chico, CA: Scholars Press, 1982. A translation of two works by St. Augustine devoted to Romans with original Latin on facing pages.

Origen. *Commentary on the Epistle to the Romans*. Translated by Thomas P. Scheck. 2 vols. FC 103–4. Washington, DC: Catholic University of America Press, 2001–2. An abridgement of the first full-scale commentary ever written on Romans. Rich in both theological insight and pastoral application.

St. John Chrysostom. *Homilies on Romans*. Vol. 11 of *NPNF*[1]. Edited by Philip Schaff. Translated by J. B. Morris and W. H. Simcox. Grand Rapids: Eerdmans, 1979. Pastoral teaching on Romans from the heart of the ancient Church and in light of the whole Bible.

St. Thomas Aquinas. *Commentary on the Letter of Saint Paul to the Romans*. Translated by F. R. Larcher, OP. Edited by J. Mortensen and E. Alaracón. Latin-English Edition of the Works of St. Thomas Aquinas 37. Lander, WY: Aquinas Institute for the Study of Sacred Doctrine, 2012. A full exposition of Romans in the scholastic style. One of the finest specimens of careful exegesis and theological insight ever captured in writing. Latin text and English translation in parallel columns.

Academic Commentaries

Dunn, James D. G. *Romans*. WBC 38a and 38b. Nashville: Nelson, 1988. A technical, two-volume commentary by a world-class Protestant scholar. Full of helpful information about the historical background of Paul's letter and theology.

Fitzmyer, Joseph A., SJ. *Romans*. AB 33. New York: Doubleday, 1993. The most detailed commentary on Romans by a Catholic scholar in recent times. Most helpful on matters of historical and linguistic background. Attention to the history of interpretation is also one of its strengths.

Matera, Frank J. *Romans*. PCNT. Grand Rapids: Baker Academic, 2010. An insightful commentary by a Catholic scholar that is less technical than Fitzmyer's but more readable and helpful for the nonspecialist.

Moo, Douglas J. *The Epistle to the Romans*. NICNT. Grand Rapids: Eerdmans, 1996. A full and clear exposition of Romans from an evangelical Protestant perspective.

Wright, N. T. "The Letter to the Romans." In *The New Interpreter's Bible*, edited by Leander E. Keck, 10:393–770. Nashville: Abingdon, 2002. A wonderfully readable commentary by a world-renowned Anglican bishop. Very good at drawing out the theological themes of the letter.

A Midlevel Commentary

Pate, C. Marvin. *Romans*. TTCS. Grand Rapids: Baker Books, 2014. An attractive volume that succeeds in explaining complex issues in Romans in clear and understandable prose. The book is especially rich in exploring the biblical theology of the letter. Interpretation is often determined by the author's Protestant perspective.

Popular Commentaries

Aranda, Gonzalo, et al. *Romans and Galatians*. 2nd ed. The Navarre Bible. Dublin: Four Courts Press, 2005. A short, devotional commentary on Romans that draws on the writings of Catholic saints and spiritual writers.

Hahn, Scott, and Curtis Mitch. *The Letter of St. Paul to the Romans*. 2nd ed. Ignatius Catholic Study Bible. San Francisco: Ignatius, 2003. A short exposition of Romans with introduction, annotations, word studies, topical essays, and study questions.

Other Resources

Fitzmyer, Joseph A., SJ. *Spiritual Exercises Based on Paul's Epistle to the Romans*. Grand Rapids: Eerdmans, 2004. A spiritual reading of Romans in the tradition of St. Ignatius of Loyola.

Pope Benedict XVI. *Saint Paul: General Audiences, July 2, 2008–February 4, 2009*. English translation by *L'Osservatore Romano*. San Francisco: Ignatius, 2009. Not an exposition of Romans per se, but a collection of lucid meditations on various aspects of Paul's ministry and theology, including justification.

Reasoner, Mark. *Romans in Full Circle: A History of Interpretation*. Louisville: Westminster John Knox, 2005. A handy volume that looks at how theologians over the centuries have understood key passages in Romans.

Glossary

Decalogue (Greek, "ten words" or "ten utterances"): another way of referring to the Ten Commandments that Moses received from the Lord on Mount Sinai. These are the most important precepts of the Torah. Observance of the Decalogue was a sacred duty for the ancient Israelites as it is for the disciples of Jesus Christ (Matt 19:16–19; Rom 13:8–10). The Old Testament lists the commandments of the Decalogue in Exod 20:2–17 and Deut 5:6–21.

Diaspora (Greek, "dispersion" or "scattering"): refers to the community of Israel living outside the promised land. The northern tribes of Israel were forcibly removed from Palestine by the Assyrians in the eighth century BC. The southern tribes of Israel were exiled to foreign lands by the Babylonians in the sixth century BC. In Paul's day, the covenant people lived throughout the Mediterranean world.

diatribe: a rhetorical technique developed among classical writers and utilized by Paul in Romans. A diatribe consists of a dialogue between a writer and a hypothetical debate partner that proceeds by means of questions, objections, and responses. Writers adopted the conversational mode of a diatribe to convince readers of their position on a disputed or confusing issue.

economy of salvation: the divine plan to save humanity from sin and separation from God. The term "economy" derives from a Greek word meaning "household law" and refers to the ways that God, as a wise and loving Father, leads his children to moral and spiritual maturity. It is a plan that unfolds gradually, stretching from creation to the consummation of history. Its major stages of development are marked by the covenants that God makes with his people.

election, elect: God's special selection of an individual or people for divine blessing. In the Old Testament, the tribes of Israel are called to be the Lord's elect or chosen people (Deut 7:6). In the New Testament, the elect of God are the chosen who believe in Jesus as the Messiah (Matt 24:31; Rom 11:7). Election in the biblical sense comes with privileges as well as responsibilities; it includes receiving divine blessings as well as mediating those blessings to others.

eschatology, eschatological (from Greek *ta eschata*, "the last things"): theological beliefs regarding the fulfillment of God's plan in the future. The eschatology of the Old Testament concerns mainly the prophetic expectations that are met in the New Testament—e.g., the coming of the Messiah and his kingdom, the restoration of Israel, and the salvation of the Gentiles. The eschatology of the New Testament anticipates events connected with the end of history—e.g., the return of Christ in glory, the general resurrection of the dead, and the last judgment.

expiation: the divine action of remitting or "taking away" sins. In the Bible, expiation is accomplished through sacrifice.

gnostics: followers of an aberrant form of Christianity, especially prominent in the earliest centuries of the Church. Among other things, gnosticism (from Greek *gnōsis*, meaning "knowledge") posits a radical dualism between matter and spirit, the former being viewed as evil and the latter as good. Consequently, gnostics denigrated the body and many things associated with it.

Mishnah: the foundational document of rabbinic Judaism after the Hebrew Bible. It is a collection of oral traditions and legal rulings that was compiled around AD 200.

Pelagian: associated with a British ascetic named Pelagius, who died about AD 425. Contrary to Paul's teaching in Romans and elsewhere, Pelagius taught that salvation was attainable apart from the grace of the Spirit empowering Christians to avoid sin and perform good works. His main theological opponent, St. Augustine of Hippo, charged him with greatly overestimating our fallen nature's ability to live as God commands without divine assistance.

remnant: a portion that remains. In the Old Testament, a remnant consists either of survivors who escape judgment and catastrophe or of those in Israel who remain faithful to the Lord in the midst of national apostasy. The concept plays an important role in Rom 9–11, where it designates the portion of Israel that believes in Jesus as the Messiah amid widespread unbelief among the covenant people.

Septuagint (abbreviated LXX): the Greek translation of the Hebrew Bible produced in the third and second centuries BC. The Septuagint was the Bible used by Greek-speaking Jews and the version of the Old Testament most often quoted by the New Testament writers and the early Church Fathers.

Servant of the Lord, Suffering Servant: a mysterious figure who appears in the latter chapters of the book of Isaiah. He is featured in at least four prophetic poems (Isa 42:1–9; 49:1–7; 50:4–11; 52:13–53:12). On the one hand, the Servant represents the collective people of Israel (Isa 49:3); on the other, he is an individual who exercises a mission on behalf of Israel and the nations (Isa 42:1; 49:6) by suffering and dying for their iniquities (Isa 53:1–12). Christian tradition from earliest times identified the Servant as Jesus, the suffering Messiah.

Shema (Hebrew, "hear!"): refers to the affirmation of Israel's monotheistic faith in Deut 6:4: "Hear, O Israel! The LORD is our God, the LORD alone!" It is closely associated with the love commandment in Deut 6:5, which spells out the highest obligation of God's people: "Therefore, you shall love the LORD, your God, with your whole heart, and with your whole being, and with your whole strength."

typology: the study of persons, places, objects, and institutions in the Old Covenant that prefigure greater realities that come with the New Covenant. The historical realities of the biblical world that point forward in time are called types, and the greater realities for which they prepare are called antitypes. The basis of typology is the providence of God, who shapes the course of history to serve as a foreshadowing of his plans for the future.

YHWH: represents the four Hebrew consonants of the divine name "Yahweh." It is generally called the Tetragrammaton (Greek, "four letters"). Out of reverence for the holiness of this name, the Jews eventually ceased to pronounce it and substituted in its place such terms as Adonai ("Lord") and Ha-Shem ("the Name").

Index of Pastoral Topics

Index of Sidebars